The Cryptid Files Unsealed

LOCHLAINN SEABROOK WRITES IN THE FOLLOWING GENRES

Adult Books	Film	Poetry
Alternate History	Folklore	Politics
American Civil War	Genealogy	Prehistory
American History	Ghost Stories	Presidential History
American Politics	Gospels	Primary Documents
American South	Health and Fitness	Quiz
American West	Historical Fiction	Quotations
Ancient History	Historical Nonfiction	Recollections
Anthologies	History	Reference
Anthropology	Humanities	Religion
Apocrypha	Humor	Revolutionary Period
Astronomy	Illustrations	Science
Aviation	Inspirational	Scripture
Aviation History	Interviews	Self-help
Biblical Exegesis	Law of Attraction	Social Sciences
Biblical Hermeneutics	Lexicography	Southern Culture
Biography	Life After Death	Southern Heritage
Children's Books	Lifestyle	Southern Narratives
Christian Mysticism	Literature	Southern Traditions
Coffee Table Books	Matriarchy	Speeches
Coloring Books	Memoir	Spirituality
Comparative History	Men's Studies	Spiritualism
Comparative Mythology	Metaphysics	Sport Science
Comparative Religion	Military	Technology
Constitutional Studies	Military History	Thanatology
Cooking	Mysteries and Enigmas	Thealogy
Cryptozoology	Mysticism	Theology
Cultural Studies	Natural Health	UFOlogy
Diet and Nutrition	Natural History	Vexillology
Education	Onomastics	Victorian Era Studies
Encyclopediography	Paleography	Victorian Medicine
Entertainment	Paleontology	War
Ethnic Studies	Paranormal	Western Civilization
Etymology	Patriarchy	Wildlife
European History	Performing Arts	Women's Studies
Evolutionary Biology	Philosophy	World History
Exposés	Photography	Writings
Family Histories	Pictorial	Young Adult

Mr. Seabrook does not author books for fame and glory, but for the love of writing and sharing his knowledge.

Be curious, not judgmental.

THE CRYPTID FILES
UNSEALED

An Illustrated Guide to the World's Most Terrifying Unknown Creatures

LOCHLAINN SEABROOK
BESTSELLING AUTHOR, AWARD-WINNING HISTORIAN, NATIONALLY ACCLAIMED ARTIST

Diligently Researched and Generously Illustrated
by the Author for the Elucidation of the Reader

2025

Sea Raven Press, Park County, Wyoming USA

THE CRYPTID FILES UNSEALED

Published by
Sea Raven Press, LLC, founded 1995
Park County, Wyoming, USA
SeaRavenPress.com

Copyright © all text, artwork, and illustrations Lochlainn Seabrook 2025
in accordance with U.S. and international copyright laws and regulations, as stated and protected under the Berne Union for the Protection of Literary and Artistic Property (Berne Convention), and the Universal Copyright Convention (the UCC). All rights reserved under the Pan-American and International Copyright Conventions.

PRINTING HISTORY
1st SRP paperback edition, 1st printing, September 2025 • ISBN: 978-1-955351-66-9
1st SRP hardcover edition, 1st printing, September 2025 • ISBN: 978-1-955351-67-6

ISBN: 978-1-955351-66-9 (paperback)
Library of Congress Control Number: 2025945409

This work is the copyrighted intellectual property of Lochlainn Seabrook and has been registered with the Copyright Office at the Library of Congress in Washington, D.C., USA. No part of this work (including text, covers, drawings, photos, illustrations, maps, images, diagrams, etc.), in whole or in part, may be used, reproduced, stored in a retrieval system, or transmitted, in any form or by any means now known or hereafter invented, without written permission from the publisher. The sale, duplication, hire, lending, copying, digitalization, or reproduction of this material, in any manner or form whatsoever, is also prohibited, and is a violation of federal, civil, and digital copyright law, which provides severe civil and criminal penalties for any violations.

The Cryptid Files Unsealed: An Illustrated Guide to the World's Most Terrifying Unknown Creatures, by Lochlainn Seabrook. Includes an introduction, illustrations, appendix, and bibliography.

ARTWORK
Front and back cover design and art, book design, layout, font selection, and interior art by Lochlainn Seabrook.
All images, pictures, photos, illustrations, image captions, graphic design, and graphic art copyright © Lochlainn Seabrook.
All images selected, placed, manipulated, cleaned, colored, tinted, and/or created by Lochlainn Seabrook.
Cover image: "The Mothman of West Virginia," by Lochlainn Seabrook © copyright.
All rights reserved.

All persons who approve of the authority and principles of Colonel Lochlainn Seabrook's literary work, and realize its benefits as a means of reeducating the world about facts left out of mainstream books, are hereby requested to avidly recommend his titles to others and to vigorously cooperate in extending their reach, scope, and influence around the globe.

The views documented in this book concerning cryptozoology are those of the publisher.
WRITTEN, DESIGNED, PUBLISHED, PRINTED, & MANUFACTURED IN THE UNITED STATES OF AMERICA

Dedication

To the proto-cryptozoologists, those early chroniclers of hidden beasts, men such as Charles Gould, Sabine Baring-Gould, Carl Hagenbeck, Elliott O'Donnell, and Abbé Lievain Bonaventure Proyart, and to the intrepid explorers and naturalists who set down accounts of creatures yet unknown to science, men like Georges Cuvier, Sir Richard Francis Burton, David Livingstone, Alfred Russel Wallace, and Henry Morton Stanley.

Epigraph

"*Under the veil of mythology lies a solid reality.*"
Sabine Baring-Gould
1865

CONTENTS

Notes to the Reader ❧ page 13
Introduction, by Lochlainn Seabrook ❧ page 15

Adaro ❧ page 19
Agogwe ❧ page 23
Ahool ❧ page 27
Ahuitzotl ❧ page 31
Akhlut ❧ page 35
Almas ❧ page 39
Altamaha-ha ❧ page 43
Am Fear Liath Mòr ❧ page 47
Barmanou ❧ page 51
Batsquatch ❧ page 55
Bear Lake Monster ❧ page 59
Beast of Bodmin Moor ❧ page 63
Beast of Bray Road ❧ page 67
Beast of Busco ❧ page 71
Beast of Exmoor ❧ page 75
Beast of Gévaudan ❧ page 79
Beithir ❧ page 83
Big Bird ❧ page 87
Bigfoot ❧ page 91
Black Dog ❧ page 99
Black Panther ❧ page 103
Brosno Dragon ❧ page 107
Bunyip ❧ page 111
Buru ❧ page 115
Cadborosaurus ❧ page 119
Cait Sidhe ❧ page 123

Champ ꝏ page 127
Chupacabra ꝏ page 131
Devon Devil ꝏ page 135
Dogman ꝏ page 139
Dover Demon ꝏ page 143
Each-Uisce ꝏ page 147
Ellén Trechend ꝏ page 151
Emela-ntouka ꝏ page 155
Enfield Horror ꝏ page 159
Fairy ꝏ page 163
Flathead Lake Monster ꝏ page 167
Flatwoods Monster ꝏ page 171
Fouke Monster ꝏ page 175
Giant Antarctic Ice Worm ꝏ page 179
Goatman ꝏ page 183
Green Man ꝏ page 187
Hairy Dwarf ꝏ page 191
Hopkinsville Goblins ꝏ page 195
Inkanyamba ꝏ page 199
Jersey Devil ꝏ page 203
Kalanoro ꝏ page 209
Kelpie ꝏ page 213
Kongamato ꝏ page 217
Kraken ꝏ page 221
Kushtaka ꝏ page 225
Lagarfljót Worm ꝏ page 229
Lake Tahoe Monster ꝏ page 233
Lake Worth Monster ꝏ page 237
Lindorm ꝏ page 241
Lizard Man of Scape Ore Swamp ꝏ page 245
Loch Lochy Monster ꝏ page 249
Loch Morar Monster ꝏ page 253
Loch Ness Monster ꝏ page 257
Loveland Frogman ꝏ page 261
Lusca ꝏ page 265
Mantis Man ꝏ page 269
Mapinguari ꝏ page 273

Merfolk ✿ page 277
Minerva Monster ✿ page 281
Mokele-Mbembe ✿ page 285
Momo ✿ page 289
Mongolian Death Worm ✿ page 293
Mono Grande ✿ page 297
Mothman ✿ page 301
Nahuelito ✿ page 305
Nandi Bear ✿ page 309
Ngoubou ✿ page 313
Ningen ✿ page 317
Nittaewo ✿ page 321
Ogopogo ✿ page 325
Onza ✿ page 329
Orang Pendek ✿ page 333
Owlman ✿ page 337
Ozark Howler ✿ page 341
Pascagoula River Aliens ✿ page 345
Phantom Kangaroo ✿ page 349
Popobawa ✿ page 353
Pterosaur ✿ page 357
Pukwudgie ✿ page 361
Reptoid ✿ page 365
Ropen ✿ page 369
Rougarou ✿ page 373
Selkie ✿ page 377
Shunka Warakin ✿ page 381
Sigbin ✿ page 385
Skunk Ape ✿ page 389
Snallygaster ✿ page 393
Squonk ✿ page 397
Storsjöodjuret ✿ page 401
Stuart's Monsters ✿ page 405
Tatzelwurm ✿ page 409
Thetis Lake Monster ✿ page 413
Thunderbird ✿ page 417
Tikbalang ✿ page 421

Trunko ❧ page 425
Tsuchinoko ❧ page 429
Van Meter Visitor ❧ page 433
Water Hound ❧ page 437
Wendigo ❧ page 441
Werewolf ❧ page 445
White River Monster ❧ page 449
Wildman ❧ page 453
Yeren ❧ page 457
Yeti ❧ page 461
Yowie ❧ page 465
Zuiyo-maru Creature ❧ page 469

Appendix: Cryptids by Continent ❧ page 473
Bibliography ❧ page 477
Meet the Author ❧ page 493
Praise for the Author ❧ page 495
Learn More ❧ page 499

NOTES TO THE READER

READER & AGE ADVISORY
☛ *The Cryptid Files Unsealed* is an encyclopedia of mystery animals written in the format of a natural history field guide. It presents detailed profiles of scientifically unclassified beasts from around the world in an evidence-based, factual, yet open-minded manner. While suitable for general readers, the book contains dramatic imagery and accounts of encounters that may be unsettling for very young children.

Recommended age range: Best suited for readers ages 13 and up. Possibly appropriate for curious and mature readers as young as 10. However, in either case parental guidance is *always* advised.

In short, this book is ideal for anyone 14 and up; in particular those who enjoy cryptozoology, natural history, and the unexplained.

SCIENCE & CRYPTOZOOLOGY
☛ As none of the creatures itemized in my book have been accepted, identified, named, or even theoretically considered by most mainstream scientists, from a zoological perspective at least, all of my cryptids must be considered hypothetical, and the information I have gathered on them and the images I have created of them must be seen as conjectural.

This being said, I believe that more weight should be given to eyewitness accounts, especially when they come from credible, even highly trained, eyewitnesses, such as military personnel, police, doctors, pilots, lawyers, etc. After all, should not a sworn testimony that would hold up in court be regarded equally valid when it comes to identifying unknown animals?

Of course, the requirements for establishing truth are more stringent when it comes to the immutable rules of the hard sciences. Here, a physical body (the holotype) is always required to irrefutably and empirically establish an animal's reality. Since few, if any, of my cryptids have ever been captured or recovered (dead or alive), understandably conventional science must reject all unsubstantiated claims—no matter how trustworthy the eyewitness may be.

Despite this, it is my view that the sheer magnitude of sightings reports concerning unclassified creatures—in many individual cases spanning over 1,000 years, numbering in the hundreds and even thousands, and which include numerous mass sightings—combined with modern photographs, video recordings, audio recordings, and physical evidence (e.g., hair, fur, feathers, tissue, blood, fingerprints, palm prints, footprints, trackways, DNA, scat, nests, etc.), provide enough proof to consider most cryptids at least biologically possible, if not entirely probable.

Thus, while I have dealt with my subject scientifically (this is, after all, a science-based reference book), I have approached it with a questioning and open mind; one that allows for the mysteries of nature to be revealed rather than concealed. For me, as a nature writer and historian, this is the most logical manner in which to explore the natural world.

In my opinion it is by combining intellectual receptivity and creative vision with the soft sciences (e.g., history, anthropology, psychology, folkloristics, sociology, ethnography, etc.), that we come closest to gaining a true understanding of the mysterious world around us. Conventional science alone cannot accomplish this, particularly if it is used simply as a permanent and unchangeable catalog of accepted, well-worn theories. *Authentic* science is a constant, ever-evolving, open-ended search for truth—whatever that truth turns out to be. And so it is with my personal approach to cryptozoology.

It was one of my childhood idols, Albert Einstein, who in 1931 uttered these words:

> "To raise new questions, new possibilities, to regard old problems from a new angle, requires creative imagination and marks real advance in science."

L.S.

INTRODUCTION

SINCE THE DAWN OF HISTORY people everywhere have spoken of animals that dwell outside the accepted zoological record. They are said to appear along isolated shorelines, in deep mountain valleys, across remote forests, and beneath the surface of uncharted lakes and seas. Generations of witnesses have described them clearly, with accounts passed down through families and preserved in local traditions. Rather than fading into obscurity, these accounts continue to surface, shaping a long tradition of testimony that demands our respect and attention.

This is not a book of myths invented for amusement, nor of dismissals designed to explain away the unknown. It is a guide to terrifying creatures reported by ordinary people in extraordinary circumstances. Some are described as resembling prehistoric animals thought to have died out long ago, others as entirely new forms of life unrecognized by modern biology. Their stories stand as reminders that the natural world is vast, and that modern science does not yet hold the final word on its inhabitants.

To approach these subjects is not to abandon logic, but to use it more reasonably. The animals chronicled here may be elusive, they may resist capture or classification, but their persistence in testimony and tradition suggests that they belong within the larger story of life on Earth. They challenge us to look beyond accepted boundaries and to consider the possibility that exciting discoveries still lie ahead. Are you ready to join the expedition with me?

For those who share my fascination with anomalous animals, *The Cryptid Files Unsealed* is meant to be both a guide and an invitation. Within these pages lies an entryway into the shadowy realm of creatures still beyond recognition: the undiscovered, the unverified, the unrecorded, the unnamed, and the unexplained. They are the legendary beasts spoken of in every land, the phantom anomalies that blur the line between folklore and reality. They are cryptids, literally "hidden animals"—the fascinating, often frightening mystery creatures with whom we share our planet.

Lochlainn Seabrook
Park County, Wyoming, USA
September 2025
Scientia est lux lucis

"Books invite all; they constrain none."
Hartley Burr Alexander (1873-1939)

The Cryptid Files
UNSEALED

ADARO

The 10 foot long South Pacific Adaro in its native habitat: the waters around the Solomon Islands. Copyright © Lochlainn Seabrook.

QUICK FACTS

NAME: Adaro.
FIRST SIGHTING: Reported in the 20th Century, though oral traditions date back centuries.
LOCATION: Solomon Islands, South Pacific Ocean.
SIZE: Length around 10 feet; humanlike upper body with a long fishlike lower half; estimated weight 300 to 400 pounds.
APPEARANCE: Merman-like being with gills, fins, and a sharp spear-shaped appendage protruding from the head.
EYES: Large, menacing, and said to glare with hostility.
SKIN/FUR: Smooth, scaly, and aquatic in appearance; often described as dark or gray.
DIET: Said to hunt and consume fish, squid, and other sea creatures; reports also suggest aggression toward humans, with legends describing attacks involving spears, stones, or whirlpools to drown victims.
MOVEMENT: Swims swiftly through open waters; can rise vertically out of the sea; believed to travel on waterspouts.
NOTABLE BEHAVIOR: Hostile toward humans; associated with sudden storms, whirlwinds, and fatal accidents at sea.
FIRST REPORTED BY: Western documentation began in the early 20th Century, but long known in islander traditions.
CREATURE CLASSIFICATION: Cryptid aquatic humanoid, possibly rooted in myth yet treated as a dangerous reality by locals.
STATUS: Still reported in modern times by fishermen and coastal inhabitants of the Solomon Islands.

CREATURE PROFILE

The Adaro is one of Oceania's most feared aquatic cryptids, occupying a space between mythic sea spirit and zoological possibility. Originating in the Solomon Islands, it is described consistently by native accounts as a human-sized being with distinctly piscine traits. Its form is generally that of an adult man, lean and powerful, but surmounted by a tall dorsal fin that extends from head to back. Lateral gill-slits line the neck. The face is angular, with a pronounced jaw and dark eyes said to flash or glimmer in bright light. The skin is smooth, gray to dusky in coloration, sometimes depicted with faint scales. Some observers describe the Adaro as bearing weapons—often a spear or spear-like growth—which it wields with deadly effect.

Its ecology is entirely aquatic. Adaros are believed to inhabit the open waters surrounding the Solomon Islands, though coastal peoples describe them surfacing near reefs, beaches, and estuaries. They are reported both as solitary individuals and in small bands. Movement is rapid and forceful; swimmers compare their propulsion to that of a shark or large dolphin. Some stories hold that Adaros are capable of emerging onto land, striding upright like humans, before returning to the sea.

Dietary reports classify the Adaro as a predator. Fish are its chief food source, but islanders insist that humans occasionally fall prey. A notorious behavior is the hurling of poisonous flying fish at victims, a singular hunting or defensive tactic not paralleled in any known marine life. These poisoned projectiles, striking swimmers or fishermen, are said to cause injury or even death. The Adaro is further linked with meteorological disturbances, especially sudden squalls and storms, which locals attribute to its wrath.

Reproductive details are absent, though some Solomon Islanders describe the Adaro as a separate "race" that once coexisted with humans but retreated beneath the sea. Others maintain that it is a transformed human spirit, born from those who die violently in water. Whatever the case, it is regarded as both physical and supernatural, overlapping categories of animal and spirit.

Communication is believed to be nonverbal. Instead, the Adaro expresses intent through violent acts or by inducing fear. Yet fishermen speak of hearing whistling or shrill cries at sea, which they attribute to the creature. Natural enemies are not recorded, though its only deterrent seems to be ritual precautions taken by islanders before venturing onto the ocean.

Some island historians note that Adaro encounters often take place during periods of transition—dawn, dusk, or seasonal change—reinforcing the belief that these beings exist at the boundary between the human world and the unseen realm. Fishermen who venture out at twilight tell of seeing the silhouette of a tall, fin-backed figure breaking the waves, watching silently from a distance before vanishing beneath the surface. Such liminal appearances strengthen the conviction that Adaros are not only animals of the sea but guardians or enforcers of its mysteries.

The role of the Adaro within Solomon Island culture extends beyond fear. In traditional narratives it functions as both a warning and a teacher, reminding people of the dangers inherent in careless behavior on the water. Oral traditions emphasize that respect for the ocean, its moods, and its hidden life is essential for survival. Thus, the Adaro serves an ecological function in folklore: a symbolic protector of marine balance, punishing waste, arrogance, or intrusion into forbidden waters. In this sense, it is a cryptid that fulfills the role of a keystone predator in myth as well as in reported reality.

Modern cryptozoologists have suggested possible zoological explanations for Adaro reports. Some propose a misidentified large fish or marine mammal altered by fear, low light, or storm conditions. Others point to the possibility of an undiscovered species of aquatic hominid or amphibious vertebrate native to the deep Pacific. Yet the specific consistency of its dorsal fin, humanoid stance, and use of projectile fish as weapons make it difficult to align with any known organism. As such, the Adaro remains among the most enigmatic of South Pacific cryptids, bridging folklore, natural history, and the enduring possibility of life forms yet unknown to science.

The Adaro pulling an unsuspecting victim underwater, a frightening scenario cited in numerous reports. Copyright © Lochlainn Seabrook.

AGOGWE

The shy and mysterious 5 foot tall African cryptid known by native people as the Agogwe. Copyright © Lochlainn Seabrook.

QUICK FACTS

NAME: Agogwe.
FIRST SIGHTING: Early 20th Century.
LOCATION: Forests and savannas of East Africa, particularly Tanzania and Mozambique.
SIZE: Height 3 to 5 feet; slender build; estimated weight 70 to 100 pounds.
APPEARANCE: Small, bipedal hominid with long arms, a short body, and humanlike hands and feet.
EYES: Dark, round, and set deep in the face.
SKIN/FUR: Covered in reddish-brown or rust-colored hair, sometimes described as woolly.
DIET: Thought to consume roots, fruits, nuts, leaves, and small animals; may forage for insects and bird eggs; reports suggest opportunistic feeding similar to primates and early hominins.
MOVEMENT: Walks upright with a shuffling gait; can run quickly when startled; adept at moving through underbrush.
NOTABLE BEHAVIOR: Shy and elusive; avoids contact with humans; occasionally seen in small groups foraging.
FIRST REPORTED BY: Captain William Hichens in the early 20th Century, with later confirmation by naturalist Cuthbert Burgoyne.
CREATURE CLASSIFICATION: Cryptid hominid, possibly a surviving relic primate or unknown small hominin species.
STATUS: Still reported into the 20th Century, though no physical evidence has been collected.

CREATURE PROFILE

The Agogwe is a cryptid from East Africa, with reports centered in Tanzania and Mozambique. It is described as a small humanlike creature standing four to five feet tall with long arms, short legs, and reddish-brown hair covering its body. Its face is said to resemble a human more than an ape, with forward-facing eyes, a flat nose, and an intelligent expression. When seen it is usually only for a few moments before vanishing quickly into dense vegetation. Among local people the Agogwe is accepted as real, and regarded as a natural animal rather than a mythical being.

European knowledge began around 1900 with Captain William Hichens, a British officer who reported seeing two small upright figures crossing a clearing. They walked steadily on two legs and disappeared into the bush. His account later published in *Discovery* magazine caused a stir among naturalists. Another Englishman, Cuthbert Burgoyne, independently described seeing similar creatures along the Mozambique coast. Because these reports came from educated and respected men they carried unusual weight, placing the Agogwe in the category of cryptids with credible witnesses.

The most distinctive trait of the Agogwe is its bipedalism. Unlike known primates, which walk upright only occasionally, it is said to move primarily on two legs. Witnesses describe its gait as swaying, with short but deliberate steps. Though it may drop to all fours when alarmed, it is most often seen erect. Its stature—larger than monkeys, smaller than humans—sets it apart as something unfamiliar.

The fossil record adds context to these claims. East Africa is the cradle of many hominin species, including *Australopithecus* and *Homo habilis*. These ancestors were small-bodied upright walkers, combining primitive and advanced features. Reconstructions of them closely match descriptions of the Agogwe. For this reason some researchers believe the Agogwe could represent a relict hominin population, while others propose it may be an unknown primate, one that has independently evolved traits of upright walking.

African traditions provide parallel testimony. Indigenous communities speak of small hairy people of the forest. They are described as shy and elusive, able to vanish swiftly when encountered. Their reddish coats blend with the scrub and woodland, helping them remain unseen until movement betrays them. Unlike legendary spirits, they are always regarded as tangible beings inhabiting the natural world.

Behavioral details suggest an omnivorous lifestyle. The Agogwe is said to forage for fruits, roots, and perhaps small animals. It is usually reported alone or in small family groups. When approached it avoids contact and retreats rapidly into cover. Its agility and caution would make it extremely difficult to pursue. Combined with the fast decomposition rates of tropical environments and the activity of scavengers, these habits explain the lack of physical remains or specimens.

Skeptics argue that sightings may be misidentified apes, such as baboons or young chimpanzees. They point to the absence of bones, photographs, or any hard evidence. Yet those who have seen the Agogwe consistently insist that it is neither ape nor human, but something in between. The agreement in details across independent witnesses and cultures makes the reports difficult to dismiss entirely.

If ever confirmed the Agogwe would represent a discovery of immense importance. Whether a surviving hominin or a new primate species, it would deepen our knowledge of both anthropology and zoology. For now it remains unconfirmed by mainstream science; an elusive reminder that East Africa's forests may still conceal secrets from humanity's deep past.

A small group of Agogwe foraging in a Tanzanian jungle, as reported by eyewitnesses. Copyright © Lochlainn Seabrook.

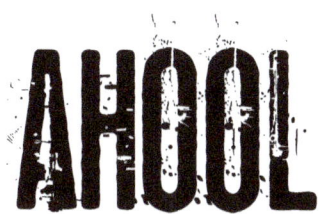

AHOOL

The 4 foot long Ahool in its native habitat: a dense Javanese rainforest. Copyright © Lochlainn Seabrook.

QUICK FACTS

NAME: Ahool.
FIRST SIGHTING: Early 20th Century.
LOCATION: Rainforests and remote river valleys of Java, Indonesia.
SIZE: Wingspan reported at 10 feet to 12 feet; body length around 4 feet; estimated weight 40 to 60 pounds.
APPEARANCE: Gigantic batlike creature with long arms, large claws, and a flat ape-like face.
EYES: Large, forward-facing, glowing red in some reports.
SKIN/FUR: Covered in short gray or brown fur with leathery wings resembling those of a bat.
DIET: Believed to feed on large insects, fish, birds, and possibly small mammals; some accounts suggest it hunts livestock and may scavenge carrion when available.
MOVEMENT: Flies with powerful wingbeats; also crawls or clambers when grounded.
NOTABLE BEHAVIOR: Emits a loud cry resembling "ahooool" as it flies, often at night over rivers.
FIRST REPORTED BY: Western zoologist Dr. Ernst Bartels in the early 20th Century.
CREATURE CLASSIFICATION: Cryptid flying mammal, possibly a surviving megabat or unknown primate-bat hybrid.
STATUS: Still reported in present-day Indonesia, though unverified by mainstream science.

CREATURE PROFILE

The Ahool is a cryptid said to inhabit the dense rainforests of Java, Indonesia. It is typically described as a massive batlike creature with a wingspan between 10 and 12 feet, dwarfing any known bat species. Witnesses describe its body as covered in short dark fur, with broad leathery wings, a flattened head, and a short tail. Its most distinctive feature is the eerie cry it produces, a loud "ahooool" call that can be heard echoing through the jungle, especially at night, and which gave the creature its name.

The first widely recorded sighting came from Dr. Ernst Bartels, a Dutch naturalist and son of the noted ornithologist M.E.G. Bartels. In 1925 while exploring along a river in western Java, Bartels reported being startled by a huge dark creature that flew low over the water with a wingspan as wide as a small aircraft. He claimed it uttered a cry unlike that of any bird or bat he had ever encountered, clearly repeating the "ahool" sound. Bartels's reputation as a serious observer made his account difficult to dismiss and his report remains one of the central pieces of evidence for the creature's existence.

Descriptions of the Ahool emphasize both its batlike and

primatelike qualities. Its wings are described as broad and membranous, suitable for sustained flight, but its face is said to resemble that of a monkey rather than a bat. Witnesses report large forward-facing eyes, a flat humanlike nose, and short ears. This combination of traits has puzzled researchers, since no known mammal exhibits them in this arrangement. Its size alone exceeds any known bat, including the giant golden-crowned flying fox of the Philippines, which reaches wingspans of six feet at most—only about half the size attributed to the Ahool.

Reports of its behavior suggest it is nocturnal and associated with rivers and streams. Witnesses often describe it flying low over water, perhaps hunting fish or aquatic insects. Its loud cry is considered one of its defining traits. The sound is said to be powerful, echoing through the jungle in a way that unnerves those who hear it. Unlike the high-pitched squeaks of bats, the Ahool's call is deep and resonant, unmistakable even at a distance.

Speculation on the Ahool's identity has ranged widely. Some suggest it may be a misidentified owl, such as the large Indonesian eagle-owl, whose call can carry far in the night. Others argue that owls cannot account for the reported wingspan or body shape. Another possibility is that the Ahool represents an undiscovered species of giant bat, perhaps related to the megabats or flying foxes. However, even the largest known bats fall far short of the reported size, leaving open the possibility of an entirely new line of flying mammal.

A more radical hypothesis suggests that the Ahool might be a surviving pterosaur, a relic from the Mesozoic era. While this idea is largely rejected by mainstream science, it is occasionally raised in cryptozoological circles because the reported size and form of the creature align superficially with reconstructions of pterosaurs. Still, without evidence such as fossils or remains, such speculation remains highly doubtful.

Local traditions treat the Ahool as part of the living landscape, not as a mythological being. For people in rural Java the creature's cry is familiar and often feared, though rarely seen directly. The consistency of reports, particularly from credible witnesses like Bartels, has helped cement the Ahool as one of Southeast Asia's most enduring cryptids.

If proven real the Ahool would represent a remarkable addition to zoology. A flying mammal with a wingspan twice that of the largest known bat would force a reconsideration of mammalian limits and adaptation. For now, it remains unconfirmed by mainstream science, an enormous batlike form glimpsed in the jungles of Java, and remembered most of all for the chilling cry that carries its name.

The Ahool goes aloft to defend its territory. Copyright © Lochlainn Seabrook.

AHUITZOTL

The dangerous, semiaquatic, 5 foot long Ahuitzotl, to this day a Mesoamerican mystery. Copyright © Lochlainn Seabrook.

QUICK FACTS

NAME: Ahuitzotl.
FIRST SIGHTING: 15th Century.
LOCATION: Central Mexico, particularly lakes, rivers, and canals once surrounding Tenochtitlán.
SIZE: Approximately 4 to 5 feet long; estimated weight 70 to 100 pounds.
APPEARANCE: Resembles a small dog- or otter-like animal with monkey-like hands and a long prehensile tail tipped with an additional claw.
EYES: Large, dark, and reflective, suited for night vision.
SKIN/FUR: Smooth, dark, seal-like hide, often described as slick when wet.
DIET: Fish, waterfowl, small mammals, and on occasion humans; legends emphasize its appetite for eyes, teeth, and fingernails, suggesting a preference for soft tissue.
MOVEMENT: Swims with agility, dives silently, and uses its tail claw to seize prey; capable of ambushing from beneath the waterline.
NOTABLE BEHAVIOR: Drags victims underwater, drowns them, and deposits their bodies on riverbanks with unusual injuries.
FIRST REPORTED BY: Aztec chroniclers, notably recorded by Fray Bernardino de Sahagún and other early Spanish historians.
CREATURE CLASSIFICATION: Semi-aquatic cryptid, possibly related to mustelids (*Lutrinae*) or a now-extinct aquatic mammal.
STATUS: Rejected by mainstream science; but rare reports still issue from rural parts of Mexico.

CREATURE PROFILE

Unlike many cryptids whose names are coined in modern times, the Ahuitzotl is known from pre-Columbian accounts. Its presence is firmly embedded in Aztec cosmology and natural history, where it is treated not as myth alone, but as a tangible predator inhabiting the waterways of central Mexico. The name itself translates as "thorny water thing" in Nahuatl, reflecting its feared reputation among those who navigated the lakes and canals around Tenochtitlán.

Descriptions consistently portray the animal as about the size of a small dog, with fur that shines when wet and a distinctively powerful tail ending in a hand-like claw. This tail feature sets it apart from known aquatic mammals and lends to its classification as a unique, undiscovered species. Reports emphasize its unusual ability to grip objects, suggesting adaptations closer to primates than to otters or seals. Its clawed tail is said to be the primary tool it uses to snatch prey from the banks or even drag fishermen directly from their canoes.

Aztec accounts are specific in their details, noting not only its physical appearance but also its predatory focus. Victims found along the waterways were sometimes reported with missing eyes, teeth, and nails. This distinctive injury pattern gave the Ahuitzotl a reputation as a soul-harvester, one tied to the rain-god Tlaloc and his underworld aquatic domain. From a modern zoological standpoint such reports may indicate a highly specialized feeding behavior, one that could involve soft-tissue consumption similar to that seen in certain bird or fish species. Alternatively, decomposition in aquatic environments could account for selective tissue loss; yet the consistency of the descriptions suggests an animal-driven cause.

Movement is another recurring feature in sightings. The creature swims quickly and with remarkable stealth, surfacing only to seize prey. Its slick, seal-like hide allows it to move without noise, an advantage in ambushing fish and waterfowl. The reflective eyes described in native accounts indicate a nocturnal or crepuscular lifestyle, matching the behavior of many aquatic hunters. Observers note that it emerges most often at dusk or during overcast weather, conditions favorable for concealment.

European chroniclers arriving in Mexico in the early 16th Century recorded Aztec testimony of the Ahuitzotl with seriousness, not dismissal. Bernardino de Sahagún, a Franciscan friar and ethnographer, documented these reports in his monumental *Florentine Codex*, placing the creature firmly within the cultural and zoological knowledge of the time. To the Aztecs the animal was as real as jaguars or coyotes, occupying a dangerous yet respected role in their environment.

Modern sightings, though sporadic, persist in rural Mexico, particularly in regions where dense reeds and quiet waterways provide cover. Fishermen and locals occasionally describe encounters with an otter-like animal larger, one more aggressive than known species. These reports often mention the same prehensile tail and black, shining skin, reinforcing continuity with earlier accounts. The Ahuitzotl may therefore represent a relict population of an unknown aquatic mammal, one adapted uniquely to the shallow lakes and canals of central Mexico.

In an unbiased cryptozoological context, the Ahuitzotl presents one of the stronger cases for authenticity among myth-linked animals. Unlike purely symbolic beings its consistent physical description, specialized behaviors, and association with real ecological niches suggest a zoological basis. If it exists, it may be an undiscovered branch of mustelids or a specialized aquatic primate, though no fossils have yet been identified. The persistence of reports into modern times strengthens the possibility that a small, elusive population survives in Mexico's wetlands, hidden among reeds and murky waters, just as the Aztecs warned centuries ago.

The Ahuitzotl prowling a shoreline seeking victims. Copyright © Lochlainn Seabrook.

AKHLUT

The bizarre and deadly 800 pound Arctic predator known as the Akhlut. Copyright © Lochlainn Seabrook.

QUICK FACTS

NAME: Akhlut.
FIRST SIGHTING: Described in Inuit traditions dating back many centuries.
LOCATION: Arctic coasts, pack ice, and tundra regions of Greenland, Canada, and Alaska.
SIZE: Estimated 6-8 feet long when in wolf form; larger and heavier than ordinary wolves or killer whales, exceeding 600-800 pounds.
APPEARANCE: Hybrid of wolf and killer whale, with the body of a large wolf and aquatic adaptations reminiscent of Orcinus orca.
EYES: Pale, luminous, and intense; often said to glow against snow or water.
SKIN/FUR: Thick dark fur on land; slick, wet appearance when emerging from the sea.
DIET: Carnivorous predator that hunts seals, fish, seabirds, and land mammals such as caribou and musk ox; may scavenge whale or walrus carcasses; believed to stalk sled dogs and occasionally follow hunters, demonstrating a broad and opportunistic feeding range that spans both sea and land.
MOVEMENT: Runs swiftly across tundra like a wolf, swims powerfully in the ocean with orca-like surges, and transitions fluidly between the two environments.
NOTABLE BEHAVIOR: Known to leave wolf tracks leading directly into the sea; said to attack sled teams; emerges without warning from icy waters to pursue prey inland.
FIRST REPORTED BY: Inuit elders and hunters preserving oral traditions across Arctic communities.
CREATURE CLASSIFICATION: Mythic cryptid; believed to be an amphibious apex predator combining traits of wolf and killer whale.
STATUS: Rejected by mainstream science; yet still part of active folklore; modern anecdotal reports continue to surface in the Arctic.

CREATURE PROFILE

The Akhlut is one of the most formidable creatures in Inuit lore, a predator whose very form defies natural classification. Said to be part killer whale and part wolf, it embodies the combined strength of two apex hunters. The Inuit envisioned it as a monstrous beast capable of striking terror both at sea and on land, making it one of the most dangerous entities of Arctic mythology. To the people who told its stories the Akhlut was not just a tale but a warning, a reminder that survival in the North required caution, respect, and humility.

Descriptions emphasize its imposing body, which carries the coloration of an orca yet the musculature and form of a wolf. Large dorsal or tail-like features connect it to its marine counterpart, while its legs and head are unmistakably lupine. Its sheer size, said to reach lengths of 20 to 30 feet, placed it far beyond any natural wolf known to science. Tales of its tracks—massive pawprints beginning at the shoreline and running inland—are among the most solid pieces of evidence cited by those who believe in its existence.

Behaviorally, the Akhlut mirrors its dual parentage. In water it swims with the same grace and predatory efficiency as the killer whale, able to pursue seals, walruses, and even beluga. On land it moves with wolf-like cunning and speed, capable of ambushing caribou herds or stalking camps under cover of darkness. It is not merely a hunter of animals but a threat to humans as well, with stories describing it dragging fishermen, hunters, and sled dogs into the sea. These habits make it a feared presence in Inuit communities, where vigilance near the ocean's edge was considered essential.

Culturally, the Akhlut functions as both a predator and a moral figure. Elders use stories of the beast to caution the young against wandering too close to dangerous waters or traveling unaccompanied along icy coasts. In this sense the Akhlut is more than myth—it is a teaching device that encodes hard-earned survival lessons into narrative form. Its role in oral tradition reflects how myth and ecology often intersect, with legends reinforcing safe behaviors in harsh environments.

Despite its roots in folklore, the Akhlut has not disappeared into the past. Modern Inuit hunters and fishermen occasionally recount unusual encounters, describing wolf-like shapes moving along remote shorelines or massive black-and-white figures just beneath the water's surface. Tracks beginning at the ocean and ending inland continue to be reported, fueling speculation that the creature may not be purely symbolic. These accounts keep the Akhlut alive as a subject of genuine curiosity and concern.

Skeptical interpretations suggest that natural events could account for the phenomenon. Wolves do travel near coastlines, and orcas sometimes beach themselves while chasing prey. The combination of such observations, magnified through oral storytelling, may have created the legend. Yet this explanation does not fully account for the recurring consistency of the reports, nor for the distinct physical descriptions passed down for generations. The lasting detail suggests something more than coincidence.

Today the Akhlut stands as a powerful example of how mythology, ecology, and possible zoology overlap. It is a creature that represents both the dangers of the sea and the wilderness of the tundra, a hybrid that transcends ordinary categories of animal life.

For cryptozoologists it remains a tantalizing prospect: if any creature could exist undetected in the vast, sparsely populated Arctic, it might be one that can thrive in both domains. For the Inuit, however, the Akhlut is less a mystery than a reality—one that continues to stalk the edges of their world, as it has for centuries.

The Akhlut menacing a pack of Canadian Eskimo dogs. Copyright © Lochlainn Seabrook.

ALMAS

The 7 foot tall Almas, one of Central Asia's most commonly reported cryptids. Copyright © Lochlainn Seabrook.

QUICK FACTS

NAME: Almas.
FIRST SIGHTING: Documented in the 15th Century.
LOCATION: Remote mountain ranges and forests of Mongolia, the Caucasus, and Central Asia.
SIZE: Typically 5-7 feet tall; estimated weight 200-300 pounds.
APPEARANCE: Upright, humanlike figure with long arms, sloping forehead, and robust body covered in hair.
EYES: Deep-set, dark, and often described as piercing.
SKIN/FUR: Reddish-brown to dark hair covering most of the body, with bare patches on the face, palms, and soles.
DIET: Omnivorous and opportunistic; believed to consume roots, berries, grasses, and wild fruits, while also hunting small mammals, birds, fish, and scavenging carrion; occasional reports suggest theft of livestock or crops, indicating adaptive feeding strategies.
MOVEMENT: Walks bipedally with a stooped gait; also capable of running quickly and climbing steep terrain.
NOTABLE BEHAVIOR: Shy but curious; avoids humans yet has been reported near villages stealing food; sometimes vocalizes with growls or cries.
FIRST REPORTED BY: Early travelers and chroniclers in Central Asia, later corroborated by local herders and hunters.
CREATURE CLASSIFICATION: Relict hominin; possibly a surviving branch of *Homo erectus* or another archaic human.
STATUS: Still reported in modern times across remote parts of Asia.

CREATURE PROFILE

The Almas is one of the best-known wild hominid cryptids of Eurasia. Unlike apes or bears it is consistently described as a fully bipedal, hair-covered humanoid that inhabits remote mountains and steppe regions. Reports from Mongolia, the Caucasus, and Central Asia describe the Almas as both a physical presence and a cultural figure, occupying a place between folklore and natural history. Its persistence into the modern era makes it a continuing subject of interest among researchers.

Descriptions of the Almas emphasize its human-like frame combined with primitive features. Witnesses state that it stands between five and seven feet tall, weighing 200 to 300 pounds. Its long arms, sloping forehead, and prominent brow ridge suggest a form reminiscent of fossil hominins such as Neanderthals. Covered in reddish-brown or black hair, with sparse patches on the face, the Almas presents a distinct and recognizable profile. Deep-set eyes, a flat nose, and a powerful jaw further distinguish it from both apes and modern humans.

Behavior attributed to the Almas reflects intelligence alongside caution. It avoids settlements but is known to approach at night to steal food or livestock. Hunters and herders sometimes report encounters near campfires or along mountain passes, where the creature is seen watching quietly before retreating into the dark. Reports of tracks—large, broad, human-like footprints—reinforce these claims. The Almas is also said to vocalize with grunts, howls, or whistles, which locals recognize as distinct from wolves or bears.

In its ecology the Almas survives as an omnivore. Accounts describe it gathering berries, roots, and wild plants while also hunting small animals or scavenging from kills. Its ability to thrive across varied environments—from alpine forests to dry steppes—suggests an adaptability similar to early human relatives. Caves, rocky slopes, and remote valleys provide shelter, making sightings rare and difficult to verify.

Folklore and oral tradition strengthen the Almas's presence. Central Asian chronicles from the 15th Century mention hairy wild people living alongside nomadic tribes. Mongolian stories describe them as dangerous if provoked but generally elusive. Some tales claim interbreeding between Almas and humans, producing hybrid offspring who could be recognized by unusual hair growth or primitive features. While these accounts cannot be proven, they reflect how deeply the Almas is woven into local memory.

In modern times the Almas continues to be reported. Expeditions in the Caucasus and Mongolia during the 20th Century collected testimonies from hunters, shepherds, and villagers who claimed direct encounters. Soviet researchers in particular gathered hundreds of accounts, noting consistencies in description across distant regions. Although no physical specimen has been captured, the survival of reports across centuries suggests the possibility of an undiscovered relict hominid species.

Skeptics propose alternative explanations, such as misidentified bears, feral humans, or folklore amplified through repetition. Yet these theories do not account for the anatomical detail provided in sightings, nor for the tracks and vocalizations reported. The convergence of cultural tradition and modern testimony gives the Almas a weight that few Eurasian cryptids carry.

Today the Almas remains a symbol of the unknown wilderness of Central Asia. For some it is living proof that human history is incomplete, a surviving branch of early hominids that persists in isolated regions. For others it is a figure of folklore that speaks to humanity's long relationship with untamed nature. Either way, the Almas continues to be encountered, described, and feared, ensuring its place in the natural history of cryptids.

Its reputation for abducting humans indicates that the Almas may be responsible for some of the thousands of people who go missing every year across Inner Eurasia. Copyright © Lochlainn Seabrook.

ALTAMAHA-HA

The 30 foot long Altamaha-ha prowling a lonely estuary in the U.S. state of Georgia. Copyright © Lochlainn Seabrook.

QUICK FACTS

NAME: Altamaha-ha.
FIRST SIGHTING: Early 18th Century.
LOCATION: Altamaha River, its tributaries, and coastal estuaries in southeastern Georgia, USA.
SIZE: Commonly described as 20-30 feet long; estimated weight 1-2 tons.
APPEARANCE: A serpentine body with multiple humps, a broad crocodile- or sturgeon-like head, and ridges along the back.
EYES: Small, dark, and positioned high on the head for surface scanning.
SKIN/FUR: Smooth gray to greenish skin that blends with the murky waters of the river.
DIET: Believed to include a wide variety of aquatic life such as mullet, shad, catfish, sturgeon, turtles, and waterfowl; some reports suggest opportunistic feeding on mammals or carrion found near the shoreline, indicating a versatile predatory strategy suited to estuarine ecosystems.
MOVEMENT: Undulating motion with several humps rising in rhythmic succession; capable of sudden dives and bursts of speed that create large wakes.
NOTABLE BEHAVIOR: Surfaces to breathe with audible exhalations; sometimes follows boats, startles fishermen, or disrupts schools of fish.
FIRST REPORTED BY: Native peoples of coastal Georgia and early European settlers.
CREATURE CLASSIFICATION: Aquatic cryptid; possibly a surviving prehistoric reptile, giant unknown fish, or unclassified marine vertebrate.
STATUS: Still sighted in modern times; considered an ongoing mystery of the American South.

CREATURE PROFILE

The Altamaha-ha, more commonly known as "Altie," is one of the best known aquatic cryptids of the American South. Said to dwell in the lower Altamaha River near the town of Darien, Georgia, this elusive creature has fascinated generations of witnesses, naturalists, and cryptozoologists alike. The Altamaha is the third-largest river basin on the East Coast of the United States, draining some 14,000 square miles of wilderness before emptying into the Atlantic. This environment of shifting channels, deep pools, and marshlands provides an ideal refuge for a large animal to remain hidden.

Accounts of the Altamaha-ha stretch back centuries. Long before Europeans settled the Georgia coast, the Muscogee (Creek) people told stories of a great water beast inhabiting the river. These oral traditions describe a powerful creature surfacing suddenly from the depths, frightening travelers and reminding them to respect the dangerous waters. Early settlers repeated similar reports in the 1700s and 1800s, describing a huge, serpentine animal rising above the surface in rhythmic undulations, only to slip beneath the water and vanish. Such continuity suggests a deep cultural memory, reinforced by modern sightings.

The creature is generally described as being 20-30 feet in length and weighing an estimated 1-2 tons. Witnesses often compare the head to that of a seal or sturgeon, with large, protruding eyes and sometimes whisker-like features. Its body is long and serpentine, with several humps three to four feet high breaking the water's surface when it moves. The skin is smooth and grayish-brown, lacking the scales of an alligator, which gives it an almost mammalian appearance. This smooth texture and undulating movement distinguish it from the many large fish that inhabit the river, such as sturgeon.

Despite its intimidating size, Altamaha-ha is consistently described as shy and non-threatening. It does not approach boats aggressively, preferring instead to surface briefly at a distance before diving back into the depths. Reports indicate it surfaces most often in quiet stretches of the river, far from heavy boat traffic, as if avoiding disturbance. Fishermen and boaters recount startling glimpses, sometimes mistaking the animal at first for a log or a line of dolphins, until its strange seal-like head becomes visible.

Speculation about the creature's identity has led to several theories. Some propose that Altamaha-ha may represent a relic population of a prehistoric marine reptile, perhaps a plesiosaur or mosasaur adapted to estuarine life. Others suggest it could be an unknown species of large fish, an undiscovered seal, or even a unique offshoot of the manatee. Skeptics argue that most sightings are misidentifications of sturgeon, alligators, or floating debris. Yet the consistency of descriptions—serpentine body, multiple humps, smooth skin, and seal-like head—suggests more than random error.

Reports have continued into the 20th and 21st Centuries, making the Altamaha-ha one of the few North American water cryptids still regularly encountered in modern times. Locals in Darien embrace the creature as part of their cultural heritage. Murals, mascots, and festivals celebrate Altie, linking the mystery to community identity while continuing to draw interest from tourists and researchers.

Though scientific proof remains absent, the persistence of sightings across centuries and the inhospitable terrain of the Altamaha estuary leave open the possibility that an undiscovered aquatic species inhabits the region. Until confirmed or disproven, Altamaha-ha remains a living mystery of the Georgia coast, a cryptid whose legend continues to ripple across the waters of the South.

The Altie lunging at its prey. Copyright © Lochlainn Seabrook.

AM FEAR LIATH MÒR

Countless outdoor enthusiasts report having encountered the terrifying 10 foot tall Am Fear Liath Mòr in the Scottish Highlands. Copyright © Lochlainn Seabrook.

QUICK FACTS

NAME: Am Fear Liath Mòr.
FIRST SIGHTING: Early 20th Century.
LOCATION: Ben MacDhui, Cairngorm Mountains, Scotland.
SIZE: Estimated height 8 to 10 feet tall, with weight possibly exceeding 600 pounds.
APPEARANCE: A towering humanoid with long arms, massive shoulders, and a looming silhouette.
EYES: Rarely described, though often perceived as dark or shadowed.
SKIN/FUR: Covered in short grey fur, giving it a spectral or mist-like appearance from a distance.
DIET: Believed to be omnivorous, capable of subsisting on mountain vegetation, small game, carrion, or opportunistic prey, though some traditions suggest it draws sustenance from energy or fear itself.
MOVEMENT: Walks with heavy deliberate strides, often matching the pace of those who encounter it, sometimes heard but not seen.
NOTABLE BEHAVIOR: Known for inducing intense feelings of dread, panic, and despair in those nearby.
FIRST REPORTED BY: J. Norman Collie, a respected mountaineer, in 1925.
CREATURE CLASSIFICATION: Relict hominid or mountain spirit.
STATUS: Rejected by science, but reported into the present day.

CREATURE PROFILE

Amid the mist-shrouded peaks of the Cairngorm Mountains in Scotland there exists a figure that is both feared and revered. Known as Am Fear Liath Mòr, or the "The Big Grey Man," this cryptid occupies a unique place in European folklore because of the consistency of its modern reports. Mountaineers who climb Ben MacDhui often speak of its overwhelming presence. Unlike many cryptids that are primarily seen, this being is most often sensed through sound, emotion, and fleeting shadowy glimpses. The weight of its legend rests not only on physical description but also on the profound psychological effects it has on those who cross its path.

The earliest widely publicized account came from J. Norman Collie in 1925 when he described a strange presence following him along the summit ridge. Though he saw nothing clearly, he heard heavy footsteps that matched his own yet seemed to belong to something much larger. Since Collie's testimony, many climbers, soldiers, and hikers have reported similar encounters. Witnesses consistently describe a sudden onset of fear, the sound of steps in the fog, and the sense of being pursued by a towering figure. Some claim to see a vast grey humanoid form moving in parallel, occasionally emerging against the skyline before vanishing into mist.

Descriptions of its size place Am Fear Liath Mòr in the same physical range as legendary North American primates such as Sasquatch. Eight to ten feet in height with immense weight, its silhouette is said to dwarf even large men. Covered in short grey fur that blends seamlessly with the granite and fog of the Cairngorms, it is well camouflaged against its environment. Observers often report only a hazy impression rather than clear anatomical details, as if the creature is partly obscured by its own natural aura of mist.

What sets this entity apart is the powerful psychological influence it exerts. Climbers often speak of being seized by terror so intense that they are forced to flee despite actually having seen nothing. The sensation is not described as ordinary fear but as an unnatural wave of despair that strikes without warning. Some theorists suggest that Am Fear Liath Mòr may generate low-frequency infrasound, a phenomenon known to cause unease and dread in humans. Others argue that it may be a guardian spirit of the mountain whose purpose is to drive intruders away from its sacred heights.

The question of diet is speculative. If a physical being, it could survive by browsing on alpine vegetation, feeding on deer or small mammals, or scavenging carrion from the slopes. Its elusive habits suggest it does not seek human food. Folkloric interpretations, however, often view it as a spectral entity that requires no traditional sustenance but rather feeds on human fear and energy. Both perspectives persist in modern accounts, underscoring the ambiguous nature of this cryptid.

Today sightings continue though they remain rare. Modern mountaineers climbing Ben MacDhui still report being shadowed by heavy footsteps or glimpsing enormous shapes in the fog. Some describe a sudden feeling of being watched followed by panic so severe that they abandon their ascent. These accounts demonstrate that Am Fear Liath Mòr remains an active phenomenon rather than a relic of past folklore. Its ongoing presence in the Cairngorms links modern witnesses with a tradition that may stretch back centuries into Gaelic legend.

Am Fear Liath Mòr lives on as one of Europe's most haunting cryptids. Neither fully spectral nor entirely physical, it bridges the worlds of natural history and the supernatural. Its combination of immense size, shadowy form, and overwhelming psychological effect ensures that those who encounter it do not soon forget. For cryptozoologists it represents a case where physical traits merge with environmental and psychological evidence, creating one of the most compelling mysteries in the field.

Am Fear Liath Mòr driving hikers from its mystery-enshrouded domain. Copyright © Lochlainn Seabrook.

BARMANOU

The 8 foot tall Barmanou, said to haunt the rugged landscapes of Pakistan and Afghanistan. Copyright © Lochlainn Seabrook.

QUICK FACTS

NAME: Barmanou.
FIRST SIGHTING: Reports trace back to the 4th Century.
LOCATION: Mountain ranges of northern Pakistan and Afghanistan.
SIZE: Estimated height between 6 and 8 feet tall, weighing 300 to 500 pounds.
APPEARANCE: Broad-shouldered biped with a stocky body, large hands and feet, and a conical head.
EYES: Deep-set and dark, often described as glaring.
SKIN/FUR: Covered in long reddish-brown or dirty gray hair.
DIET: Omnivorous, reportedly feeding on plants, fruit, roots, insects, livestock, and possibly small game or carrion. Witnesses claim it may take food from human camps.
MOVEMENT: Walks upright with a heavy stride but also climbs steep terrain with agility. It is said to run quickly when threatened.
NOTABLE BEHAVIOR: Reports suggest attempts to abduct women. Known to mimic human voices. Some accounts describe it as nocturnal and reclusive, avoiding direct encounters.
FIRST REPORTED BY: Local shepherds and villagers in ancient oral traditions, later documented by travelers and researchers in the 20th Century.
CREATURE CLASSIFICATION: Anthropoid hominin, possibly related to *Gigantopithecus blacki* or a surviving relict hominin.
STATUS: Unconfirmed by mainstream science, but still actively reported into the present day.

CREATURE PROFILE

Unlike many cryptids whose reports are scattered or vague, the Barmanou stands out as one of the few that is consistently described in the same way across centuries of oral and written records. In the high mountains that stretch between northern Pakistan and Afghanistan, shepherds, woodcutters, and villagers still speak of a tall hairy being that lives in remote valleys. Known as the Barmanou, this creature holds a firm place in local folklore yet continues to produce modern accounts that suggest a very real presence.

The Barmanou is often compared to the Yeti of the Himalayas and the Almas of Central Asia, though it has its own unique characteristics. Witnesses describe a broad body covered in long, tangled hair, reddish-brown or gray depending on the light and the season. Its head appears slightly conical, with a heavy brow ridge and a face that resembles both ape and man. Most descriptions place its height between six and eight feet, though larger individuals are sometimes claimed. Its hands and feet are reported as oversized, leaving tracks distinct from those of local wildlife.

Dietary reports indicate that the Barmanou consumes a wide range of food sources. Villagers have found evidence of excavated roots, broken branches heavy with fruit, and scavenged livestock remains near its supposed haunts. Some accounts even suggest that it raids human camps to take food, and in rare cases has been blamed for the disappearance of goats or sheep. This varied diet points to an adaptable omnivore capable of surviving in rugged mountain terrain where food can be scarce.

Behavioral accounts lend additional weight to its reputation as more than myth. Multiple witnesses over the years report hearing the creature mimic human voices, an eerie trait that aligns with abilities observed in great apes. Some villagers tell of women being stalked or even grabbed by the beast, though these stories are difficult to verify. The Barmanou is said to prefer solitude and darkness, emerging most often at night, yet sightings during the day also occur when shepherds drive their flocks into high pastures.

Scientific interest in the Barmanou increased during the 20th Century when explorers and researchers recorded testimonies directly from mountain villagers. Several expeditions gathered detailed descriptions and occasional plaster casts of footprints. Though no physical specimen has been secured, the consistency of accounts suggests that something unusual exists in this region. Some researchers propose it may be a surviving hominin, possibly related to *Gigantopithecus blacki*, the massive ape thought to have lived in Asia until relatively recent times. Others suggest it could represent a unique branch of human evolution persisting in isolation.

The cultural dimension of the Barmanou is equally important. For the people living in these remote valleys the creature is not only a zoological mystery but also a presence woven into daily life. Folktales warn children not to wander too far into the forests, and shepherds keep close watch over their herds when moving through known areas of activity. Some traditions portray the Barmanou as a guardian of the wild places, while others see it as a dangerous entity that must be avoided. These long-standing beliefs reinforce the idea that encounters are not rare inventions but part of a deep-rooted relationship between humans and an enigmatic neighbor of the high mountains.

Despite the lack of physical proof, reports continue into the present day. Villagers in Pakistan's Chitral and Swat regions still describe fresh encounters, and hunters sometimes claim to see it moving along ridgelines at dusk. The persistence of these accounts across generations makes the Barmanou one of the best candidates for a surviving unknown primate. Whether it proves to be a relic ape, an isolated population of archaic humans, or an entirely new species, the Barmanou remains an essential figure in the growing body of cryptozoological evidence that suggests relict hominins may yet share the Earth with us.

Pursued by the Barmanou, a young Pakistani woman flees for her life. Copyright © Lochlainn Seabrook.

BATSQUATCH

The 9 foot tall Batsquatch flying over the forested slopes of Mount St. Helens. Copyright © Lochlainn Seabrook.

QUICK FACTS

NAME: Batsquatch.
FIRST SIGHTING: 1980.
LOCATION: Mount St. Helens region, Washington State, USA.
SIZE: Estimated 8 to 9 feet tall, with a wingspan of up to 30 feet, weight around 600 to 700 pounds.
APPEARANCE: Resembles a massive primate with bat-like wings, broad shoulders, and muscular limbs.
EYES: Often reported as glowing yellow or red in low light.
SKIN/FUR: Covered in dark blue to black fur, with leathery wings that are largely hairless.
DIET: Likely carnivorous or omnivorous, with reports suggesting predation on deer, livestock, large birds, and possibly carrion, while some witnesses believe it scavenges opportunistically and supplements with vegetation or fruit.
MOVEMENT: Capable of both bipedal walking and powerful flight, often described as gliding silently before sudden bursts of speed.
NOTABLE BEHAVIOR: Associated with violent storms, seismic activity, and sudden power outages, with reports of it terrifying hikers and farmers, sometimes flying low over vehicles or campsites.
FIRST REPORTED BY: Residents near Mount St. Helens following the volcanic eruption in 1980.
CREATURE CLASSIFICATION: Winged humanoid cryptid.
STATUS: Unconfirmed by mainstream science; though rare, it is still being reported in the Pacific Northwest.

CREATURE PROFILE

Few cryptids combine elements of both terrestrial and aerial mastery as convincingly as Batsquatch. This creature is often described as a fusion of ape and bat, towering on the ground yet capable of flight across mountain valleys. Its emergence in the modern record begins after the catastrophic eruption of Mount St. Helens in 1980, when locals reported seeing a huge winged beast moving through the skies near the devastated landscape. From that moment Batsquatch entered Pacific Northwest folklore as one of the most terrifying yet intriguing cryptids of North America.

Eyewitness accounts remain consistent in their descriptions. The animal stands around eight or nine feet tall, its chest broad and muscular, with arms that extend into leathery wings spanning nearly thirty feet. Its body is covered in thick, dark fur that contrasts with the thin, membranous surface of its wings. Its head is often described as simian with pointed ears and glowing eyes that shift between yellow and red depending on the light. Reports emphasize the fearsome impression it creates, particularly when seen swooping overhead in silence, only to break that silence with sudden gusts of air as it surges upward.

Habitat reports place Batsquatch deep within the rugged Cascades. The dense forests, high peaks, and volcanic terrain provide an isolated environment capable of concealing a large unknown species. While skeptics claim such a beast could not remain hidden, those who live in the region understand how vast and impenetrable the wilderness remains. This creature is often associated with extreme weather, and many sightings occur just before or during thunderstorms, suggesting a behavioral link with atmospheric conditions. Its sudden appearance in areas of natural upheaval such as volcanic eruptions or lightning storms has led some to propose it is drawn to powerful energy sources, or even migrates with shifting geological activity.

Dietary habits remain educated guesswork. Witnesses describe livestock mutilations in remote farms, while others report deer carcasses torn apart in ways inconsistent with local predators. Its primate features suggest some omnivorous capacity, while its predatory behavior and enormous wingspan imply a need for high-caloric sustenance. Opportunistic scavenging is also possible, especially in rugged mountain environments where carrion is plentiful. Its diet may mirror that of large raptors and primates combined, allowing adaptability across changing seasons.

Behavioral notes from encounters often include intimidation and aggression. Campers report it circling campsites at night or swooping low over tents with a terrifying rush of air. Drivers claim to have seen it flying above roads or even pacing their vehicles. Its association with power failures, electrical disturbances, and storm fronts has led to speculation about electromagnetic sensitivity. Some theories suggest it navigates using geomagnetic cues similar to migratory birds, which could explain its link to volcanic regions rich in magnetic anomalies.

Despite its frightening appearance, there are no reliable accounts of Batsquatch killing a human. Its behavior leans more toward territorial displays, perhaps warning intruders away from hidden roosts. This suggests it is intelligent enough to avoid unnecessary risks with humans. Its continued presence into the 21st Century is supported by sporadic modern reports, though most remain local and rarely reach national media. Today, Batsquatch is seen not just as a regional legend but as a potential living remnant of an unknown branch of winged primates or giant bats, possibly an evolutionary offshoot adapted to the isolation of the Cascades.

For researchers of cryptozoology, Batsquatch remains one of the most fascinating candidates for study. It embodies traits from both mammalian and chiropteran lineages, yet stands apart as a distinct form. With each new report from Washington, Oregon, and beyond, the case strengthens that this enigmatic winged creature may indeed be real, alive, and still patrolling the storm-swept skies of the Pacific Northwest.

The Batsquatch is reported to act with swift aggression toward those who encroach on its territory. Copyright © Lochlainn Seabrook.

BEAR LAKE MONSTER

The mysterious 50 foot long Rocky Mountain cryptid known as the Bear Lake Monster. Copyright © Lochlainn Seabrook.

QUICK FACTS

NAME: Bear Lake Monster.
FIRST SIGHTING: Early 19th Century.
LOCATION: Bear Lake, straddling the Utah-Idaho border.
SIZE: Reported lengths between 20 and 50 feet, with estimates of several tons in weight.
APPEARANCE: Long serpentine body with humps rising above the surface, often described with a head resembling a cow, otter, or crocodile.
EYES: Large, protruding, and dark.
SKIN/FUR: Smooth, dark-colored skin with a glossy sheen when wet.
DIET: Likely piscivorous, feeding on large schools of fish such as cutthroat trout and whitefish, though some accounts suggest it may also prey on waterfowl and other lake-dwelling animals.
MOVEMENT: Described as swift and powerful, capable of producing wakes that resemble those of a large boat, often undulating with visible humps.
NOTABLE BEHAVIOR: Frequently reported surfacing and diving in long arcs, occasionally coming close to shore, and sometimes said to chase boats or livestock swimming in the lake.
FIRST REPORTED BY: Settlers and pioneers during the mid-19th Century.
CREATURE CLASSIFICATION: Freshwater cryptid, often compared to serpentine lake monsters such as Ogopogo or Nessie.
STATUS: Scientifically rejected; but still reported sporadically.

CREATURE PROFILE

The Bear Lake Monster is one of the great aquatic mysteries of North America. Found in the deep glacial waters of Bear Lake along the Utah-Idaho border, this Rocky Mountain cryptid has been reported for nearly two centuries. Unlike many regional legends that fade with time, sightings of this enigmatic creature continue into the modern day, maintaining its place as a subject of fascination for locals and researchers alike. The lake itself stretches 20 miles long and 8 miles wide, with depths exceeding 200 feet, making it an environment more than capable of concealing large unknown animals.

Descriptions of the Bear Lake Monster vary but generally paint a consistent image of a long-bodied creature with multiple humps breaking the surface. Witnesses compare its head to that of familiar animals such as cows, crocodiles, or even otters, suggesting a blend of mammalian and reptilian traits. Its body is said to be dark in color and glistening when wet, with skin that appears smooth rather than scaled. Observers often emphasize the size of the creature, with estimates ranging from 20 feet to an immense 50 feet. Weight is harder to judge, but based on bulkier descriptions, several tons seems likely.

Behavior reports add further intrigue. Witnesses describe the creature moving with great power, creating wakes that resemble those of a motorboat—despite the absence of vessels nearby. Its swimming motion is often undulatory, marked by successive humps rolling above the surface in rhythmic arcs. On occasion the monster has been said to follow or even pursue boats, causing fear among fishermen. Livestock driven across the lake have reportedly been attacked, fueling speculation that the creature is predatory. Its presumed diet most likely consists of the abundant fish species found in Bear Lake, such as cutthroat trout, whitefish, and Bonneville cisco, though anecdotal accounts suggest it may also feed opportunistically on waterfowl or other aquatic animals.

The first settlers to describe the monster were pioneers in the mid-19th Century. Their accounts quickly spread, drawing interest from newspapers of the time. Though skeptics dismissed the stories, the consistency among witnesses has kept the tradition alive. Native American legends of the area also describe powerful water beings, lending further depth to the lore and suggesting the phenomenon predates pioneer settlement. This convergence of indigenous tradition and settler testimony underscores the longstanding mystery surrounding Bear Lake.

Present-day sightings continue, though less frequently than in the 19th and early 20th Centuries. Modern observers still report large dark shapes surfacing unexpectedly or wakes cutting across the calm water with no apparent source. These events often occur in summer, when recreational use of the lake is highest, offering more chances for encounters. The persistence of sightings across generations strengthens the argument that something biological could inhabit Bear Lake, even if it remains officially undiscovered.

While mainstream zoology has yet to confirm the Bear Lake Monster, its case remains open due to the sheer weight of testimony. The lake's size, depth, and isolated setting make it an ideal candidate for harboring an unidentified aquatic animal. The possibility of a surviving relict species—whether a large fish, amphibian, or unknown aquatic reptile—cannot be entirely ruled out. Until hard physical evidence is obtained the Bear Lake Monster remains a cornerstone of American cryptozoology, standing alongside the world's most famous lake cryptids as a compelling reminder that even well-traveled regions may still guard ancient secrets.

As reported by credible eyewitnesses, the Bear Lake Monster sometimes pursues livestock being driven across the lake. Copyright © Lochlainn Seabrook.

BEAST OF BODMIN MOOR

The 9 foot long Beast of Bodmin Moor, Cornwall's most dangerous and enigmatic cryptid. Copyright © Lochlainn Seabrook.

QUICK FACTS

NAME: Beast of Bodmin Moor.
FIRST SIGHTING: Early 1970s.
LOCATION: Bodmin Moor, Cornwall, England.
SIZE: Body estimated 4 to 5 feet long, weighing between 60 and 120 pounds.
APPEARANCE: A large catlike animal with a long tail, rounded head, and muscular frame.
EYES: Bright yellow or green eyes that reflect light strongly at night.
SKIN/FUR: Smooth black or dark brown fur with occasional lighter markings.
DIET: Believed to prey on rabbits, deer, livestock, and smaller mammals, while also scavenging carrion when available.
MOVEMENT: Swift and agile, capable of leaping long distances and running silently across uneven ground.
NOTABLE BEHAVIOR: Frequently linked to livestock killings, silent stalking, and sudden vanishings into dense moorland.
FIRST REPORTED BY: Farmers and local residents in Cornwall.
CREATURE CLASSIFICATION: Cryptid felid, possibly related to *Panthera pardus* or *Puma concolor*.
STATUS: Scientifically unrecognized; yet it continues to be reported consistently into the present day.

CREATURE PROFILE

In the wild and windswept expanse of Cornwall's Bodmin Moor lives the long-told legend of a shadowy predator known as the Beast of Bodmin Moor. This large feline-like creature is said to roam the granite uplands, a rugged landscape of heath, bog, and ancient stone formations that provide natural cover for a reclusive carnivore. For more than half a century locals and visitors alike continue to report sightings describing a sleek dark predator with the unmistakable form of a big cat.

The earliest wave of credible reports begins in the 1970s when farmers started discovering inexplicably mutilated livestock. Sheep and calves were found with deep claw marks and precise throat wounds consistent with the hunting methods of large cats. Around the same time eyewitnesses began describing a muscular animal resembling a leopard or puma moving silently through the foggy moor. These observations are not limited to fleeting glimpses. Some witnesses claim extended views through binoculars where the animal's feline shape, long curling tail, and smooth fur were observed with clarity.

Descriptions remain remarkably consistent. The Beast's body is usually between four and five feet in length with a tail nearly as long as its body. Its coloration is predominantly black, though some accounts mention a dusky brown coat that blends seamlessly with the moor's bracken and stone. The eyes are striking and luminous, often glowing yellow or green when caught in torchlight or vehicle headlights. Witnesses stress its feline movements, the sinuous stride, and the ability to leap over obstacles with effortless precision.

Its diet appears typical of apex predators of similar size. Deer carcasses with neatly stripped ribs, sheep pulled down without human explanation, and rabbits vanishing in areas where tracks suggest the presence of a large stalking animal are all attributed to the Beast. Farmers regularly report mysterious livestock losses that align with big cat predation rather than the scattered attacks of local dogs or foxes. The frequency of these incidents has caused many in Cornwall to accept the Beast as a living reality rather than mere folklore.

Behaviorally, the animal is elusive and secretive. Sightings often last only seconds before it disappears into the mist, or retreats into bramble thickets and rocky outcrops. Some accounts mention it moving along the edges of rivers or streams, suggesting it uses waterways as hunting corridors. Tracks resembling those of large cats have occasionally been found, though casts are rare. Despite periodic official investigations no conclusive physical specimen has been obtained, a fact that adds to the mystery while not diminishing the consistency of the testimony.

Local culture has fully absorbed the Beast of Bodmin Moor into Cornish identity. Road signs, tourist attractions, and folklore all reference the animal, reflecting the widespread belief that something unusual inhabits the moor. Researchers propose that the Beast could descend from exotic pets released in the mid-20th Century following changes in British laws regarding the keeping of dangerous animals. Others believe it represents a remnant or hybrid lineage of wild cats that once roamed Britain.

The endurance of this natural history puzzle also raises important ecological questions. If the Beast is indeed a large predatory cat, its continued survival on Bodmin Moor would indicate a stable prey base and sufficient cover to sustain a breeding population or at least a long-lived individual. This makes the region not only a hotspot for folklore, but also a potentially significant location for the study of hidden wildlife populations in Britain.

Today reports still surface of a sleek black figure seen at dawn or dusk, crossing fields or standing silently on a ridge against the setting sun. The continuing consistency of these sightings, combined with livestock predation and elusive evidence, supports the possibility that the Beast of Bodmin Moor is more than legend. Whether it proves to be a surviving member of a known big cat species or an as yet undocumented population, its presence keeps alive one of the longest lasting and most mysterious natural history enigmas of modern Britain.

Cornwall's healthy deer population, which includes red deer, fallow deer, and roe deer, could easily support a creature like the Beast of Bodmin Moor. Copyright © Lochlainn Seabrook.

BEAST OF BRAY ROAD

The Beast of Bray Road, a 7 foot tall cryptid known to stalk the rural Wisconsin countryside. Copyright © Lochlainn Seabrook.

QUICK FACTS

NAME: Beast of Bray Road.
FIRST SIGHTING: Late 20th Century.
LOCATION: Elkhorn, Wisconsin, USA—and surrounding areas of Walworth County.
SIZE: Estimated 6 to 7 feet tall when upright, 400 to 600 pounds.
APPEARANCE: Wolf-like head with a long snout, broad shoulders, and muscular torso.
EYES: Often described as glowing yellow or amber.
SKIN/FUR: Covered in thick grayish brown fur resembling that of a timber wolf.
DIET: Reported to consume deer, livestock, small mammals, and carrion, with accounts suggesting opportunistic feeding on roadkill and even stored food left outside homes.
MOVEMENT: Runs on all fours like a wolf but also moves upright with a shambling gait.
NOTABLE BEHAVIOR: Observed kneeling or crouching at roadsides while feeding on prey.
FIRST REPORTED BY: Local residents, first widely covered by reporter Linda Godfrey in the early 1990s.
CREATURE CLASSIFICATION: Canid-like cryptid, sometimes compared to a werewolf or upright wolf.
STATUS: Rejected by mainstream science; yet reports continue into the 21st Century, with ongoing credible eyewitness accounts.

CREATURE PROFILE

Along rural roads and quiet fields of Walworth County in southern Wisconsin, a figure both feared and respected continues to be reported by locals. The Beast of Bray Road, named for the country road outside Elkhorn where many encounters take place, stands as one of North America's most intriguing cryptids. Unlike ambiguous shadowy figures, this creature is consistently described with detailed features that suggest something more tangible. Witnesses describe a tall wolf-like animal that behaves in ways unlike any ordinary predator native to the region.

The most striking feature of the Beast is its ability to shift between quadrupedal and bipedal locomotion. On all fours it resembles a large timber wolf, but when upright it is described as standing six to seven feet tall, with a broad chest and muscular build that more closely matches a human. Reports describe the head as distinctly lupine with a long snout, sharp teeth, and erect pointed ears. The eyes are often said to shine with an amber or yellow glow, especially when caught in headlights at night. Thick fur of a grayish brown hue covers the entire body, providing camouflage in the woodlands and fields of Wisconsin.

Its diet is consistent with that of a large omnivorous predator. Accounts note deer being dragged off roadsides, livestock vanishing from farms, and the creature crouching over carrion. Some reports describe it feeding on roadkill with human-like forelimbs holding the carcass. Such behavior suggests both physical strength and adaptability, traits that allow the creature to survive on whatever the environment provides. There are even accounts of the Beast raiding trash bins or storage sheds, indicating it is bold enough to move close to human dwellings.

Movement is often described as unnerving. Witnesses see the Beast running swiftly on four legs, only to stand up in an instant and lope forward on two. This dual style of locomotion sets it apart from natural wolves or dogs. Its upright stride is not fluid like a man's, but instead it shambles—as though the body is not fully adapted to bipedal motion. Yet its speed and agility on four legs allow it to vanish quickly into fields or tree lines, leaving observers shaken and uncertain of what they saw.

Behavioral accounts are consistent across decades. Drivers have reported the creature kneeling at roadsides, tearing at the body of a deer. Others have encountered it crossing roads in the dead of night, pausing to watch before bounding away. The Beast has also been observed standing at the edge of farm fields, seemingly watching livestock or people from a distance. These sightings suggest a cautious intelligence. It rarely attacks humans directly, yet its presence, often described as "evil" and "demonic," is intimidating enough to keep people at bay.

The modern history of the Beast began in the late 1980s and early 1990s when numerous sightings along Bray Road led to local press coverage. Journalist Linda Godfrey's reporting brought widespread attention, collecting eyewitness testimony that confirmed a pattern of encounters. Since then, new reports continue to surface, showing the phenomenon is ongoing rather than a closed chapter of folklore. This persistence indicates that whatever the Beast is, it remains active in the region and has not faded into memory.

The classification of the Beast of Bray Road remains debated. Some consider it a cryptid canid, perhaps an unknown species of wolf capable of unusual locomotion. Others view it as a living werewolf-like being, tied to centuries of European legends of upright wolves.

While scientific explanation has yet to be offered, the consistency of eyewitness accounts points to something real occupying the rural Midwest. For many in southern Wisconsin the Beast is not a myth; it is a constant presence that continues to challenge conventional boundaries between known wildlife and the unexplained.

The Beast of Bray Road has been reported keeping pace with cars traveling up to 60 mph. Here, a family tries to outrun the ferocious creature. Copyright © Lochlainn Seabrook.

BEAST OF BUSCO

The Beast of Busco: Fulk Lake's fearsome 500 pound resident monster. Copyright © Lochlainn Seabrook.

QUICK FACTS

NAME: Beast of Busco.
FIRST SIGHTING: 1898.
LOCATION: Fulk Lake near Churubusco, Indiana.
SIZE: Reports claim 12 to 15 feet long and weighing up to 500 pounds.
APPEARANCE: Gigantic snapping turtle with an unusually massive shell and thick neck.
EYES: Small, dark, and beady, said to glint just above the water.
SKIN/FUR: Rough, leathery gray skin with patches of algae and mud.
DIET: Believed to feed on large fish, waterfowl, muskrats, frogs, aquatic vegetation, and possibly small mammals near the shoreline.
MOVEMENT: Slow on land but powerful in water, gliding with strong strokes of its webbed limbs.
NOTABLE BEHAVIOR: Surfaces briefly before submerging again, often leaving large ripples and disturbances in the water.
FIRST REPORTED BY: Oscar Fulk, a local farmer who claimed to have seen the turtle in 1898.
CREATURE CLASSIFICATION: Giant cryptid reptile, possibly an outsized *Chelydra serpentina* or a prehistoric survivor.
STATUS: Still reported in modern times though rare, with the lake remaining a place of ongoing interest.

CREATURE PROFILE

Among the many aquatic cryptids of North America, the Beast of Busco holds a unique place as one of the few described as a giant turtle. Its story begins at Fulk Lake near Churubusco, Indiana, where locals report a creature of immense size surfacing from time to time. The lake itself is small and unassuming, yet its legend is large enough to rival better known mysteries like those of Loch Ness and Lake Champlain.

The earliest report traces back to 1898 when farmer Oscar Fulk described seeing a monstrous turtle in his lake. His account sparked interest, though at first it remained a local tale. By the mid 20th Century sightings multiplied and the beast was frequently said to be between 12 and 15 feet long with a shell broad enough to resemble a small boat. The descriptions match a snapping turtle but on a scale far larger than any known specimen. For comparison, the largest verified common snapping turtles rarely exceed 19 inches in shell length and 75 pounds, making the Busco turtle an outlier by many magnitudes.

The creature's physical details are remarkably consistent. Witnesses report a dark gray, rough shelled animal that sometimes carries algae on its back, lending it the look of an old and ancient creature. Its head is described as massive, with strong jaws and a thick muscular neck that rises above the water before it quickly disappears. Its eyes are said to peer from just above the surface, dark and reflective, giving the impression of an intelligent and watchful animal. When it moves through the lake it creates powerful ripples and occasionally churns the water enough to suggest the presence of something far heavier than any normal turtle.

The diet of the Beast of Busco is inferred from its size and habits. Large snapping turtles feed opportunistically on fish, amphibians, birds, and even small mammals. A turtle many times their size would require an equally broad diet, and it is easy to imagine such a predator ambushing ducks, muskrats, or larger fish that inhabit the waters. The presence of unexplained disturbances in the fish population has occasionally been linked to the creature, though no direct evidence has been collected.

Behaviorally the beast is elusive. It rarely lingers at the surface, instead surfacing briefly before sinking back into the lake. This habit has made verification difficult and has contributed to its mystery. Efforts in the mid 20th Century to capture or display the animal drew national attention. The most famous attempt occurred in 1949 when Gale Harris, Fulk Lake's then owner, constructed a massive trap and drained part of the lake in search of the creature. Despite national coverage and thousands of onlookers, the Beast of Busco evaded capture, furthering its reputation as a clever and cautious survivor. Speculation about its identity continues.

Some suggest it is a giant mutant snapping turtle, perhaps a rare individual that grew unchecked for decades. Others argue it could represent a remnant population of prehistoric turtles such as *Macrochelys temminckii* or even something older, a relic from the Pleistocene that has survived in the sheltered waters. The consistent size estimates suggest a real biological foundation behind the reports rather than exaggeration alone.

Today the legend lives on in the town of Churubusco, where the creature is celebrated as a symbol of local identity. Reports of large turtles in Fulk Lake and nearby waters still surface from time to time, ensuring that the Beast of Busco remains more than just folklore. Whether a giant snapping turtle, a prehistoric holdover, or an undiscovered species, the creature fits securely into the catalog of North American cryptids and continues to inspire curiosity and investigation.

The 6 foot long freshwater turtle known as the Beast of Busco continues to defy both categorization and capture. Copyright © Lochlainn Seabrook.

BEAST OF EXMOOR

The 7 foot long Beast of Exmoor: real, an illusion, or simply misidentification? Copyright © Lochlainn Seabrook.

QUICK FACTS

NAME: Beast of Exmoor.
FIRST SIGHTING: Early 20th Century.
LOCATION: Exmoor, Devon and Somerset, England.
SIZE: Length 6 to 7 feet, height at shoulder 2 to 3 feet, weight estimated 120 to 170 pounds.
APPEARANCE: Large panther-like creature with a long body, muscular frame, and extended tail.
EYES: Bright yellow or green, reflective in light.
SKIN/FUR: Glossy black or dark brown coat, often described as sleek and uniform.
DIET: Believed to prey on deer, sheep, livestock, and smaller mammals; opportunistic predator.
MOVEMENT: Silent, smooth, catlike gait with long leaping ability.
NOTABLE BEHAVIOR: Known for stalking livestock herds, leaving claw marks, and killing without consuming all of its prey.
FIRST REPORTED BY: Local farmers in Devon.
CREATURE CLASSIFICATION: Mystery feline, possibly related to a *Panthera* species or unknown big cat.
STATUS: Dismissed by mainstream science; yet still regularly reported and sighted today.

CREATURE PROFILE

The high moors of Devon and Somerset hold more than sweeping landscapes and quiet villages. They also carry a reputation for a predator that is not supposed to exist in England. This creature, known as the Beast of Exmoor, is described as a large black cat with the power and appearance of a panther. Its presence is a source of both fascination and fear for those who live in the region.

The earliest accounts from the early 20th Century mention farmers losing sheep in unusual circumstances, with carcasses found torn apart but not always eaten. By the mid-20th Century, sightings increased, with reports of a sleek black animal moving across the ridgelines of Exmoor. The animal is most often described as the size of a Labrador dog but longer, more muscular, and equipped with a tail that swings low like that of a leopard. Its silhouette is unmistakably feline.

Farmers across Exmoor still claim that their sheep and even calves are sometimes taken by this predator. Evidence usually includes claw marks, shredded throats, and in some cases the remains of animals hidden in sheltered areas. The fact that not all kills are consumed suggests surplus hunting behavior similar to what large cats display in the wild. This sets it apart from foxes and dogs, which tend to leave different patterns of attack.

Those who encounter the Beast describe glowing eyeshine when light strikes its face at night. The eyes are often said to be green or yellow, piercing through the darkness with an intensity beyond that of ordinary wild animals in Britain. During daylight sightings, its dark coat blends perfectly with the gorse and heather of the moorlands, allowing it to vanish almost instantly.

Movement is one of the most striking features of the Beast of Exmoor. Witnesses describe a creature that glides smoothly over rough terrain. It crouches low, stalks, and then bounds in long leaps with a speed that exceeds domestic cats. It is silent, appearing and disappearing in a way that defies explanation. Several reports describe it clearing fences more than six feet high in a single leap.

Hunters, soldiers, and police have been called in over the decades to track the Beast, but no confirmed specimen has ever been captured. Prints have been photographed, though they are often dismissed as being from large dogs. Yet some tracks show characteristics of a feline paw, such as retractable claws. The lack of definitive physical evidence does not erase the fact that hundreds of reliable witnesses continue to describe the same animal across generations.

Theories about the Beast range from the survival of a released exotic pet to an unknown species of big cat adapted to the English landscape. Britain once allowed ownership of non-native cats before strict laws were introduced in the 1970s. Some researchers suggest that abandoned or escaped animals could have survived and reproduced. Others argue the sightings represent a species not recognized by science.

Despite the uncertainty, locals continue to see and report the Beast. Sightings are still being logged in the 21st Century. Farmers remain wary of leaving young livestock unguarded on open moorland. Walkers and travelers occasionally glimpse a powerful black form crossing a field or slipping into woodland. The legend of the Beast of Exmoor endures because it is not simply a legend—it is based on repeated encounters that have yet to be disproven.

In the natural history of Britain the Beast of Exmoor stands as a reminder that the countryside may still harbor predators thought lost to this land. Whether it is a remnant of a forgotten population, an introduced species, or something entirely unknown, the Beast continues to live on in both fact and mystery.

The Beast of Exmoor is reported to prey upon livestock, including Exmoor ponies. Copyright © Lochlainn Seabrook.

BEAST OF GÉVAUDAN

Though the Beast of Gévaudan was last reported in 1767, some surmise it may still roam the countryside of southern France. Copyright © Lochlainn Seabrook.

QUICK FACTS

NAME: Beast of Gévaudan.
FIRST SIGHTING: 1764.
LOCATION: Gévaudan region, south-central France.
SIZE: Reported between 5 and 7 feet long, weighing 150 to 200 pounds.
APPEARANCE: Wolf-like body with an elongated head, broad chest, and a long, powerful tail.
EYES: Described as large, fierce, and often glowing in low light.
SKIN/FUR: Reddish-brown fur with darker streaks, sometimes with a line of bristles along the back.
DIET: Primarily carnivorous, feeding on livestock such as sheep and cattle; also reported to attack humans.
MOVEMENT: Swift and agile, capable of running long distances and leaping great bounds.
NOTABLE BEHAVIOR: Known for its boldness in attacking humans during daylight, often targeting the throat.
FIRST REPORTED BY: Peasants of Gévaudan in the mid-18th Century.
CREATURE CLASSIFICATION: Cryptid canid, possibly an unknown species related to *Canis lupus*.
STATUS: Unconfirmed by mainstream science.

CREATURE PROFILE

The Beast of Gévaudan stands out as one of the most fearsome predator mysteries in Europe. Unlike many legendary creatures that remain confined to folklore, this animal left a trail of bodies, panic, and historical documentation. From 1764 to 1767 the mountainous province of Gévaudan in south-central France suffered through an outbreak of attacks that terrified entire villages and claimed more than one hundred lives. Its sudden appearance and strange behavior placed it outside the understanding of naturalists and hunters of the period, giving rise to one of the greatest enigmas in cryptozoological history.

Contemporary reports described a beast larger than a wolf, stretching up to seven feet in length and weighing close to two hundred pounds. Its fur was said to be reddish-brown with dark streaks, and many claimed it bore a mane or bristling ridge that rose when it was angered. The head was elongated and wolf-like but with an unusual shape, possessing jaws powerful enough to crush bone. The eyes were described as large and fierce, sometimes glinting with a strange brightness in the twilight. The long tail, often noted in reports, was muscular and capable of lashing like a whip.

What set the Beast apart from ordinary predators was its method of attack. Rather than preying only on livestock, it frequently targeted humans, often in daylight and in the presence of witnesses. Its favored tactic was to spring upon its victim and seize the throat in its jaws, killing quickly and brutally. Women and children bore the brunt of the slaughter, but men were not spared. Victims were sometimes mutilated beyond recognition, leaving parish officials to record gruesome details in their registers. Livestock kills also occurred, but the preference for human prey distinguished the Beast as something abnormal in the natural order.

The killings prompted both local and national responses. Villagers formed armed hunting parties, while King Louis XV dispatched soldiers and professional huntsmen. Rewards were posted, and the Crown demanded results. Several large wolves were shot and triumphantly displayed as the Beast; yet the attacks continued unabated, often within days. This persistence convinced many that the true Beast remained alive or that there were several such animals roaming together. Despite months of tracking, laying traps, and scouring the forests, the hunters failed again and again.

Speculation about the Beast's identity abounded. Some insisted it was a monstrous wolf, though its reported size and coloring contradicted known species. Others suggested it was a wolf-dog hybrid, perhaps crossed with mastiff bloodlines to produce an abnormally large and fearless predator. A few argued it was an exotic animal such as a lion or hyena brought to France and later released. More speculative voices claimed it might represent a surviving remnant of an ancient predator line, a relic species thought to have vanished long before. Each theory reflected the desperation to explain a creature that defied classification.

In 1767 after years of carnage a large wolf was killed by a local hunter. Authorities declared the Beast destroyed. Attacks diminished sharply afterward, though occasional killings still occurred in nearby districts. Many locals believed the real Beast had never been slain, and oral traditions of strange wolf-like predators lingered across the region for decades. The legend became firmly embedded in French folklore, shaping both literature and collective memory.

Today the Beast of Gévaudan remains one of the most thoroughly documented cryptid cases. Mainstream science views the episode as wolf predation intensified by fear and rumor, but cryptozoologists point to the distinct behavior, bold hunting style, and the failure of official hunts as evidence of an unknown species or hybrid. While its historical outbreak is fixed in the 18th Century, occasional reports of oversized wolves in modern France keep speculation alive. Its survival remains unconfirmed by mainstream science, yet the possibility that descendants live on in remote areas remains a subject of serious consideration.

The story of the Beast continues to fascinate because it represents the meeting point between history, folklore, and zoology. It reveals how an unidentified predator can devastate human communities, elude large-scale hunts, and survive in memory long after official explanations close the case. Whether a giant wolf, a hybrid, or something altogether unknown, the Beast of Gévaudan reminds us that Europe's wilderness once held mysteries not yet fully explained and may still conceal predators capable of astonishing power.

The 7 foot long Beast of Gévaudan was known to stalk and kill women and children in the 18th Century. Did it leave behind modern descendants that continue the fearsome practice? Copyright © Lochlainn Seabrook.

BEITHIR

Does the 50 foot long Beithir still haunt the Scottish Highlands? Many present day eyewitnesses say yes. Copyright © Lochlainn Seabrook.

QUICK FACTS

NAME: Beithir.
FIRST SIGHTING: At least the 16th Century.
LOCATION: Highlands of Scotland, particularly glens, lochs, and mountainsides.
SIZE: Reports range from 10 feet to over 30 feet long, with some accounts suggesting greater lengths, along with estimated weights of 500 to 2,000 pounds—depending on length.
APPEARANCE: A giant serpent-like creature with a long tapering body, ridged back, and sharp spines.
EYES: Large, glowing eyes that are said to shine with a green or fiery red hue.
SKIN/FUR: Smooth, shiny, scale-covered hide, often described as dark green, brown, or black.
DIET: Believed to prey on livestock, deer, fish, and occasionally humans. Said to consume large animals whole and to strike with venom.
MOVEMENT: Slithers with great speed across land, and is also capable of swimming through rivers and lochs.
NOTABLE BEHAVIOR: Associated with thunder and lightning, appearing after storms or striking victims with venom. Said to guard hidden places and sometimes attack without provocation.
FIRST REPORTED BY: Scottish Highlanders through oral folklore and early written accounts of the Middle Ages.
CREATURE CLASSIFICATION: Giant serpent or dragon.
STATUS: Unconfirmed by mainstream science, but still reported in modern Highland folklore and also by hikers and locals.

CREATURE PROFILE

Among the rugged mountains and mystical glens of Scotland lies the legend of the Beithir (Scottish Gaelic for "serpent"), a creature spoken of with the same hushed respect as other Highland terrors. Unlike more familiar lake monsters the Beithir is not bound to the water. It moves freely across the land, slipping through the heather and over the rocks with the sinuous power of a massive serpent. For centuries its name has been uttered in warnings, its image passed down in story and song, and its reputation as one of the deadliest of Scottish beasts has carried on into the present.

Descriptions of the Beithir place it somewhere between a serpent and a dragon. It lacks wings yet bears the menace of a creature that can command storms. Its body is long and muscular, armed with ridges and sometimes spines, while its head carries wide jaws filled with sharp teeth. Its eyes are said to glow in dim light, a trait that gives it an otherworldly presence when seen against the backdrop of stormy skies.

Though accounts vary the most consistent detail is its venom, which is said to kill swiftly and with no cure once its fangs pierce the skin.

Highland communities have long regarded the Beithir as both a natural predator and a supernatural force. Folklore tells of people struck dead after disturbing its resting place, often caves or stony hillsides. Farmers told of cattle lost to the creature, dragged away in silence, leaving only crushed earth and a trail of scales. Fishermen swore that the Beithir slid into rivers and lochs to ambush prey, gliding through the water with terrifying rapidity. Because of these behaviors it became known as a hybrid monster, as comfortable in fresh water as on the rugged Highland slopes.

Its link with weather further enhances its legend. Many Highlanders believed that thunder and lightning heralded its appearance. Some stories describe the Beithir itself as a lightning spirit that took physical form, while others claimed that when struck down by a thunderbolt it would return even more powerful. For this reason it was often considered immortal or reborn after destruction, a belief that strengthened the fear surrounding its name. To encounter it in a storm was thought to mean certain death.

Modern sightings, though rare, suggest that the legend has not faded. Hikers in the Highlands have occasionally spoken of immense serpentine shapes moving across scree slopes or vanishing into mountain lochs. Others report strange patterns in the grass or earth resembling the track of a giant serpent. Though dismissed by conventional science these reports continue to echo the older traditions and keep the Beithir alive in the folklore of Scotland. The persistence of sightings indicates that some eyewitnesses still believe they have seen the monster firsthand.

The possibility of the Beithir's survival is certainly not entirely dismissed by those open to cryptozoology. A relict population of enormous serpents or eel-like creatures could theoretically inhabit the remote and sparsely populated Highland regions. The rugged terrain offers caves, lochs, and hidden valleys where such animals could exist with minimal detection. The venom attributed to it suggests that if it is real it could belong to a lineage of reptiles that developed toxic defense and offensive systems. In this sense the Beithir might represent a surviving branch of large prehistoric reptiles adapted to a harsh climate.

As with many cryptids the Beithir occupies a space between folklore and zoology. To locals, it remains a dangerous being woven into the identity of the Highlands, a warning against wandering alone after storms or disturbing wild places without respect. To researchers it stands as one of the most compelling serpent-like beings of Europe, linked as much to weather and myth as to physical encounters. Whether it is an undiscovered predator, a misunderstood natural species, or a folkloric echo of ancient fear, the Beithir remains embedded in Scotland's living tradition of mysterious creatures.

The Beithir: one of Scotland's most mysterious serpentine cryptids. Copyright © Lochlainn Seabrook.

BIG BIRD

The 7 foot tall Big Bird continues to be spotted across parts of Texas and Mexico, confounding skeptics while corroborating the many reports of eyewitnesses. Copyright © Lochlainn Seabrook.

QUICK FACTS

NAME: Big Bird.
FIRST SIGHTING: January 1976.
LOCATION: Rio Grande Valley, Texas, USA.
SIZE: Estimated wingspan 10 to 12 feet, height 5 to 7 feet, weight possibly 200 to 300 pounds.
APPEARANCE: Described as a massive birdlike creature with leathery wings, a long beak, and clawed feet.
EYES: Large and dark, often reported as intense and predatory.
SKIN/FUR: Featherless in most reports, with gray to black leathery skin resembling that of a reptile.
DIET: Believed to feed on small mammals, birds, reptiles, fish, and carrion, though some reports suggest it may prey on domestic animals.
MOVEMENT: Flies with heavy, deliberate wingbeats, capable of gliding silently for long distances, occasionally seen running on the ground.
NOTABLE BEHAVIOR: Known to circle neighborhoods at night, perch on rooftops, and chase cars and people.
FIRST REPORTED BY: Multiple independent witnesses including schoolchildren and police officers in South Texas.
CREATURE CLASSIFICATION: Possibly a surviving pterosaur, giant bird species, or unknown megafaunal avian.
STATUS: Unconfirmed by mainstream science, but still reported in Texas and northern Mexico.

CREATURE PROFILE

The Big Bird of South Texas emerges in accounts as one of the most dramatic avian cryptids in North America. Unlike many other mystery birds that have faded into distant memory, this one entered modern history with startlingly vivid encounters during the 1970s and remains a subject of occasional sightings today. Reports describe a massive winged creature, one that seems far too large to be any known living bird. Its wings, reaching ten feet or more, cast a shadow across rural highways and small towns, leaving witnesses shaken by its sheer scale.

Descriptions agree on a body more reptilian than avian, with leathery skin in place of feathers. The wings appear batlike, with thick, membranous surfaces reminiscent of prehistoric pterosaurs. Its long beak and taloned feet reinforce the impression of an ancient predator that has somehow survived into the modern era. When perched it reaches the size of a grown man, but when airborne its span gives the impression of a small aircraft.

The first major wave of reports in 1976 centered in the Rio

Grande Valley. Schoolchildren described the beast ominously circling playgrounds. Adults claimed to see it swooping low over roads. Local police officers, normally cautious about strange claims, confirmed seeing something huge and winged flying at rooftop height. Its presence was so unsettling that newspapers across Texas covered the story; residents began referring to it as the "Big Bird."

The creature's behavior is equally remarkable. Witnesses describe it gliding silently, only occasionally flapping its wings, suggesting an efficient design suited for covering long distances without tiring. At times it has been reported chasing cars, matching speeds up to fifty miles an hour before veering off. Its willingness to follow or approach humans makes it seem unusually daring, unlike the more elusive habits of known large birds, such as eagles or vultures.

Diet remains speculative but evidence suggests carnivorous habits. Farmers in South Texas reported missing livestock during the 1976 flap, including goats and chickens—though no carcasses were recovered. Some witnesses believed it scavenged roadkill, a behavior common among large birds of prey. Its strong beak and clawed feet would make it capable of seizing both living and dead animals.

Several explanations have been offered. Some argue that Big Bird represents a surviving pterosaur, perhaps related to *Quetzalcoatlus northropi*, which once inhabited Texas during the Cretaceous. Others suggest it could be an undiscovered species of giant bird, akin to a massive stork or condor adapted to the arid southern plains. Still others consider it a misidentified large bird such as a heron or crane—though the sheer size and reptilian descriptions are difficult to reconcile with known species.

Importantly, the sightings have not disappeared. Though less frequent than during the 1970s wave, locals in Texas and northern Mexico still occasionally report encounters with a giant birdlike creature. Its persistence across decades suggests either a small breeding population or lone survivors of a hidden species. The open ranchlands, deserts, and river valleys of South Texas provide wide areas of habitat where such a creature could evade detection.

The Big Bird stands as a compelling example of modern cryptozoology. It bridges natural history and folklore, recalling prehistoric skies while intruding into contemporary life. Whether a relic of deep time or an undiscovered megafaunal bird, the ongoing reports ensure that the legend remains alive. Despite the doubting claims of mainstream science, in a world where many animals once thought extinct have resurfaced, the possibility of the Big Bird's survival remains open.

Witnesses in South Texas in the 1970s gave differing descriptions of the Big Bird. Some reported a giant bird-like creature with sparse feathers, while others described a leathery, pterosaur-like beast—confusing images that only add to the beast's perplexing nature. Copyright © Lochlainn Seabrook.

BIGFOOT

A 10 foot tall (male) Bigfoot, arguably North America's most familiar, most discussed, and most often witnessed cryptid. Copyright © Lochlainn Seabrook.

QUICK FACTS

NAME: Bigfoot.

ALTERNATIVE NAMES: Sasquatch, Skookum, Oh-Mah, Wildman, Hairy Man, Forest Giant.

FIRST REPORTED SIGHTING: 1811, European (in Canada); Indigenous oral traditions predate written history.

SIGHTING LOCATION: Primarily Pacific Northwest, USA, and Canada; sightings quite common across North America; it, or countless "apeman" variants, have been seen on every continent except Antarctica.

ESTIMATED SIZE: Height generally reported between 7 and 10 feet; estimated weight 500 to 1,000+ pounds; broad shoulder width up to 3 feet; stride length 4 to 6 feet; tracks measure 14 to 24 inches long and 6 to 10 inches wide.

WITNESS DESCRIPTION: Massive, often intimidating, bipedal, ape-like or human-like figure covered in dark brown, black, auburn, reddish, blonde, white, or gray hair; conical head shape; no neck (head appears to sit directly on shoulders); deep-set eyes; long arms; powerful build; emits a strong, musky odor in some encounters.

BEHAVIOR: Primarily reclusive, avoiding human contact; observed walking smoothly with a long, swinging arm motion; occasionally emits loud vocalizations, including whoops, whimpers, growls, yells, and mournful blood-curdling screams; some surmise it may have its own language (known non-technically as "Samuri chatter"); often heard producing wood knocks (hitting trees with sticks or logs), rock clacks (smacking two rocks together), and mouth pops; known to imitate the sounds of wildlife (such as owls) and even humans; may throw pine cones, sticks, pebbles, rocks, and even boulders at would-be intruders; its foot, hand, knuckle, and body prints, as well as its trackways, are often found near water sources; it is sometimes observed in patriarchal family groups. As with humans, Bigfoot individuals seem to have unique personalities, for example, peaceful, aggressive, territorial, inquisitive, friendly, shy, extroverted, etc.

DIET: Believed to be omnivorous and opportunistic. Reports and indirect evidence suggest a diet comprised largely of berries, nuts, roots, tubers, and other plant material; fish and small to medium mammals; occasional deer predation; bird eggs; insects such as ants and grubs; and scavenging of carrion. Seasonal patterns likely influence diet, with more plant-based foods in summer and autumn and higher protein intake in winter. Anecdotal accounts include observed feeding on salmon during spawning runs, stripping bark for insect larvae, and raiding gardens or orchards. In some cases farm animals are taken. Often spotted along both green and powerline corridors. May migrate up and down in elevation (as black and

brown bears do) with the change of the seasons in search of food.
CREATURE CLASSIFICATION: Cryptid; possible undiscovered North American primate, a surviving relict hominin, or perhaps an unknown great ape—sometimes assumed to be the "extinct" *Gigantopithecus blacki*. It is also interpreted in some traditions as a spiritual, extraterrestrial (alien), or interdimensional being (e.g., the biblical Nephilim)—even possessing paranormal powers, such as cloaking, shape-shifting, teleportation, and invisibility.
STATUS: While some individual scientists argue for its reality, the creature continues to remain unrecognized by mainstream science as a whole, as no physical specimen has yet been documented. Some of our more open-minded scientists are using touch DNA on purported Bigfoot hair, scat, blood, and saliva samples in the hopes of coming closer to a definitive identification (one study that I consider legitimate found that the creature's DNA was half human, half unknown primate). In any case, thousands of eyewitness accounts, track casts, hair samples, and audio recordings spanning centuries maintain its standing as one of the most investigated cryptids in the world.

CREATURE PROFILE

Bigfoot—also widely known as Sasquatch—is arguably the most famous cryptid in North America and a central figure in modern cryptozoology. While the term "Bigfoot" originated in the late 1950s following the discovery of large humanlike barefoot tracks in California, the name "Sasquatch" comes from the anglicized form of the Halkomelem word *Sásq'ets*, used by Indigenous Coast Salish peoples of British Columbia. Oral traditions describing large apemen, or hairy man-like beings of one kind or another, extend back centuries, making this one of the oldest continuous legends on the North American continent.

The first well-documented modern sighting occurred in 1811 near Jasper, Alberta, Canada, when British explorer David Thompson recorded finding large, human-like tracks in the snow. Over time reports have come from every U.S. state and Canadian province. But the Pacific Northwest—with its dense coniferous forests, mountainous terrain, and abundant food sources—remains the epicenter of activity.

Eyewitnesses consistently describe a towering powerfully built "apeman" covered in hair, walking upright with a long swinging gait. Skin tones described (just visible beneath its hair) range from gray to dark brown. The head often appears slightly pointed or conical, while the face is usually described as more humanlike than apelike. Some witnesses report an overpowering "horrid" musky odor accompanying encounters.

Behavioral observations include rock throwing, pine cone throwing, wood knocking, rock clacking, mouth popping, tongue clicking, and a wide variety of vocalizations, from high-pitched screams to deep roars, some of the latter possibly interlaced with infrasound (also used by tigers, elephants, alligators, whales, etc.): powerful subsonic frequencies that are known to cause anxiety, nausea, fear, fatigue, hallucinations, visual distortions, memory loss, dizziness, headaches, motion sickness, vertigo, and, among other things, changes in heart rate, blood pressure, and breathing, in humans. Tracks—some exceeding 20 inches in length—remain among the persistent forms of reported evidence, with numerous plaster casts held in private and public collections.

While the creature is most often associated with remote mountain and forest regions, reports also occur surprisingly close to rural towns and even suburban areas, particularly where wilderness borders human development. Witnesses have described seeing Bigfoot raiding gardens, crossing highways at night, carrying dead deer over their shoulders, lurking behind stores and shopping malls, and following hunters and campers through the wilderness. These encounters suggest that it is both highly intelligent and adaptable, able to exploit a wide range of environments while remaining elusive enough to avoid capture.

Regional variations in description also add nuance to the mystery. In the Pacific Northwest Bigfoot is typically described as dark brown or black, while reports from the American South—where it is often referred to as the Skunk Ape—tend to describe a smaller, slimmer creature with reddish hair and an even stronger odor. In the Midwest and Appalachians witnesses often note glowing red or amber eyes, sometimes associated with nighttime encounters along backroads. These differences could suggest multiple related species or subspecies, or they might reflect environmental adaptations in different habitats.

Speculation about Bigfoot's identity ranges from an undiscovered great ape to a surviving population of *Gigantopithecus blacki*, or even a relict hominin closely related to *Homo sapiens*. Others interpret it through a supernatural lens (the "woo" factor), suggesting it may be a shapeshifter, spiritual being, nature guardian, or interdimensional traveler—an idea rooted in some Indigenous traditions. Despite decades of research, according to mainstream science at least, no physical specimen has been captured or scientifically verified, leaving the creature's true nature an open question. (Note that Bigfoot's identity continues to be hotly debated with as of yet no consensus among either mainstream scientists or cryptozoologists.)

In addition to anecdotal sightings several pieces of physical evidence have fueled the debate over the creature's existence. Among the most famous is the Patterson-Gimlin film, shot in northern California in 1967, which shows a large, upright, hair-covered figure striding fearlessly and gracefully through a creek bed. While skeptics argue it is a hoax, the footage has never been conclusively debunked and remains one of the most analyzed pieces of cryptid evidence in history. Hair samples, scat, and unusual vocal recordings have also been collected, though laboratory results have often been inconclusive or contradictory; in some cases items sent in for scientific analysis become mysteriously "lost"—for reasons that go unexplained. (One wonders what was found.)

Cultural influence is another reason for Bigfoot's enduring prominence. It has become an icon of wilderness mystery, appearing in documentaries, films, literature, and even as a marketing symbol for products ranging from jerky to sports teams. For Indigenous communities, however, Bigfoot represents more than a pop culture figure: it is often regarded as a guardian of nature, a cautionary presence reminding humans to respect the land. This dual role—part scientific mystery, part cultural archetype—has ensured that Bigfoot remains one of the most compelling and intrenched enigmas of modern times.

Beyond North America, reports of similar creatures exist worldwide; and, in fact, I would consider it one of the most, if not the most, widely dispersed cryptid in this book. The Yeti of the Himalayas, the Yeren of China, the Alma of Central Asia, and the Yowie of Australia, for example, all share strikingly parallel descriptions, suggesting that the Bigfoot phenomenon is actually the result of a global-wide species that has spawned a myriad of subspecies, each one adapted to its own particular geographic location. The near universal tradition of "wildman," "hairy man," and "apeman" lore certainly suggests as much.

Indeed, the cross-cultural consistency involved lends weight to the argument that these legends are based on a biological reality—even if unacknowledged by conventional science. This has led some serious researchers to propose that these reports point to a once-widespread hominin species that has survived into the present day in isolated pockets.

Attempts to gather definitive proof continue. Numerous organizations conduct field expeditions, setting up thermal cameras, audio recorders, and drone surveys in suspected hotspots. Citizen scientists and professional researchers alike contribute data, from footprint impressions to long-term studies of remote habitats. Advances in environmental DNA (eDNA) sampling are now being applied to soil and water collected from alleged Bigfoot sites, potentially offering a path to verification without the need for a captured body (holotype).

In recent decades more sophisticated methods of analysis have been added to the investigator's toolkit. Acoustic experts have studied recordings of alleged Sasquatch vocalizations, noting unusual ranges and frequencies that fall far outside normal human or animal capacity. Forensic analysts have examined footprint dermal ridges that appear consistent with primate physiology, yet which are unlike any known species. Field researchers have also collected hair samples that defy easy classification, sometimes showing traits consistent with both human and nonhuman primates.

Most compelling are the thousands of eyewitness testimonies, many from hunters, foresters, law enforcement officers, and other trained observers, whose accounts carry a level of credibility beyond the casual eyewitness. Together this body of data forms a mosaic that, while incomplete, suggests that something tangible is generating the phenomenon.

Some researchers also point to alleged government and military interest in Bigfoot cases. Accounts circulate of federal agencies removing evidence, seizing bodies, or discouraging witnesses from going public. Though unverifiable, these claims feed into a long-standing suspicion that authorities may know more about the phenomenon than they admit. If true, suppression could explain why conclusive physical evidence has never reached the public domain—despite centuries of encounters.

At the same time, skeptics argue that the lack of bones, bodies, or other irrefutable evidence strongly suggests that Bigfoot does not exist. They contend that most sightings can be explained as misidentifications of bears, moose, or even humans in costumes, while alleged tracks may be hoaxes or natural impressions misread as footprints. Yet despite repeated claims of hoaxing, the volume of reports remains steady and often convincing, indicating that most accounts cannot be dismissed so easily.

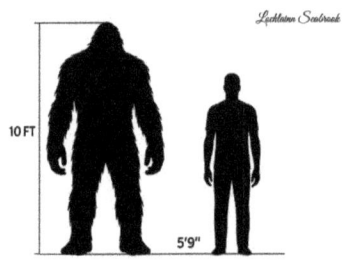

Size comparison between an adult male Bigfoot and an average man. Copyright © Lochlainn Seabrook.

One of the most intriguing aspects of the Bigfoot mystery is the consistency of its description over time. From Native American oral histories to modern encounters, the core image—a giant, hairy, human-like creature—remains remarkably stable. This has led some anthropologists to suggest that Bigfoot serves as a cultural archetype, a symbol of the untamed wilderness and humanity's lingering fear of what lurks beyond civilization's edge. In this view Bigfoot exists as both a flesh-and-blood biological species and a nebulous but powerful psychological reality.

Despite the lack of consensus across every field, Bigfoot remains one of the most reported and researched cryptids in the world. For believers the sheer volume of encounters indicates a hidden reality just beyond the margins of scientific acknowledgment. For skeptics it highlights the human tendency to mythologize the unknown.

Either way, the near constant and continuous flood of sightings, track finds, audio recordings, and countless other sometimes otherworldy phenomena associated with it—all which continue to be reported unabated into the present day—suggests that Bigfoot may be both biological *and* paranormal; an archetypal being, part animal, part human, part spirit; one that will forever remain embedded in both the wilderness lore and cultural identity of North America.

Bigfoot (and its many global variants) can occasionally display terrifying aggressive behavior, implying that it may be responsible for at least some of the literally millions of people who go missing every year around the world. Copyright © Lochlainn Seabrook.

Bigfoot is well-known for its habit of tree-peeking, as well as for paralleling hikers, ushering them (from off trail and just beyond sight) out of their territory. Its sometimes ominous presence is usually more than enough to clear an entire area of humans—many swearing they will never return. Copyright © Lochlainn Seabrook.

BLACK DOG

England's 7 foot long Black Dog hovers on the line between physical reality and ancient mythology. Copyright © Lochlainn Seabrook.

QUICK FACTS

NAME: Black Dog.
FIRST SIGHTING: At least the 12th Century.
LOCATION: Reported across the British Isles, with related sightings in Europe and North America.
SIZE: Typically described as 6 to 7 feet long, weighing an estimated 150 to 250 pounds.
APPEARANCE: A large, spectral dog often appearing solid, though sometimes semi-transparent.
EYES: Usually described as glowing red, orange, or yellow.
SKIN/FUR: Black fur, thick and coarse, sometimes described as smoky or shadow-like.
DIET: Said to feed on fear, energy, or in some accounts on livestock and carrion; rarely associated with attacking humans directly.
MOVEMENT: Moves silently on padded feet, can vanish or appear suddenly, sometimes reported floating above the ground.
NOTABLE BEHAVIOR: Often appears on lonely roads, crossroads, and graveyards; sometimes considered a death omen but also a guardian spirit in certain regions.
FIRST REPORTED BY: Medieval chroniclers and local villagers in England and Wales.
CREATURE CLASSIFICATION: Paranormal canine cryptid.
STATUS: Unrecognized by mainstream science; yet still reported in rural Britain and elsewhere today.

CREATURE PROFILE

Legends of the Black Dog live on in the rolling hills, moors, and villages of the British Isles. These mysterious canines occupy a unique place in folklore, blending qualities of ghostly apparitions with those of physical animals. People across centuries have described them as large shaggy dogs with fiery eyes and a menacing presence that lingers long after the creature vanishes. Yet their role is not always hostile. In some traditions the Black Dog serves as a harbinger of death, while in others it protects travelers from harm.

Reports usually describe an animal far larger than any natural dog. Many accounts place its length at six or seven feet, with a height at the shoulder equal to that of a small pony. Its eyes are the most striking feature, glowing brightly in the darkness, often red though sometimes golden or orange. These eyes have been said to paralyze those who meet their gaze, filling the witness with dread. The fur is nearly always reported as jet black, thick and bristling, though in some cases the body appears less substantial, more like a shifting shadow than flesh.

The Black Dog is strongly linked with liminal spaces such as crossroads, bridges, and graveyards. It is also encountered along old country lanes and lonely stretches of moorland. In East Anglia the creature is known as Black Shuck, whose name may come from an old English word for demon. In Wales it is called the Gwyllgi, or "Dog of Darkness." Similar stories echo through Yorkshire, Cornwall, and beyond. These widespread traditions suggest a phenomenon deeply ingrained in human experience rather than a localized myth.

The lasting impact of these accounts is reflected in Sir Arthur Conan Doyle's 1902 novel *The Hound of the Baskervilles*. In that work the author drew directly on Black Dog lore from Dartmoor to craft his tale of a spectral hound haunting an English family. The popularity of the novel demonstrates how deeply embedded the Black Dog is in British culture, and how eyewitness traditions provided the foundation for one of literature's most famous supernatural hounds.

Behavior varies across reports. Sometimes the Black Dog simply walks alongside travelers before vanishing at a fork in the road. In other cases it blocks a path, its glowing eyes fixed on the intruder until they flee. There are also records of the dog appearing inside churches or houses, scratching at doors, or even attacking livestock. Yet not all stories are grim. Some accounts claim the Black Dog warns of danger ahead or keeps company with lonely wanderers until they are safely home.

Diet is difficult to define since the creature rarely interacts in a naturalistic way. Witnesses describe it feeding less on physical prey than on the fear it inspires. Its presence seems tied to human emotion, as if drawing strength from dread and awe. However, isolated tales of livestock killings suggest a more material appetite in some manifestations. This duality strengthens the theory that the Black Dog may occupy both a physical and supernatural state.

The persistence of sightings into modern times supports the idea that the Black Dog is more than a medieval legend. Contemporary reports describe encounters on English roads, Scottish highlands, and even in parts of North America where British settlers carried their traditions. Many who meet the creature today describe the same chilling silence, the same fiery eyes, and the same sudden disappearance into the night.

Speculation about survival is important here. If the Black Dog is a living species rather than a purely spectral entity, it may represent an unknown large canine that has adapted to avoid detection while inspiring fear. Its apparent ability to vanish could be a misunderstanding of sudden retreat, or a genuine ability tied to a physical adaptation beyond current knowledge. If instead it is a spiritual manifestation, it demonstrates remarkable consistency across time and geography, suggesting continuity of a real phenomenon. Either way the Black Dog continues to prowl lonely paths, reminding us that some mysteries continue, outwitting both time and science.

Eyewitnesses often report that the Black Dog turns transparent before completely disappearing. Copyright © Lochlainn Seabrook.

BLACK PANTHER

The nearly ubiquitous 7 foot long Black Panther has been reported on four of our planet's seven continents. Copyright © Lochlainn Seabrook.

QUICK FACTS

NAME: Black Panther.
FIRST SIGHTING: Early 19th Century.
LOCATION: Rural regions of North America, the British Isles, and Australia.
SIZE: Estimated 5 to 7 feet long including tail, 2 feet tall at the shoulder, 100 to 200 pounds.
APPEARANCE: Large muscular cat with an elongated body, long tail, and rounded head.
EYES: Yellow or green, often reported glowing at night.
SKIN/FUR: Short dense black coat, sometimes showing faint rosettes under bright light.
DIET: Reported to prey on deer, sheep, goats, kangaroos, wallabies, livestock, wild boar, smaller mammals, birds, and occasionally carrion; opportunistic carnivore with hunting strategies similar to leopards and cougars.
MOVEMENT: Silent, agile, powerful; capable of leaping high fences and sprinting quickly over short distances.
NOTABLE BEHAVIOR: Stalks prey with stealth, leaves large paw prints, emits cat-like screams or growls at night, often vanishes suddenly without trace.
FIRST REPORTED BY: European settlers and farmers encountering unexplained predation.
CREATURE CLASSIFICATION: Elusive large feline, possible unknown population of melanistic leopards or cougars.
STATUS: Not recognized by mainstream science, but reported regularly into the present day.

CREATURE PROFILE

Few cryptids have gained as much widespread attention as the so-called Black Panther. Reports of large black cats roaming outside their recognized native ranges surface continually in newspapers, farm records, and eyewitness accounts. Unlike many legendary creatures that occupy narrow cultural or geographic niches, these big cats are seen across continents, creating one of the broadest distribution patterns of any cryptid. The consistency of descriptions from such diverse locations strongly suggests a real animal may be responsible.

Sightings are concentrated in three main regions: the rural and forested areas of the United States, particularly the South and Midwest; the British Isles, where they are often referred to as "Alien Big Cats"; and Australia, especially New South Wales and Victoria. In each of these places locals encounter animals too large to be ordinary house cats and too dark-coated to be recognized cougars or leopards known from zoos. Witnesses describe a sleek black cat of formidable size, often spotted near farmland or edges of forest, moving with predatory confidence. When farmers and ranchers find livestock carcasses stripped of flesh, along with puncture wounds consistent with feline teeth, they typically attribute the kill to the panther.

The biological identity of the Black Panther remains debated but one of the most compelling explanations involves melanism. In nature melanism is a genetic condition that produces excess dark pigmentation. Black leopards

(*Panthera pardus*) and black jaguars (*Panthera onca*) are known examples. Some believe feral populations of such cats have established themselves after escapes or releases from menageries, circuses, or private collections in the 19th and 20th Centuries. Others propose that the North American cougar (*Puma concolor*), normally tawny, may have a rare but unrecognized melanistic phase. If this is correct it would extend the range of melanism into a species previously not documented with that trait.

Physical evidence has been fragmentary but tantalizing. Large paw prints, far exceeding those of dogs, are sometimes discovered near kill sites. Sheep carcasses with cleanly sheared bones, as opposed to ragged tearing, suggest powerful feline jaws. Photographs, though often blurry, occasionally show a dark, catlike form with the distinct profile of a big cat. Video recordings in Britain and Australia have also circulated, and while some have been dismissed as misidentifications of domestic animals, others remain unexplained after professional review. Zoo officials and big cat specialists who have examined certain images admit that the proportions appear consistent with leopards or cougars.

Behavior attributed to the Black Panther parallels known big cat behavior. The creature moves silently, is mostly solitary, and is most often seen at dawn or dusk. Eyewitnesses describe sudden vanishing acts when the cat slips back into cover, leaving no more than paw prints or claw marks on trees. Its vocalizations are equally striking. Low growls, coughing roars, and piercing screams are all reported. Such sounds match those of large cats rather than small felines or foxes, further bolstering claims that we are dealing here with a real animal.

Ecologically, there is little to prevent these cats from surviving in the reported areas. North America, the UK, and Australia each host abundant prey species and suitable cover in forests, hedgerows, and mountain ranges. In Britain in particular, where native large predators have long been absent, deer and sheep populations provide an easy food base. Similarly, Australian farmland supplies sheep and kangaroos in abundance. Such resources could sustain a small breeding population if even a handful of individuals were released decades ago.

Despite this, no carcass has been officially recovered and verified by mainstream science. This absence fuels skepticism. But it also underscores the extreme elusiveness of large carnivores in human-dominated landscapes. Cougars themselves, though officially present in many parts of North America, can go unseen for years even in regions where they are common. The lack of remains, therefore, is not conclusive evidence against the Black Panther's existence.

Today reports continue at a steady pace. Farmers still find livestock killed under suspicious circumstances. Motorists claim to glimpse sleek black cats crossing rural roads at night. Hikers in both the British Isles and American backcountry occasionally encounter large cats moving silently through undergrowth. In each case, the description remains remarkably consistent: a big black cat, larger than any dog, moving with the fluid grace of a wild predator. The persistence of these accounts into the present day suggests that the Black Panther may not be a myth at all but a hidden mystery animal that has adapted to modern rural environments.

The cryptic Black Panther chasing down a wild boar in the woods of Tennessee. Copyright © Lochlainn Seabrook.

BROSNO DRAGON

The 30 foot long Brosno Dragon was first reported in the 13th Century. Sightings continue to this day. Copyright © Lochlainn Seabrook.

QUICK FACTS

NAME: Brosno Dragon.
FIRST SIGHTING: 13th Century.
LOCATION: Lake Brosno, Tver Region, western Russia.
SIZE: Estimated 15 to 30 feet long, possibly larger, weighing 1 to 3 tons.
APPEARANCE: Serpentine body with a long neck, dragon-like head, and large mouth.
EYES: Said to be large, reflective, and bright in low light.
SKIN/FUR: Described as scaly, rough, and reptilian, dark gray to brown in color.
DIET: Believed to consume fish, waterfowl, livestock near the shore, and on occasion larger animals such as horses or even humans if available. Reports also suggest it may scavenge drowned animals and carrion that sink into the lake's depths.
MOVEMENT: Undulating swimming motion across the surface, quick dives, and sudden emergences.
NOTABLE BEHAVIOR: Known for overturning boats, frightening fishermen, and attacking animals drinking at the shore. Also reputed to create whirlpools and foam when surfacing.
FIRST REPORTED BY: Medieval Russian chroniclers and villagers.
CREATURE CLASSIFICATION: Aquatic reptilian cryptid, possibly related to *plesiosauria* or large species of *varanid*.
STATUS: Unverified by mainstream science, with modern sightings continuing into the 21st Century.

CREATURE PROFILE

Unlike many cryptids that entered the public imagination only in modern times, the Brosno Dragon is rooted in folklore stretching back hundreds of years. Lake Brosno itself, a deep glacial body of water in Russia's Tver Region, has long been regarded with awe and fear. Locals describe the lake as bottomless, an impression enhanced by its extreme depth and the dark coloration of its waters. Out of this ancient setting arises the legend of the Brosno Dragon, a creature that remains alive in both tradition and ongoing eyewitness accounts.

Reports describe the animal as a massive aquatic beast with a serpentine body, a dragon-like head, and a long powerful neck. Fishermen speak of a creature large enough to rock boats, its dark scaly hide glistening just before it slips beneath the surface. Many accounts emphasize its size as extraordinary, often compared to the length of a bus or a small whale. Though descriptions can and do differ, the unifying image is of a predatory reptilian animal capable of swift and unexpected appearances.

The history of the Brosno Dragon is rich with dramatic encounters. Medieval chronicles mention a beast emerging to swallow warriors and their horses during invasions in the 13th Century. Local legends tell of villages abandoned after repeated sightings. These stories contribute to a cultural memory of the lake as the home of a dangerous predator. During later centuries travelers and soldiers alike recorded strange disturbances in the water and inexplicable losses of animals along the shore. The continuity of reports across so many generations adds weight to the possibility that a real creature lies behind the legend.

Eyewitness accounts in the modern period continue to reinforce the tradition. In the 20th Century fishermen reported seeing a huge form rolling just beneath the surface before breaking into view. Some described humps rising rhythmically above the waves, while others spoke of a great head lifting out of the water before crashing down with a splash. The animal is not confined to single brief appearances but is repeatedly described by multiple witnesses across different decades. Even into the 21st Century reports persist of disturbances in Lake Brosno attributed to this unknown animal.

Behaviorally, the Brosno Dragon is said to exhibit both predatory and territorial traits. It reportedly devours fish in vast quantities and may prey upon larger animals that stray too close to the water's edge. Stories abound of livestock disappearing near the shoreline, with villagers blaming the lake beast. Some witnesses claim the creature can create whirlpools or cause waves that overturn small craft. These descriptions suggest a strong, fast-moving body capable of displacing large volumes of water, consistent with reports of a massive reptilian aquatic predator.

From a zoological perspective theories about the Brosno Dragon vary. Some suggest it could be a surviving relic of *plesiosauria*, while others favor the idea of a giant species of monitor lizard or unknown aquatic reptile. The scaly skin, serpentine motion, and carnivorous habits described by witnesses all fit within this range of possibilities. The depth and relative isolation of Lake Brosno provide an environment where a large predator could remain hidden for centuries, surfacing only rarely and thus avoiding capture or study.

The Brosno Dragon continues to rank among Eurasia's best-known aquatic cryptids. While no specimen has ever been caught or studied, the continuity of reports from medieval times to the present indicates that something extraordinary inhabits the lake. Whether myth, undiscovered species, or prehistoric survivor, the Brosno Dragon continues to command the fascination and fear of those who live near Lake Brosno.

Eyewitness reports include attempts by the Brosno Dragon to capsize boats. Copyright © Lochlainn Seabrook.

BUNYIP

The 15 foot long, 6 foot tall Bunyip in its native habitat: the dark and mysterious wetlands of Australia. Copyright © Lochlainn Seabrook.

QUICK FACTS

NAME: Bunyip.
FIRST SIGHTING: Early 19th Century by European settlers, though Aboriginal accounts extend back Centuries.
LOCATION: Swamps, billabongs, rivers, and waterholes of Australia.
SIZE: Length 7-15 feet, height 5-6 feet upright, weight estimated 500-1,200 pounds.
APPEARANCE: Dog-like head, long neck, flippers, and powerful torso, sometimes furred or feathered.
EYES: Large, round, luminous at night, often glowing.
SKIN/FUR: Dark brown or black, smooth and slick or coarse-haired.
DIET: Fish, birds, amphibians, crustaceans, and livestock; traditions say it also preys on humans.
MOVEMENT: Swims swiftly and silently, lunges from water, moves clumsily on land.
NOTABLE BEHAVIOR: Emits booming or roaring cries, lurks near shorelines, ambushes at night.
FIRST REPORTED BY: Aboriginal Australians in oral tradition.
CREATURE CLASSIFICATION: Aquatic cryptid, possibly prehistoric survivor or undiscovered mammal.
STATUS: Still reported in rural Australia, though unverified by mainstream science.

CREATURE PROFILE

Among the most legendary creatures of Australia, the Bunyip holds a prominent place in both Aboriginal lore and modern cryptozoology. Unlike many cryptids confined to a single lake or river, the Bunyip is said to inhabit a wide range of environments across the continent. Reports come from freshwater swamps, reed-choked billabongs, winding rivers, and isolated waterholes. This broad distribution has contributed to the diversity of descriptions; yet a common thread remains: the creature is consistently feared as a predator of both man and beast.

Aboriginal Australians pass down stories of the Bunyip that long predate European settlement. These traditions often describe it as a powerful spirit-animal that rules over watery places. The presence of the Bunyip in such narratives suggests that the phenomenon has been observed for many centuries, perhaps millennia. In a number of tribes warning children about the Bunyip was a way of instilling caution around deep waters where drowning or animal attacks might occur. However, the specificity of features—such as flippers, bellowing calls, and ambush behavior—implies that witnesses were describing a genuine animal rather than a symbolic myth.

European settlers began recording encounters with the Bunyip in the early 19th Century. Accounts describe livestock vanishing from riverbanks, strange tracks leading from the water into mud flats, and unearthly cries at night that froze listeners with fear. Some reports mention bodies of drowned animals discovered with unusual wounds, fueling speculation that a large unknown predator was responsible. Drawings from this period depict a creature with a horse-like or dog-like head, a long serpentine neck, and a robust torso with seal-like flippers.

The physical form of the Bunyip remains one of its greatest mysteries. Descriptions differ so widely that some researchers propose there may be more than one type. Certain witnesses describe a shaggy-furred, quadrupedal animal reminiscent of an oversized otter or giant wombat. Others insist it is a long-necked beast resembling a freshwater plesiosaur. Another group of reports suggests a more amphibian appearance, with smooth dark skin, a broad mouth, and protruding eyes. Despite the variety, nearly all accounts emphasize its great size, aquatic lifestyle, and violent nature.

Behavioral details are consistent across both ancient and modern testimonies. The Bunyip is said to lie in wait beneath the water's surface, then erupt suddenly to seize prey. It may drag victims underwater, leaving only ripples behind. Its cry is one of its most memorable traits, likened to a booming roar, deep bellow, or unnatural booming sound that echoes across wetlands at night. Some reports suggest territorial aggression, as though the animal actively defends its waterhole against intruders.

Naturalists who consider the Bunyip seriously often suggest that it could represent a surviving relict population of a prehistoric Australian species. Fossil records reveal giant marsupials such as *Diprotodon* and immense amphibians that once inhabited the region. It is possible that one such lineage persisted in secretive aquatic environments. Others suggest a massive undiscovered pinniped-like animal adapted to inland waterways.

To this day sightings continue in rural Australia. Fishermen, campers, and farmers occasionally report encountering large dark shapes moving just beneath the water or hearing cries that cannot be traced to known animals. Aboriginal elders still pass on cautionary tales, reinforcing the idea that the Bunyip is more than just folklore.

Whether it is a surviving prehistoric animal, a yet-unknown mammal, or a formidable amphibian, the Bunyip remains one of Australia's great enigmas. Its perseverance across both traditional accounts and modern reports strongly suggests that this formidable aquatic predator may represent a real creature still waiting to be identified by conventional science.

According to both ancient and recent accounts, the Bunyip attacks and eats a wide range of prey—including humans. Copyright © Lochlainn Seabrook.

BURU

The weird, impossible-to-classify, 15 foot long Buru has inhabited the waters of northeastern India for hundreds of years. Copyright © Lochlainn Seabrook.

QUICK FACTS

NAME: Buru.
FIRST SIGHTING: Oral traditions date back hundreds of years, first written accounts in the early 20th Century.
LOCATION: Swamps and marshes of the Apa Tani Valley, Arunachal Pradesh, India.
SIZE: Reported 12 to 15 feet in length, weighing an estimated 1,000 to 1,500 pounds.
APPEARANCE: Crocodilian body with a long neck and elongated head, broad tail, and four sturdy legs.
EYES: Large, forward-facing, adapted for aquatic vision.
SKIN/FUR: Smooth, dark, reptilian scales with a slight sheen when wet.
DIET: Said to consume fish, amphibians, reptiles, small mammals, and occasionally larger animals such as pigs or deer; also reported to attack humans when threatened.
MOVEMENT: Swims swiftly with tail propulsion, walks slowly on land with a sprawling gait.
NOTABLE BEHAVIOR: Reportedly spends long periods submerged, surfacing only to breathe; linked with sudden disappearances of livestock and people near marshes.
FIRST REPORTED BY: Apa Tani tribal people of Arunachal Pradesh, India.
CREATURE CLASSIFICATION: Semi-aquatic reptile, possibly a surviving species related to giant monitor lizards or prehistoric reptiles.
STATUS: Considered unverified by mainstream science, yet regarded as real and dangerous by locals.

CREATURE PROFILE

Few cryptids are so deeply tied to the living memory of an isolated people as the Buru. In the remote Apa Tani Valley of northeastern India, this reptilian beast continues to occupy a central place in both folklore and everyday life. The accounts describe a creature that is not a ghostly spirit or myth but a tangible predator inhabiting swamps and marshes. For the people of this region the Buru is not a legend but a living animal that demands respect and avoidance.

Reports emphasize its formidable size. Length estimates consistently range from 12 to 15 feet with a body mass of more than half a ton. Its elongated form resembles a crocodile; yet its long neck and unusual head shape set it apart from known species. It possesses a broad tail designed for propulsion through water and four powerful legs that allow it to haul itself onto land when necessary. The physical combination suggests an animal well adapted to amphibious life, one similar to large reptiles of the prehistoric past.

The Buru is described as having a dark scaled hide that glistens when wet, giving it a near metallic sheen in sunlight. Witnesses note its large forward-set eyes which appear suited for seeing underwater in dimly lit environments. These features allow it to remain concealed for long stretches, surfacing only briefly to breathe. This behavior has made the creature difficult to document or photograph, yet ensures its survival in the marshy terrain of Arunachal Pradesh.

Dietary accounts are consistent with what one would expect of an apex swamp predator. Locals describe the Buru feeding on fish, turtles, frogs, and snakes, but also note that it preys upon pigs, dogs, deer, and in some cases humans who stray too near the water's edge. Its wide range of prey suggests a generalist carnivore that can exploit almost any source of protein within its environment. This adaptability would help explain the persistence of reports across many decades and align it with the feeding strategies of crocodiles or giant monitor lizards.

Movement is another defining trait. While sluggish on land, where it lumbers with a low sprawling gait, in water it becomes a robust swimmer. Using its tail for propulsion and its legs for maneuvering, the Buru is said to glide swiftly and silently through flooded valleys. Witnesses emphasize the suddenness of its strikes, comparing its ambush style to that of a crocodile. This stealth and speed make it a feared presence in rural communities.

Behavioral accounts reveal a creature that spends long periods of time underwater, surfacing only to breathe or strike prey. Livestock vanish without explanation when tethered near swampy ground, and villagers tell of people who disappeared after entering the Buru's territory. Such incidents have given the animal an aura of menace that continues to shape local practices and taboos. Tribal elders recount that traditional settlements avoided certain marshes altogether out of respect for the Buru's domain.

The first recorded reports came from the Apa Tani people themselves, who have described the Buru for generations. Later, in the early 20th Century, anthropologists documented these traditions and even attempted expeditions into the swamps. Despite scientific skepticism, local witnesses remain consistent in their testimony. They distinguish the Buru from known reptiles of the area and insist it is a separate species altogether.

Properly classified, the Buru appears to be a type of semi-aquatic reptile. Some speculate it could be a surviving lineage of large prehistoric reptiles while others consider it a giant relative of the monitor lizard. In either case it represents a biological mystery that continues to elude mainstream zoology. For the Apa Tani however, there is no mystery. The Buru is real, dangerous, and part of their everyday landscape.

The semi-aquatic Buru probably feeds mainly on fish, but is known to hunt larger animals, even mammals, as well. Copyright © Lochlainn Seabrook.

CADBOROSAURUS

The enigmatical 70 foot long Cadborosaurus, swimming casually along the British Columbia coastline. Copyright © Lochlainn Seabrook.

QUICK FACTS

NAME: Cadborosaurus.
FIRST SIGHTING: Early 19th Century.
LOCATION: Coastal waters of British Columbia, Canada, especially near Cadboro Bay.
SIZE: Typically reported 40 to 60 feet long, with some accounts suggesting up to 70 feet; estimated weight 2 to 4 tons.
APPEARANCE: Serpentine body with a long horse-like head, vertical undulating movement, and multiple humps visible above water.
EYES: Large and dark, often described as intelligent and alert.
SKIN/FUR: Smooth and scaly, usually reported as dark brown, gray, or greenish.
DIET: Likely carnivorous; reported feeding on fish, squid, octopus, seals, and seabirds, with some accounts suggesting predation on larger marine animals.
MOVEMENT: Undulates vertically with rhythmic humps rising from the surface; capable of sudden bursts of speed.
NOTABLE BEHAVIOR: Occasionally beaches itself when chasing prey; sometimes seen hunting in pairs; known for sudden dramatic surfacing events near boats.
FIRST REPORTED BY: Indigenous peoples of the Pacific Northwest, later recorded by European settlers in the 19th Century.
CREATURE CLASSIFICATION: Possible marine reptile or mammal.
STATUS: Undocumented by mainstream science, but still reported today, especially along the British Columbia coast.

CREATURE PROFILE

The animal known as Cadborosaurus is one of the most famous sea serpent-type cryptids of North America. Reports are concentrated along the rugged coastline of British Columbia, especially near Cadboro Bay from which the beast's name derives. It is widely known by locals and Indigenous peoples of the region who preserve stories of a long-bodied marine creature that has been seen for generations. Unlike many lake and sea monsters which remain obscure, Cadborosaurus is one of the most frequently sighted cryptids in Canadian waters, with hundreds of accounts spanning nearly two centuries.

Descriptions of the creature are remarkably consistent despite the diversity of observers. Witnesses describe a massive serpentine animal ranging from 40 to 70 feet in length with a horse-like head, large eyes, and a body divided into several humps that rise above the water when it swims. It undulates in a vertical motion unlike the side-to-side movement of fish, giving it an appearance closer to a mammal or reptile. Some observers compare it to a giant sea serpent, others to a prehistoric reptile reminiscent of *Plesiosaurus* or *Mosasaurus*. Its weight is estimated at several tons, making it one of the largest cryptids on record.

The skin is reported as smooth and scaly with colors ranging from dark brown to gray or greenish tones that provide camouflage in the deep coastal waters of the Pacific. Accounts of lighter underbellies are not uncommon, further reinforcing the impression that this is a marine predator with natural countershading. The eyes are frequently described as large and dark with an intelligent or watchful expression. Its head shape has been compared to both horses and camels, with some witnesses noting a mane-like ridge running down the neck.

Reports of diet are varied but consistent with a carnivorous lifestyle. Eyewitnesses have described Cadborosaurus pursuing schools of fish or surfacing among flocks of seabirds. Some claim it attacks and eats octopus or squid, while a few dramatic accounts describe seals being dragged beneath the surface by a long neck and powerful jaws. If true this suggests a formidable apex predator that operates in the same ecological niche as orcas. The possibility that it preys on larger animals, combined with its size, implies an enormous caloric demand that would explain its wide range along the Pacific coast.

Movement is one of the most striking features of Cadborosaurus. Observers consistently describe the rhythmic rise and fall of multiple humps that move in unison as the creature advances. Its vertical undulation sets it apart from known marine animals and has led some to theorize that it could represent a surviving form of ancient reptile or an undiscovered species of mammal. It is also capable of sudden bursts of speed and abrupt changes in direction, further complicating identification.

The earliest written accounts date to the 19th Century with European settlers, but Indigenous oral traditions long precede these records. The First Nations of the Pacific Northwest speak of large sea serpents with descriptions that closely match modern reports of Cadborosaurus. These traditions lend weight to the idea that the creature is not a recent invention but a long-observed inhabitant of the coast.

Sightings continue into the present day, with fishermen, ferry passengers, and coastal residents offering new reports. The combination of long historical tradition, consistent physical descriptions, and modern accounts makes Cadborosaurus one of the most compelling cryptids in marine folklore. While undocumented by mainstream science, the sheer volume of reports and the plausibility of a large marine animal eluding classification in the vast waters of the Pacific argue strongly that Cadborosaurus is very likely a real biological species awaiting discovery.

Cadborosaurus, one of the most commonly sighted cryptids in this book, continues to elude both identification and capture. Copyright © Lochlainn Seabrook.

CAIT SIDHE

The 4 foot long Cait Sidhe, a massive mystical feline that dwells somewhere between the fairy realm and the Earth plane. Copyright © Lochlainn Seabrook.

QUICK FACTS

NAME: Cait Sidhe.
FIRST SIGHTING: Early Middle Ages in Celtic folklore.
LOCATION: Scottish Highlands and throughout rural Ireland.
SIZE: Around 4 feet long (including the tail), weighing 25-40 pounds.
APPEARANCE: Large black cat with a single white patch of fur on the chest.
EYES: Luminous green or golden eyes that are often described as glowing.
SKIN/FUR: Dense black fur with a distinct white marking.
DIET: Believed to consume small mammals, birds, fish, and carrion, as well as milk offerings left by humans. In folklore it is also said to draw energy from human souls.
MOVEMENT: Moves with agility, stealth, and sudden bursts of speed. Often described as capable of vanishing or appearing instantly.
NOTABLE BEHAVIOR: Associated with stealing souls of the dead before burial, haunting wakes, and bringing blessings or curses depending on whether it is appeased with offerings of milk.
FIRST REPORTED BY: Early Celtic chroniclers and Gaelic oral tradition.
CREATURE CLASSIFICATION: Supernatural feline cryptid linked to Celtic fairy lore.
STATUS: Rarely reported in modern times, but occasionally sighted in remote parts of Scotland and Ireland.

CREATURE PROFILE

Legends of a large black cat with a white chest patch continue to circulate in the highlands of Scotland and the rural glens of Ireland. The Cait Sidhe, whose name translates from Gaelic as "fairy cat," is more than just a product of old superstition. Reports describe a creature that looks like a domestic feline in form yet is significantly larger, more intelligent in behavior, and bound to traditions that suggest powers beyond those of natural animals.

Accounts consistently emphasize its distinctive appearance. The Cait Sidhe is black from nose to tail, with a white blaze on the chest that serves as its identifying mark. Its body is stockier and longer than any ordinary cat, reaching three feet without the tail. Its eyes shine in low light with a glow that has often been compared to fire. Witnesses note a silent presence and a strange intensity in its stare, giving the impression that this being understands human activity in a way common cats do not.

In the traditions of the Middle Ages, the Cait Sidhe is feared for its connection to death. Folklore describes the creature prowling around wakes, waiting to capture the soul of the recently departed before religious rites are completed. To protect the dead people kept constant watch and used loud music or games to distract the creature. Offerings of milk were also placed outside doorways to appease it, for it was believed that if it was satisfied it would bless the household; if ignored, however, it could curse the family with misfortune. Such stories suggest a deep cultural memory of a predator whose behavior was tied closely to human ritual life.

Beyond funerary associations the Cait Sidhe is said to roam the moors and rocky slopes of the Scottish Highlands. Shepherds claim to have glimpsed its shadow moving across ridgelines at dusk. Farmers have spoken of finding paw prints larger than those of any domestic or feral cat near their barns. In Ireland traditions speak of fairy mounds where the Cait Sidhe guards hidden treasures, appearing only on certain nights of the year. These patterns of belief point to a creature that inhabits borderlands, both in geography and in human imagination, half rooted in the natural world, half in the otherworldly.

Its diet is often described as typical of large felines. Small mammals such as rabbits and hares are likely prey, as are birds and fish. Carrion may also be consumed, which would explain its presence near human settlements and graveyards. Legends expand on this naturalistic diet with the claim that it steals souls, which may be a symbolic memory of its presence near death or decay. The common theme is that it takes something vital from its environment, whether physical prey or spiritual essence.

Movement is another element that sets the Cait Sidhe apart. Witnesses report that it moves with sudden swiftness, leaping into view and then vanishing as if into thin air. Some accounts describe it appearing at windows or on rooftops without any sound or warning. Such observations might be explained by stealth; but the regularity with which these vanishings are reported keeps alive the belief that it possesses supernatural abilities.

Although mainstream science has yet to document this animal, scattered reports continue to pour in from isolated areas of Scotland and Ireland. People describe seeing a massive black cat with glowing eyes on lonely roads or in mountain passes, sometimes mistaken at first for a dog—until its feline form becomes clear. These continuing sightings show that the Cait Sidhe is not confined to the past. Whether regarded as an undiscovered species of large cat, a supernatural guardian, or a vestige of Celtic folklore, the Cait Sidhe remains a powerful presence in the natural and the cultural landscape of the Celtic world.

The Cait Sidhe attending an Irish funeral, in search of a human soul. Psychopomp or devilish entity? Copyright © Lochlainn Seabrook.

CHAMP

Champ, a 40 foot long aquatic cryptid, breaches the surface of Lake Champlain, displaying its curious dorsal humps and magnificent long neck. Copyright © Lochlainn Seabrook.

QUICK FACTS

NAME: Champ.
FIRST SIGHTING: 1609.
LOCATION: Lake Champlain, bordering New York, Vermont, and Quebec.
SIZE: Typically 20 to 40 feet long, estimated weight 2 to 3 tons.
APPEARANCE: Serpentine body with multiple humps, long neck, and horse-like or reptilian head.
EYES: Large and dark, often described as piercing or reflective.
SKIN/FUR: Smooth and dark gray, black, or brown, sometimes with lighter underside.
DIET: Reported to consume schools of fish such as perch, trout, and salmon, as well as eels, aquatic invertebrates, and possibly small mammals or waterfowl near the surface.
MOVEMENT: Undulating or serpentine swimming with visible humps breaking the surface, capable of sudden dives.
NOTABLE BEHAVIOR: Often rises partially from the water, creates wakes in calm conditions, and appears curious about boats.
FIRST REPORTED BY: French explorer Samuel de Champlain.
CREATURE CLASSIFICATION: Aquatic cryptid, possibly a surviving plesiosaur or long-bodied pinniped.
STATUS: Unverified by mainstream science, but supported by centuries of eyewitness accounts, photographs, and sonar recordings.

CREATURE PROFILE

The waters of Lake Champlain continue to produce sightings of a mysterious animal that locals and visitors alike call Champ. The lake itself is vast, stretching over 120 miles in length and reaching depths of more than 400 feet. Its size and isolation provide ample space for an undiscovered aquatic species to remain hidden while sustaining a thriving breeding population. Many who live along its shores accept Champ as part of the lake's natural heritage.

The earliest account comes from Samuel de Champlain in 1609, who recorded seeing a creature with scales and a body more than five feet thick. He described it as armed with sharp and dangerous teeth and larger than most fish. His words laid the foundation for the original legend. Reports increased during the 19th Century as steamboats brought more traffic across the lake. Many passengers observed serpentine shapes undulating through the water, often keeping pace with their vessels.

Descriptions of Champ are remarkably consistent across the centuries. Witnesses speak of a body ranging from 20 to 40 feet long with several humps rising above the surface in sequence. A long neck supports a head sometimes compared to that of a horse or reptile. The skin is usually reported as dark gray or brown and smooth, lacking fur. Some say the underside is lighter, giving the creature countershading, a feature found in many other aquatic animals. The eyes are described as large, dark, and occasionally reflective in sunlight.

Dietary habits are deduced from the fish populations of Lake Champlain. The waters hold abundant perch, trout, salmon, and eels. Eyewitnesses often note Champ appearing during large fish runs, suggesting predation. Some accounts describe waterfowl being taken from the surface, which may indicate opportunistic feeding behavior. Like many large predators Champ likely consumes whatever is most readily available within its environment.

Movement is one of its most distinctive features. Witnesses describe a rhythmic, serpentine motion with multiple humps rising and falling in a rolling sequence. At times the creature glides silently just beneath the surface, creating large wakes in otherwise calm waters. Sudden dives or breaches are also reported. Boats are sometimes followed or approached, indicating curiosity rather than aggression.

Evidence for Champ includes more than eyewitness testimony. Photographs dating back to the late 1800s show long dark shapes in the lake. Sonar studies in modern times have recorded large moving objects far below the surface, some longer than 30 feet. Audio recordings of unusual underwater sounds have also been captured, fueling speculation that an undiscovered animal inhabits the lake.

Theories about Champ's classification vary. Some propose a surviving plesiosaur, citing the long neck and fully aquatic lifestyle. Others suggest a large form of sturgeon or an unknown species of pinniped adapted to freshwater. While mainstream science has not confirmed the existence of such a creature, the continuance of sightings over more than four centuries keeps the discussion active.

Locals embrace Champ as both a cultural symbol and a biological possibility. Towns along the lake celebrate the creature through festivals, statues, and tourism, reflecting its importance to the region's identity. For many who spend time on Lake Champlain, Champ is more than folklore. It is considered a living presence whose elusive nature only adds to its mystery.

Champ exhibiting aggressive behavior, a trait consistent with eyewitness reports during close encounters. Copyright © Lochlainn Seabrook.

CHUPACABRA

The bizarre and terrifying, 5 foot tall Chupacabras as it is described in early Puerto Rican eyewitness accounts. Copyright © Lochlainn Seabrook.

QUICK FACTS

NAME: Chupacabra.
FIRST SIGHTING: 1995.
LOCATION: Puerto Rico, Mexico, southern United States, Central America, and South America.
SIZE: 3 to 5 feet tall, weighing between 40 and 110 pounds.
APPEARANCE: A small biped with a row of spines or quills running from neck to tail, a hunched back, long limbs, and a reptilian or canid face.
EYES: Large, round, and glowing red or orange when seen at night.
SKIN/FUR: Described as leathery gray-green skin or covered in sparse, coarse hair.
DIET: Said to feed on the blood of livestock such as goats, chickens, and cattle by puncturing the neck and draining fluids, occasionally reported attacking wild animals and sometimes leaving organs intact while removing blood.
MOVEMENT: Walks or hops on two legs like a kangaroo, though at times runs on all fours with speed and agility.
NOTABLE BEHAVIOR: Attacks livestock under cover of darkness, often without making noise, leaving clusters of small circular wounds on the victim.
FIRST REPORTED BY: Madelyne Tolentino, Puerto Rico.
CREATURE CLASSIFICATION: Possible undiscovered predator or misidentified hybrid of reptilian and mammalian features.
STATUS: Unverified by mainstream science; but still widely reported.

CREATURE PROFILE

When reports of a strange livestock-killing creature surfaced in Puerto Rico during the mid-1990s, few expected the story to spread across the Western Hemisphere. Yet within months the being became one of the most famous cryptids of modern times. Known as the Chupacabra, or "goat-sucker," it is feared for its unusual feeding method, leaving animals drained of blood rather than eaten. Carcasses of goats, chickens, sheep, and even cattle are found with small puncture wounds in the neck and bodies left largely intact, behavior that separates it from known predators.

The case that brought the Chupacabra into worldwide attention began in 1995 when Madelyne Tolentino, a resident of Canóvanas, Puerto Rico, reported seeing a small bipedal creature near her home. She described an animal about four feet tall with large oval eyes, a row of spines running down its back, and an appearance unlike any mammal she had ever seen. Tolentino's report coincided with a rash of mysterious livestock deaths in the region, leading to a wave of fear among farmers and ranchers. Her testimony, widely circulated in local and international news, became the foundation for the modern image of the Chupacabra.

Descriptions vary depending on region, but many accounts repeat the key features Tolentino gave. Some describe a reptilian animal with leathery gray-green skin, spines, and a lizard-like stance. Others describe a canid form with patchy hair, often associated with mange. The possibility of two forms suggests either separate species or variations of the same animal. In both versions the creature is small but menacing, with glowing red or orange eyes and a powerful flexible frame built for agile movement.

Behavior attributed to the Chupacabra is consistent with a nocturnal predator: It approaches quietly under cover of darkness, leaves behind distinctive wounds, and disappears before it can be confronted. Witnesses claim it moves in a hopping motion when on two legs, but also runs on all fours with surprising speed. A few reports mention a foul, sulfur-like odor lingering in places it has visited.

The diet reported for the Chupacabra is unusual and highly specialized. Victims are left with blood drained, sometimes partially and sometimes completely; yet the flesh is rarely eaten. Goats and chickens are most often targeted, though pigs, sheep, dogs, cats, and cattle have also been reported. In some cases organs remain untouched, supporting the idea of a unique physiology geared toward sanguivory. Few animals feed exclusively on blood, making this trait one of the most striking and difficult to explain.

After Puerto Rico reports of the Chupacabra spread quickly into Mexico, Florida, Texas, and later to Central and South America. Farmers and ranchers across the region began describing identical livestock deaths, often matching Tolentino's original details. While mainstream science attributes some of these cases to disease, wild dogs, or coyotes, those explanations fail to address the uniformity of the wounds, the lack of flesh consumption, and the frequency of glowing-eyed, spined, or reptilian descriptions.

Today, three decades after Tolentino's sighting, the Chupacabra is still being reported. It has not faded into folklore but remains part of daily life for rural communities across the Americas. Whether reptilian, canid, or something in between, it is regarded by many as a living predator yet to be studied. Until physical evidence is secured and examined, the Chupacabra will remain one of the most mysterious cryptids of the modern age.

The Chupacabra on a nighttime hunt for its favored prey: livestock. Copyright © Lochlainn Seabrook.

DEVON DEVIL

The Devil's Footprints of 1855: a mysterious cloven trackway running in a straight line through the snow of rural Devon, England. The individual prints, spaced up to sixteen inches apart, reportedly stretched for 100 miles across fields, hedgerows, and villages—and even over rooftops—in a single night. The bizarre bipedal beast that made them has never been identified. Copyright © Lochlainn Seabrook.

QUICK FACTS

NAME: Devon Devil.
FIRST SIGHTING: February 1855.
LOCATION: Devon, England.
SIZE: Hypothetical height 4 to 6 feet, weight 150 to 250 pounds.
APPEARANCE: Likely a bipedal, horned, cloven-hoofed figure inferred from folklore and tracks.
EYES: Unverified; folkloric accounts describe glowing red or orange.
SKIN/FUR: Unknown; theories suggest dark skin or coarse hair.
DIET: Hypothetical diet includes livestock such as sheep and goats; possible scavenging of carrion; folklore emphasizes attraction to blood.
MOVEMENT: Leaves hoof-shaped tracks suggesting bipedal locomotion; able to travel long distances without pause.
NOTABLE BEHAVIOR: Known only for leaving miles of unbroken tracks across varied terrain in 1855.
FIRST REPORTED BY: Villagers of Devon.
CREATURE CLASSIFICATION: Terrestrial cryptid of unknown origin; possibly a humanoid or large mammal with cloven feet.
STATUS: Still discussed in modern times though never scientifically verified.

CREATURE PROFILE

The stealthy creature, being, or entity that made these famous footprints in 1855 was never seen by human eyes, and thus the case has always been known simply as the "Devil's Footprints." However, as it is a notable cryptid that earned its way into my book, I have given it the name "Devon Devil" in order to make it easier to discuss. Here is how its story began.

In February 1855, after a heavy snowfall blanketed the county of Devon in England, residents awoke to find miles of hoof-shaped prints pressed into the snow. The tracks stretched across more than thirty distinct locations, continuing over rooftops, through fields, over walls, and across frozen rivers. They formed a nearly continuous line that spanned an estimated one hundred miles in a single night. The sheer extent and peculiarity of the impressions caused alarm throughout the countryside, and reports were carried as far as London.

The hoof-prints were described as cloven, resembling those of a goat or donkey, yet too small and precise to be attributed to either. The prints were about four inches long and three inches wide, spaced eight to sixteen inches apart, and ran in an almost straight line as though made by a creature hopping or walking with rigid regularity. The depth and clarity of the tracks suggested weight, yet no snow was displaced around them, adding to the mystery. No one saw the being responsible, leaving only physical evidence and speculation.

From this lack of direct observation locals began to construct an image of the entity. The name, the "Devil's Footprints," reflected both the fearful climate of mid-19th Century rural England and the uncanny nature of the event. Educated guesses about its form suggest a creature of moderate human-like height, perhaps four to six feet, heavy enough to impress the snow deeply yet light enough to leave minimal disturbance. Folklore added horns, glowing eyes, and leathery or furred skin; but these traits are speculative rather than reported. The hoof-marks themselves are the only firm evidence of its anatomy—and how strange they are!

Behavior can also be cautiously inferred. The length and continuity of the trail imply an organism with remarkable endurance, capable of covering immense distances in a single night. Its ability to move across varied obstacles without interruption suggests powerful leaping ability or perhaps even limited flight, though no wing marks were ever reported. The straightness of the tracks across fields and villages hints at deliberate, perhaps pre-planned, travel rather than aimless wandering.

Diet is harder to deduce. Folklore insists that the Devon Devil preys on livestock, particularly sheep and goats, echoing the agricultural fears of rural communities. While mutilated animals were sometimes attributed to it, no confirmed evidence links the tracks to predation. It is possible that if such a creature exists in our reality that it may scavenge carrion or consume small mammals and birds. Traditional accounts emphasizing its thirst for blood may be folkloric exaggerations, though they reflect the local conviction that the creature is carnivorous.

The mystery of the Devon Devil remains unsolved. Naturalistic explanations have been proposed, including escaped kangaroos, badgers, birds, or atmospheric phenomena, yet none fully account for the scale and precision of the tracks. The 1855 event stands as one of the most compelling unsolved cases in cryptozoology because it rests on physical evidence witnessed by hundreds of people across multiple towns. Unlike most cryptids, the Devon Devil has no eyewitness body description—its identity must be pieced together solely from the eerie trackways it left behind.

For classification purposes the Devon Devil is best considered a terrestrial cryptid with unknown taxonomic placement. The most likely interpretation is that it represents an undiscovered hoofed mammal or a unique humanoid adapted to bipedal movement. Its strength, precision of gait, and ability to traverse difficult terrain remain unexplained by mainstream science. This incident lives on in Devon folklore, and occasional reports of strange tracks in snow or mud revive the legend, maintaining the possibility that what I have termed the Devon Devil is more than myth.

My hypothetical reconstruction of what I have named the "Devon Devil," the English cryptid believed by some to have created the Devil's Footprints in 1855. Copyright © Lochlainn Seabrook.

DOGMAN

A 9 foot tall Dogman prowls the backroads of the Great Lakes region. Its tall, muscular frame, wolf-like head, erect ears, digitigrade legs, and dark coarse fur are common themes in American eyewitness accounts. Copyright © Lochlainn Seabrook.

QUICK FACTS

NAME: Dogman.
FIRST SIGHTING: 1887.
LOCATION: Midwestern and Northeastern United States, especially Michigan and Wisconsin.
SIZE: Stands 6 to 9 feet tall when upright, estimated weight 250 to 450 pounds.
APPEARANCE: Bipedal creature with the body of a heavily muscled man and the head of a wolf or large dog.
EYES: Often described as glowing yellow or amber, sometimes red.
SKIN/FUR: Covered in thick fur, usually dark brown, gray, or black.
DIET: Believed to be carnivorous, feeding on deer, livestock, and possibly carrion. Reports also suggest opportunistic scavenging and occasional predation on small animals.
MOVEMENT: Capable of both quadrupedal and bipedal locomotion, runs with incredible speed, sometimes compared to that of a deer.
NOTABLE BEHAVIOR: Known for terrifying vocalizations including howls, growls, and screams. Reported to stalk witnesses and even chase vehicles.
FIRST REPORTED BY: Lumberjacks in Wexford County, Michigan.
CREATURE CLASSIFICATION: Possible hominid-canine hybrid.
STATUS: Unverified by mainstream science; yet reported regularly into the present day.

CREATURE PROFILE

Unlike many cryptids confined to myth or isolated sightings, the Dogman is actively reported across large portions of North America, particularly in the Great Lakes region. Its legend gains strength from the sheer number of consistent accounts spanning more than a century. Witnesses continue to describe a towering wolf-headed humanoid that moves with an unsettling combination of human intelligence and canine agility. The Dogman is not treated as a cultural tale alone but as a phenomenon that hunters, motorists, hikers, and rural families still claim to encounter today.

The physical description remains remarkably consistent. Dogman typically stands between 6 and 9 feet tall when upright. Its shoulders are broad, its chest is barrel-like, and its limbs are proportionate to those of a tall man, though more heavily muscled. The head resembles that of a German shepherd or wolf, complete with pointed ears, long snout, and prominent fangs. Fur color varies but is most often described as black or gray. Some witnesses note a tail, while others claim none is visible, suggesting regional variations or even more than one type or subspecies.

The eyes of Dogman are particularly unsettling to those who encounter it. They are said to glow unnaturally in low light, either yellow, amber, or red, often visible before the creature itself comes into view. Many describe the sensation of being watched by a predator, a primal fear triggered by its gaze alone. The ears stand erect and seem to twitch like those of a wolf, giving the impression of heightened alertness and acute hearing.

Dogman's diet is assumed to be strictly carnivorous, as most reports link it to areas with heavy deer populations. Rural farmers claim livestock disappear without trace in regions where sightings are frequent. Scavenging from roadkill or human refuse may also sustain it, making it an opportunistic feeder. Some accounts even suggest it attacks domestic dogs, a behavior consistent with territorial dominance rather than hunger. Assuming it is real, its role in the ecosystem is likely that of a top predator, occupying a niche similar to wolves but with the added advantage of intelligence and bipedal speed.

Movement is one of Dogman's most disturbing traits. While it runs effectively on all fours, it can also rise to two legs and sprint in a humanlike fashion. Witnesses insist that the upright gait does not resemble a bear or ape, but a man moving with canine grace. Reports of it chasing vehicles, keeping pace at highway speeds, have fueled fears of its raw power. Some describe it leaping fences with ease, vanishing into forests with astonishing quickness, or standing motionless as if challenging those who see it.

Behaviorally, the Dogman is both elusive and confrontational. Most encounters involve intimidation rather than direct attack. It growls, howls, or lets out screams that witnesses describe as blood-curdling and unnatural. The creature is also known to shadow travelers, stalking them from the treeline or circling campsites. In some accounts it slaps houses, scratches walls, or rattles doors before retreating. This suggests not only animal ferocity but an element of psychological dominance, as if it takes satisfaction in frightening humans who enter its domain.

The first widely acknowledged reports came from 19th Century lumberjacks in Michigan. Since then sightings have spread outward into Ohio, Wisconsin, Pennsylvania, and beyond. Regional Native American traditions also speak of wolf-headed beings with humanlike qualities, lending further weight to the idea that this is not a modern invention. The continued frequency of sightings indicates that Dogman may represent a persistent and undiscovered species rather than folklore alone.

Unverified by mainstream science yet impossible to dismiss outright, Dogman occupies a unique place in North American cryptozoology. Its presence blends natural predation with humanlike cunning, challenging the line of demarcation between animal and man. Whether a surviving relic species, a rare genetic hybrid, a demonic entity, or an undiscovered apex predator, it remains one of the most credible and unsettling cryptids on record, with reports continuing into the present day.

The Dogman, surely one of the most physically intimidating cryptids of all time, is often seen at night lurking menacingly along roadsides and farms. Eyewitnesses describe their encounters as the most terrifying experience of their lives. Despite this, there is no record of the beast ever actually harming a human. Copyright © Lochlainn Seabrook.

DOVER DEMON

The fantastical 4 foot tall Dover Demon, as described by eyewitnesses in Dover, Massachusetts, during the 1977 sightings. Copyright © Lochlainn Seabrook.

QUICK FACTS

AME: Dover Demon.
FIRST SIGHTING: April 21, 1977.
LOCATION: Dover, Massachusetts, USA.
SIZE: Estimated 3 to 4 feet tall, weighing 40 to 80 pounds.
APPEARANCE: Thin humanoid with long limbs and oversized head.
EYES: Large, glowing orange or green eyes.
SKIN/FUR: Smooth, hairless, pale gray to peach-colored skin.
DIET: Unknown, possibly insectivorous or carnivorous, theorized to consume small mammals, birds, amphibians, reptiles, and invertebrates.
MOVEMENT: Crawls on all fours or walks upright with awkward gait.
NOTABLE BEHAVIOR: Seen perched on stone walls or crouched near roadsides, seemingly unafraid of vehicles.
FIRST REPORTED BY: William Bartlett, a 17-year-old local youth.
CREATURE CLASSIFICATION: Terrestrial humanoid cryptid, possible alien or undiscovered primate.
STATUS: Unconfirmed by conventional science; rare, with sightings limited to a single 24-hour period in the Spring of 1977.

CREATURE PROFILE

In the spring of 1977 a series of unusual encounters in a small New England town brought one of America's strangest cryptids to public attention. The Dover Demon is remembered as a short thin-bodied being with an oversized head and eerie glowing eyes. Sightings occurred over the course of two consecutive nights and involved four credible witnesses, all teenagers, whose descriptions matched closely despite being given independently. Since then the creature has remained a notable cryptozoological mystery, as no subsequent verified reports have been made; yet the consistency and detail of those first accounts continue to invite serious study.

The Dover Demon is said to stand around 3 to 4 feet in height, with a spindly frail-looking body and long fingers gripping stones, tree branches, or the ground when encountered. Its most striking feature is its disproportionately large melon-shaped head, which lacks hair, ears, or a pronounced nose. Witnesses describe the skin as smooth, either pale gray or peach in tone, and illuminated in the headlights of passing cars. The eyes are described as large, glowing orange or green, and without visible pupils. No clothing or tools were seen, suggesting the creature is either entirely feral or of a type unknown to modern science.

The first sighting was made by William Bartlett, who reported the figure clinging to a stone wall along Farm Street. He recalled the eyes glowing in the darkness as his car headlights struck it. Later that same evening John Baxter saw the creature again while walking home, this time describing it crouching near trees before retreating down a gully. The following night another pair of youths, Abby Brabham and Will Taintor, also encountered the Demon, giving descriptions in agreement with the earlier reports. The short time span and the independence of the witnesses lend weight to the probability that they all encountered the same being.

While its diet remains speculative, some researchers suggest the Dover Demon may subsist on small wildlife. Its long fingers and grasping hands could be adapted for capturing amphibians, reptiles, or insects. The smooth skin suggests either a cold-blooded physiology or a unique form of terrestrial adaptation. If mammalian, the lack of fur is highly unusual for a New England creature, though not impossible if it dwells underground or maintains a lifestyle independent of cold conditions.

Movement is described as both quadrupedal and bipedal, though awkward in the latter form. Witnesses noted its ability to cling tightly to rocks and move swiftly out of view, implying strong limbs and possibly arboreal abilities. Its preference for perching on walls or crouching in ditches suggests a cautious, observant nature rather than outright aggression.

Notably, the Dover Demon has never been connected with reports of attacks or hostile behavior. It appears more curious than threatening, pausing in the presence of humans rather than fleeing instantly. This sets it apart from other cryptids often linked with aggression. Its rarity and the brevity of its known appearances raise the possibility of a transient species, an isolated mutant individual, or even a non-terrestrial visitor from space.

The Dover Demon remains one of the most puzzling creatures in North American cryptozoology. It cannot be dismissed as a prank due to the consistency and seriousness of the witnesses. Yet it cannot be readily explained as a known animal due to its odd morphology. Whether a misidentified primate, a relict hominid, or an entity of otherworldly origin, the Demon's brief emergence continues to fascinate researchers nearly fifty years later.

For now, the Dover Demon exists in that narrow margin between folklore and zoology, with its case supported by sincere and credible testimony, yet wholly lacking the physical remains required by mainstream science. Its sudden appearance and disappearance in a single community over a short span of hours suggest that it may be migratory, subterranean, or of limited population size. Until more evidence emerges it remains a cryptid of extraordinary interest, a fleeting shadow in the annals of modern natural history whose presence defies easy classification, and which challenges assumptions about what creatures may yet dwell among us unseen.

According to the four 1977 eyewitnesses, the Dover Demon was non-aggressive, and fled for cover rather than risk human contact. Was this a one-time phenomenon, or does the creature still roam the yards of this small Massachusetts town? Copyright © Lochlainn Seabrook.

EACH-UISCE

The dangerous, 12 foot long, nearly 2 ton Each-Uisce in its horse form, haunting a Scottish loch. Copyright © Lochlainn Seabrook.

QUICK FACTS

NAME: Each-Uisce.
FIRST SIGHTING: At least the 16th Century.
LOCATION: Coastal regions and inland lochs of Scotland and Ireland.
SIZE: Reported length 8 to 12 feet, estimated weight 1,000 to 1,500 pounds.
APPEARANCE: Resembles a strong horse with aquatic traits, occasionally with webbed feet or a reptilian tail.
EYES: Large, dark, and luminous, often said to gleam with intelligence.
SKIN/FUR: Smooth seal-like skin or sleek dark fur, sometimes black, sometimes gray.
DIET: Carnivorous. Feeds on fish, seabirds, seals, and reportedly humans. Will attack livestock near the shore. Known for dragging prey underwater and devouring it.
MOVEMENT: Moves with speed and grace in water; on land appears like a normal horse, capable of running swiftly until it reaches water.
NOTABLE BEHAVIOR: Lures people to mount its back then dives into the sea or lake to drown them. Considered highly aggressive and far more dangerous than the Kelpie.
FIRST REPORTED BY: Highland and island inhabitants of Scotland and Ireland.
CREATURE CLASSIFICATION: Aquatic equine cryptid.
STATUS: Unverified by mainstream science; yet sightings by ardent eyewitnesses throughout the 18th and 19th Centuries raise it above the level of pure folklore.

CREATURE PROFILE

Unlike many cryptids whose behavior is elusive or benign, the Each-Uisce stands apart as a creature described in consistently lethal terms. It is not regarded as a mere curiosity but as a deadly predator of both animals and humans. Accounts portray it as a being that must be avoided at all costs, a reputation earned from centuries of sightings and warnings along the coasts and lochs of the British Isles. The danger it represents is emphasized in both oral tradition and recorded accounts, making it one of the most feared cryptids in Celtic regions.

The creature is said to resemble a beautiful horse when seen on land, often appearing to travelers or fishermen who mistake it for a stray or lost animal. Its deceptive appearance is part of its hunting method. Unlike the Kelpie, which is most often tied to rivers and lochs, the Each-Uisce is associated with the sea and coastal waters, though it also inhabits inland lakes. This versatility suggests an aquatic animal capable of thriving in multiple habitats, a trait found in pinnipeds and crocodilians as well. Once a rider mounts the creature its skin is said to becomes adhesive, making escape impossible. It then plunges into the nearest body of water, drowning its victims before devouring them.

Descriptions of its physical traits vary but generally suggest a hybrid form. Many reports describe a horse with unusually strong muscles, a long tapering tail resembling that of a reptile or fish, and sometimes webbed hooves. In water it swims like a seal or crocodile, with notable bursts of speed. This adaptability between land and water recalls the behavior of semi-aquatic predators. Its eyes are frequently described as intelligent, shining with a strange gleam, hinting at a mind that may be more than mere animal. Such intelligence may explain its use of deception to lure prey.

The diet of the Each-Uisce sets it apart from other equine cryptids. It is portrayed as fully carnivorous, feeding not only on fish and seabirds but also on seals and domestic livestock near the shore. Disturbingly, numerous accounts describe it as preying on humans. The reports are striking in their consistency, suggesting that this is not merely symbolic but based on actual experiences or encounters. Its feeding method of dragging prey into deep water parallels the tactics of crocodiles, further strengthening the view that it may represent a real aquatic predator misclassified through the lens of folklore.

Behaviorally, the Each-Uisce is aggressive and territorial. It does not seek coexistence but domination of its environment. Villagers warned children not to approach strange horses near lakes or the sea, a cultural adaptation to the possibility of its reality. Unlike more neutral water spirits, this creature is portrayed without ambiguity as dangerous. It is perhaps the only cryptid in Celtic tradition regarded as purely malevolent.

The classification of the Each-Uisce remains debated. Some see it as a mythologized memory of real animals, such as large seals or marine reptiles. Others argue it is an unknown species of aquatic mammal with equine characteristics, an adaptation to environments where deception is a hunting strategy. While mainstream science has not confirmed its existence, the consistency of reports across centuries and regions gives weight to the possibility of a genuine biological basis.

In the modern era sightings are rare but not absent. Fishermen occasionally report horse-like shapes moving in coastal waters, and unexplained livestock drownings continue in some rural areas. Whether viewed as folklore, survival warnings, or evidence of an undiscovered species, the Each-Uisce remains one of the most formidable and frightening cryptids known to mankind.

A young Irish woman, having fallen for the beauty and charm of the Each-Uisce, has mounted the baleful steed, blissfully unaware of the deadly fate that momentarily awaits her. Copyright © Lochlainn Seabrook.

ELLEN TRECHEND

The 50 foot long Ellén Trechend, a mythic three-headed Celtic monster, could be based on genuine but now lost ancient animals. Copyright © Lochlainn Seabrook.

QUICK FACTS

NAME: Ellén Trechend.
FIRST SIGHTING: 10th Century.
LOCATION: Ireland, particularly the region near Cruachan in Connacht.
SIZE: Estimated 40 to 50 feet in length, standing 12 to 15 feet high, with a possible weight of 20 to 25 tons.
APPEARANCE: A monstrous beast with three massive serpent or dragon-like heads attached to a single body.
EYES: Described as fiery and glowing, casting light like burning embers.
SKIN/FUR: Scaly, reptilian hide with dark or mottled coloration.
DIET: Carnivorous, capable of consuming livestock, humans, and possibly entire herds; likely opportunistic and indiscriminate.
MOVEMENT: Capable of both slithering and lizard-like strides; reports suggest it can swim or cross water when necessary.
NOTABLE BEHAVIOR: Associated with widespread destruction, attacks on settlements, and leaving entire regions devastated.
FIRST REPORTED BY: Early Irish chroniclers in the medieval text *Cath Maige Mucrama*.
CREATURE CLASSIFICATION: Multi-headed dragon or draconic cryptid.
STATUS: Legendary, yet possibly representing an undiscovered or misidentified reptilian species.

CREATURE PROFILE

Among the many creatures preserved in Irish lore Ellén Trechend stands out as one of the most fearsome. It is said to rise from the caves of Cruachan, known in myth as Oweynagat or the "Cave of Cats," a site long regarded as a gateway to the Otherworld. The creature's very name suggests terror, combining ancient Gaelic terms that have been translated as "three-headed monster." From its lair it unleashes destruction on the countryside, striking fear into entire populations.

The defining feature of Ellén Trechend is its three immense heads, each serpent-like, attached to a massive reptilian body. The three heads may serve both as weapons and as a form of heightened sensory perception, allowing it to track prey over long distances. Accounts emphasize the glowing nature of its eyes, suggesting a bioluminescent or reflective quality. This feature would have made it visible at night, an imposing sight for villagers who encountered it near settlements or fields.

Descriptions of its hide are consistent with a scaled creature, dark in tone, possibly armored. Such attributes would make it resistant to conventional weapons of the time. The enormous length and bulk recorded in tales suggest an animal far larger than known European reptiles, more akin to the great sea serpents or dragons described in other traditions. If measured by modern standards its mass has been compared to that of medium-sized sauropod dinosaurs or the largest marine reptiles.

Its diet, as described in old Irish stories, is horrendous. Ellén Trechend reportedly consumed livestock, leaving fields barren of cattle and sheep. There are also claims of direct human predation, entire communities fleeing its approach. Unlike other cryptids known for shy or reclusive behavior, this creature is depicted as aggressive and wide-ranging. If taken literally this behavior aligns with apex predators that dominate their ecosystems and exert control over prey numbers.

Movement is described as both slithering and walking, a confusing combination that may indicate a hybrid body plan. Some witnesses imply that it can swim across rivers or lakes. This versatility would allow it to extend its range far beyond a single location. Reports of its rapid assaults, combined with its immense weight, suggest a powerful musculature capable of propelling its massive body with speed and force.

Notably, Ellén Trechend is not merely a solitary predator but one whose appearances are linked with catastrophe, suffering, and mistery. Accounts describe the devastation of entire regions, with fires, ruined villages, and dead livestock marking its path. These destructive episodes place the beast within the same tradition as other world-threatening dragons; yet its setting is uniquely Irish, tied to the sacred landscape of Connacht.

The earliest written reference to the creature appears in the medieval saga *Cath Maige Mucrama*, where it is slain by the hero Amergin. This account shows that the Ellén Trechend was already a firmly established part of oral history by the 10th Century. While its origins are recorded in mythic texts, it is possible that the stories preserve memory of an actual encounter with a now-lost animal. Fossil evidence in Ireland does not support large reptiles surviving into historical times, yet the persistence of dragon-like cryptids across the world suggests a recurring pattern worth considering.

Modern classification places Ellén Trechend within the broad category of draconic cryptids. Though some dismiss it as purely legendary, others argue that oral memory may encode encounters with extraordinary animals now extinct or hidden. Until further evidence emerges Ellén Trechend remains an open case: a monstrous, three-headed predator of Ireland that defies simple explanation.

According to ancient legend, the carnivorous Ellén Trechend fed on a host of prey items, including humans. Copyright é Lochlainn Seabrook.

EMELA-NTOUKA

The 16 foot long mystery animal known as the Emela-ntouka in its native habitat: the Likouala swamps of the Congo River Basin. Copyright © Lochlainn Seabrook.

QUICK FACTS

NAME: Emela-ntouka.
FIRST SIGHTING: Early 20th Century.
LOCATION: Remote swamps, rivers, and lakes of the Congo Basin, Central Africa.
SIZE: Length estimated at 12 to 16 feet, height at the shoulders 4 to 5 feet, weight around 2,000 pounds.
APPEARANCE: Large quadruped with a heavy body, short legs, and a single forward-facing horn.
EYES: Small and dark, positioned on the sides of the head.
SKIN/FUR: Smooth, grayish-brown skin resembling that of a rhinoceros; no fur reported.
DIET: Reported to feed on aquatic plants such as Malombo leaves, though some accounts suggest territorial aggression toward animals, including elephants and hippos.
MOVEMENT: Slow-moving on land, but powerful in water, often described as capable of overturning canoes.
NOTABLE BEHAVIOR: Aggressive toward other animals, highly territorial, particularly hostile to elephants.
FIRST REPORTED BY: Local tribes and hunters of the Congo Basin, accounts later collected by explorers and missionaries.
CREATURE CLASSIFICATION: Possible surviving ceratopsian dinosaur such as *Monoclonius* or *Centrosaurus*, or an unknown species of large aquatic herbivore.
STATUS: Unverified by mainstream science, though reports continue into the present.

CREATURE PROFILE

In the heart of Central Africa, deep within the remote river systems of the Congo Basin, the Emela-ntouka is still spoken of with both fear and respect. Its name, drawn from the native Lingala language, translates as "killer of elephants," a title that reflects its reputed strength and hostility toward even the largest creatures of the forest. Unlike many cryptids that occupy a murky place in folklore, the Emela-ntouka is consistently described by multiple tribes across a wide region, strongly suggesting a biological rather than mythical origin.

The most striking feature of this animal is its single horn, placed at the center of its head and directed forward like that of a ceratopsian dinosaur. Witnesses describe it as long and sharply pointed, a weapon used to defend its territory and attack perceived rivals. The rest of its body is said to resemble a rhinoceros or an oversized buffalo, with thick legs, a broad torso, and a sturdy tail. Its hide is smooth and hairless, resembling leather, and typically colored gray or brown to blend with the muddy waters it inhabits.

The Emela-ntouka is primarily associated with water. Hunters and fishermen report seeing the animal submerged in rivers, with only part of its back and head breaking the surface. It is described as slow and deliberate when walking on land but swift and dangerous in aquatic environments. Accounts describe the beast as capable of overturning dugout canoes and frightening away hippos, animals that usually dominate such waters. Its sheer presence inspires caution among locals, who often avoid certain stretches of river said to be inhabited by the beast.

Dietary habits attributed to the Emela-ntouka suggest it is primarily herbivorous. Tribes consistently report the creature feeding on Malombo plants, large aquatic vegetation common to the region. Despite this, the Emela-ntouka is also said to display violent behavior toward elephants, a rare quality in herbivorous animals. Witnesses claim it attacks these giants with its horn, leaving deep puncture wounds and sometimes killing them outright. Whether this hostility is linked to competition for food, territory, or another factor is not known, but the behavior is consistent across multiple accounts.

The first collected reports of the Emela-ntouka came in the early 20th Century from missionaries and explorers traveling through the Congo Basin. They relayed accounts from local tribes who regarded the animal as a real and dangerous presence. Since then occasional modern expeditions have attempted to gather evidence, but the vast and inaccessible swamps of the region make research extremely difficult. No photographs or physical remains have yet been confirmed by science, but sightings from tribes and hunters continue into the present.

In terms of classification, cryptozoologists often compare the Emela-ntouka to ceratopsian dinosaurs such as *Monoclonius* or *Centrosaurus*. The forward-pointing horn, large size, and semi-aquatic behavior fit broadly with what such animals may have been like if they survived into the present. Others suggest it could be an unknown species of large semi-aquatic mammal, unrelated to dinosaurs but equally formidable. Either explanation places it among the most extraordinary cryptids of the modern age.

The Emela-ntouka remains unverified by mainstream science. Yet the consistency of reports, the detailed descriptions, and the continuing sightings suggest that an undiscovered species could be concealed within the swampy heart of Central Africa. Until thorough investigation is possible the Emela-ntouka will continue to live as one of the most compelling possibilities of a prehistoric survivor still walking the Earth.

The Emela-ntouka is notoriously territorial and uses its horn to drive out intruders, animal or human. Copyright © Lochlainn Seabrook.

ENFIELD HORROR

The 5 foot tall Enfield Horror, a three-legged monstrosity that terrorized the village of Enfield, Illinois, in 1973. Copyright © Lochlainn Seabrook.

QUICK FACTS

NAME: Enfield Horror.
FIRST SIGHTING: April 25, 1973.
LOCATION: Enfield, Illinois, USA.
SIZE: Between 4 and 5 feet tall, weighing around 80 to 120 pounds.
APPEARANCE: Small, stocky, with short arms and three long legs ending in talon-like feet.
EYES: Red and glowing.
SKIN/FUR: Smooth, pale, or grayish skin without fur.
DIET: Likely carnivorous or opportunistic; may prey on rabbits, pets, livestock, and wild animals. Possibly scavenges.
MOVEMENT: Leaps great distances, using all three legs for balance and propulsion. Moves in sudden bursts of speed.
NOTABLE BEHAVIOR: Scratches at doors, emits eerie screeches, frightens residents, and has been reported attacking animals.
FIRST REPORTED BY: Henry McDaniel.
CREATURE CLASSIFICATION: Terrestrial cryptid with possible extraterrestrial or interdimensional qualities.
STATUS: Vague reports continue to come in, but nothing verifiable; after 1973 the creature seems to have largely disappeared.

CREATURE PROFILE

In the small rural community of Enfield, Illinois, the 1970s brought reports of a creature unlike any other in American folklore. Known today as the Enfield Horror, it is described as a strange nightmarish entity that continues to stand apart from other Midwestern cryptid reports. Its most distinctive trait is its unusual locomotion: Witnesses describe it moving with three legs, bounding with an almost insect-like rhythm that defies ordinary biology. These accounts suggest a creature well adapted for sudden bursts of speed, able to cover ground quickly and unpredictably, often startling those who encounter it.

The first widely accepted report came from Henry McDaniel, a resident of Enfield, who claimed on April 25, 1973, that the creature scratched violently at his door during the night. When he investigated, he saw a small figure with glowing red eyes, short forelimbs, and three massive legs ending in clawed feet. McDaniel insisted the animal leaped away at a tremendous speed when he fired a gun at it. His description remains the foundation of nearly all later reports.

The Enfield Horror is estimated at 4 to 5 feet in height, suggesting a body plan smaller than most other cryptids of the region. Witnesses emphasize its stocky frame and unnatural gait. It does not move like a quadruped or a biped, but rather in an unearthly triple-step motion. This unique method of locomotion makes it difficult to categorize within any known animal family.

Its eyes are consistently described as red and glowing, appearing luminous even in darkness. This has led to speculation that the creature may possess specialized vision suited for nocturnal hunting. Combined with its small stature, sudden speed, and clawed feet, the animal appears to be a predator that hunts small game or domestic animals. Reports of mutilated pets and frightened livestock in the area lend weight to the idea that the Horror feeds opportunistically on whatever prey is most accessible.

Its skin is said to be pale or gray, smooth rather than furred. This detail is striking as it does not align with typical mammals of the region. Smooth skin might suggest a reptilian or amphibian lineage, though no known species matches the full description. Others propose that the creature is an undiscovered terrestrial predator, possibly highly adapted to nocturnal life in rural environments. A minority of researchers consider it an extraterrestrial visitor or even an interdimensional being due to its bizarre morphology.

The creature is known for its alarming behavior around humans. Witnesses claim it scratched at doors and windows, emitted loud screeches, and moved in a way that seemed calculated to terrify. The sound has been compared to a high-pitched cry or shriek, unnerving enough to drive residents to arm themselves against it. Yet there is no verified record of it attacking a person directly. Its primary interactions appear to be intimidation and predation upon smaller animals.

Following McDaniel's initial report sightings occurred sporadically in the same region, though they quickly diminished in frequency. Some locals dismissed it as hysteria, while others believed they had glimpsed something real and dangerous.

Today any and all credible reports concerning the Horror remain isolated to the Enfield area, suggesting either a very small population of these creatures or a single individual wandering through. While ambiguous sightings continue today, after the spring of 1973 the creature appears to have vanished, with no further reliable encounters recorded.

The Enfield Horror stands as one of the more puzzling American cryptids of the 20th Century. Its strange anatomy, disturbing behavior, and localized presence resist easy explanation. Whether considered a flesh-and-blood animal yet to be classified by science, or a phenomenon with more unusual origins, it remains a uniquely chilling part of Illinois folklore and one of the most bizarre creatures ever documented in modern cryptid research.

The frightening entity known as the Enfield Horror was famous for scratching on people's doors and emitting blood-curdling screams. Copyright © Lochlainn Seabrook.

FAIRY

The Fairy: sometimes mischievous, sometimes treacherous, always beguiling. Copyright © Lochlainn Seabrook.

QUICK FACTS

NAME: Fairy.
FIRST SIGHTING: Antiquity, earliest references appear in pre-Christian European folklore.
LOCATION: Primarily Europe, though sightings are reported worldwide.
SIZE: Generally between 6 inches and 3 feet in height, with weight ranging from less than 1 pound to around 30 pounds.
APPEARANCE: Small humanoid body, delicate features, often with insect-like or bird-like wings, sometimes glowing or surrounded by light.
EYES: Large, luminous, and expressive, often described as unusually bright or radiant.
SKIN/FUR: Human-like skin, usually pale but sometimes described as greenish, golden, or shimmering. Rare reports note fur or a soft down-like covering.
DIET: Commonly linked with nectar, honey, fruit, seeds, and flowers, though some traditions record a carnivorous diet of small animals, insects, or even human blood. Folklore also speaks of their fondness for milk, cream, and bread offerings.
MOVEMENT: Can fly swiftly with wings, also walk or run with agility; some are said to vanish instantly or teleport.
NOTABLE BEHAVIOR: Known for trickery, mischief, and abduction, but also for guiding, healing, and bestowing gifts. Frequently associated with nature guardianship and protection of sacred sites.
FIRST REPORTED BY: Celtic and pre-Christian oral traditions, later chronicled by medieval monks and early European writers.
CREATURE CLASSIFICATION: Elemental humanoid cryptid.
STATUS: Still reported in modern times, particularly in rural Europe and among those who live close to natural landscapes.

CREATURE PROFILE

In countless traditions across the globe stories of small winged beings dwelling in forests, meadows, and gardens stubbornly persist. The Fairy is one of the most deeply archetypal cryptids in human memory, with its image preserved across centuries of storytelling, ritual, and recorded sightings. While often reduced in modern culture to whimsical children's characters, the accounts of actual Fairies describe a species of small, intelligent, and highly secretive humanoids that are deeply connected to the natural world.

Fairy encounters are reported in rural landscapes where forests meet pastures, near streams, and within areas considered sacred or ancient. Witnesses describe them as vividly real beings, distinct from imagination, with glowing skin or an aura that suggests a natural bioluminescence. The wings, when present, resemble those of dragonflies, moths, or birds, moving so quickly that they are sometimes seen as blurs. Their movements in flight are reported to be silent and precise, with the ability to dart in and out of view in the blink of an eye.

Descriptions of their diet are strikingly consistent across cultures. Fairies are closely tied to flowering plants and are observed feeding on nectar, honey, and seeds. Farmers of earlier centuries often left bowls of milk, cream, or sweetened bread to appease them, believing that these gifts ensured good harvests and protection from mischief. Yet other accounts emphasize a darker side, telling of Fairies who hunt small animals or drain livestock of blood in a manner disturbingly similar to modern reports of vampiric cryptids.

Behavior attributed to Fairies ranges from benevolent to dangerous. Some are healers and teachers, offering herbal remedies, guiding lost travelers, or gifting insight into hidden aspects of nature. Others are said to steal human food, sabotage equipment, or even abduct people, most often children or adults who stumble too close to their hidden dwellings. Time anomalies are a frequent theme, with those who claim to have visited Fairy gatherings reporting that minutes among them equated to days or years in the human world.

The first reports of Fairies appear in the oral traditions of Celtic peoples, where they were regarded as guardians of nature and remnants of earlier races displaced by human expansion. Medieval monks recorded testimonies of strange diminutive beings encountered near abbeys and villages, treating them as real entities rather than myth. By the time of the Renaissance sightings were common enough that early natural historians speculated about their existence as an undiscovered form of humanoid life.

Modern sightings, though rarer, still occur, especially in Europe where traditions remain strong. Witnesses often describe brief encounters at dusk or dawn, in woodland glades or gardens, where tiny winged figures are glimpsed before vanishing into the air. The consistency of these reports, stretching from ancient history to the present day, suggests that Fairies may represent a genuine species, highly adept at concealment, whose presence has intertwined with human imagination and belief for millennia.

Highly credible eyewitnesses from across Europe have solemnly testified that they have seen fairies dancing in circles on moonlit moorlands. Science continues to question, but actual sightings quickly convert nonbelievers. Copyright © Lochlainn Seabrook.

FLATHEAD LAKE MONSTER

The 40 foot long Flathead Lake Monster is no idle myth. Trustworthy sightings continue to be reported into the present day. Copyright © Lochlainn Seabrook.

QUICK FACTS

NAME: Flathead Lake Monster.
FIRST SIGHTING: 1889.
LOCATION: Flathead Lake, Montana, USA.
SIZE: Reported lengths range from 20 to 40 feet, with estimated weights up to 4,000 pounds.
APPEARANCE: Long, serpentine body with humps rising above the waterline.
EYES: Large, dark, and often described as unblinking.
SKIN/FUR: Smooth, dark gray to black skin, sometimes said to glisten in sunlight.
DIET: Believed to feed on fish such as whitefish, lake trout, perch, and possibly waterfowl; may also prey on other aquatic animals when available.
MOVEMENT: Swift, undulating motion similar to that of a snake or eel; capable of sudden dives and rapid bursts across the surface.
NOTABLE BEHAVIOR: Frequently surfaces in calm conditions; has been seen creating large wakes without boats present; occasionally described as following or circling watercraft.
FIRST REPORTED BY: Captain James C. Kerr and over 100 passengers aboard the steamer U.S. *Grant* in 1889.
CREATURE CLASSIFICATION: Freshwater cryptid, often categorized with lake monsters similar to Ogopogo and Champ.
STATUS: Undocumented by mainstream science; yet reported sightings continue today.

CREATURE PROFILE

Few cryptids in North America command as much attention as the Flathead Lake Monster of Montana. With Flathead Lake being one of the largest freshwater bodies west of the Mississippi, its depths provide an ideal habitat for an elusive aquatic animal of unusual size. Reports spanning more than a century continue to describe a long, serpentine creature moving powerfully beneath the surface, fueling the region's greatest cryptozoological mystery.

The first widely recognized account dates to 1889, when Captain James C. Kerr of the steamer U.S. *Grant*, along with more than one hundred passengers, claimed to witness a massive creature swimming through the lake. The event marked the beginning of public awareness of the monster, and its legend has persisted ever since. Sightings are still made today by fishermen, recreational boaters, and lakeside residents. This continuity over time provides strong evidence that the animal may be a permanent resident of Flathead Lake rather than a chance visitor.

Descriptions of the Big Sky Country beast are remarkably consistent. Witnesses often report a dark form between 20 and 40 feet long, surfacing in a rolling manner that suggests an elongated flexible body. Many speak of distinct humps breaking the water in sequence, reminiscent of a giant eel or snake. The animal's size, coupled with its quick diving ability, makes it difficult for observers to capture more than fleeting glimpses. Some accounts include mention of large unblinking eyes or a shiny skin that reflects the sun as the monster moves close to the surface.

The diet of the creature, assuming it is real, would logically consist of the plentiful fish species within Flathead Lake. Whitefish, lake trout, northern pike, and perch form the base of the lake's food chain and would supply adequate sustenance for a large predator of this kind. Witness reports occasionally mention flocks of waterfowl scattering when the monster surfaces, which raises the possibility that birds may sometimes be taken as prey. The animal's impressive size suggests it may require large quantities of food, making its presence more compatible with the fish-rich waters of a lake the size of Flathead.

Movement is consistently described as serpentine and undulating, with sudden bursts of speed that produce large wakes. On calm days observers have reported wide ripples spreading across the surface of the lake without any visible boats or natural causes. In some cases the monster appears to follow watercraft, either out of curiosity or for reasons unknown. These behavioral patterns align closely with other well-documented lake monster traditions around the world, strengthening its classification among freshwater cryptids.

Local Native American tribes, including the Kutenai, also possess oral traditions describing giant water-dwelling creatures in Flathead Lake long before the arrival of European settlers. These accounts may represent early encounters with the same animal now called the Flathead Lake Monster, or they may point to a broader cultural memory of unusual aquatic species in the region.

Though skeptics have attempted to attribute the sightings to large sturgeon or misidentified logs, the sheer number of credible eyewitnesses—which often include group sightings—suggests that something extraordinary is present. Thus the possibility that a remnant species of large fish or prehistoric creature survives in the depths of Flathead Lake cannot be dismissed.

Until conclusive evidence is gathered the Flathead Lake Monster remains one of North America's most compelling cryptids, a living mystery inhabiting the clear cold waters of the Treasure State.

In pursuit of its piscine prey, the Flathead Lake Monster sometimes surfaces abruptly near startled boaters. Copyright © Lochlainn Seabrook.

FLATWOODS MONSTER

The Flatwoods Monster: This strange, otherworldly, 14-foot tall being appeared in the rural woods near Flatwoods, West Virginia, in 1952. Its luminous eyes, clawed hands, spade-shaped hood-like head, and weird metallic body left a deep and indelible impression on all who saw it. Copyright © Lochlainn Seabrook.

QUICK FACTS

NAME: Flatwoods Monster.
FIRST SIGHTING: September 12, 1952.
LOCATION: Flatwoods, Braxton County, West Virginia, USA.
SIZE: Estimated height between 10 and 14 feet, weight possibly 500 to 800 pounds.
APPEARANCE: Tall, humanoid figure with a spade-shaped head covering, dark body, and metallic-looking features.
EYES: Large, glowing, round eyes that emitted a green or orange hue.
SKIN/FUR: Reported as metallic or armor-like plating, with no visible skin or fur.
DIET: Unknown, though theorized to have been carnivorous, insectivorous, or energy-feeding based on behavior and environment.
MOVEMENT: Glided rather than walked, floating above the ground with smooth, mechanical motion.
NOTABLE BEHAVIOR: Emitted hissing sounds, released a pungent mist or gas, and caused illness in witnesses.
FIRST REPORTED BY: Kathleen May and six local boys in Flatwoods, West Virginia.
CREATURE CLASSIFICATION: Possibly extraterrestrial, interdimensional, or undiscovered terrestrial species.
STATUS: Unverified by mainstream science, with no confirmed capture, body, or remains.

CREATURE PROFILE

The Flatwoods Monster was one of the most distinctive cryptids ever reported in the United States. Its appearance in West Virginia in the mid-20th Century was sudden and dramatic, and the encounter quickly became a cornerstone of American cryptid and UFO lore. The creature was remarkable not only for its unusual form but also for the physical effects it produced on its environment and on human witnesses.

Witnesses described the Monster as towering over them at a height greater than ten feet, with a body cloaked in what appeared to be armor or a mechanical suit. Its head was reported as shaped like an ace of spades: broad at the top and narrowing to a point below the chin. Within this helmet-like feature were two luminous eyes that glowed with a piercing brightness. The body beneath was dark and mechanical-looking, with long, spindly arms and claw-like fingers. Its movements were smooth and gliding, as if it floated above the ground without using legs.

A central feature of the sighting was the noxious mist that the creature released. Witnesses consistently reported a pungent metallic odor and a choking fog that lingered in the air. Those who breathed it suffered nausea, burning eyes, and throat irritation. These symptoms were sometimes compared to reactions from chemical exposure; yet no known chemical was ever recovered from the site.

The physical aftereffects experienced by the witnesses remain one of the most compelling aspects of the case. Several of the children and Kathleen May suffered from nausea, throat irritation, and temporary eye inflammation for days after the encounter. These symptoms resembled chemical exposure or even mild radiation sickness, suggesting that the Monster, or its equipment, emitted some form of toxic substance or energetic field. The consistency of these reports lent weight to the possibility that the Flatwoods Monster represented more than folklore, as few known natural animals could produce such widespread physiological impacts on humans.

The Flatwoods Monster was first encountered by a group of local boys who observed a fiery object streak across the evening sky and land on a nearby hill. With Kathleen May, they ascended the slope and found the enormous creature standing among the trees. Startled by its size and presence, they fled, later describing the terrifying experience to neighbors and authorities. Subsequent investigations uncovered tracks, a lingering odor, and reports of military interest in the area.

What made the Flatwoods Monster unique among cryptids was the mixture of biological and mechanical characteristics. Some descriptions suggested that the creature was not a living organism but rather a being encased in a protective suit. This led to speculation that it may have been extraterrestrial in origin—perhaps a visitor or scout from another world. Others proposed that it was interdimensional, an entity that slipped briefly into our realm before vanishing again. Still others maintained that it may have represented an undiscovered terrestrial animal, albeit one with highly unusual traits.

Though the primary sighting occurred in 1952, occasional later reports described similar beings in West Virginia and beyond. These accounts reinforced the idea that the Flatwoods Monster was not an isolated event but part of a broader phenomenon. Even today the creature is remembered in the region, where it is celebrated in festivals, artwork, and local lore.

The Flatwoods Monster remains unclassified and unconfirmed. Yet its size, shape, and associated effects placed it firmly within the realm of serious cryptid research. Whether it was alien, mechanical, or a still-undiscovered earthly species, the reports showed consistency and detail that suggested a real encounter with something unknown.

Its mystery continues to intrigue investigators, keeping alive the possibility that the Monster of Braxton County was not just a story but a genuine presence.

The Flatwoods Monster: The memory of this bizarre, towering, spade-headed figure lingers in the haunted hills of Appalachia to this day. Copyright © Lochlainn Seabrook.

FOUKE MONSTER

The 8 foot tall Fouke Monster: This strange apeman hybrid with glowing red eyes and distinctive three-toed feet, is said to inhabit the misty swamps of Boggy Creek, Arkansas. Copyright © Lochlainn Seabrook.

QUICK FACTS

NAME: Fouke Monster.
FIRST SIGHTING: 1908.
LOCATION: Fouke, Arkansas, USA.
SIZE: Height 7-8 feet, weight estimated 250-400 pounds.
APPEARANCE: Tall, ape-like, broad shoulders, long arms, cone-shaped head, often hunched.
EYES: Red or yellow, glowing at night.
SKIN/FUR: Covered in long, dark brown or black shaggy hair.
DIET: Believed to be omnivorous, feeding on deer, livestock, small animals, fish, fruit, roots, and possibly carrion. Known livestock losses in the area suggest predatory behavior.
MOVEMENT: Bipedal but with a shambling gait, long strides, capable of moving quickly through thick swamps and forests.
NOTABLE BEHAVIOR: Emits loud howls and screams, strong odor described as rancid or skunk-like, leaves large three-toed tracks, raids farms, and approaches rural houses at night.
FIRST REPORTED BY: Local residents near Fouke, Arkansas.
CREATURE CLASSIFICATION: Hominid cryptid, often linked to regional Bigfoot-type beings.
STATUS: Unverified by mainstream science, yet reported sightings continue.

CREATURE PROFILE

Among the many American forest-dwelling cryptids, the Fouke Monster holds a distinct place as one of the most frequently reported and most deeply embedded in local culture. Associated with the small town of Fouke in southwest Arkansas, the creature came to national attention in the early 1970s, but accounts stretch back decades earlier. Its reputation has made Fouke a focal point for researchers, folklorists, and eyewitnesses who insist the animal is far more than rural legend.

Witness descriptions are consistent and striking. The Fouke Monster is said to stand between 7 and 8 feet tall, covered in thick, dark hair, and moving with a lumbering gait that is both awkward and unnervingly fast. Its head is often described as somewhat pointed, more conical than human, and its arms unusually long. The creature's eyes are reported as red or yellow, glowing in the dark, giving it a fearsome appearance during nighttime encounters. Its odor is frequently compared to that of rotting flesh mixed with a skunk-like musk, an olfactory signature that has become one of its defining traits.

The creature's diet is assumed from both reported sightings and circumstantial evidence. Farmers have claimed missing livestock and chickens, while hunters have reported finding unusual tracks near deer kills. It is also thought capable of foraging on wild plants, berries, roots, and river fish, making it an adaptable omnivore well suited to the swampy terrain of Arkansas. Its capacity to leave large, unusual tracks has drawn attention, with three-toed impressions being a particularly distinctive feature, setting it apart from other North American Sasquatch-type cryptids.

Movement reports emphasize the monster's ability to travel quickly through dense undergrowth and waterlogged ground. Although lumbering in appearance, it can cross roads in a matter of seconds, vanish into forests, or retreat into swamp channels where humans cannot easily follow. Its speed and stealth have prevented any conclusive capture or photograph, further adding to its mystique.

The Fouke Monster first entered broader awareness in 1971 after a family reported a violent encounter near their home. This incident, combined with ongoing sightings, became the subject of newspaper reports and later inspired the cult film *The Legend of Boggy Creek* (1972). Since then numerous sightings have continued in the surrounding Sulphur River bottoms, a vast wilderness of swamp, forest, and creeks ideally suited for harboring an elusive species. These reports span from hunters and fishermen to ordinary townspeople who describe seeing the creature at night along roadsides or near rural dwellings.

Behaviorally, the creature is known for loud piercing screams and howls that echo across the bottomlands, sounds that defy identification with any known local wildlife. It has been reported to approach homes, peer through windows, and strike fear into families living on the fringes of Fouke. The combination of auditory, olfactory, and visual evidence has built a strong local tradition of belief in the creature's reality.

Despite this extensive body of testimony, no specimen has ever been collected and no physical proof has been universally accepted by the scientific community. Local tracks, clawed trees, and livestock attacks remain circumstantial but compelling for many. For the residents of Fouke the monster is not merely a tale but a real and present feature of the Arkansas landscape. Ongoing reports ensure that the Fouke Monster remains one of America's best-known regional cryptids and a subject of continued interest to cryptozoologists and natural historians alike.

The Fouke Monster is known chiefly for its lurking presence, blood-curdling screams, and horrid smell. Its odd three-toed feet sharply distinguish it from North America's many other Sasquatch-like creatures. Copyright © Lochlainn Seabrook.

GIANT ANTARCTIC ICE WORM

The bizarre 50 foot long, 1 ton Giant Antarctic Ice Worm has been reported since the first scientific explorations of the area began nearly 70 years ago. Copyright © Lochlainn Seabrook.

QUICK FACTS

NAME: Giant Antarctic Ice Worm.
FIRST SIGHTING: 1960s.
LOCATION: Antarctica.
SIZE: Length 10 to 50 feet, weight estimated between 500 and 2,000 pounds.
APPEARANCE: Long cylindrical worm-like body with a slightly tapered head and blunt tail.
EYES: Small black eyes or eye-like spots sometimes reported, other witnesses describe eyeless specimens.
SKIN/FUR: Smooth pale skin ranging from white to translucent blue, occasionally described as glossy or glistening.
DIET: Believed to feed on microbial mats, algae, frozen invertebrates, fish, and possibly scavenged remains of penguins and seals. Some reports suggest it bores into ice layers to feed on trapped organic matter.
MOVEMENT: Slow undulating crawling through ice tunnels, with sudden bursts of speed when emerging to the surface.
NOTABLE BEHAVIOR: Known for burrowing through dense ice, leaving large smooth tunnels. Occasionally rises from fissures and crevasses during Antarctic thaws.
FIRST REPORTED BY: Early polar explorers in the Ross Sea region.
CREATURE CLASSIFICATION: Undiscovered annelid or nemertean, possibly adapted megafaunal worm.
STATUS: Unverified by mainstream science; yet sightings reports continue today.

CREATURE PROFILE

In the frozen expanses of Antarctica, where few forms of complex life survive, comes the striking account of the Giant Antarctic Ice Worm. It is described as a massive elongated invertebrate capable of surviving deep within glacial layers. The creature is said to emerge from fissures, crevasses, or exposed ice faces, presenting a disturbing yet remarkable spectacle for those who have encountered it. Its appearance challenges what is considered biologically possible in such an extreme environment, yet its recurring reports suggest that it may be one of the most unusual cold-adapted organisms on Earth.

Mid 20th Century explorers moving across the Ross Sea region noted strange rounded tunnels appearing overnight in solid ice, as if something large and cylindrical had moved through it. These were not small melt channels caused by water but rather smooth tubes wide enough for a man to crawl into. Some claimed to see great pale forms withdrawing into cracks when disturbed, suggesting a living animal. These accounts gave rise to the idea that an immense worm-like creature was responsible. Subsequent expeditions recorded similar anomalies, with tunnels and surface disturbances appearing where no known animal could have been active.

Descriptions of the ice worm vary, yet most agree on its overall form. Witnesses describe a long cylindrical body between 10 and 50 feet in length, with a thickness of two to three feet. The head region is said to be blunt and tapered, giving it an almost featureless look. Some observers mention small black eyes, while others insist the animal is eyeless and moves by sensing vibration and temperature gradients in the ice. Its skin is commonly described as white or translucent blue, often shining with a moist gloss, which may assist in reducing friction as it pushes through ice.

Diet is another point of interest. Naturalists who have studied similar but much smaller Arctic worms note that they consume algae and microorganisms locked within ice crystals. By scaling this pattern upward, it is suggested that the giant worm feeds on microbial mats, algal blooms within frozen layers, and the occasional invertebrate or small fish trapped beneath. There are even reports that carcasses of penguins or seals left near crevasses have been drawn into ice holes overnight, raising the possibility that the animal is opportunistically carnivorous.

Movement is typically slow and undulating, with the worm pushing its way through dense ice with surprising ease. However, it is said to move quickly when surfacing, rising suddenly from fissures as if forced upward by inner pressure. This behavior contributes to its frightening reputation, as encounters often occur without warning. Its tunneling ability remains unexplained, but theories suggest secretion of a chemical antifreeze or abrasive structures along its body that allow it to bore through compact ice.

The Giant Antarctic Ice Worm remains unverified by science, but the repeated discovery of unexplained tunnels in Antarctic glaciers, combined with scattered eyewitness accounts, keep the legend alive. Whether it is an undiscovered giant annelid, a form of nemertean worm, or a unique lineage adapted to Earth's harshest continent, the fact remains that Antarctica almost certainly conceals megafauna yet unknown. The stark and isolated conditions of the southern polar region provide both the challenge and the opportunity for such a creature to persist undetected into the present day.

Personnel stationed at Antarctic research stations continue to report sightings of the extraordinary Gigantic Antarctic Ice Worm. What it is, how it lives, feeds, and breeds, is unknown. Copyright © Lochlainn Seabrook.

GOATMAN

The Goatman, a bipedal hybrid cryptid reported in Maryland since the 1950s, is described as standing up to 7 feet tall with a muscular humanlike torso, cloven hooves, curling horns, and glowing eyes. Witnesses say it prowls rural backroads at night seeking unsuspecting victims. Copyright © Lochlainn Seabrook.

QUICK FACTS

NAME: Goatman.
FIRST SIGHTING: 1957.
LOCATION: Prince George's County, Maryland, USA.
SIZE: Stands 6-7 feet tall, estimated weight 250-350 pounds.
APPEARANCE: Humanoid body with the head and legs of a goat, broad chest, muscular arms, cloven hooves, and sharp horns.
EYES: Red or yellow, often described as glowing.
SKIN/FUR: Covered in coarse dark brown or black hair, with patches of exposed skin on chest and face.
DIET: Carnivorous and omnivorous; reported to kill livestock such as dogs, sheep, and goats, but also scavenges carrion and raids garbage, suggesting opportunistic feeding habits.
MOVEMENT: Walks upright with a shambling gait, capable of dropping to all fours for speed, sometimes reported leaping long distances.
NOTABLE BEHAVIOR: Associated with livestock mutilations, car attacks, and sudden appearances along rural roads; often lets out high-pitched screeches or goat-like bleats.
FIRST REPORTED BY: Local residents in Prince George's County, Maryland, USA.
CREATURE CLASSIFICATION: Cryptid humanoid, possibly related to primates or an unknown ungulate-hominid hybrid.
STATUS: Unverified by conventional science, yet reported intermittently from the mid-20th Century to the present.

CREATURE PROFILE

Few modern cryptids generate as much fear in rural communities as the Goatman. This bizarre man-beast hybrid is said to roam the backwoods and lonely roads of Maryland, especially around Prince George's County, where reports stretch back to the 1950s. The creature is consistently described as standing between six and seven feet tall, with the shaggy fur, horns, and hooves of a goat fused with the upright body and powerful arms of a human. Witnesses frequently remark on its unnatural strength, its ability to leap onto vehicles, and its chilling screams that echo through the woods at night.

The epicenter of Goatman activity lies near the Maryland town of Bowie, where locals still exchange stories of livestock found dead and torn apart under mysterious circumstances. Farmers in the area report animals vanishing from pens, their remains discovered mutilated with unusual precision. Dogs in particular are said to be targets, with accounts of entire packs destroyed in a single night. While predators such as coyotes or feral dogs might be responsible in some cases, the sheer ferocity and accompanying sightings of a towering goat-like figure convince many that another explanation is required.

Travelers describe encounters along secluded stretches of Fletchertown Road and near bridges crossing local creeks. In several instances cars have been damaged by a massive horned figure that charged from the roadside, pounding on hoods and roofs before vanishing back into the forest. The creature is also said to stalk teenagers parked in lovers' lanes, a detail that has fueled both local cautionary tales and genuine fear among those who live near the reported hot spots. In these encounters glowing eyes and the rank smell of musk or decay are often noted.

Beyond Prince George's County, sightings spread into Virginia, Kentucky, and even Texas, suggesting that Goatman may not be confined to a single location. These regional variations sometimes differ in detail, but the central image of a horned, human-goat hybrid remains constant. This widespread pattern hints at either a migrating population of creatures or a recurring archetype preserved in local folklore yet reinforced by ongoing sightings.

Scientific speculation has occasionally been entertained. Some researchers suggest the Goatman might represent a surviving offshoot of an unknown primate, adapted to local environments with ungulate-like features. Others propose genetic mutation, possibly tied to experimental mishaps at nearby facilities—though such theories remain unverified. What is striking, however, is the consistency of physical descriptions across decades and regions: a creature large enough to overpower livestock, mobile enough to evade capture, and distinct enough to be instantly recognizable.

The creature's vocalizations are among its most disturbing traits. Witnesses describe piercing screams blending human-like cries with goat bleats, sometimes erupting without warning in otherwise quiet forests. Hunters and hikers report freezing at the sound, convinced they are hearing something unnatural. Combined with sudden appearances and swift retreats, these calls contribute to the Goatman's reputation as an aggressive yet elusive predator.

Reports continue into the present day. Sightings are less frequent than during the peak decades of the 1960s and 1970s, but scattered encounters still surface from residents and travelers in Maryland and beyond. These modern accounts reaffirm that Goatman is not a figure of fading folklore but an active part of North American cryptid tradition. Whether an undiscovered species, a genetic anomaly, or a remnant of ancient myth given flesh, the Goatman persists as one of the most unnerving creatures in contemporary natural history.

The Goatman: An aggressive bipedal hybrid with a goat-like head, horns, and hooves; reported attacking cars near bridges and lover's lanes in Prince George's County, Maryland. Copyright © Lochlainn Seabrook.

GREEN MAN

The Green Man: Long dismissed by skeptics as nothing more than folklore, or perhaps an aesthetically pleasing but meaningless architectural symbol, actual sightings appear to have begun in the Medieval period, with eyewitness reports continuing into the present day. Copyright © Lochlainn Seabrook.

QUICK FACTS

Name: Green Man.
First Sighting: Medieval period carvings beginning in the 11th Century (suggestive of sightings as long as 1,000 years ago), with modern reports into the 20th and 21st Centuries.
Location: Europe, particularly Britain, and in Pennsylvania, United States.
Creature Type: Humanoid nature entity.
Size: Reports describe human-sized figures, 5 to 7 feet tall, 150 to 250 pounds.
Appearance: Human-like form covered in leaves, vines, moss, or with a leafy face.
Eyes: Glowing or shadowed, sometimes hidden beneath foliage.
Skin/Fur: Bark-like skin, moss-covered body, or green-tinged human flesh.
Diet: Uncertain; some traditions suggest a plant-based diet, others imply energy drawn from nature.
Movement: Walks upright, slow or silent, sometimes described as gliding.
Notable Behavior: Appears near forests, tunnels, or old roads; sometimes waves or accepts offerings.
First Reported By: European stonemasons and carvers, later by locals in Pennsylvania.
Status: Dismissed as purely folkloric by mainstream science; yet sightings reports continue into the present day.

CREATURE PROFILE

The Green Man is a prominent figure bridging folklore, architecture, and cryptozoology. His likeness appears across medieval European churches, where artisans carved foliate heads into stone, blending human faces with leaves and vines. These images—beginning in the 11th Century and becoming widespread from the 12th Century onward—suggest a deep cultural memory of a being associated with forests, fertility, and the cycles of life. While mainstream scholars interpret the Green Man as purely symbolic, his persistence in legend and modern sightings suggests a more complex reality.

In Britain the Green Man appears not only in church carvings but also in seasonal celebrations such as May Day and Jack-in-the-Green festivals. Here he is portrayed as a living embodiment of spring, cloaked in leaves and flowers, leading processions through towns. Yet outside of pageantry and parades witnesses have occasionally reported encounters with leafy, humanlike figures in woodland settings. Drivers have claimed to glimpse a tall, green-hued man at the edges of darkened roads, while others describe a silent apparition that seems to merge with the surrounding vegetation. Such accounts, while anecdotal, add to the probability that the Green Man is more than an artistic motif.

Modern testimonies continue to surface, often describing a tall humanoid whose body is covered in leaves, moss, or vines, blending seamlessly into the forest. In some cases, witnesses have reported the figure stepping partially out of dense undergrowth, only to retreat when approached, leaving no trace behind. Others tell of a shadowy presence seen in rural lanes, particularly at dusk or dawn, where the figure is described as motionless until noticed, then vanishing without sound. These encounters, scattered across the British Isles and occasionally reported in North America, keep alive the belief that the Green Man is not merely a decorative figure but a living being.

Some observers describe a face half-hidden by greenery, with glowing or unusually reflective blue eyes. A few accounts claim the Green Man gestures, waves, or simply watches from a distance before dissolving back into foliage. The consistency of these reports over decades suggests that witnesses are describing a similar phenomenon rather than random hallucinations or inventions. While skeptics dismiss such stories as illusions caused by pareidolia or imagination, the testimonies continue, pointing to the reality of an elusive humanoid adept at camouflage and rarely lingering long enough for study.

The Green Man's association with foliage and forests connects him to a wider tradition of wild men and forest guardians found in many cultures: the Leshy in Russia, the Waldschrat in Germany, and the Woodwose of medieval England. These beings, half-man and half-nature, blur the boundary between human and environment. In every case they embody a reminder that the forest is alive, watchful, and inhabited by intelligences beyond modern recognition.

Skeptics maintain that all such figures are symbolic, artistic, or mistaken identities, yet, to repeat, the consistency of reports across centuries suggests that the Green Man represents a real but unclassified being. His silent appearances at forest edges, tunnels, and ancient roads evoke the possibility of a species evolved to camouflage with vegetation, or perhaps an elemental presence intertwined with the life force of trees themselves.

Whether regarded as a decorative motif or a living cryptid, the Green Man occupies a unique space between art and reality. His face stares down from stone arches, yet his shadow lingers on forest paths and country roads. For those open to the mysteries of nature, he is more a hidden but authentic guardian of the world's green places than a folkloric myth.

The Green Man is far more than an antiquated aspect of ancient iconography, art, mythology, and folklore. Like Bigfoot, he seems to serve as a guardian of the natural world, a reminder that, as Henry David Thoreau said: "In wildness is the preservation of the world." Copyright © Lochlainn Seabrook.

HAIRY DWARF

The 4 foot tall Hairy Dwarf: one of South America's strangest, most territorial, and most aggressive cryptids. Copyright © Lochlainn Seabrook.

QUICK FACTS

NAME: Hairy Dwarf.
FIRST SIGHTING: Late 19th Century.
LOCATION: Central and West Africa.
SIZE: Height 3 to 4 feet, weight 80 to 120 pounds.
APPEARANCE: Short, powerfully built humanoid with long arms and broad chest.
EYES: Dark, round, and reportedly glowing in firelight.
SKIN/FUR: Covered in thick dark brown or reddish-brown hair, with leathery skin beneath.
DIET: Omnivorous, feeding on roots, tubers, fruits, insects, small mammals, and occasionally scavenged meat. Known to raid farms for crops and poultry.
MOVEMENT: Walks bipedally with a slightly stooped posture, sometimes runs on all fours when threatened.
NOTABLE BEHAVIOR: Aggressive when cornered, known to attack humans with stones or sticks, but also reclusive and quick to vanish into dense vegetation.
FIRST REPORTED BY: European explorers and colonial officials in Africa.
CREATURE CLASSIFICATION: Cryptohominid.
STATUS: Unverified by mainstream science, but still reported in modern times.

CREATURE PROFILE

Reports of the Hairy Dwarf surface from some of the most impenetrable regions of Central and West Africa, where the dense forests conceal a variety of poorly understood species. Witnesses describe an unusual creature that is humanlike in form yet distinct enough to stand apart from any known primate. The Hairy Dwarf is consistently depicted as short in stature but muscular, with long arms and a thick coat of hair. Its body proportions give it a rugged and powerful appearance that does not match pygmy human groups or ordinary apes.

The accounts often come from villagers who claim to have seen the creature raiding crops or stealing poultry. Farmers describe small but heavy footprints pressed into the soil, sometimes alongside clawed or stick impressions that suggest tool use. This behavior points toward a level of intelligence not generally found in wild primates. Some local traditions describe the Hairy Dwarf as nocturnal, appearing mainly at dusk or after dark when villages are less active. Its eyes are said to reflect light in the darkness, creating an eerie glow that adds to its fearsome reputation.

The diet of the Hairy Dwarf is varied. Many accounts describe it pulling up roots and tubers or stripping fruit from trees, but there are also reports of it consuming insects and even raiding animal pens. In certain regions hunters speak of finding partially eaten carcasses of antelope or bush pigs in places where no leopard or hyena activity was present, suggesting that the creature scavenges or may hunt opportunistically. This adaptability in diet likely explains how it has survived for so long in environments where food sources shift seasonally.

Locomotion is another detail that sets this cryptid apart. Witnesses often describe a strange, shuffling walk when it moves upright, but with sudden bursts of speed it can drop to all fours and vanish into the undergrowth. The transition between bipedal and quadrupedal movement gives it a hybrid quality that makes classification difficult. Some researchers suggest it may represent a relic hominin species, while others believe it could be an undiscovered large primate uniquely adapted to the forests of Africa.

Its behavior is equally complex. Villagers warn that the Hairy Dwarf is not merely a timid forest dweller, but a being capable of overt aggression. When cornered or threatened it has been known to hurl stones, shake branches, and brandish sticks in ways that resemble primitive weapon use. This quality makes it one of the more formidable cryptids of Africa, feared not just for its strangeness but for its potential danger. Despite this, most encounters end with the creature retreating rapidly into the forest rather than engaging humans directly.

European explorers of the late 19th Century recorded some of the earliest written reports, often dismissing them as folklore. Yet the consistency of descriptions across vast geographic areas strengthens the possibility that a real species underlies the tradition. Local names for the creature vary by region, but all point to a wild hairy little man who inhabits the margins of human settlement. The persistence of such stories over more than a century suggests a cultural memory of genuine encounters.

Today, reports still arise from rural African communities, though they rarely reach the wider world. To villagers the Hairy Dwarf is as real as any other forest animal, a troublesome presence that must be watched for at night. For cryptozoologists, however, it represents a tantalizing clue to the survival of an unknown hominid or primate line. Whether the Hairy Dwarf is eventually proven to exist or not, it remains one of the central mysteries of African cryptozoology.

A Hairy Dwarf making war on a Brazilian farm, a not uncommon occurrence. Copyright © Lochlainn Seabrook.

HOPKINSVILLE GOBLINS

A mysterious 3 foot tall Hopkinsville Goblin, standing in a moonlit Kentucky field. Its metallic skin, glowing eyes, and alien-like features reflect witness reports from the infamous 1955 encounter. Copyright © Lochlainn Seabrook.

QUICK FACTS

NAME: Hopkinsville Goblins.
FIRST SIGHTING: August 21, 1955.
LOCATION: Kelly-Hopkinsville, Kentucky, USA.
SIZE: Around 3 feet tall, estimated 35 to 50 pounds.
APPEARANCE: Small humanoid bodies with long arms, clawed hands, and oversized heads.
EYES: Large, round, glowing yellow or orange eyes.
SKIN/FUR: Shiny metallic or silvery-gray skin, smooth and reflective.
DIET: Unknown, but theorized to have included small animals, insects, or energy sources such as electromagnetic or psychic fields. Opportunistic omnivory was also suggested.
MOVEMENT: Witnesses said they glided or floated across the ground, with the ability to leap and climb with agility.
NOTABLE BEHAVIOR: Approached a rural farmhouse, peered into windows, resisted bullets, showed no fear of humans. Often linked to hovering lights in the sky.
FIRST REPORTED BY: The Sutton family and their guests.
CREATURE CLASSIFICATION: Extraterrestrial humanoid or interdimensional entity.
STATUS: No modern reports; unverified by mainstream science.

CREATURE PROFILE

The Hopkinsville Goblins entered the record on a summer night in 1955 when a Kentucky farm family reported being surrounded by small beings unlike any known animals. The account quickly became one of the most detailed and striking incidents in cryptid and UFO history because of the number of witnesses, the length of the encounter, and the dramatic behavior of the creatures involved. Unlike ambiguous "lights in the sky" or distant vague shapes, the Goblins were observed at close range for hours, leaving a strong impression on all who saw them.

Descriptions were consistent across the witnesses. The creatures stood about 3 feet tall, with thin bodies, spindly arms, and hands ending in claws. Their heads appeared large in proportion to their bodies, and their ears jutted out to the side like bat wings. Their most striking feature was their enormous glowing eyes, which reflected light in shades of yellow or orange. Their bodies seemed smooth and metallic, with a silver-gray sheen that reflected gunfire and flashlight beams.

Witnesses said the Goblins moved in strange ways. They sometimes floated or glided just above the ground rather than walking, and when they did move with their limbs they showed unusual agility, climbing onto rooftops, peering through windows, and gripping doorframes with ease. When shot at repeatedly with rifles and shotguns, they were knocked backward but never appeared injured, producing metallic sounds when hit and then retreating into the shadows. Their resistance to bullets convinced some that they were armored or possessed bodies of an unknown hardened substance.

The skin was described as reflective and metallic in appearance, unlike the flesh of any terrestrial animal. No hair was seen and the creatures' surfaces appeared entirely smooth. Their hands seemed well adapted for climbing and grasping, with elongated digits that easily hooked onto objects—including buildings. The witnesses were certain that these were not animals native to Kentucky.

The diet of the Hopkinsville Goblins was never determined. No feeding was witnessed, but researchers speculated afterward that they might have been capable of consuming insects, small animals, or possibly drawing sustenance from energy sources in the environment. Others suggested they might have been opportunistic omnivores able to adapt to available food. More speculative theories proposed that, if alien or non-terrestrial, they may not have required conventional nourishment at all, instead using electromagnetic or psychic energy as sustenance.

Behavior during the 1955 siege was persistent yet nonaggressive. The goblins circled the farmhouse for hours, peering inside, crawling over the roof, and retreating when fired upon, only to return minutes later. Their curiosity seemed focused on observing the humans within, not harming them. Although the family was terrified and fired countless rounds at the beings the creatures never attempted to break into the house or attack.

The event was first reported by the Sutton family and their friends, who eventually fled to the Hopkinsville police station in fear. When officers returned with them they confirmed bullet holes, torn screens, and panicked witnesses, though no physical trace of the creatures remained. The sheer number of adults and children providing matching testimony added weight to the account.

The Hopkinsville Goblins were generally classified as extraterrestrial humanoids or interdimensional visitors, their form and behavior aligning with later reports of "little gray" alien entities. Mainstream science dismissed the story due to lack of physical specimens, but the incident remains one of the best-documented close encounters of the 20th Century.

No confirmed sightings have taken place since the original 1955 encounter, leaving the Hopkinsville Goblins as a singular yet powerful case in cryptozoological and ufological study.

Thankfully the 1955 event is the only known report of the weird and disturbing creatures that came to be known as the Hopkinsville Goblins. Copyright © Lochlainn Seabrook.

INKANYAMBA

The unpredictable and powerful 30 foot long Inkanyamba is said to haunt the rivers, waterfalls, and lakes of South Africa. Copyright © Lochlainn Seabrook.

QUICK FACTS

NAME: Inkanyamba.
FIRST SIGHTING: 19th Century.
LOCATION: Howick Falls, KwaZulu-Natal, South Africa.
SIZE: Reported length up to 20 to 30 feet, weight estimated at over 1,000 pounds.
APPEARANCE: Giant serpent-like body with a horse-like head and finned appendages.
EYES: Large, round, and luminous, often said to glow at night.
SKIN/FUR: Smooth, scaled, and slick, often described as dark brown, gray, or black.
DIET: Fish, birds, amphibians, and possibly livestock or other large animals taken near water.
MOVEMENT: Swims powerfully in rivers and waterfalls, coils and thrashes violently when disturbed.
NOTABLE BEHAVIOR: Associated with violent storms, tornadoes, and floods; feared for its destructive powers.
FIRST REPORTED BY: Zulu and Xhosa people through oral traditions.
CREATURE CLASSIFICATION: Aquatic cryptid serpent.
STATUS: Considered folklore by mainstream science; yet sightings continue to be reported into the present day.

CREATURE PROFILE

Among the waterfalls of KwaZulu-Natal there are ongoing stories of a creature so powerful that locals link its presence to violent storms. This being is the Inkanyamba, a massive serpent-like animal said to live in the deep waters of Howick Falls in South Africa. It is regarded with deep respect and fear by the Zulu and Xhosa people who have passed down their knowledge of it for generations. Unlike many water cryptids that remain obscure, the Inkanyamba is described with specific traits and a strong association with destructive weather, making it one of the most distinctive cryptid serpents in African tradition.

The physical appearance of the Inkanyamba is consistently reported as immense. Witnesses describe a body between 20 and 30 feet long, thick-bodied, and resembling an eel or serpent. What sets it apart is its unusual head which is often compared to that of a horse. This peculiar combination of traits has been cited repeatedly, reinforcing the possibility that it represents an unknown species rather than a misidentified common animal. The creature's skin is said to be smooth, slick, and dark in color, with shades ranging from deep brown to black. Observers also mention large luminous eyes that shine in the dark, a feature suggesting possible bioluminescence or reflective membranes adapted for low light environments.

Behaviorally, the Inkanyamba is tied to violent meteorological events. Oral traditions claim that when the creature moves between bodies of water it stirs up great storms, whirlwinds, and even tornadoes. Farmers in KwaZulu-Natal historically blamed crop damage from gales on the Inkanyamba's temper. Seasonal flooding was also connected to the animal's movements. Such attributions indicate a long-standing cultural understanding of the creature's role in the natural environment. Some modern witnesses describe the animal thrashing in the river during heavy rains, which aligns with its storm-related reputation.

Its diet is thought to include a wide range of prey. Fish are a natural staple given its aquatic habitat, but reports also mention it taking water birds, frogs, and sometimes even domestic animals that venture too close to the falls. The scale of its reported size suggests it would need large quantities of food, possibly leading it to feed opportunistically on anything within reach. This places it in the role of an apex predator within its environment, capable of influencing the populations of multiple species.

Movement is described as serpentine yet more powerful than any known eel or fish. It swims with violent thrashing motions, creating turbulence in the water, and has been seen rising partially above the surface. Accounts of it moving across land between rivers are rarer, but the belief that it leaves the water during seasonal rains continues. Such behavior may have led to its strong association with storms, since sudden sightings often coincide with destructive weather.

Though first formally recorded by European settlers in the 19th Century, the Zulu and Xhosa have preserved knowledge of the Inkanyamba for far longer. In their traditions the animal is not merely a beast but a spiritual force tied to weather and natural disasters. This dual role as both physical creature and elemental power gives it a unique place in cryptid study. Unlike other lake or river monsters it is both a zoological mystery and a cultural symbol of nature's unpredictable fury.

Skeptics and mainstream science, of course, dismisses the Inkanyamba as folklore, arguing that sightings could be large eels or misinterpretations of storms themselves. Yet the consistency of descriptions across generations and the continued reports from modern witnesses suggest that something unusual exists in these waters.

Whether a yet-undiscovered giant eel, a new species of aquatic reptile, or a cryptid that bridges biology and legend, the Inkanyamba remains one of the most formidable water creatures still spoken of today.

The South African Inkanyamba is especially known for its predatory behavior toward livestock. Copyright © Lochlainn Seabrook.

JERSEY DEVIL

The 7 foot tall Jersey Devil in its native habitat: the ominous cryptid hotspot known as the Pine Barrens of southern New Jersey. Copyright © Lochlainn Seabrook.

QUICK FACTS

NAME: Jersey Devil.
FIRST SIGHTING: Early 1700s.
LOCATION: Pine Barrens, New Jersey, USA.
SIZE: Height 5 to 7 feet, weight estimated 150 to 250 pounds.
APPEARANCE: Kangaroo-like body with wings, long neck, horse-like head, horns, cloven hooves, and long tail.
EYES: Large, bright, glowing red when seen at night.
SKIN/FUR: Dark leathery skin or sparse coarse hair depending on reports.
DIET: Reports suggest omnivorous feeding habits including livestock, poultry, small mammals, carrion, and possibly wild plants or fruits.
MOVEMENT: Hops, glides, or flies with strong wingbeats; can also run quickly on land.
NOTABLE BEHAVIOR: Known to emit loud screeches, shrieks, and growls; frightens animals; attacks farm animals; leaves strange tracks.
FIRST REPORTED BY: Local settlers and early colonists of southern New Jersey.
CREATURE CLASSIFICATION: Winged cryptid, possibly an unknown species of large bat-like or reptilian mammal.
STATUS: Considered folklore by mainstream science, but reported consistently into the present day.

CREATURE PROFILE

The Jersey Devil stands out among cryptids because of its unusual longevity in folklore paired with an active presence in modern eyewitness reports. While many regional monsters fade into memory this creature remains firmly embedded in both local culture and the continuing natural history of New Jersey's Pine Barrens. What makes it unique is the remarkable consistency of descriptions over more than three centuries, combined with the frequency of new encounters, which indicates the possibility of a stable breeding population rather than a single anomalous sighting.

Most detailed accounts describe an animal with a height of 5 to 7 feet, equipped with wings, cloven hooves, and a long tail. The head is compared most often to that of a horse, but observers stress its unnatural aspect, with a thinner snout, sharp teeth, and glowing red eyes visible at night. The wings are said to be leathery, bat-like, and strong enough to rapidly lift the creature into the air. Its body is lean, with a kangaroo-like stance and long limbs capable of hopping or bounding. These features give it an unsettling hybrid appearance, as though it combines elements of mammal, reptile, and bird in one form.

The Pine Barrens provide an ideal environment for such a cryptid to survive. Covering more than one million acres, this spooky region of southern New Jersey consists of dense forests, swamps, and remote sand roads. Large stretches are uninhabited and visibility within the thickets can be limited to only a few feet. Wildlife thrives in these habitats, from deer and wild turkey to raccoons and foxes. A large omnivore such as the Jersey Devil could subsist comfortably, feeding on smaller prey, raiding farms, and supplementing its diet with fruits, berries, or carrion. Its reputation for attacking livestock aligns with the behavior of opportunistic predators such as coyotes, but the winged and bipedal elements set it apart.

Reports of its movement emphasize versatility. On the ground it can run on all fours, bound on two legs, or leap with surprising agility. In the air it uses its wings to fly rapidly, sometimes circling before gliding off into the distance. Witnesses note that the creature can ascend almost vertically from a standing position, a maneuver requiring immense wing power. This accounts for its ability to leave sudden tracks that start or stop without logical explanation. Modern drivers have reported the Jersey Devil keeping pace with cars along lonely stretches of road before veering upward into the night sky, an ability unmatched by any known mammal.

Behaviorally, the creature is often associated with chilling vocalizations. Eyewitnesses consistently describe its scream as inhuman, a piercing wail or high-pitched shriek that unsettles both people and animals. Farmers recount how their livestock panic violently when these cries echo through the Barrens. Dogs refuse to chase or approach it—and in some accounts are killed when they do. The creature is said to be bold, sometimes approaching farmhouses or circling populated areas. During the so-called "flap" of 1909, hundreds of reports came in within a single week, many from law enforcement officers and civic leaders, suggesting that "mass hysteria" is not a sufficient explanation.

The cultural history of the Jersey Devil is tied to the legend of Mother Leeds, a woman who allegedly cursed her thirteenth child in the early 1700s, dooming it to transform into a monster. While folklorists emphasize this tale, it is important to distinguish between narrative embellishment and zoological evidence. The existence of consistent physical descriptions, independent of the Leeds story, demonstrates that people were seeing something tangible long before the legend was codified. Similar winged, red-eyed cryptids appear in other parts of the world, hinting that the Jersey Devil may belong to a broader class of as-yet-unrecognized animals.

Modern encounters keep the story alive. Hikers, hunters, and motorists in the Pine Barrens continue to report sightings. In some cases the Jersey Devil is seen crossing roads, flying overhead, or perching briefly in trees before disappearing. In others, livestock killings are blamed on the creature when tracks and sounds do not match coyotes or bears. The New Jersey State Police have files containing reports dating into the late 20th Century, and local newspapers still occasionally print witness accounts. The persistence of these reports into the 21st Century strengthens the case that the Jersey Devil is not a myth alone but a genuine biological mystery.

If real, its classification is uncertain. The combination of hooves, wings, and mammalian body structure does not fit any recognized taxonomic category. Some theorize it could represent a large bat with unusual mutations, perhaps surviving from a prehistoric lineage. Others suggest a marsupial or reptilian mammal with convergent features. The glowing eyes may result from a reflective retinal layer similar to the tapetum lucidum found in many nocturnal animals. Such traits would aid a predator or scavenger active at night in dense forests.

The skepticism of mainstream science stems from the lack of physical remains. No body, skeleton, or preserved specimen has yet been produced. However, this absence is not unusual among cryptids. Dense forests, scavengers, and rapid decomposition often erase evidence quickly. I myself have hiked many thousands of miles in the wilderness and have yet to come across the bones of any large predatory animal. The Pine Barrens' acidic soils are particularly poor for preserving bones. Many known animals were once dismissed as myths until specimens were discovered, such as the okapi and the giant squid. The Jersey Devil could represent another case in which folk memory preserves knowledge of a real but elusive creature.

Ultimately the Jersey Devil continues to resist simple classification. Its place in both folklore and field reports highlights the need for unbiased study. Rather than dismissing centuries of consistent testimony, a scientific approach would involve systematic tracking of vocalizations, examination of tracks, and the use of camera traps in areas with frequent sightings. Until then the Jersey Devil remains one of the most enigmatic cryptids of North America—feared by some, dismissed by others, yet still seen and heard in the dark foreboding forests of the Pine Barrens.

The Jersey Devil in flight, underscoring reports of its frightening presence and supernatural aura. Copyright © Lochlainn Seabrook.

The Jersey Devil lurking near a rural roadway, its luminescent eyes and grotesque form evoking the fear and dread reported by countless credible witnesses. Copyright © Lochlainn Seabrook.

KALANORO

One of Madagascar's most aggressive and dangerous cryptids: the 3 foot tall, human-like Kalanoro. Copyright © Lochlainn Seabrook.

QUICK FACTS

NAME: Kalanoro.
FIRST SIGHTING: Reported in Madagascar in the 18th Century.
LOCATION: Madagascar.
SIZE: Height 2 to 3 feet, weight estimated at 40 to 60 pounds.
APPEARANCE: Dwarf-like humanoid with long arms, clawed fingers, and a hunched posture.
EYES: Large and round, glowing at night.
SKIN/FUR: Covered in coarse hair, usually described as gray or brown.
DIET: Believed to be omnivorous, feeding on small animals, insects, fruits, roots, and occasionally livestock. Reports claim they sometimes attack humans for food.
MOVEMENT: Walks upright though stooped, climbs with ease, runs quickly, and is a skilled swimmer.
NOTABLE BEHAVIOR: Known for stealing food, abducting children and women, and lurking near rivers or caves. Said to let out loud cries at night.
FIRST REPORTED BY: Malagasy villagers, later by European explorers and missionaries.
CREATURE CLASSIFICATION: Cryptid hominin, possibly a surviving relict population of early humans or primates.
STATUS: Unverified by mainstream science; yet belief in the creature remains strong, and sightings—though rare—continue, with oral traditions persisting in some communities.

CREATURE PROFILE

In Madagascar there is an ongoing story of small wild people who live deep in the forests, known as the Kalanoro. Local accounts describe them as dwarf-like beings with a terrifying presence, feared and respected by villagers for generations. Unlike many cryptids, the Kalanoro is not merely a shadow of folklore but a creature that witnesses insist is still encountered in remote parts of the island today. Reports continue to come in from isolated regions, where dense jungle and hidden rivers provide the kind of refuge few humans enter.

Descriptions of the Kalanoro show remarkable consistency across the centuries. Witnesses say these beings stand no more than 3 feet tall, with long arms that reach nearly to their knees. Their hands bear sharp claws that are used both for climbing and for tearing into prey. Their bodies are covered in rough hair, usually gray or brown, which helps them blend into the shadows of the forest. At night their large round eyes are said to glow, betraying their presence to startled travelers. Their faces are human-like but twisted, with protruding mouths and sharp teeth, giving them a feral and disturbing appearance.

The diet of the Kalanoro is one of the most troubling features attributed to them. Though they feed on fruits, roots, and forest animals, villagers say they also steal goats, chickens, and even pigs. More unsettling are accounts that they sometimes attack humans, targeting lone travelers or sleeping women. Oral traditions claim they have carried off women to the forest, sometimes keeping them alive for unknown purposes. Such stories raise the question of whether the Kalanoro is purely myth or a real and dangerous predator.

Behaviorally, the Kalanoro shows traits common to both humans and animals. They walk upright—though with a hunched back—moving with surprising speed when threatened. They are also adept at climbing and swimming, which makes them well-suited to Madagascar's rugged terrain. Villagers report hearing them at night near rivers, their cries echoing through the darkness. These cries are described as neither human nor animal, a chilling sound that causes locals to avoid the area. Such accounts, passed down for generations, form a strong case that there is something real behind the legend.

European missionaries and explorers of the 18th and 19th Centuries wrote of strange wild men described to them by the Malagasy. These reports often matched what the locals had already long believed, that small hairy people lived apart from humans, feared for their violence and unpredictability. Missionaries in particular repeated tales of abductions and attacks, reinforcing the perception that the Kalanoro was not only real but dangerous. These accounts have become part of the written record, supporting what oral tradition has claimed for ages. (Note that in some regions of Madagascar the Kalanoro is also referred to as the Kapa—though the descriptions remain essentially the same.)

From a scientific perspective, the Kalanoro has been interpreted in several ways. Some researchers suggest it may be a relict hominin, a surviving branch of early humans such as *Homo floresiensis*. Others think it could be an unknown species of primate adapted to Madagascar's environment. Another possibility is that the creature represents an amalgam of myths and real encounters with unusual forest dwellers, possibly small groups of outcast humans who lived apart from society. However, none of these theories address all of the creature's characteristics and behaviors, and the Kalanoro remains beyond the grasp of mainstream science.

Today the legend of the Kalanoro is still alive in Madagascar. Hunters, farmers, and villagers occasionally report sightings of small figures moving quickly through the trees or hearing strange cries near the rivers at night. Whether myth, memory, or reality, the Kalanoro continues to occupy a firm place in both Malagasy culture and global cryptozoological study. Its persistence suggests that there may yet be truths hidden within the forests of Madagascar, awaiting our discovery.

The Kalanoro's reputation for abducting human children makes it particularly frightening. Copyright © Lochlainn Seabrook.

KELPIE

Lochlainn Seabrook

An unsuspecting Scottish girl succumbs to the alluring but deadly beauty of the 9 foot long, half ton Kelpie. Copyright © Lochlainn Seabrook.

QUICK FACTS

NAME: Kelpie.
FIRST SIGHTING: 6th Century.
LOCATION: Scotland.
SIZE: 7-9 feet in length, 5-6 feet in height, estimated weight 800-1,200 pounds.
APPEARANCE: Equine shape with dark mane, sometimes shifting into a human-like form.
EYES: Large, luminous, often reported as fiery or glowing.
SKIN/FUR: Sleek black or dark gray coat that appears wet, sometimes slimy to the touch.
DIET: Aquatic vegetation, fish, deer, livestock, and humans; opportunistic feeder capable of consuming both plant and animal matter. Reported to drag prey underwater before consumption.
MOVEMENT: Swift swimmer with powerful lunges; runs on land with the speed of a racehorse; capable of moving silently through water.
NOTABLE BEHAVIOR: Known for shape-shifting, luring humans, and dragging victims into water; leaves behind only waterlogged remains. Often neighs with an unnatural echo near lochs and rivers.
FIRST REPORTED BY: Early Christian monks and Celtic oral tradition.
CREATURE CLASSIFICATION: Aquatic equine cryptid with shape-shifting abilities.
STATUS: Classified as folklore by mainstream science, though sightings continue into modern times.

CREATURE PROFILE

When describing the Kelpie, one must begin with its close connection to the waterways of Scotland. This aquatic equine is said to inhabit deep lochs, fast-moving rivers, and even coastal estuaries. It is not regarded as a mere legend alone, for reports continue into the present day. Eyewitnesses speak of a large horse-like creature with a dripping black coat, standing silently near the water's edge as if inviting the curious to draw nearer. Once mounted the victim finds him or herself bound to the animal's back by an unnatural adhesion. It is then that he or she is carried without mercy into the depths where the Kelpie feeds.

The earliest accounts of the Kelpie emerge in Celtic oral traditions that predate written records. By the 6th Century Christian scribes recorded stories of water horses in their attempts to describe the supernatural dangers of Scotland's wild landscape. The creature is not confined to a single loch but ranges widely, inhabiting nearly every major body of freshwater across the Highlands and Lowlands. In this sense the Kelpie may represent a widespread species rather than a single isolated phenomenon. Its adaptability to rivers and lakes suggests a highly mobile predator, capable of moving across large distances in short spans of time.

Descriptions vary, yet common features remain. The Kelpie is usually seen as a large black horse with an unnatural shine to its skin, sometimes slick as though covered in oil. Its eyes glow with a pale light and its mane often appears tangled with weeds and river grasses. In certain encounters the Kelpie assumes human form, often as a tall dark-haired man who exudes a magnetic presence near water. Witnesses claim that even in this guise, a trace of aquatic vegetation or water dripping from the figure betrays its true identity. The ability to change shape suggests an advanced survival strategy, blending deception with predation.

The diet of the Kelpie is varied, further establishing it as a versatile creature. Some accounts describe it feeding on reeds, grasses, and freshwater vegetation, indicating it can graze like a true horse. Yet—oddly for a traditionally herbivorous animal—it is more often associated with carnivory. Sheep, deer, and cattle found near rivers are said to vanish mysteriously, with drag marks leading into the water. Human victims are also well documented in Scottish folklore. Survivors of near encounters claim the Kelpie attempted to lure them into the water with hypnotic sounds or a strangely beckoning neigh.

Its movement is described as both terrestrial and aquatic. On land it gallops faster than any horse, its hooves striking sparks from stone. In water it swims with immense force, creating whirlpools and surges that can overturn small boats. Some reports state that when the creature submerges with its prey, the surface of the loch remains eerily still, as if it has swallowed both noise and motion.

Behavioral accounts portray the Kelpie as highly territorial. It guards stretches of river and certain loch inlets, returning to the same locations across generations. Many Highland families recount encounters passed down through centuries, often tied to a specific bridge, ford, or riverbank. The creature's neigh is considered a warning sign: an echoing call that carries on the wind just before a drowning.

The Kelpie remains a notable subject of study for cryptozoologists. Its widespread presence in Scottish tradition, coupled with modern sightings, suggests that the phenomenon is not solely mythological. Whether the Kelpie is a surviving aquatic species, a shape-shifting equine entity, or an undiscovered natural predator, its consistency across the centuries gives weight to its reality. Mainstream science dismisses it as folklore, but the continuing flow of credible reports ensures that the Kelpie remains a serious candidate for further investigation.

The Kelpie dragging another victim into the murky depths of a Scottish loch. Copyright © Lochlainn Seabrook.

KONGAMATO

The elusive, 4 foot long Kongamato hunting along the edge of a Zambian wetland. Copyright © Lochlainn Seabrook.

QUICK FACTS

NAME: Kongamato.
FIRST SIGHTING: Late 19th Century.
LOCATION: Zambia, Angola, and Congo.
SIZE: Wingspan 4 to 7 feet, body length 3 to 4 feet, estimated weight 20 to 35 pounds.
APPEARANCE: Large batlike flying creature with leathery wings, elongated beak, and sharp teeth.
EYES: Large, round, and reddish.
SKIN/FUR: Smooth, hairless, dark brown or reddish skin resembling that of a bat.
DIET: Believed to prey on fish, small reptiles, amphibians, birds, and occasionally larger animals. Some reports suggest scavenging behavior at carrion sites.
MOVEMENT: Strong rapid wingbeats. Flies low over rivers and swamps. Walks awkwardly on the ground when landed.
NOTABLE BEHAVIOR: Aggressive toward humans when disturbed. Said to overturn boats and attack fishermen. Often associated with remote waterways.
FIRST REPORTED BY: Indigenous peoples of Zambia. Later documented by British explorers in the early 20th Century.
CREATURE CLASSIFICATION: Possible surviving pterosaur such as *Pteranodon* or *Rhamphorhynchus*.
STATUS: Considered mythical by mainstream science; yet it is still reported.

CREATURE PROFILE

Among the rivers and swamps of central Africa there are still reports of a flying beast known as the Kongamato. Local traditions describe it not as a spirit or metaphor but as a real animal with physical form capable of injuring and killing those who intrude upon its territory. This distinction sets it apart from many other legendary creatures of Africa. The people of Zambia in particular regard the Kongamato as a flesh-and-blood predator that requires no supernatural explanation.

The most striking feature of the Kongamato is its resemblance to a pterosaur. Witnesses speak of wings without feathers, stretched by skin like those of a bat. The wingspan is consistently described as between four and seven feet. A long snout lined with sharp teeth allows it to seize fish from the water with precision. Its eyes are said to glow red in certain light, enhancing its sinister reputation. Unlike birds its body lacks feathers. Instead its skin is smooth and dark, sometimes tinged with red, giving it an almost reptilian appearance.

Dietary habits of the Kongamato are pieced together from both sightings and the damage it leaves behind. Fishermen describe sudden attacks on canoes and missing catches that vanish in a flash of leathery wings. Some accounts describe the creature taking fish directly from nets or lines, while others suggest it will scavenge carcasses left near water. Small reptiles, frogs, and waterfowl likely provide regular food sources. Its dentition suggests a versatile carnivorous diet, not restricted to any one prey type.

In flight the Kongamato moves with swift, forceful wingbeats. It is often observed skimming the surface of rivers, flying low as though patrolling for prey. When it lands it becomes clumsy, walking with difficulty as if its body is designed more for flight than terrestrial movement. Its aggressiveness is well noted. Witnesses report it attacking those who disturb it, overturning boats and even leaving deep wounds on victims with its beak and claws. This hostility has led to deep caution among local tribes, who avoid certain areas known to harbor the beast.

The Kongamato is also linked to seasonal patterns. Villagers say it is seen more often during the rainy season when rivers flood and fish are abundant, suggesting that its behavior may be tied to water levels and food availability. Sightings are less frequent in the dry season, which may indicate either migration or retreat into deeper swamp habitats. This seasonal rhythm further strengthens the view that it is a living animal with consistent long term ecological needs.

Reports entered Western awareness during the colonial period, when British explorers collected stories from villagers and in some cases claimed to have seen the animal themselves. Descriptions in these reports aligned so closely with pterosaur reconstructions that some scientists speculated whether an unknown species of large bat or bird might explain the sightings. Others suggested a surviving remnant of a pterosaur line, though this interpretation remains rejected by mainstream science. Nevertheless, the parallels between ancient fossils and modern reports are difficult to ignore.

The cultural impact of the Kongamato is significant. It is feared and respected as a dangerous animal rather than worshiped as a spiritual being. Its name translates roughly to "breaker of boats," a reminder of its reputation along African waterways. Local knowledge stresses avoidance of its nesting areas and waterways where it has been seen most often. Unlike purely mythical cryptids the Kongamato inspires real world responses: people change behavior and routes to avoid confrontation.

Today sightings continue to be reported, though rarely. Remote regions of Zambia, Angola, and the Congo still hold vast stretches of unexplored wetlands where such a creature could remain hidden. Whether it represents an undiscovered species of giant bat, an exaggerated stork, or a true living fossil, the Kongamato occupies a firm place in the zoological mysteries of Africa. Its persistence in both local tradition and modern accounts keeps alive the possibility that the skies of central Africa are shared with a predator from another age.

The pterosaur-like Kongamato, reported by both native peoples and European explorers, is known to attack people and overturn boats. Copyright © Lochlainn Seabrook.

KRAKEN

A 100 foot long Kraken spots one of its favorite meals in the distance: a pod of sperm whales. Copyright © Lochlainn Seabrook.

QUICK FACTS

NAME: Kraken.
FIRST SIGHTING: 12th Century.
LOCATION: North Atlantic Ocean, particularly off Norway, Greenland, and Iceland.
SIZE: Length estimated between 40 feet and 100 feet, weight possibly exceeding 50 tons.
APPEARANCE: Gigantic cephalopod-like creature with multiple massive tentacles, central body, and beak-like mouth.
EYES: Very large, round, and forward-facing.
SKIN/FUR: Smooth, rubbery, and slick skin ranging from dark gray to reddish-brown.
DIET: Feeds on large fish, whales, seabirds, and humans when encountered. Tentacles capture prey and draw it toward a sharp beak. May consume enormous schools of fish at once. Known for creating whirlpools that pull marine life downward for easy feeding.
MOVEMENT: Propelled by jetting water from siphons and by undulating tentacles. Can move quickly upward to seize prey near the surface or lie dormant in the deep.
NOTABLE BEHAVIOR: Reported to capsize ships while seizing their crews, dragging sailors into the sea, and create whirlpools by diving rapidly. May surface suddenly with tentacles spread wide, terrifying sailors. Frequently associated with sudden mass disappearances of fish or the vanishing of entire boats.
FIRST REPORTED BY: Norse sailors and chroniclers.
CREATURE CLASSIFICATION: Marine cryptid, cephalopod-like.
STATUS: Considered mythical by mainstream science, yet modern sightings continue.

CREATURE PROFILE

The Kraken holds a prominent place in maritime natural history. For generations sailors crossing the cold and dangerous waters of the North Atlantic have described a massive cephalopod rising from the depths without warning. The creature is known by its Scandinavian name but parallels exist in seafaring traditions across Europe. Its form is so vast and its presence so sudden that it has influenced seafaring culture for nearly a thousand years.

Reports of the Kraken focus on its immense size. Descriptions often depict a creature large enough to rival a small island, its body concealed beneath the water while its tentacles stretch skyward. Many encounters tell of masts being snapped and decks ripped apart as its limbs curl over the sides of wooden ships. The central body is said to be bulky and rounded with a strong beak hidden beneath. Such proportions suggest an animal of enormous weight, capable of sinking vessels that were the pride of the sailing age.

The eyes of the Kraken are frequently emphasized. Accounts describe them as round, forward-facing, and as wide as shields. A gaze from these eyes is said to unsettle men who otherwise spent their lives at sea. Large eyes would be practical for an animal dwelling in the deep where light is scarce. Such details reinforce the possibility that these observations are based on a real creature rather than pure legend.

Its diet is described in remarkable detail by sailors and early naturalists. Entire schools of fish vanish when the Kraken is nearby. Fishermen sometimes note sudden abundance before a collapse, as if prey were driven upward before being consumed in a single sweep. Whales are said to fall victim to its grasp, pulled down and suffocated before being devoured. The beak, always mentioned with dread, is the focal point of its feeding. The idea of the Kraken creating whirlpools by its own descent may represent a natural hunting tactic to trap prey in currents and turbulence.

Movement is equally dramatic. At times it drifts near the surface with little visible effort, its bulk hidden below while tentacles writhe slowly above. At other times it propels itself with astonishing speed, surging upward or diving sharply. The use of jet propulsion through siphons is a plausible explanation, aligning with known cephalopod mechanics. Its ability to vanish quickly into the depths adds to its mystery and the absolute terror it inspires.

Behavioral accounts include striking details. Ships have been seized and destroyed, not through storm or reef, but through the sudden assault of the Kraken's limbs. Sailors tell of decks wrapped and pulled apart, of men swept into the sea, and of the ocean itself churned into chaos. The whirlpool effect is among its most famous traits. Whether the result of its sheer size or a method of descent, sailors often viewed these maelstroms as inescapable.

The first written reports come from Norse and Scandinavian sailors in the 12th Century. Chroniclers describe the animal not as fanciful but as a known danger. Early natural histories, such as those of Bishop Pontoppidan in the 18th Century, catalogued it in the same manner as whales or sharks. For centuries the Kraken remained a very real concern to mariners. Modern scientists attribute these accounts to giant squids, but the descriptions often surpass the limits of known species.

Today sightings are ongoing. Deep-sea fishermen, sailors, and submersible operators still speak of colossal tentacled forms in the depths. While mainstream science regards the Kraken as mythical, the survival of such reports across the centuries suggests an underlying reality. After all, if giant squids and colossal squids exist, it is not unreasonable to accept that an even larger relative may still patrol the darkest reaches of the North Atlantic.

In either case, the Kraken remains one of the most compelling marine mysteries of all time.

If modern fishermen, divers, and sailors are to be believed, frightening encounters with the Kraken continue into the present day. Copyright © Lochlainn Seabrook.

KUSHTAKA

The terrifying 8 foot tall otter-like Kushtaka, one of Alaska's many shapeshifting cryptids, is reported to prey on humans. Copyright © Lochlainn Seabrook.

QUICK FACTS

NAME: Kushtaka.
FIRST SIGHTING: Reported in Tlingit oral tradition for many centuries.
LOCATION: Southeastern Alaska, USA.
SIZE: Between 6 and 8 feet tall, estimated 200 to 400 pounds.
APPEARANCE: Humanlike form with the ability to shift into an otter or hybrid shape.
EYES: Dark and often described as glistening or reflective in low light.
SKIN/FUR: Thick brown to black fur when in otter form, rough humanlike skin when in anthropoid form.
DIET: Fish, shellfish, and small to medium-sized mammals, though also said to prey on humans.
MOVEMENT: Walks upright on two legs in humanoid state, swims with great agility in otter form.
NOTABLE BEHAVIOR: Mimics human voices to lure victims; physically transforms to confuse or frighten; known to steal souls or convert humans into Kushtaka.
FIRST REPORTED BY: Indigenous Tlingit and Tsimshian peoples.
CREATURE CLASSIFICATION: Shapeshifting anthropoid cryptid.
STATUS: Unverified by mainstream science; yet reports and sightings continue into the present.

CREATURE PROFILE

Among the cryptids of the Pacific Northwest, few are as feared or as culturally significant as the Kushtaka. This shape-shifting being is firmly rooted in the traditions of the Tlingit and Tsimshian peoples of southeastern Alaska. Unlike many other regional cryptids the Kushtaka is not merely seen as an animal of unusual size or behavior, but rather as a supernatural predator that blurs the line between the natural and the spiritual. It stands as a powerful example of how cryptids can serve both as folkloric warnings and as possible reflections of actual biological entities.

The Kushtaka is most often described as a humanoid creature capable of taking on the form of a large river otter or an unsettling hybrid between man and otter. Sightings usually place its size between 6 and 8 feet tall with a muscular build and dense fur. Witnesses claim that in humanlike form it retains otter features such as whiskers, sharp teeth, and webbed hands. This unsettling blend of human and animal characteristics may explain why it remains so deeply feared within Indigenous traditions.

Behavioral reports of the Kushtaka consistently emphasize its deceptive and dangerous nature. It is said to mimic the cries of distressed children or the voices of friends and family in order to lure humans to rivers or coastlines. Once in proximity the creature may seize its victim and either drown them, tear them apart, or transform them into another Kushtaka. This act of transformation is seen by many Tlingit elders not only as a frightening physical change but as a theft of the human soul. Because of this, the Kushtaka has long been regarded as a spirit of death and misfortune.

Dietary accounts vary but typically include salmon, trout, shellfish, and other local aquatic life. However, human predation is a recurring theme in the reports. Whether this is literal or symbolic remains an open question. Some believe the Kushtaka represents the real threat of drowning in Alaska's icy waters, where a person lured off-course could easily perish. Others maintain that the sheer number of accounts, coupled with the consistency of their details across different tribes, suggests that the Kushtaka is a genuine predatory species that has avoided scientific classification.

Modern sightings continue to surface, often from remote villages or wilderness travelers. Fishermen claim to have seen large otterlike figures standing upright along shorelines before disappearing into the forest. Others describe strange unearthly vocalizations calling them toward the water. These encounters reinforce the idea that the Kushtaka is not confined to myth but remains an active presence in Alaskan wilderness today.

Cultural defenses against the Kushtaka include the use of copper, which Tlingit tradition regards as a protective material. Shamans were also believed to have the power to ward off or drive away the beings. Accounts suggest that Kushtaka avoid dogs and can be repelled by loud noises or fire. Such details point toward survival strategies passed down for generations, offering practical guidance for those living in close contact with these strange dangerous entities.

In evaluating the Kushtaka one must acknowledge both its folkloric role and the possibility of its biological reality. The idea of an intelligent semi-aquatic hominid adapted to Alaska's coastal environment is not beyond scientific speculation. If such creatures exist, their ability to blend into both water and forest would make them extraordinarily difficult to document. For now, the Kushtaka remains both a terrifying legend and a potential North American cryptid, a reminder that the cold waters of Alaska may yet conceal beings unknown to science.

Emerging suddenly from the frigid waters of an Alaskan bay, a 400 pound Kushtaka launches an unprovoked attack on a group of horrified canoeists. Copyright © Lochlainn Seabrook.

LAGARFLJÓT WORM

According to sightings reports, the Lagarfljót Worm may attain lengths of up to 90 feet, making it one of the world's largest cryptids. Copyright © Lochlainn Seabrook.

QUICK FACTS

NAME: Lagarfljót Worm.
FIRST SIGHTING: 1345.
LOCATION: Lake Lagarfljót, near Egilsstaðir, Iceland.
SIZE: Between 30 feet and 90 feet in length, weighing several tons.
APPEARANCE: Long serpentine body with humps rising above the water, dark or pale in color.
EYES: Rarely observed, sometimes described as faintly glowing.
SKIN / FUR: Smooth eel-like surface without scales or fur.
DIET: Believed to feed on fish including trout and char, possibly waterfowl, and occasionally larger aquatic animals. Some accounts suggest opportunistic feeding on carrion near the shoreline.
MOVEMENT: Undulates through the water in a serpentine manner, sometimes appearing as rolling coils or multiple humps.
NOTABLE BEHAVIOR: Surfaces during cold weather, ice melts, or flooding events. Often linked with local disasters. Sometimes thrashes violently at the surface.
FIRST REPORTED BY: Farmers and residents of East Iceland.
CREATURE CLASSIFICATION: Aquatic cryptid, serpent-like animal.
STATUS: Existence unacknowledged by mainstream science, but still reported today.

CREATURE PROFILE

The waters of Lake Lagarfljót in eastern Iceland are home to one of Europe's most famous aquatic mysteries. Known as the Lagarfljót Worm, this enormous serpentine animal is said to glide through the glacial depths and emerge only on rare occasions. Unlike many lake monster traditions that began in recent centuries, sightings of this creature extend back to the early 14th Century, making it one of the oldest recorded aquatic cryptids in the Northern Hemisphere. Reports first appeared in 1345 when townsfolk described a massive worm-like being inhabiting the lake, terrifying both farmers and travelers who passed along its shores.

Lake Lagarfljót itself forms the perfect setting for such a creature to thrive. It is a glacial-fed body of water more than 80 feet deep, long and narrow, with a silty opacity that makes visibility almost nonexistent below the surface. The cold mineral-heavy water combined with the great depth provides excellent concealment for any large animal. This natural cover may explain how such a creature could survive in relative secrecy for centuries, surfacing only when environmental changes or disturbances in the lake stir it upward.

Accounts consistently describe the Worm as a serpentine figure with a body large enough to produce humps or coils across the surface of the water. Eyewitnesses sometimes report multiple ridges breaking the waves in sequence, giving the impression of a colossal rope being pulled across the lake. The color is usually dark gray or pale white, with an eel-like smoothness and no visible fins. On rare occasions glowing eyes are mentioned; but in most cases observers see only the immense length and movement.

Its diet remains speculative but is generally believed to include the lake's trout and Arctic char populations. Fishermen occasionally report losing catches to sudden disturbances beneath their boats, while other witnesses suggest the Worm may also prey upon waterfowl or small mammals near the shoreline. Some oral traditions claim it feeds on carrion or livestock carcasses swept into the lake by floods. This opportunistic feeding behavior, combined with the abundance of fish, would provide the nutritional base necessary to sustain an animal of such enormous size.

Behavioral reports highlight the Worm's tendency to appear during specific natural events. Many sightings occur in winter or early spring when ice begins to thaw and break apart, releasing currents that may drive the animal closer to the surface. Some observers link its appearances to flooding, with the creature described as thrashing violently in the water as if disturbed by the rising levels. These patterns suggest that the Worm is responsive to environmental shifts rather than being a constant surface presence.

One of the most significant modern reports occurred in 2012 when a video captured a long, undulating figure moving beneath the ice of Lake Lagarfljót. The form advanced with rhythmic serpentine motion, resembling descriptions of the Worm passed down for hundreds of years. The footage received national and international attention, with many Icelanders affirming its likeness to traditional accounts. Even though mainstream science attributed the phenomenon to ice movements or debris, the official commission of study gave the sighting legitimacy few cryptids have achieved.

Beyond the 2012 video other modern encounters strengthen the Worm's credibility. In 1963, workers constructing a hydroelectric power station near the lake reported seeing a massive serpentine form rise and submerge repeatedly, describing loops of its body as large as barrels. In the late 1980s, schoolchildren and teachers on a field trip claimed to witness ridges undulating across the water for several minutes, with several students sketching nearly identical shapes afterward. These incidents demonstrate a continuity of testimony across age groups and occupations, reducing the likelihood of fabrication. Many Icelanders hold that the Worm is not a legend confined to the past but an animal that occasionally reveals itself to the observant. Local folklore even speaks of the creature as a guardian of hidden treasure at the bottom of the lake, blending myth with natural observation. This dual role as both folkloric guardian and living serpent reinforces its unique place in Icelandic tradition and sets it apart from other European water monsters.

Today sightings remain sporadic but ongoing. Locals continue to share stories of dark coils sliding through the water, while visitors sometimes claim to see unexplained ridges across the surface. Whether a giant unknown species of eel, a relict serpent-like fish, or an undiscovered aquatic vertebrate, the Lagarfljót Worm holds a firm place in Icelandic natural history. Its presence, sustained through seven centuries of credible testimony, continues to inspire respect and caution from those who live near the frigid waters of one of Iceland's most mysterious lakes.

Though humans do not seem to be on the Lagarfljót Worm's menu, it is said that the beast will defend its territorial waters when necessary. Copyright © Lochlainn Seabrook.

LAKE TAHOE MONSTER

Sightings of the 80 foot long Lake Tahoe Monster date back several hundred years, with new reports continuing into the modern era. Copyright © Lochlainn Seabrook.

QUICK FACTS

NAME: Lake Tahoe Monster.
FIRST SIGHTING: Mid-1800s.
LOCATION: Lake Tahoe, Nevada and California, USA.
SIZE: Reported length between 15 and 80 feet, estimated weight from 1,500 to 5,000 pounds.
APPEARANCE: Long serpentine body, bulky midsection, and tapering tail with humps breaking the surface.
EYES: Described as large, round, and luminous when seen near the surface.
SKIN/FUR: Smooth, dark gray to black skin, sometimes described as scaled.
DIET: Said to feed on large fish such as trout and salmon, waterfowl, aquatic mammals, and possibly carrion. Some accounts suggest it may scavenge drowned animals.
MOVEMENT: Undulating serpentine motions, gliding smoothly with visible humps, sometimes creating strong wakes.
NOTABLE BEHAVIOR: Surfaces suddenly; frightens fishermen; occasionally seen resting near piers; reported to overturn boats.
FIRST REPORTED BY: Early settlers and Washoe Tribe members.
CREATURE CLASSIFICATION: Aquatic cryptid, possibly a relict marine reptile or giant eel-like species.
STATUS: Unverified by mainstream science; yet sightings continue into the present day.

CREATURE PROFILE

Among the clear blue waters of Lake Tahoe lurks a mystery that has lasted for over a century. Locals and visitors alike continue to report sightings of a massive aquatic animal known as the Lake Tahoe Monster. Washoe tribal stories describe a large creature inhabiting the lake long before European settlers arrived, indicating that the belief in its presence is deeply rooted in regional tradition. With a depth of over 1,600 feet, Lake Tahoe provides a perfect environment for an animal of great size to exist undetected, and it is here that eyewitnesses claim the creature appears.

Accounts often describe a massive serpentine form moving just below the surface, long enough to produce several humps visible at once. The animal is said to rise without warning, frightening boaters who sometimes describe it as large enough to capsize small craft. The dark smooth body and undulating motion suggest a streamlined predator adapted to a deep freshwater habitat. Observers sometimes compare it to a giant eel, while others insist it resembles a prehistoric marine reptile. Its eyes, reported as large and reflective, add to the impression of an ancient predator perfectly suited to the dim underwater world of Tahoe's depths.

Dietary habits are difficult to verify, yet many reports agree that the monster feeds on large trout and salmon, abundant in the lake. There are also claims that it takes ducks or geese from the surface and may scavenge drowned animals, which could explain stories of bodies never recovered from the lake. Its movements are usually silent and smooth, though sudden breaches and strong wakes have startled fishermen. In several accounts entire schools of fish scatter as the monster passes, reinforcing its image as a dominant predator within its ecosystem.

Encounters with the Lake Tahoe Monster, affectionately known as "Tessie," continue into the present day. Fishermen, tourists, and lakeside residents provide testimony of something vast moving beneath the waves. A few boaters have reported being shadowed by the creature, while swimmers describe the unsettling sight of a huge dark mass gliding past them in the water. The consistency of these reports, despite being separated by decades, suggests a recurring biological reality rather than coincidence or illusion.

Explanations vary. Some researchers propose that the monster could be a giant sturgeon, an ancient fish known for its size and armored appearance—though no specimen of such magnitude has been confirmed in Tahoe. Others theorize the existence of a relict plesiosaur or mosasaur, species thought to have vanished millions of years ago yet often linked to lake monster traditions. Another hypothesis is that it is an unknown species of oversized eel, capable of navigating both deep waters and surface hunting. None of these possibilities can be proven, yet the persistence of sightings keeps all options open.

Lake Tahoe's unique geology may help explain the mystery. Its immense depth, steep cliffs, and cold dark waters make it one of the least explored large lakes in North America. Such an environment could conceal a breeding population of large creatures for generations. Tribal traditions and modern accounts together build a strong case that the lake holds more secrets than science has yet uncovered.

The Lake Tahoe Monster remains a prime candidate for cryptozoological study. Continued reports affirm its existence in the eyes of locals, and the combination of depth, size, and habitat makes the lake one of the most likely places in the United States for a large undiscovered species to survive. For now the creature remains unverified by mainstream science, yet those who have seen it emerge from the lake's deep cobalt blue depths are convinced that something extraordinary still swims beneath Tahoe's surface.

Swimmers and boaters on Lake Tahoe are usually completely unaware of what may be lurking beneath them: a cryptic monster the length of a bowling alley lane. Copyright © Lochlainn Seabrook.

LAKE WORTH MONSTER

The outlandish yet terrifying 7 foot tall Lake Worth Monster, sighted by dozens of eyewitnesses, combines the traits of Bigfoot, Goatman, human, and even reptile. Copyright © Lochlainn Seabrook.

QUICK FACTS

NAME: Lake Worth Monster.
FIRST SIGHTING: 1969.
LOCATION: Lake Worth, Fort Worth, Texas, USA.
SIZE: Around 7 feet tall, estimated weight 300-400 pounds.
APPEARANCE: Large humanoid figure with goat-like head, horns, and shaggy body.
EYES: Described as large, glaring, and reflective in car headlights.
SKIN/FUR: White to gray fur covering most of the body, sometimes described as scaly in patches.
DIET: Reported to attack fish and livestock, possibly scavenges human food left near the lake. May also consume small wild animals such as rabbits, birds, and amphibians.
MOVEMENT: Walks upright on two legs, capable of running quickly. Sometimes reported leaping from trees or rocks.
NOTABLE BEHAVIOR: Throws large tires and rocks at cars; frightens couples parked near the lake; approaches fishing areas at night.
FIRST REPORTED BY: Local residents of Fort Worth, Texas, in newspaper accounts and police reports.
CREATURE CLASSIFICATION: Cryptid humanoid, possibly a hybrid form or undiscovered primate.
STATUS: Existence denied by mainstream science; nonetheless, sporadic sightings continue.

CREATURE PROFILE

Unlike many older lake legends, the Lake Worth Monster arises in modern times, its first reports dating to the late 1960s. Its presence in a heavily populated urban area sets it apart from other cryptids that dwell in remote forests or secluded mountain ranges. The monster is said to live in and around Lake Worth, a large reservoir west of Fort Worth, Texas. Witnesses continue to claim sightings today, describing a shaggy, horned, half-man, half-goat creature that prowls the shoreline and occasionally emerges to startle or even threaten humans.

Accounts describe it as a bipedal being over 7 feet tall with massive strength. The most famous incident involves the creature hurling a car tire more than 500 feet, landing it on the hood of a parked vehicle with two people inside. This level of power suggests extraordinary musculature. Some have suggested the creature is not merely goatlike but may have reptilian traits, with scales seen around its chest and arms. This odd combination of mammalian and reptilian features fuels theories of hybridization, mutation, or even an undiscovered species adapted to the wetlands and limestone cliffs of the area.

The monster is mostly nocturnal, mainly showing itself in the hours after sunset. Couples in parked cars, fishermen by the lake, and campers in the woods report frightening encounters where the creature runs toward them or emerges suddenly from trees or water. Its glowing eyes are often the first feature spotted in the darkness, giving a sense of being watched. In some reports it has leapt onto cars or chased frightened witnesses into nearby neighborhoods.

While its diet is debated there are stories of mutilated livestock near the lake, with goats and sheep found with strange wounds. Witnesses also claim to have seen it clutching fish along the shoreline, suggesting a semi-aquatic feeding habit. Scavenging behavior is possible, as garbage bins in the parklands have been overturned; though whether this is the work of the monster or mundane wildlife is unknown.

Behavioral reports consistently emphasize aggression and territorial defense. The Lake Worth Monster appears to use intimidation to frighten humans away from its habitat. The ability to throw heavy objects with precision is rare among animals and points to high intelligence or at least unusual problem-solving skills. Loud growls and humanlike screams have also been recorded, adding to its terrifying reputation.

Some researchers speculate that the rocky bluffs and caves surrounding Lake Worth could provide shelter—which would explain how the monster avoids detection despite the area's popularity. Others suggest the creature may use the lake itself as a refuge, slipping into deep water when pursued or threatened.

Eyewitness descriptions vary, which is common with cryptid sightings; but the majority point to a consistent image: tall, humanoid, muscular, white-furred, horned, and menacing. The horns in particular distinguish it from other ape-like cryptids such as Bigfoot. Horns suggest either a misidentified goat-like animal or a truly unique being with features never before catalogued in zoology.

For many residents of Fort Worth the monster is more than a legend. During the height of sightings in 1969 crowds gathered at Lake Worth hoping to see it, and police took multiple reports. Even today it is a subject of local lore and occasional modern sightings. If real the Lake Worth Monster would represent one of the few known cryptids dwelling near a major American city.

The persistence of accounts into the present indicates that whatever the creature is, it continues to maintain a foothold in the woodlands and waters of north Texas.

The Lake Worth Monster is particularly known for its aggressive behaviors, including jumping on, chasing, and trying to break into cars. Copyright © Lochlainn Seabrook.

LINDORM

According to reports, the 60 foot long Lindorm has been terrorizing Scandinavia for at least 400 years, right into the present day. Copyright © Lochlainn Seabrook.

QUICK FACTS

NAME: Lindorm.
FIRST SIGHTING: 16th Century.
LOCATION: Scandinavia.
SIZE: Length reported between 20 and 60 feet, weight estimated from 1,000 to 4,000 pounds.
APPEARANCE: Serpentine body, often described with two clawed forelimbs, long tail, and dragonlike head.
EYES: Large, bright, and glowing, often described as yellow or green.
SKIN/FUR: Covered in hard scales ranging from black to dark green with lighter undersides.
DIET: Said to prey on livestock, deer, fish, and occasionally humans; also reported to feed on carrion and other large animals available in its range.
MOVEMENT: Slithers like a giant snake but can rear up on its limbs and coil when threatened; reported to swim powerfully in rivers and lakes.
NOTABLE BEHAVIOR: Guards treasures, blocks travelers on roads, attacks livestock, and is said to appear suddenly from underground dens or water sources.
FIRST REPORTED BY: Scandinavian chroniclers and local villagers in medieval sagas and folklore accounts.
CREATURE CLASSIFICATION: Giant serpentlike dragon.
STATUS: Considered mythical by mainstream science, but sightings continue right into the present day.

CREATURE PROFILE

In the deep forests and waterways of Scandinavia there are lingering accounts of a colossal serpentlike beast known as the Lindorm. The name itself translates as "serpent dragon," appropriate for a creature that is deeply rooted in the Nordic landscape of myth and eyewitness tradition. Unlike smaller folkloric animals that fade into tall tales, the Lindorm is continually described in ways that give it the weight of a living predator still haunting rural lands and waterways. Its presence is not restricted to ancient tales but extends into more modern reports from the 19th and 20th Centuries, where farmers, hunters, and travelers continue to speak of encounters with a reptilian colossus.

Descriptions of the Lindorm vary slightly across regions but remain consistent in their overall form. It is a serpentine animal of immense proportions, usually said to stretch from 20 to as much as 60 feet in length. Its body is muscular and armored with scales, sometimes dark like wet stone and sometimes shining green when caught in daylight. Unlike ordinary snakes witnesses often describe it as possessing two short but strong forelimbs with clawed digits, giving it the ability to rear up from the ground and display a more dragonlike stance. The head is commonly likened to that of a great reptile, with a broad jaw and large eyes that shine at night. When coiled it can block entire pathways and its movements are said to be accompanied by a low hissing or rumbling sound.

The Lindorm is not confined to land alone. Some sightings place it in rivers and lakes, where it is reported to swim with surprising speed and strength. Fishermen tell of nets ripped apart and boats rocked by unseen forces beneath the water, later followed by glimpses of a serpentine back or a sinuous tail breaking the surface. In these aquatic settings the creature shows its versatility, moving between terrestrial lairs and watery hunting grounds with ease. Its behavior has been described as territorial, emerging to defend stretches of road, old burial grounds, or remote passes in the mountains.

Dietary reports give the Lindorm the profile of a large apex predator. Farmers recount livestock disappearing after nighttime disturbances, and hunters tell of deer vanishing in areas where tracks lead to disturbed soil or waterlogged banks. Some tales speak of human victims, particularly lone travelers who vanish without trace in regions long associated with the beast. Less dramatic reports suggest scavenging habits, with the creature feeding on carrion as well as fresh kills. This varied diet aligns with what would be expected of a giant predator needing to maintain its bulk in isolated wilderness areas.

The cultural role of the Lindorm is also significant. In sagas it is sometimes described as a guardian of treasure, buried hoards, or sacred places, lending a supernatural aspect to its identity. Yet even here the descriptions remain grounded in physical traits: coiled bodies, armored hides, and ferocious behavior. Such consistency across the years strengthens the case that eyewitnesses are not merely passing down symbolic images but may be describing encounters with a real zoological species—perhaps a relic from an older era.

Modern science places the Lindorm in the category of myth, alongside dragons and other legendary serpents. However, the persistence of reports, the detailed anatomical features, and the spread of sightings across both medieval and modern times suggest the possibility of an undiscovered species.

Whether the Lindorm represents a surviving lineage of giant snake, a semi-aquatic reptile, or a unique animal altogether, it continues to occupy an important place in the living folklore of Scandinavia.

The Lindorm is known for dominance displays, such as blocking forest trails and menacing boats. Copyright © Lochlainn Seabrook.

LIZARD MAN OF SCAPE ORE SWAMP

The horrifying 7 foot tall Lizard Man, said to stalk South Carolina's Scape Ore Swamp. Copyright © Lochlainn Seabrook.

QUICK FACTS

NAME: Lizard Man of Scape Ore Swamp.
FIRST SIGHTING: June 29, 1988.
LOCATION: Bishopville, South Carolina, USA.
SIZE: Height around 7 feet, weight estimated between 200 and 250 pounds.
APPEARANCE: Upright reptilian humanoid with long limbs, three clawed fingers, and a powerful build.
EYES: Large, round, glowing red eyes.
SKIN/FUR: Green, leathery, lizard-like scales covering the entire body.
DIET: Believed to feed on fish, frogs, turtles, waterfowl, small mammals, livestock, and possibly carrion; also known to attack vehicles and structures suggesting a highly opportunistic diet.
MOVEMENT: Walks upright with a shambling but powerful gait; can run quickly on two legs and leap great distances.
NOTABLE BEHAVIOR: Known to attack cars, claw metal, rip through trim and bumpers, and leave unusual three-toed tracks in mud and sand.
FIRST REPORTED BY: Christopher Davis, a local teenager.
CREATURE CLASSIFICATION: Cryptid reptilian humanoid, possibly a surviving relic reptile species or unique swamp-dwelling hominid.
STATUS: Ignored by mainstream science; yet still seen and reported.

CREATURE PROFILE

In the sultry wetlands of South Carolina dwells a truly strange creature: the Lizard Man of Scape Ore Swamp. It is one of the most distinctive cryptids reported in the United States, and remains a cultural landmark of Bishopville. Sightings center around the cypress-draped waterways of Lee County where marshland, forest, and farmland meet in a tangled and mysterious landscape that hides countless forms of life.

The modern history of the Lizard Man begins in June 1988 when seventeen-year-old Christopher Davis reported a terrifying encounter. After changing a flat tire on a country road near Scape Ore Swamp, Davis claimed a seven-foot reptilian humanoid rushed from the trees. It allegedly clawed at his car and attempted to seize the vehicle. Davis managed to drive away; but deep scratches and bite marks were later found on the car's body. This incident sparked an outpouring of media attention and multiple witness accounts, creating a modern legend that continues to grow.

Descriptions from eyewitnesses remain consistent. The creature is said to be tall, muscular, and fully scaled, with greenish skin that glistens like wet leather. Its three clawed fingers are capable of shredding metal and leaving distinctive impressions in mud. Many reports emphasize the glowing red eyes which suggest either reflective tissue similar to a tapetum lucidum or an unknown biological adaptation for night vision. Its appearance and behavior mark it as something different from folkloric swamp monsters. Witnesses describe a living being with physical presence and force.

Tracks attributed to the Lizard Man are some of the most striking evidence. Large three-toed prints have been found in sand and mud, sometimes accompanied by damage to vehicles and farm equipment. These tracks do not resemble those of any known reptile native to South Carolina. The length, width, and depth of the impressions suggest a powerful bipedal animal weighing at least 200 pounds. Unlike alligators, which leave belly and tail drags, the Lizard Man's prints are clean, upright, and distinctly humanoid in posture.

Its diet is a matter of speculation, though reports of attacks on livestock and observations near waterways suggest an opportunistic predator. The swamp ecosystem provides fish, amphibians, waterfowl, turtles, snakes, and small mammals, all of which could sustain a large carnivorous or omnivorous reptile. The damage done to vehicles may be explained by territorial defense or attempts to reach stored food—though no single theory has been confirmed.

The Lizard Man continues to be seen into the present day. Modern reports place it in the same region, emerging from dense vegetation near the swamp. Some sightings describe it chasing cars at night or moving rapidly across the road before vanishing into the darkness. Others mention its lingering presence around bridges, culverts, and isolated backroads where it remains hidden until startled.

The swamp itself provides the perfect refuge for such a being. Thick walls of cypress, tupelo, and pine shelter dark pools of water where visibility is low and human access is difficult. Muddy channels, fallen logs, and tangled vegetation create countless hiding places, while an abundance of prey ensures a steady food supply. At night the chorus of frogs, insects, and birds could easily mask the movements of a large predator. In such an environment, a reptilian humanoid could remain concealed for years while still ranging far enough to encounter humans on the outskirts of its territory.

Although dismissed by mainstream science as folklore or hoax, the persistence of sightings across decades cannot be ignored. For the people of Bishopville the Lizard Man has become more than just a monster. It is a local guardian of mystery, a symbol of the swamp's untamed heart, and a lasting reminder that not every creature of this Earth has been named.

With terrifying speed and agility, the Lizard Man easily chases down cars on the backroads of Lee County, South Carolina. Copyright © Lochlainn Seabrook.

LOCH LOCHY MONSTER

Gliding silently and powerfully through the cold, murky depths of Loch Lochy, its resident 40 foot long monster provides a chilling reminder of the incredible mysteries that still lay hidden beneath Scotland's waters. Copyright © Lochlainn Seabrook.

QUICK FACTS

NAME: Loch Lochy Monster.
FIRST SIGHTING: 1929.
LOCATION: Loch Lochy, Scottish Highlands.
SIZE: Reported between 20 and 40 feet in length, estimated weight 1 to 3 tons.
APPEARANCE: Long-bodied aquatic creature with a serpentine form, described with humps rising above the surface.
EYES: Said to be dark and set close to the top of the head.
SKIN/FUR: Smooth dark gray to black skin, sometimes reported as shiny when wet.
DIET: Believed to prey on salmon, trout, and other fish species common to the loch. Some accounts suggest waterfowl and possibly small mammals near the shoreline.
MOVEMENT: Undulating motion with rolling humps, able to submerge quickly and move at surprising speeds.
NOTABLE BEHAVIOR: Frequently surfaces in calm water, often producing wakes or splashes without visible boats. Known to vanish abruptly when approached.
FIRST REPORTED BY: Multiple eyewitnesses, including local fishermen, in 1929.
CREATURE CLASSIFICATION: Freshwater cryptid, possibly related to other Highland lake monsters.
STATUS: Existence unconfirmed by mainstream science; yet modern sightings continue unabated.

CREATURE PROFILE

Among the hidden waters of the Scottish Highlands Loch Lochy holds a reputation for harboring a mysterious inhabitant. Locals speak of a large animal that moves beneath the surface, a creature that has been reported for nearly a century. The Loch Lochy Monster is not nearly as famous as its southern neighbor Nessie of Loch Ness; yet those who live near its waters regard it as just as real and significant.

The earliest modern reports begin in 1929 when three witnesses saw an enormous beast breaking the loch's surface. Its body rolled in long curves that resembled a serpent, and its bulk suggested a creature of massive weight. Since that time fishermen, visitors, and residents alike continue to describe a dark aquatic form that appears unexpectedly, sometimes for only seconds before sinking again. These accounts often include humps or ridges rising and falling in the water—details consistent across decades of testimony.

The size estimates are impressive, ranging from 20 feet to as much as 40 feet in length. Witnesses often describe a thick body that seems too large for any known fish in Scotland. This description places the Loch Lochy Monster among the large-bodied freshwater cryptids of the Highlands, alongside the creatures reported in Loch Ness, Loch Morar, and other deep lakes of the region. Its possible relationship to these others is often suggested, though each loch's monster maintains a distinct history and personality in local tradition.

Observers usually report smooth skin, dark gray to nearly black, with a sheen that reflects the light when the creature surfaces. Its eyes are small and dark, positioned high on the head in a way that allows it to keep watch while mostly submerged. This adaptation would make sense for an aquatic predator needing to stay hidden while scanning above water.

Dietary speculation focuses on the abundant fish of Loch Lochy. Salmon and trout thrive in these waters, providing an ample food supply for a large carnivorous animal. Several accounts describe schools of fish scattering moments before the creature rises, suggesting predatory activity. Some stories add that it may prey on waterfowl or small mammals that approach the shoreline, though fish remain the most likely staple of its diet.

Movement is most often described as rolling or undulating, with a series of humps breaking the surface in rhythmic motion. The Monster is said to move with surprising speed when disturbed, diving steeply and leaving a large wake behind. The ability to vanish suddenly contributes to its elusive reputation and fuels speculation that it possesses extraordinary swimming power for a freshwater creature.

Behaviorally, it is known for surfacing in still conditions. Calm waters are suddenly broken by splashes or waves that cannot be traced to boats or wind. Eyewitnesses describe feelings of awe and fear as the animal glides into view then slips beneath the surface as if deliberately avoiding close contact. These behaviors echo those of other Highland lake monsters yet remain distinct enough to identify it as a unique phenomenon.

Today reports continue, keeping the legend alive. Locals remain cautious and respectful of the loch's gigantic hidden resident. While mainstream science has yet to verify its existence, the consistency of accounts across nearly 100 years suggests that Loch Lochy may indeed harbor a living mystery.

To those who have seen it, the creature is more than folklore. It is a real and vital presence in the loch, an animal adapted to secrecy, and perhaps a survivor from an earlier age.

The Loch Lochy Monster may appear without warning near unwary boaters. Copyright © Lochlainn Seabrook.

LOCH MORAR MONSTER

The haunting golden mists of Loch Morar hide a reclusive 30 foot long monster that may be related to the prehistoric plesiosaur. Copyright © Lochlainn Seabrook.

QUICK FACTS

NAME: Loch Morar Monster.
FIRST SIGHTING: 1887.
LOCATION: Loch Morar, Highlands, Scotland.
SIZE: Reported between 20 and 30 feet in length, with estimates of 2,000 to 3,000 pounds.
APPEARANCE: Long, serpentine body with multiple humps visible above the water, often described with a horse-like or crocodilian head.
EYES: Large, dark, and sometimes said to shine in low light.
SKIN/FUR: Smooth, dark gray to black skin, occasionally reported as glistening.
DIET: Believed to feed on fish such as trout, salmon, and eels; possibly waterfowl, otters, and larger prey when available. Some accounts suggest scavenging behavior on carrion.
MOVEMENT: Undulating, serpentine motions with the ability to dive deeply and remain submerged for long periods. Sometimes seen gliding smoothly at the surface.
NOTABLE BEHAVIOR: Known to surface in calm weather; occasionally follows boats; startles swimmers. Its appearances often occur in still waters with little wind.
FIRST REPORTED BY: Alexander MacDonald, a crofter, who saw the creature in 1887.
CREATURE CLASSIFICATION: Unidentified aquatic cryptid, possibly a surviving prehistoric reptile or giant eel.
STATUS: Existence unacknowledged by mainstream science, though sightings continue.

CREATURE PROFILE

The waters of Loch Morar hold one of Scotland's most lasting cryptid mysteries. Known as the Loch Morar Monster, or "Morag," this creature has been reported for well over a century. Unlike Loch Ness, however, Morar is far less commercialized and receives fewer visitors, which makes its sightings both rarer and more compelling. The loch itself is remote, wild, and among the deepest bodies of freshwater in Europe, plunging to depths of more than 1,000 feet. These features provide an ideal refuge for an elusive animal.

Witnesses describe Morag as a long serpentine creature with multiple humps breaking the surface as it moves. Its head has been said to resemble both that of a horse and a crocodile, with some reports noting a gaping mouth. Its body length is generally given as between 20 and 30 feet, though some observers suggest even larger. Its mass is estimated at several thousand pounds, and its ability to move quickly despite its size suggests streamlined adaptations for deep-water living.

One of the earliest detailed encounters occurred in 1887 when Alexander MacDonald, a crofter, claimed to have seen the monster rise out of the loch. Since then sightings have been recorded sporadically through the 20th Century and into modern times. Unlike the Loch Ness Monster, which is seen more frequently, the Loch Morar Monster is rarely encountered, adding to its aura of mystery. Witnesses who have seen it agree that it is not a simple misidentification of a seal, otter, or wave formation. To the contrary, its behavior and shape set it apart from known animals.

Diet is an important consideration in understanding how such a creature could survive in a freshwater loch. Loch Morar has a healthy stock of salmon, trout, char, and eels, which could sustain a large predator. Some reports suggest that Morag may also take waterfowl or otters and even scavenge carrion along the shoreline. Its deep-diving ability allows it to exploit food resources unavailable to surface animals, making survival in such an isolated loch more plausible.

Notable behavior includes smooth gliding at the surface, sudden dives, and long periods of submersion. Witnesses report that it sometimes appears during calm weather, rising without ripples to show several humps at once. On rare occasions boats have been followed. In at least one case, in 1969, two men claimed to have accidentally struck the creature with their boat, after which it became aggressive before diving away.

Cultural context is also important. Local tradition holds that Morag is not only a physical creature but sometimes an omen. Folklore suggests that its appearance foretells death among the people living near the loch. This intertwining of myth and natural history is common with cryptids, but in Morag's case it reinforces the seriousness with which locals regard the creature.

From a scientific perspective, several possibilities have been proposed. These include a relic population of prehistoric reptiles such as *plesiosaurs*, an unknown species of giant eel, or a type of sturgeon or other large fish that has remained undiscovered. None of these theories have been confirmed, but the long term consistency of eyewitness testimony makes the case impossible to dismiss. The Loch Morar Monster continues to be seen into the present day, always elusive yet always convincing to those who encounter it. Its remote habitat, immense loch depth, and reliable fish population make its existence plausible. Whether it represents a prehistoric survivor, an oversized known animal, or a completely new species, Morag stands as one of the most compelling aquatic cryptids in Europe.

Scotland's enigmatic Loch Morag Monster surfaces next to a small boat. Whether motivated by curiosity or territoriality is unknown. Copyright © Lochlainn Seabrook.

LOCH NESS MONSTER

Arguably the world's most famous lake cryptid, the 40 foot long Loch Ness Monster continues to evade both capture and positive identification. Copyright © Lochlainn Seabrook.

QUICK FACTS

NAME: Loch Ness Monster.
FIRST SIGHTING: 6th Century.
LOCATION: Loch Ness, Scotland.
SIZE: Between 20 and 40 feet long, weighing up to 2,500 pounds.
APPEARANCE: Long neck, bulky body, flippers, sometimes reported with a humped back.
EYES: Large, dark, and reflective, occasionally described as glowing in low light.
SKIN/FUR: Smooth dark gray or black skin, sometimes said to appear slimy.
DIET: Large fish including salmon and trout, waterfowl, aquatic mammals, and possibly carrion or other lake-dwelling animals. May also feed opportunistically on schooling fish, surface birds, and decaying organic matter when food is scarce.
MOVEMENT: Powerful undulating swimming motion, sometimes breaking the surface with long rolling movements or multiple humps.
NOTABLE BEHAVIOR: Frequently surfaces in calm weather, leaves wakes without visible craft, occasionally reported to lunge or dive suddenly.
FIRST REPORTED BY: Saint Columba, 565 A.D.
CREATURE CLASSIFICATION: Aquatic cryptid, often compared with prehistoric plesiosaurs (*Plesiosauria*).
STATUS: Existence unconfirmed by mainstream science, but still regularly seen and reported.

CREATURE PROFILE

Among the many cryptids of the world few hold as much fame as the Loch Ness Monster. This creature is reported from Loch Ness in the Scottish Highlands, a body of water over twenty miles long, more than 700 feet deep, and noted for its dark, peat-stained waters. It is an environment large enough and secluded enough to conceal a sizeable unknown animal. The monster is still seen in modern times, with eyewitness reports continuing into the present era.

Descriptions consistently center on a large aquatic animal with a long neck, a bulky body, and powerful flippers. Some accounts note a series of humps that rise above the surface before sliding beneath again. The head is sometimes compared to that of a horse or serpent, while others describe a more rounded shape. The skin is said to be dark gray or black and often has a wet, slick look.

Such features strongly resemble ancient marine reptiles such as plesiosaurs—though the possibility exists that the Loch Ness Monster represents a unique species adapted to the loch.

The eyes are an important detail in many reports. Witnesses describe them as large and dark, with a reflective or glowing quality under low light conditions. This suggests the presence of a tapetum lucidum, the reflective eye structure found in nocturnal and deep-water animals. If true the Loch Ness Monster may be well adapted to the murky depths of the loch, which admits little sunlight even during the day.

Dietary habits are inferred from both witness accounts and ecological logic. Loch Ness supports a steady population of salmon and trout, along with eels, smaller fish, waterfowl, and mammals along the shore. A creature of Nessie's reported size would require large amounts of protein. Observers suggest it feeds on fish schools, water birds, and carrion, moving between deep water and surface zones depending on prey availability. The possibility of feeding on migratory salmon runs explains seasonal spikes in reported activity.

Behavioral reports often note smooth undulating motion when the animal breaks the surface. Long wakes are observed across calm water, with no boats in sight. These wakes suggest a large body in motion beneath the surface. At times the monster is described as lunging upward before diving, which has led to theories of feeding strikes. Calm weather sightings are common, likely because smooth water makes disturbances more visible.

The first documented encounter dates to 565 A.D., when Saint Columba was said to have encountered a water beast in the River Ness, just downstream of the loch. Since then thousands of reports have followed.

Modern sightings surged in the 20th Century, particularly after the construction of roads along the loch that provided unobstructed views of the water. Despite skepticism the volume and persistence of these reports over many centuries indicate a real phenomenon, one of extreme biological interest.

Scientific expeditions have deployed sonar and underwater cameras in an effort to locate the creature. Some sonar scans have shown large moving targets, though definitive evidence remains elusive. Photographs and videos exist, but none have satisfied critics. Regardless, the Loch Ness Monster remains one of the most fascinating, elusive, and perennial cryptids on record.

What sets Nessie apart from other lake monsters is not only the frequency of sightings but also the sheer fame of the loch itself. The Scottish Highlands have embraced the legend; yet behind the folklore there remains the strong likelihood of a living animal. Whether a relict species of marine reptile, a massive unknown fish, or a specialized aquatic mammal, the Loch Ness Monster continues to invite study and attention.

Though Nessie has been seen by hundreds of individuals over the past 1,500 years, spotting her remains an extraordinary privilege granted only to a fortunate few. Copyright © Lochlainn Seabrook.

LOVELAND FROGMAN

The bizarre, 4 foot tall, humanoid-like Loveland Frogman lurks on the banks of the Little Miami River—an unsettling reminder of the mysteries that continue to haunt Ohio's waterways. Copyright © Lochlainn Seabrook.

QUICK FACTS

NAME: Loveland Frogman.
FIRST SIGHTING: 1955.
LOCATION: Loveland, Ohio, USA.
SIZE: Height 3 to 4 feet, weight estimated 60 to 90 pounds.
APPEARANCE: Humanoid frog-like being with webbed hands and feet, leathery body, and broad head.
EYES: Large, circular, and reflective with a yellowish glow at night.
SKIN/FUR: Smooth amphibian-like skin, mottled gray, green, or brown in color.
DIET: Believed to consume fish, amphibians, crustaceans, insects, and possibly small mammals and carrion. May also opportunistically scavenge human food near water sources.
MOVEMENT: Walks upright on two legs, can leap long distances, swims with strong strokes, and moves stealthily on land.
NOTABLE BEHAVIOR: Sometimes observed holding a rod or wand-like object. Reported to hiss at humans when threatened. Frequently seen near bridges and riverbanks at night.
FIRST REPORTED BY: A traveling salesman.
CREATURE CLASSIFICATION: Amphibious humanoid cryptid.
STATUS: Unverified by mainstream science; yet sporadic sightings continue.

CREATURE PROFILE

Southwestern Ohio is home to one of America's most unusual cryptids, a small amphibious being that has become known as the Loveland Frogman. Unlike larger lake or swamp creatures, this cryptid is described as distinctly humanoid with both frog-like and man-like qualities. Its reported behavior, appearance, and repeated sightings suggest that something more than simple folklore may be present along the Little Miami River and its tributaries. Witnesses continue to describe a creature with features that place it outside the known animal kingdom, yet consistent enough across reports to point toward a single type of being.

The first known encounter occurred in 1955 when a traveling salesman claimed to see several of the creatures clustered together on a bridge outside Loveland. According to his account they stood upright and seemed to be engaged in some form of interaction, with one holding a rod that emitted sparks. The strangeness of this detail has become one of the lasting mysteries of the Frogman legend. Later sightings, though fewer in number, have reinforced the description of a small but distinctly humanoid amphibian.

The most famous modern reports came from two separate police officers in March of 1972. Both claimed to encounter a bipedal frog-like creature on different nights near the Little Miami River. One officer described the animal crouched on the roadside before it leapt over a guardrail and vanished into the water. The second officer reported a nearly identical being a few weeks later. Such consistency in description from trained observers gave the Frogman case unusual weight in cryptozoological circles and continues to fuel interest today.

The physical characteristics most often given include a height of three to four feet, long muscular legs, webbed extremities, and a wide mouth across a flat face. The skin is described as smooth and moist like that of a frog or salamander. Colors range from dull green to grayish brown, likely providing camouflage along the muddy riverbanks. Large eyes with a reflective quality are said to glow when caught in light, suggesting a nocturnal lifestyle.

Habitat reports consistently place the Frogman near rivers, creeks, and drainage systems in and around Loveland. The Little Miami River, with its wooded banks and slow-moving waters, offers abundant food and cover. It is possible that the creature uses culverts and tunnels for shelter during the day and emerges at night to hunt. Its diet is believed to be opportunistic, including fish, frogs, crayfish, and insects. Some accounts speculate it may take small mammals or even carrion, much like other amphibious predators.

Movement is another distinctive feature. Witnesses often stress its ability to walk upright for extended periods, though it can also drop to all fours or swim powerfully when threatened. Reports of it leaping over barriers in a single bound suggest strong hind limbs similar to a frog's. This versatility of motion may explain how it has managed to evade capture despite multiple encounters across decades.

Behaviorally, the Frogman is usually shy and avoids humans. However, when cornered or surprised, it has been described as hissing or raising its body in a defensive posture. The most puzzling element is the early report of it carrying a rod or wand, which has never been adequately explained. Whether this was a natural object, a tool, or an exaggeration remains unknown, yet it adds an element of mystery unlike most other cryptid accounts.

Today, the Loveland Frogman continues to be sighted sporadically, usually at night and often near water. While mainstream science dismisses it as a misidentified animal, possibly a large frog, iguana, or escaped pet, the number of credible reports over seventy years makes outright dismissal impossible. For cryptozoologists the Frogman represents the possibility that a small amphibious humanoid species has managed to survive in the waterways of Ohio largely undetected.

The disconcerting form of the Loveland Frogman is still seen by frightened eyewitnesses along the banks of Ohio's Little Miami River. Copyright © Lochlainn Seabrook.

LUSCA

The gargantuan Lusca, reported to be as long as 200 feet, reigns over the depths of Bahamian blue holes. Copyright © Lochlainn Seabrook.

QUICK FACTS

NAME: Lusca.
FIRST SIGHTING: 1700s.
LOCATION: Blue Holes, caves, and coastal waters of the Bahamas and Caribbean.
SIZE: Length reported between 50 and 200 feet, weight estimated between 10 and 40 tons.
APPEARANCE: Massive sea creature with features of both an octopus and a shark, with long tentacles, a powerful body, and large jaws.
EYES: Large, lidless, reflective, adapted for low-light aquatic environments.
SKIN/FUR: Smooth, rubbery, and slimy, ranging from reddish-brown to dark gray or blue.
DIET: Large fish, sharks, sea turtles, rays, dolphins, squid, and occasionally humans; said to drag entire boats below the surface.
MOVEMENT: Propelled by jetting water and powerful strokes of long tentacles, capable of rapid bursts of speed and sudden vertical lunges.
NOTABLE BEHAVIOR: Associated with whirlpools and sudden violent waterspouts in blue holes; attacks boats and swimmers without warning; lurks in underwater caves.
FIRST REPORTED BY: Indigenous Caribbean islanders and later European sailors.
CREATURE CLASSIFICATION: Giant cephalopod-like cryptid, possibly related to *Architeuthis dux* or an unknown colossal octopus.
STATUS: Unverified by mainstream science; but still seen and reported.

CREATURE PROFILE

In the waters of the Bahamas and throughout the Caribbean, fishermen and divers speak of a predator that dominates the blue holes and reef passages: the Lusca. This panic-induing cryptid is described as one of the ocean's most fearsome mysteries, a creature that blends the traits of giant octopus, shark, and squid into a single terrifying form. Many accounts describe not just a large animal but one that commands its environment, capable of creating whirlpools and violent currents to disorient its prey.

Reports place the Lusca at sizes far beyond known cephalopods. Estimates suggest lengths of 100 feet or more with some witnesses claiming as much as 200 feet. The weight of such a monster would be measured in tens of tons. Tentacles are said to be strong enough to crush the hull of a small fishing boat. Its central body is often described as wider than a man is tall, with a gaping jaw armed with shark-like teeth, a feature not typical of ordinary octopuses. This combination of characteristics is what makes the Lusca so distinct from any known marine species.

Sightings most often occur in and around the Bahamas' blue holes. These underwater caves and sinkholes provide deep vertical passages that connect to the ocean, forming ideal hiding places for a predator that ambushes prey from below. Local divers speak of sudden shifts in current, strong downward pulls, and the unexplained disappearance of animals and even people. Some of these losses are attributed directly to the Lusca, which is said to seize victims with its tentacles and drag them into the depths where escape is impossible.

The behavior of this cryptid suggests a highly opportunistic hunter. Witnesses claim it attacks sharks, devours schools of fish, and even confronts boats. There are accounts of vessels being pulled under so quickly that no survivors remain to tell the story. In calmer moments fishermen describe seeing immense shadows pass beneath their boats, followed by a sudden stillness in the water that signals the presence of the Lusca. It is said to wait silently in its lair until the right moment to strike.

Appearance reports emphasize the contrast between its long, octopus-like arms and the muscular bulk of its shark-like torso. Some say its coloration shifts in the water, from deep blue to rusty red, perhaps a form of camouflage. Its eyes are often described as unnervingly large, fixed, and glowing in dim conditions, an adaptation for hunting in the dark passages of the blue holes. The skin is slick and rubbery, typical of cephalopods, but in some descriptions it has a mottled, scale-like texture along its back.

Caribbean folklore connects the Lusca with natural oceanic phenomena. Sudden whirlpools, violent spouts, and unexplainable rips in calm water are often attributed to the beast's movements. In this way it functions not only as a predator but as a force of nature in local tradition, embodying the danger of venturing too close to the hidden entrances of the blue holes. Divers today still report sudden disappearances of fellow explorers in these regions, fueling belief that the Lusca remains active.

Though mainstream science has not confirmed the Lusca, its continued presence in reports from locals, fishermen, and divers keeps it at the forefront of Caribbean cryptid lore. Whether it represents an undiscovered species of colossal octopus, a misidentified giant squid, or something unique to the waters of the Bahamas, the Lusca remains a real possibility in the eyes of those who live by the sea.

Eyewitnesses report entire boats and their crews being dragged underwater by the Lusca, the Bahama's most infamous giant underwater cryptid. Copyright © Lochlainn Seabrook.

MANTIS MAN

One of cryptozoology's most disturbing creatures: New Jersey's 7 foot tall insect-humanoid hybrid, the Mantis Man. Copyright © Lochlainn Seabrook.

QUICK FACTS

NAME: Mantis Man.
FIRST SIGHTING: Early 2000s.
LOCATION: Musconetcong River, Hackettstown, New Jersey, USA.
SIZE: Reported height 6 to 7 feet, estimated weight 120 to 200 pounds.
APPEARANCE: Resembles a giant praying mantis with a long body, triangular head, and thin arms.
EYES: Large, bulbous, and insect-like, often glowing in dim light.
SKIN/FUR: Smooth exoskeleton-like covering, green or brown in color.
DIET: Thought to be carnivorous, possibly preying on fish, amphibians, insects, and small mammals; some accounts suggest it may consume carrion or plants opportunistically.
MOVEMENT: Upright bipedal stride, with rapid bursts of insect-like agility; occasionally hovers or vanishes abruptly.
NOTABLE BEHAVIOR: Seen silently watching fishermen and passersby, then retreating quickly; appears to avoid human contact.
FIRST REPORTED BY: Local fisherman in Hackettstown, New Jersey.
CREATURE CLASSIFICATION: Humanoid insect cryptid, possibly related to arthropods of Order *Mantodea*.
STATUS: Existence denied by mainstream science, but sightings stubbornly continue.

CREATURE PROFILE

Mantis Man sightings in northern New Jersey stand out as some of the most unsettling cryptid encounters reported in modern times. Along the Musconetcong River, near Hackettstown, fishermen and locals describe encounters with a towering figure resembling a humanoid praying mantis. Unlike many lake or forest cryptids tied to centuries-old folklore, the reports of Mantis Man appear relatively recent, with most accounts originating in the early years of the 21st Century. Despite the modern timeframe, the descriptions remain consistent, suggesting the presence of a real creature rather than unrelated misidentifications.

The being is described as standing between 6 and 7 feet tall, with a thin elongated body and a triangular head characteristic of true mantises. Its arms are long and spindly, often bent as if in the posture of a mantis at rest. Witnesses consistently describe its insect-like eyes, large and bulbous, sometimes reflecting or glowing in dim light. Its coloration ranges from a muted green to earthy brown, giving it camouflage along the forested banks and reeds of the Musconetcong. Its body covering is smooth and appears more like an exoskeleton than skin, adding to the impression of an insect enlarged to impossible size.

Mantis Man's behavior is notable for its avoidance of confrontation. Witnesses report that the creature is often spotted standing silently near the river, apparently watching fishermen, hikers, or casual passersby. When noticed, however, it tends to retreat rapidly, either through a swift, insect-like dash into the brush or by vanishing so quickly that witnesses struggle to describe its departure. This has led to speculation that Mantis Man possesses unusual speed, or even abilities beyond normal biology, such as cloaking or leaping with great force. While such claims are extraordinary, the repeated accounts of sudden disappearance suggest at least an uncanny agility.

The diet of Mantis Man is unknown, but based on its resemblance to mantises, some suggest it may be carnivorous. It could prey on river fish, amphibians, or small mammals, ambushing them with speed before devouring them. Others propose it might feed opportunistically, scavenging carrion or consuming plant matter as camouflage requires. Reports of it lingering near the water's edge may indicate a reliance on aquatic food sources, or at least a preference for hunting grounds rich in prey.

Though Mantis Man reports are few, their consistency has made the creature a fixture of New Jersey cryptid lore. Its classification is difficult, as it appears to be neither wholly human-like nor fully insectoid, but rather a combination of both. Some researchers speculate it could be a remnant of an unknown species related to *Mantodea* but adapted to a larger, more humanoid form. Others consider it a possible interdimensional entity or extraterrestrial, citing the creature's strange movements and sudden disappearances as evidence. Despite these theories mainstream science continues to dismiss the reports, attributing them to misidentification or exaggeration.

Nonetheless, though they remain rare, sightings continue sporadically into the present day. The Musconetcong River and surrounding forests remain quiet and sparsely populated, giving such a creature ample cover. Locals familiar with the legend often treat the riverbanks with caution, avoiding being alone in certain stretches where sightings have occurred.

For those who claim to have seen it, the experience is both terrifying and awe-inspiring, for the idea of a mantis the size of a man is so foreign that it challenges the very boundaries of not only natural history, but reality itself.

Eyewitnesses describe the Mantis Man as a human-sized, insectoid-like being that induces high-level fear and even paralysis. Copyright © Lochlainn Seabrook.

MAPINGUARI

The frightening, 10 foot tall, cyclopean-eyed Mapinguari, as described in Amazonian cryptid accounts. Copyright © Lochlainn Seabrook.

QUICK FACTS

NAME: Mapinguari.
FIRST SIGHTING: 18th Century.
LOCATION: Amazon rainforest, Brazil and Bolivia.
SIZE: Height reported between 7 and 10 feet, weight estimated between 500 and 1,000 pounds.
APPEARANCE: Large sloth-like body, potbelly, long shaggy hair, single large mouth in stomach, occasional reports of backward-facing feet.
EYES: Small and dark, usually described as deep-set and animal-like.
SKIN/FUR: Coarse reddish or brown fur covering most of the body, thick and matted.
DIET: Omnivorous, feeding on leaves, roots, fruits, and possibly small animals, with occasional reports of raiding human crops.
MOVEMENT: Walks slowly and heavily on two legs, though sometimes reported on four, leaves large tracks.
NOTABLE BEHAVIOR: Emits a foul odor, produces loud roaring calls, tears apart vegetation, sometimes reported to attack humans and livestock.
FIRST REPORTED BY: Indigenous tribes of the Amazon, later documented by European explorers.
CREATURE CLASSIFICATION: Possible surviving giant ground sloth (*Megatherium*) or unknown mammal.
STATUS: Considered mythical by mainstream science; yet credible sightings continues.

CREATURE PROFILE

The Amazon rainforest conceals a creature that locals describe with both fear and awe. The Mapinguari is one of the most infamous cryptids of South America, and accounts of its existence continue to be reported from remote jungle regions. Unlike many creatures of folklore that are seen only in passing, the Mapinguari is frequently said to leave behind evidence in the form of tracks, torn vegetation, and an overpowering smell that lingers long after it has moved on. These details give weight to the probability that something real inhabits the deep forests.

The Mapinguari is typically described as a massive sloth-like beast, standing upright and towering at nearly 10 feet when fully erect. Witnesses often speak of its large potbelly and long shaggy hair that hangs in thick mats. Perhaps the most unusual feature is its stomach-mouth, a large gaping orifice located in the abdomen that is said to serve as a second or even primary mouth. Some reports also describe backward-facing feet, a trait that confuses trackers and makes following the creature through the jungle nearly impossible.

These anatomical oddities give the Mapinguari a reputation as a supernatural guardian of the forest; others, however, argue they could simply be exaggerations of a biological reality.

Indigenous peoples of the Amazon have passed down knowledge of the Mapinguari for generations. They view the beast not only as a danger but also as a spirit tied to the jungle's balance. To many, the creature represents a guardian meant to punish those who exploit or disrespect the rainforest. Early European explorers, upon hearing these accounts, considered them strange native legends, but modern cryptozoologists point out that descriptions strongly resemble the giant ground sloth, *Megatherium*, thought to have gone extinct around 10,000 years ago. The size, posture, claws, and dietary habits of Megatherium align closely with Mapinguari reports, leading to speculation that a relict population may still survive in inaccessible parts of the Amazon Basin.

Accounts describe the creature as both terrifying and unmistakable. Witnesses report an intense foul odor so strong it causes nausea. Its calls are said to echo like a long roar or bellow that carries far through the forest canopy. Farmers occasionally accuse the Mapinguari of raiding manioc fields and orchards, tearing down trees in its path and consuming fruits, roots, and leaves. While most reports suggest it avoids humans, some encounters describe aggression when people enter its territory. A number of hunters claim to have been chased or nearly attacked—though such stories are rare compared to those of simple sightings.

The Mapinguari's slow and lumbering movement on two legs mirrors the known locomotion of extinct sloths; but it is also said to drop onto all fours when threatened or when moving across uneven ground. Its tracks are enormous, sometimes measuring more than a foot across, with strange patterns caused by its supposed backward feet. These unusual impressions fuel debate, as they do not match known jungle animals; yet they are consistent across separate reports.

For centuries the Mapinguari has remained deeply ingrained in Amazonian culture. Some scientists dismiss it as a myth blending sloth, bear, and folkloric imagination; yet others remain open to the idea of a surviving prehistoric species hidden within one of the world's last great wildernesses. Until a body or clear photographic evidence is produced, the Mapinguari continues to walk the line between natural history and legend, stalking the rainforests in both physical sightings and the living memory of those who encounter it.

The South American Mapinguari, in a territorial rage, confronts human intruders who dared enter its domain. Note the gaping mouth-like orifice on its abdomen, a preternatural anomaly often featured in eyewitness reports. Copyright © Lochlainn Seabrook.

MERFOLK

An 8 foot long mermaid: sometimes gentle and helpful toward humans, sometimes aggressive and harmful. Copyright © Lochlainn Seabrook.

QUICK FACTS

NAME: Merfolk.
FIRST SIGHTING: At least the 9th Century.
LOCATION: Coastal waters, rivers, and lakes worldwide, with concentrated traditions in Europe, Africa, Asia, and the Americas.
SIZE: Commonly 5 to 8 feet in length, with an estimated weight of 150 to 250 pounds.
APPEARANCE: Humanlike upper body with hair, arms, and a face showing subtle nonhuman traits, lower body ending in a scaled fish tail.
EYES: Large, reflective, and well suited for low-light aquatic conditions.
SKIN/FUR: Smooth and pale, sometimes gray, greenish, or shimmering, with scales on the lower half.
DIET: Feeds on fish, mollusks, and seaweed. Known to scavenge drowned animals. Many reports accuse them of consuming humans through direct predation or drowning. Traditions in Africa and the Caribbean describe offerings of food to appease them, hinting at a dietary connection to ritual.
MOVEMENT: Fast and agile swimmers; can breach the surface and may move short distances on land by dragging the body or assuming a humanlike form in certain accounts.
NOTABLE BEHAVIOR: Famous for singing or vocalizing to lure sailors. Sometimes capsizes boats or drags swimmers underwater. Other times warns of storms or aids fishermen. Shows both helpful and hostile tendencies depending on culture.
FIRST REPORTED BY: Norse sailors and Medieval chroniclers.
CREATURE CLASSIFICATION: Aquatic humanoid cryptid.
STATUS: Unverified by mainstream science, but continually reported around the world into the present day.

CREATURE PROFILE

Reports of Merfolk appear across oceans and continents, making them one of the most widespread cryptid types. From early Medieval writings to current eyewitness accounts, descriptions remain consistent enough to suggest a genuine biological presence rather than simple folklore. The creature is described in both remote fishing villages and modern coastal cities, showing that its legend and sightings go well beyond isolated oral traditions.

Morphological descriptions are highly uniform. Witnesses usually see a being with a humanlike head, torso, and arms. Differences from humans include longer jaws, larger eyes, and sharp or irregular teeth. The lower half of the body is scaled and muscular, ending in a strong tail fin that propels it with great speed. Hair is often long and flowing. Many accounts mention webbed fingers, a clear aquatic adaptation. Colors range from pale gray to green, with iridescent or shimmering tones more common in warm waters. Such recurring details strongly suggest more than coincidence.

Merfolk behavior is as notable as their appearance. In some traditions they approach humans with curiosity, surfacing near boats or along shores. In other accounts they display aggression, overturning vessels or pulling swimmers into the depths. Their voices are central to their reputation. Their Siren-like songs are said to be haunting, beautiful, and dangerous. Sailors across cultures claim that these calls lure people closer to peril. At the same time some reports speak of warnings or protective acts, with Merfolk alerting fishermen to storms or hazards. The dual nature of their actions mirrors the sea itself, both a giver and taker of life.

Dietary accounts emphasize their predatory and scavenging roles. Fish, shellfish, and sea plants are primary foods. Reports also describe Merfolk feeding on drowned animals or human corpses, linking them to death at sea. Some traditions state that they actively hunt humans, pulling them into the water to consume them. In parts of Africa mami wata beings are offered food and drink in ritual settings, suggesting an accepted role in human ecology and religion. Caribbean tales describe similar practices, where failing to respect them is believed to provoke disaster. These details imply that Merfolk may occupy the role of apex predator within their domains.

Their ecological patterns are worth noting. Most sightings take place near shallow coastal waters, river mouths, or estuaries. Some witnesses claim they migrate along with schools of fish. This could explain sudden flurries of sightings in particular places that later go quiet. The association with food-rich zones supports the view of Merfolk as predators integrated into marine ecosystems.

Contemporary accounts keep the subject alive. In 2009 reports from Israel described dozens of witnesses at Kiryat Yam seeing a half-human half-fish creature leaping from the sea before vanishing again. In Papua New Guinea fishermen speak of humanoid figures with piercing eyes that surface in moonlight. In the Caribbean sailors still report hearing voices calling from calm waters. These stories strengthen the probability that Merfolk are not only remembered from old tales but still active today.

Skeptics sometimes suggest seals, manatees, or dugongs as mistaken identities. However these animals do not fit the majority of descriptions. They lack the humanoid facial features, the distinctive voice, and the dual behavior most often reported. A more plausible explanation is that Merfolk may represent an unknown aquatic branch of hominins that adapted to the sea, or a marine mammal that developed striking convergent traits resembling humans—the webbing between our own 4th and 5th fingers suggesting a possible distant ancestral link. Either way, the persistence of sightings worldwide points to a genuine mystery that remains unsolved and worthy of serious study.

A pod of porpoising merfolk cutting swiftly through the water, a sight sometimes reported by boaters and fishermen. Copyright © Lochlainn Seabrook.

MINERVA MONSTER

The 8 foot tall, quarter ton Minerva Monster: Ohio's own Bigfoot. Copyright © Lochlainn Seabrook.

QUICK FACTS

NAME: Minerva Monster.
FIRST SIGHTING: August 21, 1978.
LOCATION: Minerva, Ohio, USA.
SIZE: Height 7-8 feet, estimated weight 300-400 pounds.
APPEARANCE: Ape-like creature with broad shoulders, long arms, and a bulky build.
EYES: Large, glowing, often described as orange or red in color.
SKIN/FUR: Covered in thick dark brown to black hair.
DIET: Reported to feed on livestock, small game, vegetation, and possibly fish; observed scavenging and raiding human food sources.
MOVEMENT: Walks upright with long strides; capable of moving quickly through rough terrain.
NOTABLE BEHAVIOR: Associated with strange howls, strong odors, and throwing stones at intruders. Often seen near family homes, barns, and wooded creek beds.
FIRST REPORTED BY: The Caton family of Minerva, Ohio.
CREATURE CLASSIFICATION: Unknown hominid, possibly related to regional Bigfoot-type beings.
STATUS: Classified as folklore and misidentification by mainstream science; no confirmed sightings since 1978.

CREATURE PROFILE

While there are countless reports of ape-like cryptids in North America, the Minerva Monster stands out, for its sightings are tied closely to one Ohio family whose accounts remain consistent over time. The creature is described as a massive, hairy, upright beast that emerges from the woods and creeks near the small town of Minerva. Eyewitnesses report that the animal often comes very near to homes and livestock, making it one of the more intrusive cryptids recorded in modern American history.

The first widely reported encounter occurred on August 21, 1978, when the Caton family saw the beast outside their house, observing their children through a window. This frightening experience sparked media attention and soon police officers and neighbors also claimed to have witnessed the same figure in the area. Accounts state that the creature stood about 7 to 8 feet tall and weighed 300 to 400 pounds, its body completely covered in long black or dark brown hair. Its glowing orange-red eyes and broad silhouette gave it a distinctly imposing presence.

Behavioral reports from the period are notable. The Minerva Monster was said to emit loud, eerie screams that echoed through the countryside. Witnesses also described a pungent smell, similar to rotting garbage or sulfur, that lingered when the beast was nearby. On multiple occasions large rocks were thrown at the Caton family's home, suggesting an opposable thumb as well as deliberate action rather than random animal disturbance. These behaviors parallel those attributed to Bigfoot-type creatures in other parts of the United States, which strengthens the probability that the Minerva Monster may be part of a larger class of unidentified primate or hominid species.

The habitat surrounding Minerva at the time of the sightings was ideal for a secretive animal. The region contained dense woods, rolling farmland, and winding creeks that provided cover, food, and water. Farmers often raised chickens and small livestock, which could have been tempting food sources. Reports mention that the Caton family lost animals around the time of the encounters, which they attributed to the monster. Though no physical remains were ever recovered the consistency of the sightings over several weeks suggests that something tangible was active in the area.

Law enforcement officers were called to the property more than once. In at least one incident police reported that they too observed a large hairy creature retreating into the brush when flashlights were shined toward it. This outside confirmation lends additional weight to the eyewitness testimony, since the accounts were not limited to a single family. Investigators at the time did not dismiss the case outright, though no scientific evidence was collected that could provide absolute proof.

For the people of Minerva the monster became part of local folklore, but unlike older legends passed down through generations, this case was fresh and documented within living memory. The probability that such a creature exists, at least in isolated rural areas, is reinforced by the fact that reports of tall hairy hominids are widespread across North America and often share strikingly similar details. The Minerva Monster therefore may represent a regional expression of a broader species, much like other localized Bigfoot-type beings.

To this day, locals and researchers occasionally revisit the story, and some continue to report strange sights and sounds in the Ohio woodlands. The creature is not considered extinct or relegated only to history, but rather part of an ongoing phenomenon of unexplained encounters with apemen-like creatures. While dismissed by mainstream science the Minerva Monster remains an active subject of investigation by cryptozoologists who recognize that its behavioral consistency, physical description, and credible eyewitness testimony all suggest a real animal is probably at the heart of the original reports.

As with similar Sasquatch-like creatures all over North America, the Minerva Monster had a penchant for peering curiously into the windows of rural Ohio homes. Does it still haunt the area? Possibly. Copyright © Lochlainn Seabrook.

MOKELE-MBEMBE

The mysterious 35 foot long Mokele-Mbembe feeding on aquatic vegetation in a Congolese swamp. An unclassified modern cryptid or a prehistoric holdover from the era of sauropod dinosaurs? Copyright © Lochlainn Seabrook.

QUICK FACTS

NAME: Mokele-Mbembe.
FIRST SIGHTING: Late 18th Century, with continuous reports through the 19th and 20th Centuries.
LOCATION: Congo River Basin, Central Africa.
SIZE: Length 15 to 35 feet, height 6 to 10 feet, weight estimated at 2,000 to 10,000 pounds.
APPEARANCE: Large quadruped with long neck, small head, bulky body, and long muscular tail.
EYES: Small and dark, positioned on the sides of the head.
SKIN/FUR: Smooth, hairless, gray to brown hide resembling that of an elephant or hippopotamus.
DIET: Primarily aquatic vegetation including Malombo plants, leaves, and fruit, with reports of aggressive behavior toward hippos and crocodiles suggesting territorial defense.
MOVEMENT: Moves slowly on land but with strength, more agile in water, capable of swimming and submerging for long periods.
NOTABLE BEHAVIOR: Reported to block river passages, overturn canoes, destroy fishing nets, and guard feeding areas aggressively.
FIRST REPORTED BY: French missionaries and local Congolese tribes.
CREATURE CLASSIFICATION: Cryptid, often compared to sauropod dinosaurs, such as *Apatosaurus*.
STATUS: Reported into the present day, though considered legendary by mainstream science.

CREATURE PROFILE

Accounts of Mokele-Mbembe begin with oral traditions passed down for generations by the peoples of the Congo River Basin. In the late 18th Century, French missionaries and explorers recorded these stories and compared the animal to a living dinosaur. Over the following centuries, new testimonies from locals, travelers, and colonial officials steadily added detail, forming one of the oldest and most intriguing cryptid records on the African continent.

For those interested in etymology the name Mokele-Mbembe comes from the Lingala tongue and translates as "one who stops the flow of rivers." This is a fitting description, as the animal is said to block canoes, frighten fishermen, and even alter the course of river travel through its presence.

The animal is described as a massive semi-aquatic quadruped with a bulky body, long muscular tail, extended neck, and small head. Descriptions often recall the appearance of a sauropod dinosaur, though adapted for riverine life. Unlike hippopotamuses, which it superficially resembles in bulk, Mokele-Mbembe has no tusks, no visible ears, and a longer neck. Its hide is smooth, hairless, and gray or brown, giving it a reptilian look.

Across villages and tribes of the Congo Basin the creature is consistently described in almost identical terms. Its presence is taken as fact rather than folklore and it is regarded with a mixture of fear and respect. Many locals recount encounters where it overturned canoes, destroyed fishing nets, or guarded patches of aquatic plants. Fishermen often avoid areas known to be its feeding grounds, showing how much the creature influences daily life.

Mokele-Mbembe is believed to be herbivorous, feeding mainly on Malombo plants, leaves, and fruits found along riverbanks. Despite its plant-based diet it is not a gentle animal. Reports claim it will attack hippos that stray into its territory and even charge boats that venture too close. This aggressive behavior, combined with its size and power, has cemented its reputation as a dangerous inhabitant of the swamp and river systems.

European and later American explorers of the 19th and 20th Centuries carried these reports back to the wider world. By the early 1900s organized expeditions were being mounted to confirm the animal's existence. None returned with definitive proof, yet all gathered consistent testimonies from villagers and hunters who described the same physical traits and behaviors. The probability of misidentification is difficult to accept, given the uniformity of descriptions across so many independent sources.

The Congo Basin's geography explains why such a large animal could remain undetected by mainstream science. Dense forests, vast swamps, and waterways that stretch for thousands of miles form a natural refuge for elusive species. The difficulty of travel and the lack of modern surveying equipment in much of the region means large areas are still virtually unexplored. In this setting the survival of a relict megafaunal species remains a viable probability.

For the peoples who live in this part of Africa, Mokele-Mbembe is not a mystery but a reality. They continue to adapt their lives around its presence, warning travelers and passing down stories of danger and awe. Cryptozoologists and explorers consider it one of the strongest candidates for being a living fossil, with reports suggesting survival into modern times.

Naturally mainstream science dismisses the creature as a legend or a cultural myth; yet the persistence of reports for more than two centuries tells a different story. Whether it is a relict sauropod, a unique semi-aquatic mammal, or an undiscovered reptilian species, Mokele-Mbembe continues to capture attention as one of the most plausible and important cryptids in the world.

The Mokele-Mbembe: To this day its huge size and fierce territorial nature make it one of the most feared inhabitants of the Congo Basin. If it is a myth, as conventional scientists claim, what is generating this region-wide fear? And what exactly is the large dinosaurian-like creature the native people are seeing? Copyright © Lochlainn Seabrook.

MOMO

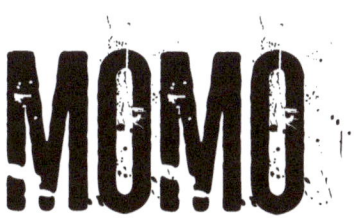

The 8 foot tall apeman known as Momo appears to be Missouri's own peculiar breed of Bigfoot. Copyright © Lochlainn Seabrook.

QUICK FACTS

NAME: Momo.
FIRST SIGHTING: 1971.
LOCATION: Missouri, USA.
SIZE: Height around 7 to 8 feet, estimated weight 500 pounds.
APPEARANCE: Large ape-like creature with a round head, long arms, and a massive body covered in thick dark hair.
EYES: Large, glowing orange or reddish eyes that stand out at night.
SKIN/FUR: Entirely covered in shaggy black or dark brown fur, often described as dirty and matted.
DIET: Thought to be omnivorous, feeding on small animals, livestock, fish, fruits, berries, and stolen human food. Reports describe it eating dog carcasses and raiding trash.
MOVEMENT: Walks upright like a human but with a loping, heavy stride. Sometimes described as running quickly despite its size.
NOTABLE BEHAVIOR: Emits a foul odor, shrill cries, and leaves behind three-toed tracks. Associated with livestock killings, trash scattering, and frightening howls.
FIRST REPORTED BY: Children near Louisiana, Missouri, in July 1971.
CREATURE CLASSIFICATION: Large North American apeman or Bigfoot-type cryptid.
STATUS: Considered unverified by mainstream science, but still reported by locals and investigators.

CREATURE PROFILE

Missouri's most famous cryptid is a hulking apeman known as Momo—short for "Missouri Monster." The creature first gained wide attention in the early 1970s when frightened children report seeing it standing at the edge of their yard, watching them in silence. What sets Momo apart from other regional apemen is not just its unusual appearance but also the distinctive details that witnesses consistently describe. Its shaggy dark coat of hair hangs long and unkempt, obscuring much of its face, while two luminous orange-red eyes glow visibly from beneath the fur. Standing around 7 to 8 feet tall and weighing perhaps 500 pounds, it is a formidable figure that continues to inspire reports across the American Midwest.

Eyewitnesses describe Momo's movements as upright and manlike but somewhat lumbering, its arms swinging heavily with each step. Despite its bulk it is capable of sudden bursts of speed, running swiftly into the cover of Missouri's thick woods and hills. Locals often note that Momo is accompanied by an overpowering odor, compared to rotting meat or sulfur, which lingers after encounters. Investigators find three-toed tracks in the area, a trait atypical for Bigfoot-type cryptids and one that fuels debate about its identity.

The creature's diet appears wide-ranging and opportunistic. Reports associate it with scavenging dog carcasses, stealing poultry, raiding trash cans, and even pulling fish from streams. Other accounts suggest it consumes wild berries, roots, and other natural foods. This omnivorous feeding habit allows it to survive in the rural and forested environment of Missouri, where farmland and river valleys provide easy access to both wild and domestic resources. Locals frequently worry about livestock disappearances in connection with sightings.

Behaviorally, Momo is both elusive and confrontational. While it avoids prolonged human contact, it often frightens witnesses with piercing shrieks or low moans. Some observers claim that glowing eyes shine out of the darkness at night, even before the massive figure is seen. In certain cases people describe feeling watched or followed, only to later discover tracks or clawed-up ground near their homes. This pattern of behavior suggests that Momo may be highly territorial, with encounters often taking place near wooded ridges and rivers around Louisiana, Missouri.

The first well-documented encounter in July 1971 involved two children who saw the monster near their home. Soon after their family dog vanished, with reports spreading of a strange apeman roaming the region. Sightings peak in 1972 when dozens of locals claimed to see the beast; some armed themselves and went searching for it. Investigators from across the country descended upon Missouri, and national headlines briefly focused on the town. Despite hunts and searches, no body or physical remains were found, though footprints, strange hair, and reports of terrible odors remained part of the evidence.

Unlike many cryptids whose legends fade, Momo continues to surface in modern accounts. Sightings stretch beyond the 1970s into later decades, with occasional reports of a large, hair-covered humanoid wandering through Missouri's backwoods.

Today Momo is not just part of Missouri folklore but also a subject of ongoing cryptid research, seen as one of the strongest regional cases for the existence of a North American apeman. Though dismissed by mainstream science, the probability remains that an undiscovered primate species inhabits the river valleys and forested highlands of the Midwest, where Momo sightings still occur.

Momo's petrifying otherworldly screams are often the only sign of the presence of this secretive beast. Copyright © Lochlainn Seabrook.

MONGOLIAN DEATH WORM

Lochlainn Seabrook

The 5 foot long Mongolian Death Worm emerges from the barren sands of the Gobi Desert. Feared by nomads for its lethal reputation, it is said to appear in the burning dunes of the "Land of the Eternal Blue Sky" during the region's hottest summer months. Copyright © Lochlainn Seabrook.

QUICK FACTS

NAME: Mongolian Death Worm.
FIRST SIGHTING: Early 20th Century.
LOCATION: Gobi Desert, Mongolia.
SIZE: Reported length 2 to 5 feet, thickness up to 6 inches, weight estimated at 5 to 15 pounds.
APPEARANCE: A large worm-like body, blood-red in color, smooth and limbless, with a blunt head and tail.
EYES: No visible eyes reported.
SKIN/FUR: Smooth, leathery, segmented skin, red or dark crimson.
DIET: Said to prey on small mammals, livestock, and potentially humans; reported to consume rodents, snakes, and carrion.
MOVEMENT: Slithers through sand like a worm; burrows quickly beneath the surface.
NOTABLE BEHAVIOR: Allegedly capable of ejecting corrosive acid or venom, and in some reports, generating electrical discharges that kill on contact.
FIRST REPORTED BY: Mongolian nomads.
CREATURE CLASSIFICATION: Terrestrial invertebrate cryptid.
STATUS: Unverified by mainstream science; but the legends surrounding it are still very much alive.

CREATURE PROFILE

A number of bizarre creatures have been reported from the deserts of Central Asia. However, none stirs more fascination than the Mongolian Death Worm. This enigmatic being is said to inhabit the Gobi Desert, one of the most remote and inhospitable landscapes on Earth. Accounts describe it as a bright red worm-like animal, living beneath the sands and surfacing only during the hottest months of summer, when desert storms are most intense. The secrecy of its habitat, combined with its unusual reported features, makes it one of the most legendary and elusive cryptids in the world.

The earliest widely shared information about the Mongolian Death Worm comes from the testimony of nomadic herders who for generations have spoken of a dangerous subterranean beast. They call it *olgoi-khorkhoi*, which translates as "large intestine worm," a reference to its tubular body. Its alleged size is modest, usually reported between two and five feet in length, yet its reputation is far more menacing than its physical dimensions would suggest. The creature is considered lethal to approach and local accounts emphasize its ability to kill either by spitting an acidic substance that corrodes flesh and metal or by discharging a form of electric shock powerful enough to fell a camel or horse instantly.

Descriptions of its physical appearance remain consistent across reports. Witnesses insist it is uniformly blood-red, with no discernible eyes, mouth, or external organs, giving it the impression of a featureless tube. This appearance reinforces its association with worms, though some observers suspect it may belong to an unknown branch of reptiles or amphibians that adapted to desert life. The absence of visible sensory organs is sometimes explained as an evolutionary adaptation to its subterranean existence, relying on vibrations and chemical cues rather than sight.

The Mongolian Death Worm is credited with behaviors unusual even among cryptids. It is said to rise to the surface only during the driest months, lying coiled in the sand before ambushing prey. When disturbed it can rear up and discharge its alleged defenses with alarming accuracy. Some reports claim the animal can kill from a distance without physical contact, making it an object of fear to those who encounter it. Nomadic traditions warn of livestock collapsing without wounds after the worm appeared, and herders often avoid specific stretches of desert believed to be its range.

Attempts to investigate the creature have been made by explorers from the early 20th Century onward; but the vastness of the Gobi Desert and the secrecy of its nomadic witnesses have kept direct evidence scarce. Expeditions consistently note the seriousness with which Mongolian locals regard the Death Worm. Unlike many cryptid tales, which may be dismissed as folklore or entertainment, the accounts of the Death Worm are often delivered with grave caution, underscoring the probability that these people have experienced encounters they regard as authentic.

Speculation about the creature's identity includes theories that it could be an unknown species of burrowing reptile, a large type of worm or annelid unknown to science, or even a surviving line of venomous amphibians. Some zoologists point out that the ability to discharge electricity is extremely rare among land animals, while corrosive fluids are known in some insects and reptiles, suggesting the Death Worm may combine traits observed separately in other organisms. This unusual combination of abilities is partly why the creature has not been easily placed into known taxonomic groups.

Today the Mongolian Death Worm remains unrecognized by mainstream science; yet it continues to occupy a strong place in regional culture with the last known sighting (unverified) occurring in 2004. Expeditions by Western researchers have so far returned without proof, but local testimonies continue with striking consistency. Whether it represents an undiscovered species adapted to one of Earth's harshest deserts or a cultural memory of encounters with lethal but known animals, the Mongolian Death Worm stands as one of the most compelling cryptids of Asia. Its legend reinforces the idea that the deserts of the world, though barren in appearance, may still conceal secrets waiting to be uncovered.

The Mongolian Death Worm is capable of both spitting venom and releasing a fatal electrical discharge, making it one of the most feared cryptids in East-Central Asia. Copyright © Lochlainn Seabrook.

MONO GRANDE

The 7 foot tall Mono Grande: an aggressive South American version of Bigfoot. Copyright © Lochlainn Seabrook.

QUICK FACTS

NAME: Mono Grande.
FIRST SIGHTING: 1533.
LOCATION: South America.
SIZE: Height between 5 and 7 feet. Weight estimated between 200 and 400 pounds.
APPEARANCE: Ape-like body, broad chest, long arms, short legs, large head with a flat face.
EYES: Large, dark, forward-facing.
SKIN/FUR: Covered in thick brown or black fur.
DIET: Reported to consume fruit, roots, leaves, small animals, fish, and possibly carrion. Some accounts describe livestock predation.
MOVEMENT: Walks both bipedally and quadrupedally. Swift and powerful when running or climbing.
NOTABLE BEHAVIOR: Known to throw stones, break branches, and display aggression when threatened. Sometimes vocalizes with loud howls or guttural roars.
FIRST REPORTED BY: Spanish conquistadors in South America.
CREATURE CLASSIFICATION: Unverified large primate, possibly related to *Homo* or a surviving giant New World monkey.
STATUS: Sightings continue into the present day, but the creature remains unverified by mainstream science.

CREATURE PROFILE

The remote jungles of South America have spawned a legend of a great ape-like beast known as the Mono Grande—meaning "large monkey" in Spanish. Accounts of this mysterious animal span nearly five centuries and continue to this day. Unlike many cryptids that dwell in lakes or oceans the Mono Grande inhabits thick forests, swamps, and mountainous jungles where human access is limited and visibility is poor. It is within these shadowy habitats that the animal is said to emerge, often startling hunters, travelers, or villagers who come too close to its territory.

Descriptions of the Mono Grande are remarkably consistent across time and culture. Witnesses speak of a powerful creature covered in dark fur, larger than any known monkey or ape of the Americas. Standing upright it reaches heights of 5 to 7 feet, with an estimated weight between 200 and 400 pounds. Its chest is described as wide and muscular, with long arms extending nearly to the knees. The face is often said to resemble that of both man and ape, flat with a heavy jaw, wide nostrils, and large forward-facing eyes. This hybrid appearance is one of the features that makes the Mono Grande stand out from other primates.

Its diet appears to be varied and opportunistic. Some reports describe the animal raiding fruit trees or stripping leaves from branches. Others tell of the Mono Grande catching fish from streams or seizing small mammals and birds. Several rural stories suggest that it occasionally preys on livestock such as goats or pigs, behavior that would mark it as both an omnivore and a potential competitor with humans. Bones and carcasses found torn apart in areas of sightings have been attributed to its feeding habits, though these claims remain unverified.

Movement is another striking feature. Observers state that the Mono Grande is able to walk upright like a man but also drops to all fours to sprint with tremendous speed. Its arms are described as exceptionally strong, capable of hurling stones with accuracy. In some encounters it reportedly charges at intruders, breaking branches, and shouting guttural roars to frighten them away. Villagers in certain regions describe the night filled with unsettling howls and screams that they attribute to the beast. Such aggressive territorial displays are consistent with primate behavior in general, adding weight to the credibility of these accounts.

The first written record comes from 1533, when Spanish conquistadors mentioned large man-like apes in the South American interior. Since then missionaries, naturalists, and explorers have continued to record testimony. In the 18th and 19th Centuries European travelers returning from the Amazon reported frightening encounters with hairy giants. More recent sightings have occurred throughout the 20th and 21st Centuries, particularly in Brazil, Venezuela, and Colombia. Indigenous groups often have their own names for the creature, integrating it into their traditions as a dangerous but real inhabitant of the forest.

Scientists dismiss the Mono Grande as folklore, reasoning that no ape species is native to the New World. Yet its consistent description suggests the probability of an undiscovered primate. It could be a surviving offshoot of *Homo* that migrated earlier than expected, or an unknown species of large New World monkey that evolved gigantism in isolation. The possibility of a remnant population persisting in unexplored jungle regions cannot be entirely ruled out, given the vastness of the Amazon and Orinoco basins. Whether classified as myth or fact, the Mono Grande continues to be reported, ensuring that this South American giant remains a subject of fascination and fear.

Known for its extreme territorial nature, the Mono Grande may in fact be a relic hominin, a prehistoric humanlike creature once thought extinct. Sightings of the beast continue into the 21st Century. Copyright © Lochlainn Seabrook.

MOTHMAN

The 7 foot tall Mothman of West Virginia, to me the strangest, most intimidating, most spine-chilling entity to ever grace the pages of cryptozoology—which is precisely why it made the cover of my book. Copyright © Lochlainn Seabrook.

QUICK FACTS

NAME: Mothman.
FIRST SIGHTING: November 1966.
LOCATION: Point Pleasant, West Virginia, USA.
SIZE: Height about 7 feet, wingspan 10 to 15 feet, weight estimated at 400 to 600 pounds.
APPEARANCE: Humanoid body with enormous wings, broad chest, no visible neck, and pointed head.
EYES: Large, round, and glowing red.
SKIN/FUR: Dark gray or black, smooth or feathered in some reports.
DIET: Unknown, though some speculate carnivorous feeding on small mammals, birds, or carrion. Others suggest it is non-predatory and may feed opportunistically.
MOVEMENT: Capable of both walking upright on two legs and rapid flight, often described as gliding without flapping.
NOTABLE BEHAVIOR: Appears suddenly, often near disaster sites, sometimes chases vehicles, frequently linked to warnings of impending tragedy.
FIRST REPORTED BY: Two young couples driving near the TNT area outside Point Pleasant.
CREATURE CLASSIFICATION: Winged hominid or unknown avian-type cryptid.
STATUS: Classified as folklore and legend by mainstream science; yet sightings of the creature (or similar winged beings) continue, not only in West Virginia and other states, but around the world.

CREATURE PROFILE

Mothman became known to the public in the autumn of 1966, when locals around Point Pleasant, West Virginia, began reporting a large winged figure unlike any known animal. These accounts were consistent and vivid, describing a humanoid creature with glowing red eyes, immense wings, and a terrifying presence. For those who lived in the area, the sheer volume of sightings in a short span of time made it impossible to dismiss.

Most early encounters took place near the abandoned munitions plant known as the TNT area. This site, with its empty igloos, water-filled pits, and surrounding woods, provided a natural hiding place. Witnesses stated that the creature perched on rooftops, lifted vertically into the air without effort, and on occasion pursued cars at high speeds. These descriptions set it apart from ordinary birds and suggested a being with unusual physical abilities.

The eyes were a defining characteristic: witnesses described them as large, round, and glowing with their own internal light, not as reflections of headlights. Many people reported that once they saw the red eyes they were overcome with fear or even paralysis. The head appeared small or sunken into the shoulders, giving the impression that the eyes were set into the chest. This odd configuration added to the sense that Mothman was not a misidentified crane or owl.

The wingspan was estimated at up to 15 feet, surpassing any native bird in North America. The body was bulky, with long legs and a broad chest. On the ground it moved with awkward strides; yet in the air it glided smoothly, rising vertically with little or no wing movement. Eyewitnesses emphasized that the silence of its creepy moth-like flight was one of the most unsettling details.

By the end of 1967, many residents linked Mothman with tragedy. On December 15 of that year, the Silver Bridge collapsed into the Ohio River, killing 46 people. Several individuals claimed to have seen Mothman near the bridge in the days before the disaster. After the collapse reports in Point Pleasant diminished, leading to speculation that the creature had served as a harbinger of doom.

The diet of Mothman remains unconfirmed. No evidence of feeding was discovered during the original flap, though some speculated it preyed on small animals or birds. Others suggested it might scavenge carrion, while a few proposed that it did not require ordinary food. The lack of concrete evidence has left its ecological role undefined.

Although the concentrated wave of sightings in Point Pleasant ended with the bridge disaster, Mothman has not disappeared from history. Reports of large winged humanoids continue to emerge in various parts of the United States and in other countries. Modern witnesses still describe the same basic features: towering size, glowing red eyes, and immense wings. In these more recent accounts the creature often appears near sites of impending disaster—maintaining its reputation as a menacing forerunner or omen of death, destruction, and sorrow.

Though mainstream science explains the Mothman away as folklore and misidentification, the persistence of consistent sightings and the sheer number of credible witnesses leave open the probability that something extraordinary was and still is being seen. For believers and researchers, Mothman remains one of the most notable, singular, ghastly winged cryptids in North America.

The Mothman in mid-flight, chasing down a speeding car full of horrified occupants. Copyright © Lochlainn Seabrook.

NAHUELITO

The 30 foot long, 2 ton Nahuelito gliding silently through the dark depths of Lake Nahuel Huapi. Eyewitnesses describe a massive long-bodied aquatic creature with a serpentine body and leathery skin. Copyright © Lochlainn Seabrook.

QUICK FACTS

NAME: Nahuelito.
FIRST SIGHTING: Early 20th Century.
LOCATION: Lake Nahuel Huapi, Patagonia, Argentina.
SIZE: Between 15 and 30 feet long, estimated weight 2,000 to 4,000 pounds.
APPEARANCE: Serpentine body with humps visible above the water. Often described with a long neck and a rounded or reptilian head.
EYES: Large and dark, positioned to allow above-water vision.
SKIN/FUR: Smooth, dark, seal-like skin with a glossy or wet sheen.
DIET: Likely fish, freshwater crustaceans, and possibly waterfowl. Could also include aquatic plants when other food sources are limited.
MOVEMENT: Swims with strong lateral undulations producing large surface wakes. Often seen gliding smoothly, but capable of sudden speed.
NOTABLE BEHAVIOR: Surfaces suddenly, sometimes leaving multiple humps visible. Occasionally approaches boats but usually avoids direct contact.
FIRST REPORTED BY: Early settlers and fishermen in Patagonia.
CREATURE CLASSIFICATION: Aquatic cryptid; possibly a surviving relict species such as a plesiosaur or giant pinniped.
STATUS: Existence unconfirmed by mainstream science, yet sightings continue into the present day.

CREATURE PROFILE

Unlike many lake monster traditions that began in ancient times, the story of Nahuelito came into focus during the early 20th Century. Lake Nahuel Huapi, located in the cold clear waters of the Argentine Andes, became the setting for reports of an immense aquatic animal. The lake itself is glacial, deep, and isolated, providing an environment where a large unknown species could survive undisturbed. From the beginning local witnesses claimed encounters, and reports continued into later decades, establishing Nahuelito as one of South America's most notable cryptids.

These descriptions of Nahuelito varied; but most early reports agreed on a creature measuring between 15 and 30 feet in length. The animal's body was often said to be serpentine, with several humps breaking the surface as it moved. Some accounts noted a thick neck rising above the water, while others described a more rounded seal-like head. Its skin was reported as smooth and dark, with a texture and sheen resembling the hide of a seal or whale. In some instances it was seen at close range—large eyes visible above the waterline—before it slipped back into the depths.

The diet of Nahuelito can be inferred from the ecology of Lake Nahuel Huapi, which contains large populations of fish such as trout and perch, along with crustaceans, waterfowl, and aquatic vegetation. Witnesses and researchers have concluded that a large predator would have had ample food sources, likely feeding primarily on fish and birds while supplementing its diet with plant matter during lean seasons. This adaptability would give the animal the ability to remain hidden for generations within the lake's ecosystem.

Nahuelito's movement is almost always described as powerful and deliberate. Early witnesses claimed the creature created long wakes across still waters, with humps rising and falling in rhythmic succession. Unlike fish or otters, the size of the disturbances suggest an animal of unusual proportions. It is said to glide silently beneath the surface, accelerating rapidly when disturbed. Boats report sudden near-encounters, though no credible account mentions attacks on humans, for the animal seems to favor retreat over aggression.

What separates Nahuelito from many other lake monsters is the persistence of reports into modern times. Photographs and eyewitness accounts circulated throughout the 20th Century, with some images showing large dark shapes in the water. While skeptics suggested logs or waves, many locals held that the photographs captured a genuine animal. The continued frequency of such reports makes it difficult to dismiss the phenomenon as mere legend.

To this day sightings still occur, with visitors and residents occasionally reporting disturbances that they attribute to Nahuelito. The probability remains that an undiscovered aquatic species inhabits the cold depths of the lake.

Early settlers and fishermen provided the first documented accounts, but Indigenous traditions had already spoken of powerful beings within Lake Nahuel Huapi. These stories suggested that unexplained encounters had taken place long before European settlement. The blending of Indigenous lore with modern reports provides cultural depth, implying a long history of interaction between people and the mysterious lake monster.

Classification of Nahuelito remains speculative. Some researchers argue it could be a surviving relict species resembling a plesiosaur or another prehistoric aquatic reptile. Others suggest a giant pinniped or an undiscovered long-bodied freshwater mammal. Whatever the case may be, descriptions do not match any known species in the region. With sightings still being reported today, Nahuelito continues to stand as one of South America's most longstanding aquatic cryptids.

Of course, mainstream science has yet to confirm the existence of Nahuelito—which is to be expected. However, the combination of historical reports, cultural traditions, ongoing eyewitness accounts, and photographic evidence ensures that the mystery remains open-ended and continuous. For many in Patagonia, Nahuelito is not a legend of the past. It is a living creature that still occasionally rises from the deep forbidding waters of Lake Nahuel Huapi.

The Nahuelito surfacing near a fishing boat full of astonished local Argentinian fishermen. Copyright © Lochlainn Seabrook.

NANDI BEAR

The 8 foot long, quarter ton Nandi Bear is completely out of place in East Africa. Yet credible sightings of the aberrant creature were reported for nearly 100 years before tapering off in the late 1990s. Copyright © Lochlainn Seabrook.

QUICK FACTS

NAME: Nandi Bear.
FIRST SIGHTING: Early 1900s.
LOCATION: Western Kenya and surrounding regions of East Africa.
SIZE: Height about 4 to 5 feet at the shoulder, length about 6 to 8 feet, estimated weight 400 to 600 pounds.
APPEARANCE: Large hyena-like or bear-like creature with sloping back, massive forequarters, and short hindquarters.
EYES: Small and reddish, often described as glowing at night.
SKIN/FUR: Thick shaggy dark brown to reddish fur covering the body.
DIET: Said to be carnivorous, preying on livestock such as goats, sheep, and cattle. Also reported to consume carrion. Some accounts suggest it attacks humans and feeds on the brain.
MOVEMENT: Moves with a lumbering gait on all fours but is reportedly able to rear up and run short distances bipedally.
NOTABLE BEHAVIOR: Known for attacking people at night, raiding herds, and vanishing back into the bush. Reports emphasize its ferocity and preference for eating brains.
FIRST REPORTED BY: European settlers and colonial officials in Kenya during the early 20th Century, though local tribes had spoken of it for generations.
CREATURE CLASSIFICATION: Cryptid mammal, possibly a relict species of giant hyena (*Pachycrocuta*), chalicothere (*Chalicotherium*), or other Pleistocene survivor.
STATUS: Sightings continued into the late 1990s; considered mythical or misidentified by mainstream science.

CREATURE PROFILE

Few African cryptids inspire as much fear as the Nandi Bear. Stories of this beast surface most frequently in western Kenya, where both tribal memory and colonial-era records describe a predator of great size and savagery. Known locally as *Chemosit* in some traditions, the creature has become embedded in regional folklore as well as in cryptozoological study. Unlike many cryptids that are seen fleetingly and dismissed as mistakes, the Nandi Bear is consistently described with particular physical and behavioral details that demand closer attention.

Witnesses describe the animal as heavily built in the forequarters, giving it a hunched or sloping profile similar to that of a hyena. Its hindquarters are shorter, which emphasizes this appearance and suggests a powerful digging or pouncing adaptation. Standing 4 to 5 feet at the shoulder and weighing several hundred pounds, it is larger than any known hyena species living in Africa today.

Its shaggy dark brown or reddish coat adds to its wild and threatening presence, while its small glowing eyes are often mentioned in nighttime encounters. The overall impression is one of primal ferocity, as if the creature represents a survivor from another age.

Dietary accounts are consistent with carnivory. Herdsmen frequently accuse it of killing goats, sheep, and cattle, usually at night. Some describe it as a scavenger not unlike the spotted hyena, tearing apart carrion left behind by other predators. Yet the most chilling claim is that the beast attacks humans and consumes only the brain. This recurring detail has been repeated in multiple local traditions, suggesting that even if exaggerated it has some cultural foundation. The combination of livestock predation and supposed brain-eating behavior has secured the Nandi Bear's reputation as one of the most feared animals in East African lore.

Movement patterns are also distinctive. Reports describe it moving in a heavy lumbering gait when on all fours, with a bear-like shuffle. Yet at moments it is said to rise onto its hind legs and charge short distances bipedally. This dual mode of locomotion places it outside the category of known African carnivores. It also links it to theories that it may be a relict of an extinct species. Suggestions have included *Pachycrocuta brevirostris*, the giant hyena of the Pleistocene, or even a chalicothere, an unusual prehistoric mammal with sloping back and elongated claws. Both possibilities fit at least some of the reported features.

The first widely circulated reports in writing came from British settlers and officials in the early 20th Century. They documented local accounts, noted livestock losses, and in some cases claimed to have seen the creature themselves. Tribes in the region, including the Nandi, had long warned of the animal, embedding it within myths of monsters that lurked beyond village boundaries. These traditional beliefs were reinforced by modern reports of violent livestock raids, which gave new urgency to the old stories. It was not a creature confined to the imagination but a threat that seemed to intrude into daily life.

Mainstream science has remained skeptical, attributing the reports to exaggerated sightings of hyenas, leopards, or other known predators. Yet the consistent and ongoing descriptions across time and culture suggests that something more unusual is at work. Unlike fleeting lights in the sky or obscure shapes in the water, the Nandi Bear is reported in direct confrontation with humans and animals. It is encountered up close, not at a distance, which lends weight to the idea that witnesses are seeing something biological, something real. If so, it may represent either a highly aggressive unknown carnivore or a relic from Africa's prehistoric past.

Although sightings have not been verified since the 1990s the Nandi Bear is still present in regional memory and oral tradition. Indeed, it remains a subject of fascination in both local storytelling and cryptozoological study, both in which it is considered one of Africa's most frightening and unusual mystery animals.

The Nandi Bear's fearsome reputation for eating the brains of its victims lends the beast an extra disturbing and terrifying aspect. Copyright © Lochlainn Seabrook.

NGOUBOU

Central Africa's aggressive cryptid, the 2 ton, 15 foot long Ngoubou—reported by both natives and European explorers—may be a surviving ceratopsian dinosaur. Copyright © Lochlainn Seabrook.

QUICK FACTS

NAME: Ngoubou.
FIRST SIGHTING: Reported by native tribes for generations.
LOCATION: Central African Republic.
SIZE: Estimated 12-15 feet long, 5-6 feet tall at the shoulder, weight around 2,000-4,000 pounds.
APPEARANCE: Large quadruped with a bony frill, horned face, and massive body resembling a ceratopsian dinosaur.
EYES: Dark and forward-facing, reported as intense and alert.
SKIN/FUR: Thick gray or brown skin, rough and armor-like, sometimes described as scale-like.
DIET: Herbivorous; said to consume shrubs, grasses, reeds, and low trees; uproots plants with its horns or sheer bulk.
MOVEMENT: Walks on four legs with a heavy gait; can charge quickly when threatened.
NOTABLE BEHAVIOR: Extremely aggressive toward elephants, reported to attack them and fight to the death; territorial and solitary by nature.
FIRST REPORTED BY: Baya and Banda tribes of the Central African Republic.
CREATURE CLASSIFICATION: Probable relict ceratopsian dinosaur such as *Styracosaurus* or *Centrosaurus*.
STATUS: Unverified by mainstream science; yet it continues to be seen—particularly in Cameroon and the Congo basin.

CREATURE PROFILE

The Ngoubou is one of the most imposing cryptids of Central Africa. It is described as a massive horned beast, unlike any animal known to modern zoology, and is feared by those who claim to have encountered it. Accounts from the Baya and Banda tribes, both past and present, place this creature in the savannas of the Central African Republic, where dense vegetation borders open plains. These habitats would provide both the cover and food supply necessary for a large herbivore to survive, particularly one with a body form reminiscent of prehistoric horned dinosaurs.

Reports emphasize the Ngoubou's size and strength. Villagers describe it as being about the size of a large rhinoceros yet distinct in form, bearing a broad frill behind its head and multiple horns jutting forward. Such details suggest a resemblance to ceratopsians, a group of dinosaurs that include *Triceratops* and *Styracosaurus*. Witnesses insist it is not a rhinoceros, pointing out its frill, its horn arrangement, and its aggressive interactions with elephants. The animal is said to stand 5 to 6 feet tall at the shoulders, stretch up to 15 feet in length, and weigh several tons, placing it squarely in the range of known prehistoric horned herbivores.

Dietary accounts portray the Ngoubou as a strict plant-eater. It reportedly feeds on tall grasses, shrubs, and small trees, often uprooting entire bushes as it eats. Its heavy jaws are said to grind vegetation, while its horns and sheer force allow it to break apart obstacles. Such descriptions match what is known about ceratopsians, which used their beaks and teeth to process fibrous plants. This is consistent with the Ngoubou's environment, as the Central African savannas are rich in such vegetation.

The creature's behavior is one of the most striking aspects of its lore. Villagers maintain that the Ngoubou is not only territorial but openly hostile toward elephants. Stories describe violent battles in which the Ngoubou uses its horns and bulk to gore and topple elephants, sometimes killing them outright. This reputation as an elephant-slayer sets it apart from other African cryptids. It is said to be solitary, rarely seen in groups, and quick to charge when disturbed. Such behavior fits with the survival of a powerful but rare relic animal competing for resources with the largest mammals of Africa.

The first reports of the Ngoubou were passed down through oral tradition, long before modern researchers began to document them. Missionaries and explorers in the early 20th Century recorded local testimony, noting the consistency of descriptions between different villages. The fact that multiple tribes recognize the same creature by name, and distinguish it clearly from both elephants and rhinoceroses, lends weight to the argument that the Ngoubou is a real biological animal rather than a mythical monster.

Eyewitnesses indeed insist that the Ngoubou is not a fleeting shadow or vague figure but a solid living beast whose presence commands attention. Tracks are sometimes described as broad and round with deep impressions that suggest great weight. Local hunters speak of hearing its movements at night accompanied by the sound of heavy breathing and the breaking of branches. These details contribute to the lingering belief that the Ngoubou still roams the remote heartlands of Central Africa beyond the reach of modern surveys.

Mainstream science considers the Ngoubou to be a legend, as no physical remains have been recovered and ceratopsians are believed to have vanished at the end of the Cretaceous Period. Yet the persistence of detailed reports into the present day, the consistency of features that align with paleontological knowledge, and the specific descriptions of its anatomy and habits, raise the probability that the Ngoubou may represent a prehistoric survivor. Whether a living ceratopsian or an unknown species of giant horned mammal, the Ngoubou remains one of Africa's most formidable cryptids. The natural world still holds many secrets waiting to be revealed.

The highly territorial Ngoubou attacking a herd of panic-stricken water buffalo. Copyright © Lochlainn Seabrook.

NINGEN

A 100 foot long, 30 ton Ningen glides noiselessly beneath the frigid waters of Antarctica. This massive, eerie, pale humanoid-like beast is certainly one of the Southern Ocean's most appalling and alarming cryptids. Copyright © Lochlainn Seabrook.

QUICK FACTS

NAME: Ningen.
FIRST SIGHTING: Early 20th Century.
LOCATION: Southern Ocean near Antarctica.
SIZE: Length 60-100 feet, weight unknown but likely in excess of 20-30 tons.
APPEARANCE: Vast humanoid form with a head, torso, and limb-like extensions resembling arms and sometimes legs.
EYES: Small, dark, and round, often described as lifeless or expressionless.
SKIN/FUR: Smooth, pale, and white, resembling human skin but rubbery in texture.
DIET: Unknown, though speculated to include fish, squid, or planktonic organisms; some reports suggest opportunistic feeding on larger prey near the surface.
MOVEMENT: Glides slowly and silently through icy waters, surfaces occasionally; capable of sudden deep dives.
NOTABLE BEHAVIOR: Exhibits a tendency to follow vessels, surface near ships, and rise partially out of the water; sometimes seen resting motionless beneath the ice.
FIRST REPORTED BY: Japanese whalers and fishermen.
CREATURE CLASSIFICATION: Aquatic humanoid cryptid, possibly a giant undiscovered marine mammal or cephalopod-related species.
STATUS: Unverified by mainstream science, yet sightings continue to be reported into the present day by sailors, fishermen, and marine research scientists.

CREATURE PROFILE

The Ningen stands out for both its size and its strikingly humanlike form, two traits unheard of in the animal world—especially true as it is found only in remote waters. The name itself means "human" in Japanese, chosen by sailors and fishermen who recognized its uncanny resemblance to a person, but magnified to colossal scale. Sightings occur primarily in the Southern Ocean near Antarctica, one of the least explored regions on Earth, which has long concealed mysteries beneath its shifting ice and freezing waters. The Ningen is not seen frequently but when it is the impression it leaves is profound due to both its vast physical size and its chilling shape.

Witnesses describe a creature that often exceeds 60 feet in length, with some accounts pushing its size closer to 100 feet. Its white body blends seamlessly with the surrounding ice floes and snowfields, making it nearly invisible until it surfaces or drifts close to ships. Its head is typically rounded and humanlike, sometimes with a barely perceptible nose or mouth. Extending from its torso are massive limb-like appendages that look like arms, and in some cases legs—though whether these structures are functional or vestigial remains unclear. The animal's immense size and ghostly pallor have caused sailors to mistake it at first for drifting icebergs, only to realize the ice was moving against the current with purpose.

The eyes of the Ningen are described as small and dark, contrasting starkly with its pale body. Observers report that these eyes give off no expression or intelligence that can be read; but the simple fact that they are forward-facing adds to the impression that this is a being closely related in appearance to humans. Its smooth rubbery skin further enhances the illusion of flesh, though scaled up to monstrous proportions. No reports exist of hair, fur, or other ornamentation, making it one of the most featureless cryptids ever recorded.

Its diet remains speculative. Given its size, however, the Ningen must consume vast quantities of food to sustain itself. Some researchers propose it may feed on the same prey as baleen whales, consuming schools of krill, plankton, or small fish. Others suggest a more predatory role, with arms adapted for grasping larger prey such as squid or seals. The cold waters of the Antarctic teem with biomass, which could easily support a small population of gargantuan but elusive animals.

Movement is slow and deliberate, with the creature gliding beneath the waves or surfacing for extended periods near ships. It has been described lying still beneath the ice, as if camouflaging itself or resting. At times it follows vessels for long distances, raising questions about whether it is curious, territorial, or simply opportunistic. Its ability to dive suddenly to great depths makes it difficult to track or document, even when spotted.

The earliest known reports came from Japanese whalers in the early 20th Century. As with many sailor accounts these stories spread among crews and eventually found their way into popular circulation in Japan, where they were later amplified in the late 20th and early 21st Centuries. While some dismiss the accounts as mistaken sightings of icebergs, whales, or large rays, the consistency of details—such as humanlike features, pale skin, and great size—suggest a biological entity yet unrecognized.

If genuine the Ningen could represent a highly specialized aquatic mammal evolved for Antarctic waters; or perhaps a massive member of an entirely unknown lineage of marine animals. Its humanoid shape may be an example of convergent evolution, where certain forms are repeated in nature due to functional advantage.

Because the Antarctic remains one of the least studied marine ecosystems, the probability that such a creature could exist undetected remains real. Until actual physical evidence emerges, however, the Ningen will continue to glide stealthily through the waters of cryptozoology, a truly unnerving and colossal enigma lurking at the bottom of the world.

Unbeknownst to its crew, a curious Ningen surfaces quietly beside a research vessel under the cold light of an Antarctic moon. Copyright © Lochlainn Seabrook.

NITTAEWO

Credible evidence suggests that the 4 foot tall Nittaewo once lived alongside Sri Lanka's Indigenous peoples, making it one of the country's most zoologically plausible cryptids. Copyright © Lochlainn Seabrook.

QUICK FACTS

NAME: Nittaewo.
FIRST SIGHTING: Documented in the 18th Century.
LOCATION: Sri Lanka.
SIZE: Height 3 feet to 4 feet, weight estimated 50 to 75 pounds.
APPEARANCE: Small, stocky hominin with short arms, long claws, and broad shoulders.
EYES: Dark and deep-set, adapted for both daylight and twilight activity.
SKIN/FUR: Covered in reddish-brown hair with a coarse texture.
DIET: Omnivorous, reported to consume fruits, roots, insects, birds, reptiles, and occasionally small mammals. Accounts suggest they may scavenge and have been linked to opportunistic hunting.
MOVEMENT: Bipedal but capable of clambering into trees and moving through dense forest undergrowth with agility.
NOTABLE BEHAVIOR: Said to live in small groups, build simple shelters, and show aggression toward intruders. Noted for attacking with clawed hands rather than using tools.
FIRST REPORTED BY: Indigenous Veddas of Sri Lanka.
CREATURE CLASSIFICATION: Relict hominin.
STATUS: Not recognized by mainstream science; recently gone extinct—though persistent local traditions affirm its past existence.

CREATURE PROFILE

Reports of the Nittaewo describe a small but formidable hominin that once roamed the island of Sri Lanka. Unlike the towering giants of other traditions, this being is remembered for its diminutive height yet muscular build and sharp claws that gave it a fearsome reputation. Oral history maintains that it lived alongside humans in relatively recent centuries, not as a ghost or a spirit, but as a living creature with physical needs, habits, and a tangible presence in the forests and rocky uplands.

The Nittaewo is depicted as stocky and powerful, standing upright on two legs. Its broad chest and long-clawed hands are adaptations well-suited for survival in dense jungle terrain. Covered in coarse reddish-brown hair, with a heavy brow and deep-set eyes, it resembles an archaic hominin rather than a modern human. The combination of primitive features and predatory ability makes it a striking figure in Sri Lanka's natural history traditions.

Accounts emphasize its varied diet. The Nittaewo feed on fruit, roots, and honey when those are available, but they also hunt small animals and birds, tearing into flesh with their claws rather than using tools. They scavenge when possible and may raid nests or carcasses for nourishment. This adaptability demonstrates intelligence and opportunism, hallmarks of a species capable of surviving in both lean and plentiful seasons.

Group behavior is another defining trait. Nittaewo are said to live in small bands that cooperate in hunting and defending territory. They build crude shelters in caves or rocky crevices and show hostility toward outsiders, particularly humans. Traditions describe violent clashes with the Veddas, Sri Lanka's indigenous people, who eventually viewed the Nittaewo as rivals. Stories of entire groups being trapped in caves and exterminated suggest a final conflict that may have driven them to extinction within the last few centuries.

Descriptions place them squarely within the framework of zoology rather than mythology. They are not depicted as magical beings but as flesh-and-blood creatures. Their size, lack of tool use, and distinctive features align with theories that they may have been related to *Homo floresiensis* or another small-bodied hominin species. If true, the Nittaewo represent one of the most recent surviving branches of humanity's extended family, existing in isolation until cultural and ecological pressures ended their line.

Eyewitness testimony collected from Vedda traditions strengthens the case for their reality. These accounts are detailed and consistent, focusing on physical traits and behavior rather than supernatural qualities. The clarity of description suggests memory of a real species rather than invention. While no skeletal remains have been recovered, the combination of oral history and ecological plausibility has kept the Nittaewo at the center of cryptozoological interest in South Asia.

Today the Nittaewo are regarded as extinct by most who take the stories seriously; though some believe remnants may still linger in hidden forests of Sri Lanka. Their story is more than folklore; it is a reminder of how recently other hominin species may have walked beside us. Whether extinct or undiscovered, the Nittaewo stand out as one of the most compelling cryptids in the world, embodying both the fragility and resilience of humanity's ancient kin.

Whether the Nittaewo are extinct or still hidden in some remote forest, their legend continues as one of the most intriguing cryptid accounts from South Asia. They occupy a unique space among reported beings: neither giant nor monster, but a small, wild cousin of humanity whose memory refuses to fade.

Vedda oral traditions and folklore recorded the biological existence of the Nittaewo up to as late as the 18th Century. Presumably conflicts between the two groups eventually pushed the small hominin to extinction in the late 1700s or early 1800s. Copyright © Lochlainn Seabrook.

OGOPOGO

The 2 ton, 50 foot long Ogopogo steaming across the surface of Okanagan Lake, creating a large boat-like wake so often described by eyewitnesses. Copyright © Lochlainn Seabrook.

QUICK FACTS

NAME: Ogopogo.
FIRST SIGHTING: Late 19th Century.
LOCATION: Okanagan Lake, British Columbia, Canada.
SIZE: Length reported between 20 and 50 feet, estimated weight 1 to 2 tons.
APPEARANCE: Serpentine body with multiple humps rising several feet above the water, horse-like or goat-like head, long neck.
EYES: Dark, large, and set forward on the head.
SKIN/FUR: Smooth dark skin, usually described as green, black, or dark brown.
DIET: Reports suggest predation on fish such as salmon and trout, occasional speculation of feeding on waterfowl or small mammals that enter the lake, with a possibility of opportunistic scavenging.
MOVEMENT: Undulating swimming motion with humps breaking the surface; capable of sudden dives and rapid changes in direction.
NOTABLE BEHAVIOR: Frequently seen crossing the lake, creating large wakes without boats present, sometimes rising partially out of the water.
FIRST REPORTED BY: Settlers of the Okanagan Valley in the late 1800s, though Indigenous Syilx people recorded oral traditions centuries earlier.
CREATURE CLASSIFICATION: Aquatic cryptid, lake monster.
STATUS: Unverified by mainstream science; yet sightings reports continue into the present.

CREATURE PROFILE

The deep waters of Okanagan Lake conceal more than just salmon and trout. For generations, reports describe a creature of great size surfacing from its depths, a being known today as Ogopogo. The lake itself is immense, stretching nearly 84 miles with a maximum depth exceeding 750 feet. Such proportions create an environment capable of hiding an animal that surfaces only occasionally. For the Syilx First Nation, this is not surprising. Their ancestors told of N'ha-a-itk, the spirit of the lake, a powerful force that demanded offerings from travelers before safe passage could be made across its waters.

When European settlers began to populate the valley in the late 19th Century they too recorded strange encounters. Witnesses described a long dark animal that moved with an undulating motion and displayed humps rising several feet above the surface. The head was compared to that of a horse or sometimes a goat, with an estimated length ranging anywhere from 20 to 50 feet. The consistency of these reports over more than a century indicates that the phenomenon is not the product of imagination alone.

Sightings remain common into modern times. Boat passengers describe wakes forming suddenly in calm water, cutting across waves with unnatural speed. Multiple humps have been seen traveling in rhythmic sequence, often three or more, producing the impression of a massive serpentine body. At times part of the torso or head emerges, frightening swimmers and astonishing onlookers. Eyewitness accounts often come from groups rather than single individuals, reinforcing the strength of the testimony.

Zoological speculation has offered several possible identities. Some argue Ogopogo could represent a surviving line of ancient whales such as *Basilosaurus*, which bore serpentine features. Others propose giant eels, oversized sturgeon, or a yet-undescribed freshwater species with reptilian characteristics. Okanagan Lake contains large reserves of fish and other prey, suggesting the food supply is more than sufficient to sustain a small population of large predators. Observers have even described waterfowl or small mammals disappearing in areas of sudden disturbance, consistent with opportunistic hunting.

Some cryptozoologists also suggest Ogopogo could be an unusually large form of sturgeon. These ancient fish already inhabit Canadian lakes and rivers, growing to lengths of over 12 feet, with ridged backs that might appear as humps when breaking the water. However, many witnesses insist the animal they saw was far larger, moved differently, and displayed features not consistent with any known fish. This disagreement highlights the possibility that Ogopogo represents a species distinct from sturgeon, one that has yet to be recognized by science.

What distinguishes Ogopogo from many other cryptids is the sheer number and regularity of its sightings. Unlike the Loch Ness Monster, which is elusive and infrequently reported, Ogopogo has been witnessed with remarkable consistency. Many of the residents of the Okanagan Valley regard it as a normal part of life rather than as folklore. The city of Kelowna has embraced the animal in its cultural image, acknowledging its strong presence in both local heritage and everyday conversation.

Mainstream science attributes the sightings to misidentified animals, floating debris, or natural wave formations. While such explanations may cover isolated cases, they fail to address the uniformity of descriptions and the persistence of reports over decades. The corroboration between Indigenous oral history and modern accounts creates one of the most robust records of any lake cryptid.

From a natural history standpoint, Ogopogo represents the possibility of an undiscovered aquatic vertebrate. Its large size, elusive habits, and dependence on deep cold waters would explain why it remains unverified despite frequent surface activity. Until conclusive evidence is brought forth Ogopogo continues to occupy its place in cryptozoology.

New reports arise every few years, often from fishermen, recreational boaters, and even law enforcement officers. These accounts reinforce the probability that Okanagan Lake conceals a species not yet described by science. The merging of Syilx traditions, settler testimony, and modern observations positions Ogopogo as more than myth. It remains one of the best-documented and most culturally significant aquatic cryptids in the world.

A curious Ogopogo surfaces next to a boat of shocked onlookers. Copyright © Lochlainn Seabrook.

ONZA

Mexico's 6 foot long Onza: an unidentified mystery cat that, strangely, is more similar to an African cheetah than a North American cougar. Copyright © Lochlainn Seabrook.

QUICK FACTS

NAME: Onza.
FIRST SIGHTING: 1757.
LOCATION: Mexico.
SIZE: Length 5 feet, height 2.5 feet, weight 60-70 pounds.
APPEARANCE: Slender body, long legs, elongated face, short tail.
EYES: Large, almond-shaped, golden or amber in color.
SKIN/FUR: Short, reddish-brown fur with faint striping on the flanks.
DIET: Medium-sized mammals such as deer, rabbits, peccaries, and rodents. Birds, reptiles, and carrion also reported as food; occasionally preys on livestock including goats, sheep, and chickens when wild game is scarce.
MOVEMENT: Agile and swift runner, capable of leaping long distances; moves with feline stealth.
NOTABLE BEHAVIOR: Said to attack prey by biting at the neck and face. Reported to be more aggressive than jaguars and pumas.
FIRST REPORTED BY: Spanish colonists in northern Mexico.
CREATURE CLASSIFICATION: Unknown feline, possibly related to *Puma concolor*.
STATUS: Unverified by mainstream science, but sightings continue into the present day.

CREATURE PROFILE

When considering the carnivores of Mexico few attract as much intrigue and attention as the Onza. This mysterious feline is described as similar to the cougar yet distinctly different in its proportions and behavior. Reports from hunters, ranchers, and villagers place the animal in remote parts of northwestern Mexico, particularly in Sonora and Sinaloa, where rugged mountains and arid scrublands provide the cover and prey it requires. The continuation of sightings into modern times keeps the Onza at the forefront of discussions about unknown cats of the Americas.

The Onza is not a new discovery to local people. Accounts trace back to the 18th Century, when Spanish settlers documented encounters with a strange cat that did not match the jaguars or pumas they already knew. They referred to it as "onza," a term sometimes loosely applied to large cats, but here used in a more specific sense. Descriptions emphasized its narrow body, long legs, and notably thin frame compared to the heavyset mountain lion. These details have remained consistent across reports through the centuries.

Physical differences set the Onza apart from known felines. Witnesses describe a body around 5 feet in length with relatively long limbs that give it a greyhound-like appearance. The head is said to be smaller and more elongated than that of a cougar, with large ears and sharp facial features. Its tail appears shorter than the cougar's, often less than half the length of its body. The fur is usually reddish or tawny with faint stripes, though some accounts note a uniform brown coat. Golden or amber eyes, intense and penetrating, are frequently mentioned in sightings.

Dietary habits point to a carnivore adapted to both wild and domestic prey. Observers report the Onza preying on deer, peccaries, rabbits, and small mammals in the wild. When forced into human territory it will raid livestock pens, taking goats, sheep, or poultry. Its hunting style is described as direct and aggressive, often aiming for the throat or head of its victim. This boldness has earned the Onza a reputation among rural communities as more dangerous than either jaguar or puma.

Movements of the Onza are said to be quick and fluid. Hunters recount seeing it leap across arroyos and climb rocky slopes with ease. Its lean build and long legs suggest speed, which no doubt gives it an advantage in open terrain. Unlike the stealthier puma, the Onza sometimes pursues prey openly, a trait that adds to the perception of its fierceness.

Speculation about the Onza's identity has taken several directions. Some zoologists propose it may represent a subspecies of *Puma concolor*, adapted to drier and more open habitats. Others suggest it could be a surviving form of an extinct American cat, preserved in isolated pockets of northern Mexico. Genetic testing on a specimen killed in Sinaloa in 1986 yielded results pointing toward puma, yet the morphological differences recorded in photographs and measurements continue to puzzle researchers. Local hunters insist it is not the same animal as the mountain lion, maintaining that side-by-side comparison reveals clear distinctions.

Despite ongoing interest the Onza has yet to be formally recognized by mainstream science. Skeptics attribute the reports to variations within cougar populations. However, the consistency of features described across generations strengthens the case that something unusual is present in the region. With sightings continuing into the present day the Onza remains an open file in the study of North American wildlife. Surprises still lurk in the shadows of the mountains.

The agile, fast-running, greyhound-like Onza is known to prey on livestock. Copyright © Lochlainn Seabrook.

ORANG PENDEK

The 5 foot tall, bipedal Orang Pendek in its native habitat: the dense Sumatran rainforest. The creature is described in eyewitness accounts as a small but powerfully built hominid that moves with a distinctly humanlike gait. Copyright © Lochlainn Seabrook.

QUICK FACTS

NAME: Orang Pendek.
FIRST SIGHTING: Early 20th Century.
LOCATION: Sumatra, Indonesia.
SIZE: Height 4 to 5 feet, estimated weight 100 to 150 pounds.
APPEARANCE: Small bipedal primate with broad shoulders, long arms, and short legs.
EYES: Dark and round, set forward giving binocular vision.
SKIN/FUR: Covered in dense brown, gray, or black hair with lighter patches on chest or face.
DIET: Reported to eat fruit, roots, insects, small animals, and occasionally cultivated crops such as corn or cassava.
MOVEMENT: Walks upright on two legs with surprising agility and also climbs trees with ease.
NOTABLE BEHAVIOR: Said to avoid humans yet sometimes raids gardens or plantations; tracks resemble small human footprints.
FIRST REPORTED BY: Local Sumatran tribes and later Dutch colonists in the early 1900s.
CREATURE CLASSIFICATION: Unverified hominid, possibly a surviving hominin related to *Homo floresiensis* or another unknown human relative.
STATUS: Unverified by mainstream science; despite this, sightings continue into the present day.

CREATURE PROFILE

Throughout the mountainous forests of Sumatra, there exists accounts of a mysterious small primate. Locals know it as Orang Pendek, meaning "short person" in Indonesian. This being is consistently described as walking upright like a human yet retaining a compact and muscular primate form. The habitat of Orang Pendek centers on the Kerinci Seblat National Park region, an area of dense rainforest, steep terrain, and limited human access, conditions favorable for concealing an undiscovered hominid.

Orang Pendek stands between 4 and 5 feet tall, making it smaller than an adult human but larger than most monkeys. Eyewitnesses emphasize its disproportionately long arms, powerful shoulders, and short legs. Its body is cloaked in thick hair that ranges in color from dark brown to gray, with occasional lighter patches on the face or chest. Unlike an ape the face is often said to appear more human-like, with forward-facing eyes that give it an intense gaze. Tracks attributed to the creature display short humanlike toes, further fueling the view that this is neither monkey nor gibbon but something closer to a hominin.

Dietary habits reported by locals show a broad omnivorous range. The Orang Pendek is said to forage for forest fruits, dig up roots, and consume insects and small animals. Farmers complain that it sometimes steals corn or cassava from their fields, evidence that the animal is willing to enter cultivated areas when food is available. These behaviors suggest opportunistic feeding similar to that of both great apes and early humans.

Locomotion patterns also set this cryptid apart. It moves upright with ease and confidence, in a manner distinct from chimpanzees or orangutans, whose bipedal gait is awkward. The Orang Pendek can stride swiftly on two legs across uneven forest paths and then scramble up trees with agility, combining traits of humanlike locomotion and arboreal adaptation. Reports often mention its silence and ability to vanish quickly into cover, indicating both caution and intelligence.

Witnesses span different communities and time periods. Indigenous groups have long spoken of Orang Pendek as a real animal, part of the living landscape. Dutch settlers in the early 20th Century recorded the same descriptions, providing some of the earliest written testimony. More recently, Indonesian villagers, rangers, and even foreign researchers claim to have seen the animal or its tracks. Several expeditions in the late 20th and early 21st Centuries collected footprint casts and hair samples, though none have been accepted as conclusive by the scientific establishment.

The creature's classification remains open to debate. Some researchers suggest it could be a surviving population of *Homo floresiensis*, the small-bodied hominin discovered on the nearby island of Flores. Others propose it may represent a new species of great ape adapted to Sumatra's forests. Local traditions consistently portray it not as a spirit or myth but as a tangible living being encountered in daily life. This contrasts with many folkloric creatures that inhabit only legend.

Researchers also note that Orang Pendek is often reported near rivers, ridgelines, and fruiting trees, suggesting it follows natural food and travel corridors within the forest. These recurring patterns give weight to the idea of a resident breeding population rather than scattered chance encounters. Some observers have remarked on its cautious but deliberate behavior, as if it possesses an awareness of being watched, further distinguishing it from ordinary wildlife.

The persistence of sightings into modern times maintains the credibility of Orang Pendek as a candidate for biological discovery. Despite surveys and attempts at photographic documentation, definitive proof is still absent. Yet the consistency of witness reports, the environmental suitability of its habitat, and the parallels to other small-bodied hominins discovered in Southeast Asia suggest that this cryptid may well represent a genuine, though rare, species awaiting confirmation.

The Orang Pendek stands as one of the most compelling cases in cryptozoology, bridging the gap between folklore, science, and the uncharted corners of natural history.

An Orang Pendek stealthily food-raiding a farm at night, evidence of both its opportunistic diet and its reputation as an elusive but highly intelligent forest dweller. Copyright © Lochlainn Seabrook.

OWLMAN

The unlikely 6 foot tall Owlman is closely associated with Cornwall's ancient Mawnan Church, where it is often reported walking human-like around the grounds. Copyright © Lochlainn Seabrook.

QUICK FACTS

NAME: Owlman.
FIRST SIGHTING: 1976.
LOCATION: Mawnan, Cornwall, England.
SIZE: Stands 5 to 6 feet tall, with wingspan estimated at 10 to 15 feet, weight around 200 pounds.
APPEARANCE: Humanoid body with large feathered wings, clawed feet, pointed ears, and an owl-like head.
EYES: Large, glowing red or orange eyes.
SKIN/FUR: Dark gray to black feathers covering most of the body.
DIET: Reported to prey on small mammals, birds, and fish, with the probability of scavenging. Witnesses also describe an interest in livestock and the occasional suggestion of carrion feeding.
MOVEMENT: Capable of both bipedal walking and powerful flight, often reported gliding silently between treetops.
NOTABLE BEHAVIOR: Known to hover near church towers, make eerie hissing or screeching sounds, and follow or observe humans without direct contact.
FIRST REPORTED BY: Two young girls visiting Mawnan Church in 1976.
CREATURE CLASSIFICATION: Winged humanoid cryptid, possibly related to *Strigiformes*.
STATUS: Unaccepted by scientific institutions, yet recurring observations argue for its reality.

CREATURE PROFILE

Encounters with Owlman emerge most often around Mawnan Church in Cornwall, where the wooded surroundings and ancient stone tower provide a striking backdrop for this cryptid's presence. The first detailed accounts come from 1976 when young witnesses described a giant owl-like being perched in the trees near the church. Since then reports have recurred at intervals, maintaining Owlman's place among Europe's most intriguing winged cryptids.

Eyewitnesses consistently describe a figure that combines human and avian traits. Its body is humanoid but covered in dark feathers, with powerful wings stretching 10 to 15 feet across. The head is distinctly owl-like, with pointed ears, a flat face, and piercing forward-facing eyes that glow in red or orange tones. Feet end in sharp talons, suitable for gripping or slashing; several witnesses have remarked on its silent movement through the night air. In terms of size reports place the creature at roughly the height of a grown man, but broader and more formidable due to its wings.

The diet of such a being is inferred from both witness accounts and ecological logic. Owlman is thought to feed on rodents, small birds, and fish, paralleling the habits of large raptors. Reports of it watching over livestock suggest possible opportunistic hunting, while its occasional appearance near carrion may indicate scavenging tendencies. This wide dietary range would allow it to survive in the Cornish countryside without detection, much as owls and other nocturnal predators do.

Behavioral patterns are striking in their consistency. Owlman is frequently linked to Mawnan Church, where it is often seen perched on the tower or gliding between surrounding trees. The sounds attributed to it include shrill screeches and low hissing, noises that unsettle listeners and reinforce its connection with predatory birds. Witnesses also note its tendency to watch humans from a distance, sometimes following individuals without attack. Such behavior implies intelligence and curiosity, but not necessarily aggression.

Theories about Owlman's origins vary. Some researchers propose it as a surviving species of giant bird, perhaps related to extinct Pleistocene raptors. Others suggest a hybrid organism, with avian and humanoid characteristics combined in unknown ways. Folklorists point out the similarities with older Cornish legends of bird-like spirits, noting that the church itself stands on land long associated with local myths. The blending of folklore and modern reports supports the idea that Owlman belongs to a deep-rooted tradition of winged guardians or watchers tied to sacred spaces.

Sightings continue intermittently into modern times, with both locals and tourists claiming encounters. Descriptions remain consistent, lending credibility to the probability that the same creature type is being observed rather than unrelated misidentifications. The area around Mawnan Church retains a mystical aura, drawing cryptid researchers who treat the site as a focal point for fieldwork.

While mainstream science does not yet accept Owlman as a recognized species, the ongoing reports, the clarity of descriptions, and the concentration of sightings in one location suggest that further study is warranted. The probability of an undiscovered nocturnal predator living discreetly in Cornwall's wooded valleys cannot be dismissed. Owlman thus remains an open case in cryptozoology, a winged humanoid that challenges conventional understanding of avian evolution and continues to inspire serious investigation.

The massive Owlman gliding soundlessly above a graveyard, a sight sure to terrify even the most fearless individual. Copyright © Lochlainn Seabrook.

OZARK HOWLER

The strange and frightening 7 foot tall Ozark Howler—seemingly part felid, part ursid, part bovid—has been reported haunting the Ozark Mountain wilderness for nearly 200 years. It is said to be an omen of ill luck and even death. Copyright © Lochlainn Seabrook.

QUICK FACTS

NAME: Ozark Howler.
FIRST SIGHTING: Early 19th Century.
LOCATION: Ozark Mountains, Arkansas, Missouri, Oklahoma, and Texas, USA.
SIZE: Length 4 to 7 feet, height 2 to 3 feet at the shoulder, weight 200 to 300 pounds.
APPEARANCE: Large catlike body with short legs, long tail, and prominent horns or antlers.
EYES: Glowing red, visible in darkness.
SKIN/FUR: Thick black or dark brown fur with a coarse texture.
DIET: Reported to prey on deer, livestock, and smaller mammals. May also scavenge carrion when prey is scarce; some accounts suggest opportunistic feeding on domestic animals and wild turkeys.
MOVEMENT: Runs with a feline stride, leaps powerfully, and climbs rocky slopes with ease. Often described as swift yet deliberate.
NOTABLE BEHAVIOR: Emits a terrifying unearthly howl said to resemble a cross between a wolf's cry and a woman's scream. Avoids humans yet approaches farmsteads during the night; associated with death omens in local folklore.
FIRST REPORTED BY: Early European settlers in the Ozarks.
CREATURE CLASSIFICATION: Unidentified mammal, possibly related to large cats or an unknown branch of *Carnivora*.
STATUS: Not confirmed by mainstream science, but reported consistently into the present day.

CREATURE PROFILE

Reports of the Ozark Howler most often occur at night, when the forests of the Ozark Mountains are silent and movement is easiest to detect. Locals describe a beast that can make even seasoned hunters retreat in fear, its presence revealed less by sight than by its piercing unnatural cry. This vocalization, a blend of wolf howl, elk bugle, and human wail, is the sound that has earned the creature its chilling name. Witnesses emphasize that hearing the howl at close range is a physical experience, said to vibrate through the chest like the roar of a predator.

Sightings place the Ozark Howler across a wide territory that includes northern Arkansas, southern Missouri, eastern Oklahoma, and even into Texas. The terrain here is dominated by thick oak-hickory forests, rocky ridges, and hidden caves, providing natural shelter and hunting grounds for an animal that avoids open country. Accounts typically describe the Howler as panther-like in shape but bulkier, with short muscular legs. The most unusual feature remains the presence of horns or small antlers on its head, a trait not known in any cat species but repeated often enough by witnesses to warrant inclusion.

Eyewitnesses note the creature's glowing red eyes. These are often reported shining from the edges of woods or from high rocks overlooking trails, a feature that has led many to compare the Howler to a demon or spectral beast. Yet many zoologists who examine the accounts consider that eyeshine may be natural tapetum reflection, amplified by fear and local legend. Regardless of explanation, the eyes play a central role in encounters and add to the animal's unsettling reputation.

The Ozark Howler's diet is said to be diverse but centered on deer, which are abundant throughout the region. Farmers sometimes blame it for missing livestock, especially goats and calves. Reports also suggest opportunistic scavenging, with the creature feeding on carcasses and gut piles left by hunters. A few accounts describe it stalking turkeys or smaller mammals, suggesting that like a mountain lion it adapts its diet to available prey. Its size and musculature imply a predator capable of ambush attacks, striking from concealed vantage points before dragging its prey into cover.

Behaviorally the Howler tends to avoid direct conflict with humans. Many reports involve hunters or hikers who catch sight of it at a distance before it disappears into the forest. Still, its unearthly howl brings it close to human settlements, often during winter months when prey is scarce. Folklore throughout the Ozarks has long linked its call to misfortune and death. Families tell stories of the cry being heard before a tragedy, embedding the beast deeply into local tradition as both physical animal and supernatural omen.

While mainstream science has not accepted the Ozark Howler as a recognized species, sightings have not diminished. In fact, modern hunters and outdoor enthusiasts continue to describe encounters, often supported by photographs or recordings of its howl. These are usually inconclusive but consistent enough to sustain belief. The persistence of reports across multiple states, combined with strong cultural memory of the animal, suggests a real foundation behind the legend.

Taken as a whole, the evidence points to a predator both elusive and enduring. Whether an undiscovered branch of feline adapted to the Ozarks or a unique mammal outside known classification, the Ozark Howler remains one of North America's most compelling cryptids. Its deep association with the mountains ensures that, real or not, the creature continues to exist in both the wilderness and the minds of those who call the Ozarks home.

Unbeknownst to a group of peacefully sleeping hikers, the monstrous Ozark Howler silently stalks their campsite in the heart of Arkansas. Copyright © Lochlainn Seabrook.

PASCAGOULA RIVER ALIENS

The 5 foot tall Pascagoula River Aliens are among the weirdest, scariest, and most inexplicable creatures in the annals of cryptozoology. Copyright © Lochlainn Seabrook.

QUICK FACTS

NAME: Pascagoula River Aliens.
FIRST SIGHTING: October 11, 1973.
LOCATION: Pascagoula, Mississippi, USA.
SIZE: Approximately 5 feet tall, estimated weight around 150 pounds.
APPEARANCE: Humanoid with no visible neck, carrot-shaped head, slits for a mouth, and claw-like hands.
EYES: Small, slit-like, often described as piercing but not luminous.
SKIN/FUR: Gray, wrinkled, and leathery, with a texture compared to elephant hide.
DIET: Unknown. No reports of feeding behavior, though their focus on humans suggests interest in biological study rather than nutrition.
MOVEMENT: Gliding or floating across the ground and water without visible effort.
NOTABLE BEHAVIOR: Silent approach, physical contact with humans, apparent use of advanced craft, possible examination or abduction activity.
FIRST REPORTED BY: Charles Hickson and Calvin Parker.
CREATURE CLASSIFICATION: Extraterrestrial humanoid (*Homo extraterrestrialis* hypoth.).
STATUS: Not validated by mainstream science, though ongoing witness testimony keeps the case active.

CREATURE PROFILE

The Pascagoula River Aliens stand apart from most cryptid reports because they are tied not only to fleeting sightings but to one of the most detailed and lasting abduction cases on record. The creatures were first encountered on a quiet Mississippi night in 1973, when two shipyard workers, Charles Hickson and Calvin Parker, reported being seized while fishing on the banks of the Pascagoula River. Their testimony has since become a benchmark in the study of unidentified beings associated with UFO phenomena, giving these aliens a distinct place in cryptozoological inquiry.

To this day descriptions of the beings are remarkably specific. Standing about 5 feet tall, they lack a visible neck, their heads rising in a pointed shape that tapers back in an almost vegetable-like form. Witnesses emphasize the absence of typical human features: the creatures' mouths appear only as narrow slits, and their hands end in claw-like appendages resembling pincers. The entire body is covered in gray wrinkled skin, often compared to the hide of an elephant. Their legs are described as fused or stump-like, yet the beings move effortlessly, often said to float or glide both on land and over water. This mode of motion separates them from conventional humanoid descriptions and adds a sense of otherworldly locomotion.

The encounter details behavior that suggests purposeful interaction with humans. According to Hickson and Parker, the beings approached without sound, paralyzed their captives, and transported them aboard a waiting craft. Once inside the humans were subjected to examination under bright lights, with the beings apparently using both their claws and unknown instruments to probe the captives. No vocal sounds were reported, suggesting either telepathic communication or a species without a need for speech. After a period of examination the men were returned to their original location on the riverbank, physically unharmed but psychologically shaken.

Dietary habits are entirely speculative. With no evidence of feeding the assumption is that the Pascagoula River Aliens are either uninterested in local biological resources or that their nourishment comes in ways not recognizable to humans. The most consistent interpretation is that their interest in humans is research-driven, whether medical, biological, or psychological. This places them within a classification of "scientific observers"—though their invasive methods suggest a predator-prey relationship that cannot be dismissed outright.

Sightings of similar beings have continued in the decades following the 1973 case, with some witnesses in Mississippi and surrounding states claiming encounters with identical forms. The persistence of reports points toward an ongoing presence rather than a single isolated event. Unlike other cryptids tied solely to rural folklore, the Pascagoula River Aliens are documented with police reports, lie detector tests, and medical examinations of the witnesses, creating a case file that is impossible to dismiss.

Within cryptozoology and ufology these beings occupy an unusual position. They are neither the classic "small gray" archetype nor the reptilian or insectoid figures reported elsewhere. Their distinctive wrinkled skin, carrot-shaped heads, and clawed limbs set them apart, providing a consistent morphology not seen in other alien reports. For many researchers this uniqueness adds weight to their authenticity, suggesting that Hickson and Parker were not borrowing from preexisting cultural templates.

The status of the Pascagoula River Aliens remains scientifically unverified; yet the case is without doubt one of the most credible alien encounters in the United States. Eyewitness testimony, corroborating details, and continued modern reports lend strong probability to the conclusion that something unknown operates along the Pascagoula River. As far as cryptid classification goes, they remain in the category of extraterrestrial humanoids whose presence challenges conventional zoology and offers a rare glimpse into what may be a millennia-old interaction between humans and otherworldly life.

The silent, robot-like Pascagoula River Aliens are famous for "floating" their human victims into waiting spacecraft, where they are scanned by a massive eye-like instrument, then later returned to the ground unharmed. Copyright © Lochlainn Seabrook.

PHANTOM KANGAROO

The ghostly, out-of-place, 8 foot tall Phantom Kangaroo unsettles all who are unlucky enough to encounter it. Copyright © Lochlainn Seabrook.

QUICK FACTS

NAME: Phantom Kangaroo.
FIRST SIGHTING: Early 1800s.
LOCATION: Various parts of the USA, especially the Midwest, South, and Northeast.
SIZE: Height 4 to 8 feet, weight 50 to 300 pounds.
APPEARANCE: Large kangaroo-like body with long muscular tail and powerful hind legs.
EYES: Dark, round, and reflective at night.
SKIN/FUR: Short brown, gray, or black fur, sometimes patchy in appearance.
DIET: Reported feeding on grass, crops, small animals, insects, and in some cases scavenged carrion. Diet varies by location and availability.
MOVEMENT: Leaps in long hops; can move rapidly in bursts; often seen bounding across open fields or roads.
NOTABLE BEHAVIOR: Appears suddenly and vanishes just as quickly, often traveling alone; occasionally described as aggressive or predatory.
FIRST REPORTED BY: Early European settlers in frontier areas.
CREATURE CLASSIFICATION: Terrestrial marsupial cryptid, possibly related to *Macropus* or an unknown North American analog.
STATUS: Not acknowledged by mainstream science, though modern sightings continue across the USA.

CREATURE PROFILE

Encounters with the Phantom Kangaroo stand out because they occur in places where kangaroos are not supposed to exist. Unlike creatures tied to a single region, these animals are seen across the United States in both rural and suburban areas, often to the shock of motorists and farmers who witness them. The earliest accounts trace back to the 19th Century, when settlers in the Midwest described large leaping animals that resembled kangaroos moving swiftly through tall grass. These reports continue into the present day, demonstrating remarkable consistency in both description and behavior.

One of the most striking aspects of the Phantom Kangaroo phenomenon is the geographical spread of sightings. Reports surface from Wisconsin and Illinois to Pennsylvania and New Jersey, as well as from Texas, Kentucky, and other states. The animals are typically observed in farmlands, forest edges, or near roads, where their hopping locomotion makes them stand out from native wildlife. Their presence in multiple environments suggests either an introduced population that remains hidden or a still-unknown species that has adapted to living in North America.

Witnesses consistently describe a creature between 4 and 8 feet tall with muscular hind legs, a long balancing tail, and short fur. While many match the general outline of a kangaroo, some are said to have unusual proportions such as shorter arms or broader heads. Their eyes shine in the dark when caught by headlights, often startling drivers who then watch the animal bound away into fields or tree lines. Unlike deer they move in long deliberate hops that leave distinctive impressions in soil; yet these tracks rarely last long enough to be examined by zoologists.

Feeding habits appear diverse, with reports of Phantom Kangaroos grazing in cornfields, or on hay or wild grass. Others are seen rummaging through garbage or preying on small animals such as chickens, rabbits, or even stray cats. Some accounts speak of them scavenging carrion, giving them a more omnivorous profile than their Australian counterparts. This variability may reflect either multiple undiscovered species or simply the adaptive diet of a large animal living outside its expected environment.

Behavioral patterns suggest both elusiveness and boldness. While many Phantom Kangaroos vanish quickly upon being seen, others approach farmyards or linger on rural roads. Isolated cases describe aggressive encounters where the animal reportedly attacked dogs or attempted to defend itself against humans. These incidents recall the power of known kangaroos, whose hind legs and sharp claws can inflict serious injury.

Explanations range from escaped zoo animals to feral descendants of imported kangaroos; yet the sheer number of sightings over many decades indicates a more complex reality. If these were simply isolated escapees one would expect the population to dwindle without breeding; yet new reports continue to surface. The consistency of description across states separated by thousands of miles raises the question of whether an undiscovered North American marsupial exists alongside more familiar wildlife.

Though mainstream science does not recognize the Phantom Kangaroo, the animal remains firmly reported in both older folklore and present-day accounts. Its ability to appear suddenly, thrive across different climates, and disappear without leaving conclusive traces places it among the most baffling cryptids in North America. Until physical remains are recovered the Phantom Kangaroo will continue to occupy a space between documented zoology and unexplained reality, a creature that resists easy classification yet persists across generations of witnesses.

According to eyewitness reports the Phantom Kangaroo is known to pursue and attack livestock, pets, and even humans, with an unnatural ferocity. Copyright © Lochlainn Seabrook.

POPOBAWA

The eerie, bat-like, 6 foot tall Popobawa, as described by the terrified villagers of Tanzania. Copyright © Lochlainn Seabrook.

QUICK FACTS

NAME: Popobawa.
FIRST SIGHTING: 1970s.
LOCATION: Zanzibar and Pemba Island, Tanzania.
SIZE: Height 5 to 6 feet, wingspan 10 feet, weight 200 to 300 pounds.
APPEARANCE: Humanoid figure with large bat-like wings, pointed ears, sharp claws, and distorted facial features.
EYES: Large, glowing, and red or yellow depending on the report.
SKIN/FUR: Dark gray to black skin, often described as leathery and rough.
DIET: Said to feed on blood, psychic energy, and human fear; attacks include both physical assault and draining of vitality.
MOVEMENT: Walks on two legs, flies with strong wingbeats, sometimes glides silently.
NOTABLE BEHAVIOR: Targets people in their homes at night, often attacking entire households during outbreaks of sightings. Known for violent encounters and poltergeist-like activity.
FIRST REPORTED BY: Residents of Pemba Island during a wave of attacks in the 1970s.
CREATURE CLASSIFICATION: Winged humanoid cryptid, often compared to *Chiroptera*-like beings—but with supernatural attributes.
STATUS: Not recognized by mainstream science, though widespread testimonies continue to affirm its presence.

CREATURE PROFILE

Few cryptids inspire the same level of community-wide terror as the Popobawa. Unlike lake or forest beings that can be avoided through distance, this winged predator is said to invade homes directly, leaving little chance for escape. Its name translates as "bat-wing" in Swahili, a fitting description for a figure remembered for its broad wings and nocturnal assaults. The accounts originate on the Tanzanian islands of Pemba and Zanzibar, where whole villages have reported being visited by the creature in sudden waves of sightings. These episodes continue into modern times, often lasting several nights before fading again into silence.

The physical descriptions of Popobawa remain remarkably consistent across decades of reports. Witnesses describe a humanoid form standing about 5 or 6 feet tall with a wingspan that can reach 10 feet. Its wings resemble those of a bat, leathery and strong enough to support rapid flight. The head is sometimes human-like but distorted, with pointed ears, fangs, and an elongated face. Its eyes glow in the darkness, most often red but occasionally yellow, giving it an unmistakable presence when sighted in poorly lit rooms or open skies. Skin is described as rough, gray to black, and without hair.

What sets Popobawa apart from many winged cryptids is its behavior. Rather than remaining an elusive shadow seen only on rare occasions, the creature is feared for entering homes at night and attacking entire households. Families claim that if one person is attacked, others in the household often follow, suggesting a pattern of targeted intimidation. The assaults vary from poltergeist-like disturbances to direct physical aggression, sometimes accompanied by a suffocating odor or the sound of flapping wings. Witnesses frequently speak of paralysis, terror, and in some cases physical wounds. This has led to the widespread belief that Popobawa feeds on both the physical body and the fear it generates, suggesting a mixed diet of blood, life force, and psychic energy.

Its movement is equally threatening. Reports indicate that Popobawa can walk upright like a man, its heavy claws scraping against the floor. When airborne it either beats its wings with enough force to shake roofs or glides in silence until it lands. People claim that doors and windows provide no protection, as the creature can simply pass through barriers—another detail that blurs the line between cryptozoology and the supernatural. Still, many eyewitnesses emphasize its solid weight, great strength, and physical presence, treating it as a creature of flesh and bone.

The first widespread outbreak occurred on Pemba Island in the mid-1970s. Since then waves of sightings have recurred every few years. Villagers describe the same winged humanoid, and during such outbreaks whole communities may sleep outside in groups to avoid nighttime assaults. The persistence of testimony across generations, combined with the consistency of the description, provides compelling evidence that something more than folklore is involved.

In classification terms Popobawa is best placed among winged humanoid cryptids, loosely compared to giant bats of the order *Chiroptera*, yet exhibiting abilities beyond any known animal. It stands outside scientific recognition. Yet eyewitness accounts and the intensity of local tradition lend it a powerful reality. While unverified by mainstream science, Popobawa continues to be feared and spoken of as an active predator whose presence can unsettle entire islands.

The East African Popobawa is said to easily gain access to homes, whereupon it traps and attacks unsuspecting people in their sleep. This has prompted entire communities to sleep outside for protection, suggesting that the horrifying creature is not a myth but a real biological entity. Copyright © Lochlainn Seabrook.

PTEROSAUR

A variety of pterosaur-like creatures have been reported, and continue to be reported, around the world—including in the United States. Could they all be hoaxes and misidentifications? Copyright © Lochlainn Seabrook.

QUICK FACTS

NAME: Pterosaur.
FIRST SIGHTING: 16th Century.
LOCATION: Global, with reports in the USA, Africa, Papua New Guinea, and Latin America.
SIZE: Wingspans from 6 feet to over 30 feet, with weight estimates between 40 and 500 pounds.
APPEARANCE: Large flying reptile with leathery bat-like wings, long pointed beak, and often a cranial crest.
EYES: Large, forward-facing, adapted for night or low-light vision.
SKIN/FUR: Predominantly scaly or leathery, sometimes reported with sparse hair-like filaments.
DIET: Said to feed on fish, carrion, livestock, and occasionally small to medium land animals; opportunistic hunter and scavenger.
MOVEMENT: Powerful aerial glider with strong flapping ability; awkward on the ground but capable of hopping or short walks.
NOTABLE BEHAVIOR: Frequently linked to livestock attacks, fish snatching, and terrifying vocalizations; often reported flying in pairs or solitary.
FIRST REPORTED BY: Early European explorers, sailors, and tribal peoples in multiple regions.
CREATURE CLASSIFICATION: Surviving member of *Pterosauria*.
STATUS: Not accepted by mainstream science, though accounts continue into modern times.

CREATURE PROFILE

Across many lands there are stories of winged reptiles that resemble the prehistoric order *Pterosauria*. These accounts are not confined to a single culture or location, which suggests that the phenomenon is more than a localized legend. From the forests of Africa to the swamps of Papua New Guinea and the deserts of the American Southwest, witnesses continue to describe enormous creatures that evoke the imagery of fossilized pterosaurs thought to have vanished 66 million years ago.

Reports vary in detail yet share common features. The wings are usually leathery, stretched taut like those of a bat, rather than feathered. Lengths of 6 to 30 feet across are often cited, with bodies proportionately slender and lightweight for flight. Observers frequently mention elongated beaks with sharp teeth and, in some cases, prominent cranial crests reminiscent of known pterosaur genera such as *Pteranodon* or *Rhamphorhynchus*. The eyes are described as unusually large, glowing at night, which may indicate an adaptation to hunting in darkness or twilight.

Sightings have been consistent for centuries. European sailors of the 16th and 17th Centuries claimed to see giant flying reptiles over the oceans. In the 19th Century pioneers in the USA reported creatures dubbed "thunderbirds"—though their morphology often matched pterosaur characteristics more than avian ones. In the 20th and 21st Centuries modern witnesses in Papua New Guinea describe the "Ropen," a bioluminescent winged reptile that locals insist is a living pterosaur. Similarly, in Africa the "Kongamato" terrifies those who encounter it, with attacks on canoes and fishermen being a recurrent theme. In Texas and Arizona eyewitnesses continue to claim encounters with creatures that match these descriptions, suggesting a broader distribution than folklore alone can explain.

Feeding behavior attributed to pterosaurs in these reports is varied but plausible for a large aerial predator. Accounts mention the seizing of fish directly from rivers and lakes, swooping down on small mammals, and occasionally attacking domestic animals such as goats or chickens. Some stories describe the creatures feeding on carrion, circling over carcasses like vultures before landing awkwardly to feed. This opportunistic diet would allow survival across many ecosystems, from tropical jungles to arid deserts.

Movement in flight is often characterized by long glides punctuated with slow but powerful wingbeats. Witnesses describe the sound of leathery wings cutting the air. When grounded, pterosaurs are said to move awkwardly, hopping or shuffling, consistent with their anatomy as reconstructed from fossils. Their behavior can be aggressive when threatened, with accounts of hissing, shrieking, or growling vocalizations that frighten both people and animals.

Cultural interpretations vary. In New Guinea the Ropen is tied to ancestral traditions and warnings of danger. Among some Native American tribes Thunderbird legends may have overlapped with sightings of giant winged reptiles, though many tribes distinguished between birds and reptilian forms. African traditions treat the Kongamato as a genuine predator still inhabiting rivers and marshes. These independent streams of testimony, separated by geography and culture, strengthen the argument that eyewitnesses are describing a real creature rather than a shared myth.

Mainstream zoology currently dismisses the idea of living pterosaurs, regarding them as long extinct. Yet the persistence of sightings into the present day challenges this conclusion. While no specimen has been captured, the consistency of descriptions across centuries suggests the probability of a surviving lineage. Whether they represent relict populations hidden in remote habitats or occasional migrants that traverse great distances, the evidence from human encounters cannot be easily ignored. For now, the living pterosaur remains unverified; yet the volume of accounts points to an extraordinary natural mystery still unfolding, one that may connect the prehistoric world to the modern one.

Conventional science tells us that pterosaurs disappeared during the Cretaceous–Paleogene extinction event some 66 million years ago. What then are people seeing in the skies today? Copyright © Lochlainn Seabrook.

PUKWUDGIE

Lochlainn Seabrook

Frightening encounters with New England's mischievous, even dangerous, Pukwudgie have been reported for some 400 years, right into the present. Copyright © Lochlainn Seabrook.

QUICK FACTS

NAME: Pukwudgie.
FIRST SIGHTING: 17th Century.
LOCATION: New England, particularly Massachusetts, Rhode Island, and surrounding regions.
SIZE: Between 2 and 4 feet tall, estimated weight 40 to 90 pounds.
APPEARANCE: Small humanoid with exaggerated facial features (large nose, pointed ears), spiny back, short limbs, and long fingers.
EYES: Large, glowing, often described as red or yellow in the dark.
SKIN/FUR: Rough grayish skin that may give off a soft glow; sometimes said to be covered with short fur or spines.
DIET: Opportunistic omnivore; feeds on berries, nuts, small game, insects, fish, and scavenged human food; in darker traditions, said to consume human flesh or feed on spiritual energy.
MOVEMENT: Walks upright like a human; capable of vanishing, teleportation, or rapid darting through woods; known to move silently when stalking.
NOTABLE BEHAVIOR: Uses trickery, ambush, and illusions; throws sand to blind, creates disorienting lights, lures travelers into danger, and in hostile encounters is said to shoot arrows tipped with poison.
FIRST REPORTED BY: Wampanoag people of Massachusetts.
CREATURE CLASSIFICATION: Small humanoid cryptid with supernatural traits; better known as Little People (*Homo sylvestris folklorica*).
STATUS: Rejected by mainstream science, but oral tradition and eyewitness testimony remain strong and active, particularly in New England and the Great Lakes regions.

CREATURE PROFILE

Among the most notable of North America's "Little People" legends, the Pukwudgie is described as a small, humanoid being with both physical and supernatural traits. Though diminutive in stature it is widely regarded by Native American tribes, particularly the Wampanoag, as a dangerous presence in the forests of New England. The name Pukwudgie roughly translates to "person of the wilderness" in Algonquian languages, underscoring its role as a wild, elusive forest dweller. Unlike benign folklore figures, however, the Pukwudgie is feared for its hostility toward humans.

Oral traditions describe the Pukwudgie as once living in harmony with the Wampanoag people, but eventually turning against them. According to tribal accounts this shift led to an ongoing antagonism: the beings began ambushing travelers, stealing food, setting fires, and even killing those who disrespected them. This reputation remains intact today, as modern witnesses continue to report unsettling encounters with small humanoid shapes darting through woodlands, glowing eyes peering from underbrush, or mysterious lights leading hikers astray. The persistence of such accounts suggests that the Pukwudgie phenomenon is not a relic of folklore alone but an active element of the region's unexplained natural history.

Descriptions are consistent across centuries. Pukwudgies are generally two to four feet tall, with gray or ashen skin, typically giving off a faint shimmer in moonlight. Their features are exaggerated—large noses, pointed ears, and elongated fingers suited for manipulation and mischief. Some reports describe them carrying primitive weapons, such as spears or bows with poisoned tips. Their glowing eyes, most often red or yellow, are said to paralyze or instill dread in those who meet their gaze. Witnesses often note that these creatures appear suddenly and vanish just as quickly, leading to speculation about their ability to become invisible, teleport, or move between dimensions.

Behaviorally, Pukwudgies are complex. They are tricksters and thus sometimes mischievous; yet they are also often malevolent. Common accounts include throwing sand or dust into the eyes of victims, creating phantom lights to lure travelers into swamps or over cliffs, or mimicking voices to draw people deeper into the woods. In Wampanoag tradition they were once linked to fatal disappearances, and in some modern cases they have been blamed for sudden accidents or falls occurring on trails associated with their lore. Yet not all encounters are violent—some people report merely being watched, followed, or unsettled by fleeting glimpses of small odd looking figures in the trees.

Dietary traditions vary, but all emphasize opportunism. Pukwudgies are believed to forage on berries, roots, nuts, and small animals. Some accounts portray them as scavengers of human camps, stealing food at night. More sinister stories describe them preying upon humans, either physically or spiritually. In certain tribal narratives they are said to feed on human life force or souls, lending a supernatural dimension to their menace.

Modern sightings continue to cluster in Massachusetts, especially near Freetown State Forest and the broader Bridgewater Triangle region, an area already known for concentrated paranormal reports. Here hikers, campers, and locals alike describe glowing-eyed figures, phantom lights, and unexplained assaults attributed to Pukwudgies. These ongoing accounts, paired with the long tribal record, lend weight to the idea that these beings may represent an undiscovered species of small hominin or a folkloric entity with real-world manifestations.

Whether considered spirit, cryptid, or something between, the Pukwudgie occupies a distinct category among North America's unexplained creatures. Its history of hostility, combined with centuries of consistent descriptions and present-day reports, makes it one of the most compelling examples of the Little People tradition in global cryptozoology.

Does the Pukwudgie still inhabit the shadowy forests of New England? Many believe so.

The 4 foot tall Pukwudgie is known to creep into campsites in nighttime scavenging raids. Copyright © Lochlainn Seabrook.

REPTOID

The Reptoid: a powerful and scary 9 foot tall reptilian-hominid known to engage in telepathic communication and the brutal abduction of humans. Copyright © Lochlainn Seabrook.

QUICK FACTS

NAME: Reptoid.
FIRST SIGHTING: Ancient records traceable to Sumerian and Mesopotamian carvings, with modern reports emerging in the mid-20th Century.
LOCATION: Global, with concentrations in North America, South America, Europe, and Australia.
SIZE: Typically 6 to 9 feet tall, weighing between 200 and 400 pounds.
APPEARANCE: Humanoid body with strong musculature, reptilian head and snout, clawed hands, and long tail reported in some encounters. Covered with scales, sometimes with a crest or ridged skull.
EYES: Large, slit-pupiled eyes that glow red, yellow, or green depending on the account.
SKIN/FUR: Scaled, often described as green, brown, or gray, with sheen ranging from matte to oily. No fur reported.
DIET: Reported as omnivorous but with strong carnivorous tendencies; alleged to consume livestock, wild game, and in some accounts, human flesh. Some witnesses claim they subsist partly on underground or aquatic resources.
MOVEMENT: Bipedal with a digitigrade stance, though some reports note quadrupedal movement when running. Capable of great agility, climbing, and stealth.
NOTABLE BEHAVIOR: Often described as secretive and territorial. Associated with subterranean tunnels, caves, or underground bases. Some reports link them to abductions, encounters with military personnel, and possible telepathic communication.
FIRST REPORTED BY: Ancient Mesopotamian scribes; in modern times, witnesses include miners, military servicemen, and civilians.
CREATURE CLASSIFICATION: Cryptohominid, possibly a surviving reptilian lineage or an intelligent subterranean species
STATUS: Unconfirmed by mainstream science, but consistently reported from antiquity into the present day.

CREATURE PROFILE

Among the most unsettling cryptid reports are those describing reptilian humanoids, more commonly known as Reptoids. Unlike many creatures that remain tied to a single landscape or culture, accounts of these beings stretch across continents and millennia. Ancient carvings from Mesopotamia and Mesoamerica show serpent-headed deities or reptilian humanoids, suggesting that the phenomenon is deeply embedded in human memory. In modern times sightings describe living, flesh-and-blood entities that continue to appear in wilderness regions, underground systems, and occasionally even near human settlements.

Witnesses generally describe Reptoids as tall, muscular humanoids with distinctly reptilian features. Their skin is scaly, rough, and often tinged with green or gray hues. Many observers remark upon their eyes, which are almond-shaped with vertical slit pupils and a phosphorescent glow visible in the dark. This feature is often cited as the most terrifying aspect of encounters, giving the impression of an intelligent predator watching from the shadows.

Reptoids are frequently associated with subterranean environments. Testimonies from spelunkers, miners, and construction workers reference contact with reptilian figures emerging from caves or deep tunnels. Some encounters describe their presence in abandoned mines or natural caverns, as if the creatures maintain a hidden organized existence beneath the Earth's surface. Reports from desert and mountainous regions often describe them appearing suddenly, only to vanish into rocky crevices or underground passageways.

Movement is another defining feature. Despite their size Reptoids are said to move with surprising speed and agility. Witnesses claim they are able to leap great distances, climb sheer rock faces, and even run on all fours when necessary. This combination of stealth and power suggests a creature evolved for both predation and evasion. Accounts also indicate that they may emit low hissing sounds, guttural growls, or even use telepathic communication—reinforcing the idea that they are more than mere animals.

Dietary habits are reported with disturbing detail. Farmers in rural areas recount livestock disappearing, with evidence of predation resembling reptilian bites. Some researchers suggest a varied diet that includes meat, fish, and possibly plants or fungi found underground. More sinister accounts propose that Reptoids may prey upon humans, a claim bolstered by stories of abductions and missing persons tied to areas where sightings are common.

Behaviorally, Reptoids are described as highly intelligent, secretive, and territorial. Some reports claim they display coordinated group activity, suggesting a form of social hierarchy. In certain encounters witnesses describe an uncanny sense of being observed or influenced mentally, leading to speculation about telepathic capabilities. Military and government-related sightings in the 20th Century add further intrigue, with personnel describing encounters near restricted zones or subterranean facilities.

Encounters often leave witnesses with a sense of intelligence and watchfulness. Unlike other cryptids that flee from contact, Reptoids sometimes remain in place, studying humans with an unbroken gaze. This behavior, coupled with reports of communication and planning, has led some researchers to propose that Reptoids are not merely surviving reptiles but part of an organized, intelligent species that has maintained its secrecy for millennia.

Today, reports of Reptoids continue, particularly in North America and South America, where remote forests, deserts, and mountains provide ample concealment. Whether they represent an undiscovered branch of hominin evolution, a surviving lineage of ancient reptilian life, or something more otherworldly remains uncertain.

Though excluded from the catalogs of mainstream science, the evidence from Sumerian records through to modern abduction narratives forms a continuous chain of testimony. Reptoids remain one of the strongest cases for the existence of an intelligent non-human lineage, possibly predating or evolving alongside mankind. Whether they are the same beings honored and feared by ancient Mesopotamians or a related species that lives on today, the Reptoid stands as one of the most compelling mysteries in cryptozoology.

Some eyewitnesses report observing Reptoids working in secret underground research facilities. What they are doing, and why, is unknown. Copyright © Lochlainn Seabrook.

ROPEN

The 8 foot long Ropen, a nocturnal flying cryptid of Papua New Guinea, is described as glowing in the night sky with leathery wings and a long spade-tipped tail. Copyright © Lochlainn Seabrook.

QUICK FACTS

NAME: Ropen.
FIRST SIGHTING: Recorded by missionaries in the early 20th century.
LOCATION: Papua New Guinea.
SIZE: Wingspan estimated at 12-20 feet, body length about 6-8 feet, weight possibly 40-60 pounds.
APPEARANCE: Large leathery-winged creature resembling a pterosaur with a long tail and head crest.
EYES: Reported as large, round, and reflective, sometimes glowing red or orange at night.
SKIN/FUR: Described as hairless with dark gray or brown reptilian skin.
DIET: Believed to feed on fish, carrion, large insects, small reptiles, and possibly small mammals or birds. Eyewitnesses have also linked it to attacks on human remains.
MOVEMENT: Flies with strong batlike wingbeats, sometimes glides silently for long distances. Said to perch in tall trees or caves by day.
NOTABLE BEHAVIOR: Emits a bioluminescent glow during nocturnal flights. Reported to raid graves, attack livestock, and pursue canoes at sea. Locals also note its distinctive croaking or screeching call.
FIRST REPORTED BY: Western missionaries and native islanders.
CREATURE CLASSIFICATION: Considered by witnesses to be a surviving *Pterosauria*, often compared to *Pteranodon* or *Rhamphorhynchus*.
STATUS: Not recognized by mainstream science, though sightings continue into modern times.

CREATURE PROFILE

Legends surrounding the Ropen remain some of the most striking in the South Pacific. Accounts from Papua New Guinea describe a massive flying creature that bears a strong resemblance to the extinct pterosaurs of the Mesozoic era. Unlike many cryptids that are linked only to ancient folklore, the Ropen is still reported today, particularly by islanders living in remote coastal villages. These reports emphasize that the creature is no myth but a real presence that commands both awe and fear.

The Ropen is said to patrol the skies at night, often appearing with a glowing underside or tail tip that witnesses describe as bioluminescent. This unusual feature sets it apart from other cryptids. The glow is not random but consistent in reports, usually flashing or pulsing while the animal is in flight. Islanders believe the light serves either to startle prey or to signal other Ropen in the area. This detail has drawn particular attention from researchers because it suggests a biological adaptation not usually associated with reptiles of its supposed lineage.

Eyewitness descriptions of the Ropen depict a leathery body covered in reptilian skin, devoid of feathers or fur. Its wings are said to stretch 12-15 feet across, with a muscular build that allows for powerful wingbeats followed by long silent glides. The tail is often noted as long and ending in a diamond-shaped or bulbous structure, consistent with reconstructions of certain long-tailed pterosaurs such as *Rhamphorhynchus*. The head is described as elongated, sometimes with a crest, while the eyes appear large and reflective in torchlight. These physical traits are reported with remarkable consistency across different islands and generations.

Dietary habits attributed to the Ropen are diverse. Fishermen recount the creature swooping low over rivers and reefs to seize fish, while others describe it as a scavenger that digs into shallow graves or raids livestock pens. Its association with disturbed graves has made it an object of dread, leading many villagers to bury their dead under heavy stones. Reports of carrion feeding reinforce the view that the Ropen is an opportunistic predator, capable of surviving on whatever food is most available in its environment.

Movement is another aspect often emphasized by witnesses. In flight the Ropen is said to combine heavy flapping with periods of smooth gliding, much like modern seabirds but with a distinctly reptilian form. When perched it prefers cliffs, caves, or the upper branches of tall trees. Villagers traveling at night sometimes report being shadowed by the glowing creature as it circles above them, creating an atmosphere of deep unease.

Notably, the Ropen has a strong cultural presence among the islanders. For them it is not a mythical being but a dangerous animal that must be respected. Missionaries stationed in Papua New Guinea during the early 20th Century were among the first outsiders to record reports of the creature. Since then modern cryptozoologists have made expeditions to the region in hopes of capturing photographic or physical evidence; but so far only anecdotal accounts, blurry images, and native testimony have emerged.

The classification of the Ropen has centered on the idea that it may be a living descendant of the order *Pterosauria*. Eyewitness descriptions align with reconstructions of ancient flying reptiles, fueling speculation that small populations might have survived in isolated tropical environments. Mainstream science rejects this conclusion, citing the absence of fossil continuity and physical remains. Yet the persistence of sightings, the uniformity of descriptions, and the cultural significance of the Ropen keep the debate alive.

While no specimen has been captured the Ropen remains an active subject of field study. Expeditions continue, and villagers maintain that the animal is a real and dangerous part of their environment. Whether considered a living fossil, a misidentified bird or bat, or an undiscovered reptile, the Ropen continues to inspire serious interest. It represents one of the most compelling examples of how ancient forms may still linger in the modern world.

The eerie Ropen, with its massive 20 foot wingspan, is reported to dig up human graves for food, just one of many reasons the creature fills native Papua New Guineans with panic and horror. Copyright © Lochlainn Seabrook.

ROUGAROU

The 8 foot tall Rougarou in its Louisiana bayou habitat, its glowing eyes and lupine-humanoid features evoking both mystery and menace. Copyright © Lochlainn Seabrook.

QUICK FACTS

NAME: Rougarou.
FIRST SIGHTING: 18th Century.
LOCATION: Mainly Louisiana swamps, but also Texas, Mississippi, Florida, Arkansas, and Alabama, USA.
SIZE: Height 6-8 feet, weight estimated 250-400 pounds.
APPEARANCE: A bipedal beast with a human-like body and a wolf or dog-like head.
EYES: Large, glowing red or orange eyes.
SKIN/FUR: Covered in coarse dark brown or black fur.
DIET: Believed to feed on livestock, deer, small mammals, fish, and occasionally humans. Known to scavenge carrion when prey is scarce. Feeds heavily at night and is drawn to blood and fresh kills. Diet is opportunistic and adaptable to the swamp environment.
MOVEMENT: Walks upright on two legs but can drop to all fours when chasing prey. Swift and agile with long strides.
NOTABLE BEHAVIOR: Associated with shapeshifting. Said to prowl at night, avoid fire, and target those who break oaths. Roams bayous silently but lets out loud howls when hunting.
FIRST REPORTED BY: French settlers and Cajun communities.
CREATURE CLASSIFICATION: Cryptid canid-hominid hybrid.
STATUS: Not acknowledged by mainstream science, though sightings in Louisiana continue into the present day.

CREATURE PROFILE

The Rougarou is most often spoken of in Cajun communities as a creature that embodies both legend and lived experience. The Rougarou indeed carries the weight of cultural tradition, extending its reach across families who have passed down accounts for generations. In Louisiana's swamp country the name is known and feared, not as a distant myth but as an active warning. Farmers, fishermen, and trappers share stories of encounters with a tall, furred predator whose eyes glow brightly in the night.

The creature's body is described as upright and humanoid in frame, yet capped by the unmistakable head of a wolf or large dog. Witnesses report that it moves comfortably on two legs, striding with surprising speed through marshy ground, but when necessary it drops to all fours and accelerates in short violent bursts. These descriptions mark the Rougarou as an adaptable hunter, one that thrives in both thick forests and open wetlands. The combination of height, strength, and agility places it among the most formidable cryptids said to inhabit North America.

Its feeding habits draw particular attention. Accounts stress that it takes livestock such as cattle, goats, and chickens, though this often occurs near the edge of human settlement where opportunity is greatest. In deeper swamp territory it preys on deer, fish, and small mammals. Local accounts even suggest it consumes carrion when conditions demand it, demonstrating an ability to survive lean periods by scavenging. What unites all descriptions is the Rougarou's attraction to fresh blood and recent kills. Hunters who lose deer to an unseen predator often point to the Rougarou as the culprit.

Sightings are not limited to a distant past. Reports continue in rural Louisiana, especially around Acadiana and the Atchafalaya Basin. Witnesses claim to see tall wolf-headed figures crossing roads, watching from treelines, or approaching livestock pens under cover of night. These accounts are consistent with older traditions that warn of a beast that comes for those who break oaths or turn from faith. Such cultural framing suggests the Rougarou holds a dual role: a real predator in the eyes of many and a moral enforcer in local belief.

The origin of the name traces to French settlers who brought stories of the *loup-garou*, a werewolf of European folklore. In Louisiana the tale evolved under Cajun influence into the Rougarou, shaped by the environment of bayous and swamps. The fusion of European legend and New World setting produced a unique cryptid identity, distinct from other werewolf traditions. Unlike European werewolves bound to the cycle of the moon, the Rougarou appears at will and often remains in bestial form for prolonged periods.

Behavioral details reveal further data. The creature is said to fear fire and can be repelled by light. Yet it prowls most effectively in the heavy darkness of swamp nights, when its glowing eyes are the only warning sign before an encounter. Howls echo through the cypress trees, serving both as a hunting tactic and as a signal that the predator is near. For many Cajun residents this blend of physical and supernatural traits strengthens belief in its reality.

While mainstream science does not recognize the Rougarou, the continuity of reports and their alignment across generations argue for a foundation beyond mere legend. Whether a surviving relic species, a shapeshifting being, or an as-yet undocumented predator, the Rougarou remains one of the most persistent cryptid figures in the United States. Its reputation is not confined to books but is alive in the warnings and stories of those who still live among the swamps it is said to roam.

The flesh-eating, blood-drinking Rougarou is said to prowl the mist-enshrouded swamps of the American South, threatening all who encroach on its domain. Copyright © Lochlainn Seabrook.

SELKIE

Haunting, beautiful, and mysterious, a 7 foot long Selkie (in its human female form) rests on the rocky shores of a Scottish island. Copyright © Lochlainn Seabrook.

QUICK FACTS

NAME: Selkie.
FIRST SIGHTING: Recorded in oral tradition as early as the 10th Century.
LOCATION: Coastal regions of Scotland, Ireland, and Northern Europe.
SIZE: In seal form 5-6 feet long and 200-300 pounds. In human form 5-7 feet tall and 120-180 pounds.
APPEARANCE: As seals in the water or as attractive men and women when on land.
EYES: Large, dark, and expressive.
SKIN/FUR: Thick gray or brown fur as seals; pale smooth skin in human guise.
DIET: Fish, squid, and other marine life as seals; in human form they may consume standard human foods.
MOVEMENT: Swift swimming with powerful flippers; upright bipedal gait on land in human form.
NOTABLE BEHAVIOR: Transformation by shedding or donning a seal skin; attraction to shorelines; reported unions with humans.
FIRST REPORTED BY: Norse and Celtic seafarers.
CREATURE CLASSIFICATION: Shape-shifter with marine mammal and human forms and characteristics.
STATUS: Not recognized by mainstream science, though sightings and traditions are ongoing.

CREATURE PROFILE

Accounts of the Selkie differ from many cryptids because the being is said to exist both in the sea and on land, changing form depending on circumstance. Along the coasts of Scotland, Ireland, and the Northern Isles, fishermen and islanders continue to share descriptions of these beings as seals that remove their skins to reveal men and women of striking beauty. These stories are not static folklore alone, for people in these regions still claim to witness unusual encounters that support the long tradition of Selkies as real and living entities.

The transformation is central to the Selkie identity. Eyewitnesses often describe seals coming ashore, then shaking off a skin and walking inland as humans. The skin is considered vital, for without it the Selkie cannot return to the sea. Tales warn that stolen or hidden skins prevent the creature from resuming its seal form, binding it permanently to human existence. Though this has been written down as legend, some coastal dwellers regard these reports as grounded in real phenomena, suggesting that Selkies represent a species adapted to life in both environments.

Dietary habits align with their dual existence. In seal form Selkies feed upon the same resources as ordinary pinnipeds, including fish shoals, squid, and crustaceans. In their human guise, however, they are said to join coastal households and consume common terrestrial foods. Such adaptability points toward a biological model of an amphibious shapeshifter whose digestive system can function in both domains.

Behavioral reports are consistent across the centuries. Selkies are often associated with romance, either initiating contact with humans or being drawn into relationships when their skins are stolen. Some family lineages in the North Atlantic Isles even claim descent from Selkie-human unions, citing physical traits such as webbed fingers or an unusual affinity for the sea as evidence of hybrid ancestry. This continuity strengthens the view that the Selkie phenomenon is more than myth, being instead a record of repeated encounters across generations.

Movement is another defining feature. In the water Selkies swim with a speed and grace exceeding normal seals, some witnesses insisting they seem to understand and respond to human presence with awareness. On land in human form they move with agility, though often described as slightly unworldly, as if unused to prolonged terrestrial life. This dual locomotion adds further support to the classification of Selkies as true shape-shifters rather than ordinary marine animals.

The earliest references trace back to Norse sagas and Celtic songs, which both contain detailed depictions of seal-folk whose skins grant them passage between two worlds. These accounts predate later folkloric elaborations and suggest a deeper root in cultural memory, possibly born from genuine observations of an undiscovered marine-humanoid species. Given that coastal communities were highly observant of their environment for survival, such testimony carries weight.

Modern sightings, though less publicized, continue to surface. Fishermen occasionally report seals behaving in unusual ways, seemingly more aware and anthropomorphic than normal. Some coastal families continue to pass down stories of strangers who appeared after storms, only to vanish near the waterline leaving behind a seal skin. These testimonies, though not formally documented by science, form part of a persistent living tradition.

Mainstream zoology excludes the Selkie from accepted classifications; yet consistent descriptions, cultural continuity, modern reports, and the webbing between our 4th and 5th fingers (part of the Aquatic Ape Hypothesis), argue that the subject deserves continued study.

Whether viewed as a symbolic representation of human-sea relationships or as a living cryptid with real biological foundations, the Selkie stands as one of the most enduring figures of the North Atlantic coasts. Its dual identity as seal and human distinguishes it from most other cryptids and keeps it firmly embedded in the natural history of the region.

A Selkie in its seal form, manifesting one of its most uncanny dualistic traits: the warmth of a human and the coldness of wild animal. Copyright © Lochlainn Seabrook.

SHUNKA WARAKIN

The 7 foot long, morphologically weird Shunka Warakin on a moonlit Montana prairie, its otherworldly gaze radiating both danger and enigma. Copyright © Lochlainn Seabrook.

QUICK FACTS

NAME: Shunka Warakin.
FIRST SIGHTING: Mid-19th Century.
LOCATION: Montana, USA, and surrounding Northern Plains.
SIZE: Length 6-7 feet, height 3 feet at the shoulder, weight 120-150 pounds.
APPEARANCE: Wolf-like body with sloping back, long jaws, and shorter legs than a wolf.
EYES: Small, round, and often reported as glowing in low light.
SKIN/FUR: Dark shaggy fur, usually black or brown with a coarse texture.
DIET: Opportunistic carnivore; feeds on livestock, wild game, carrion, and possibly fish; kills sheep, horses, and dogs but also scavenges when necessary.
MOVEMENT: Runs low to the ground with a bounding gait, faster than domestic dogs; often reported leaping rather than trotting.
NOTABLE BEHAVIOR: Stalks herds and farmsteads, carries off animals, shows boldness toward humans, and sometimes attacks without fear.
FIRST REPORTED BY: Native American tribes of the Northern Plains and early European settlers.
CREATURE CLASSIFICATION: Canid-like cryptid, possibly related to prehistoric hyena (*Chasmaporthetes*) or an unknown wolf species.
STATUS: Not recognized by mainstream science, but eyewitness sightings continue into the present day.

CREATURE PROFILE

In the windswept prairies of the Northern Plains a predator unlike any known wolf or dog is said to move silently among the shadows. The Shunka Warakin is a creature both feared and respected, described as a powerful beast that raids livestock and challenges the authority of hunters and ranchers. While wolves, coyotes, and wild dogs are common in the region, this animal is consistently portrayed as something apart. Its body is longer and lower than a wolf's, with a sloping back that gives it a hyena-like appearance. Its jaws are reported as unusually elongated, capable of seizing and carrying off sheep or even small horses.

Accounts of the Shunka Warakin extend back to the oral traditions of Native American tribes. Among the Ioway the animal was named *Shunka Warakin*, which loosely translates as "carries off dogs." Their stories describe a relentless predator that moved quickly, struck boldly, and could not be easily tracked or killed. These tales were later repeated by European settlers who soon added their own encounters, often linked to missing livestock or unexplained attacks on farm animals.

Descriptions of the animal emphasize its odd shape. It is roughly 6 to 7 feet long, with shoulders no higher than 3 feet, making it appear low-slung yet powerful. Its fur is dark and shaggy, usually black or deep brown. The eyes are often described as round and glowing when caught in lantern light, adding to its reputation as a supernatural menace. Witnesses say it moves differently from wolves or coyotes. Instead of a smooth lope it bounds with sudden bursts, springing across open ground with a speed that domestic dogs cannot match. This peculiar gait has led some to compare it with African hyenas.

The diet of the Shunka Warakin is that of an opportunistic carnivore. It preys upon sheep, calves, dogs, and even young horses. Farmers report finding animals carried away entirely or left half-eaten near the edges of fields. In lean times it scavenges carrion, feasting on dead cattle or wild deer. Hunters have found evidence of large canid tracks near carcasses, yet the stride and shape of these tracks often differ from wolves known to the area.

Behavioral reports consistently point to its extreme boldness. Unlike wolves, which usually avoid human settlements, the Shunka Warakin ventures near barns and corrals, and is sometimes even seen pacing along fences at dusk. It shows little hesitation in attacking when threatened. Some accounts describe it confronting hunters directly before bounding away into the plains. This lack of fear sets it apart from other wild predators of the region.

Speculation about its identity has ranged widely. Some zoologists suggest that if real it could represent a surviving remnant of an extinct species such as the North American hyena *Chasmaporthetes*. Others believe it may be an unknown branch of wolf, perhaps a relic population of a prehistoric canid. Locals simply regard it as a predator that defies classification but continues to kill livestock and trouble ranchers.

Modern sightings have not ceased. Ranchers in Montana and surrounding states still speak of large dark canids that do not match wolves or dogs. In recent years taxidermied specimens resembling the Shunka Warakin have surfaced, lending weight to claims that the creature has been hunted more than once. For many these examples prove that the Shunka Warakin is not myth but a genuine predator that science has yet to properly acknowledge.

The Shunka Warakin therefore occupies a unique position in North American folklore and natural history. It is feared as a livestock killer, discussed as a possible prehistoric survivor, and remembered in Native traditions as a beast with power beyond ordinary animals. Though not accepted by mainstream science, its legend continues across generations. In fact, present day sightings suggest that this shadowy predator is not only real, but continues to roam the wide open prairies of the American West.

The 150 pound, hyena-wolf-like Shunka Warakin is reported to prey on pet dogs, the origin of its Native American name. Copyright © Lochlainn Seabrook.

SIGBIN

The elusive, 4 foot tall, blood-sucking Sigbin, a Filipino cryptid said to possess supernatural powers. Copyright © Lochlainn Seabrook.

QUICK FACTS

NAME: Sigbin.
FIRST SIGHTING: 16th Century.
LOCATION: Philippines.
SIZE: Around 2 feet to 4 feet tall, weighing 30 to 60 pounds.
APPEARANCE: Goat-like body with large ears, long flexible tail, and backward-facing hind legs.
EYES: Often described as glowing red or green.
SKIN/FUR: Hairless or thinly furred, usually dark gray or black.
DIET: Said to be vampiric: consumes the blood and entrails of freshly killed animals; also reported to feed on the breath of sleeping children.
MOVEMENT: Walks backwards with head lowered, legs bent in reverse orientation. Capable of sudden bounding leaps.
NOTABLE BEHAVIOR: Draws life force from victims, collects hearts, and is linked to witchcraft. Emits a foul sulfurous odor when nearby.
FIRST REPORTED BY: Early Spanish colonists and local Filipino villagers.
CREATURE CLASSIFICATION: Supernatural predator with mammalian features.
STATUS: Not acknowledged by mainstream science, though modern encounters continue to be reported.

CREATURE PROFILE

In the dense rainforests and remote villages of the Philippines one of the most unusual cryptids is said to roam: the Sigbin. This creature is remembered for its distinctive way of moving, walking backward with its head lowered and hind legs bent in reverse. Unlike other regional cryptids that take familiar animal forms, the Sigbin blends traits of goat, kangaroo, and reptile into a singular and unsettling figure.

Descriptions emphasize its long floppy ears, flexible whip-like tail, and lean body often without fur. Its most disturbing feature is its inverted gait, which immediately sets it apart from any known mammal. Witnesses claim its eyes shine in the dark with a green or blood-red glow, and many insist that a sulfurous odor announces its approach. This smell is said to be so strong that it clings to areas long after the animal has passed.

The diet attributed to the Sigbin reinforces its role as a feared nocturnal predator. Locals report that it kills livestock by draining their blood or removing their entrails. Other accounts describe it stealing the breath of children as they sleep, leaving them sick or in some cases dead. Older traditions hold that it collects human hearts, storing them in a container for use by witches or sorcerers. In this sense the Sigbin is not only a predator, but also a spiritual agent tied to darker practices.

Accounts trace back to the 16th Century when Spanish colonists recorded hearing of a mysterious beast from villagers. The animal was said to appear most often at night during Holy Week, linking it to times of heightened spiritual significance. Farmers and herders warned that a Sigbin could decimate small flocks in one evening, killing goats and chickens without leaving clear wounds—other than punctures near the chest.

Its method of movement continues to draw the attention of modern researchers. Walking backwards with bent legs requires anatomical structures not known in any standard mammal, yet eyewitnesses remain consistent on this point. Some suggest it moves in sudden jerks, then leaps forward in bursts like a kangaroo, vanishing quickly into thick foliage. This agility would explain why it has never been captured despite generations of reported sightings.

Connections with witchcraft remain strong. In many regions the Sigbin is believed to serve witches as a familiar. It may be summoned, commanded, or even kept in enchanted jars when small. Some families are rumored to secretly own Sigbins, passing them down through generations as guardians or sources of power. Whether physical or supernatural, this belief maintains the animal's presence in daily life, with rural households still leaving protective charms outside their doors.

Modern sightings still occur in isolated villages of the Visayas and Mindanao. Farmers describe hearing odd rustling in fields, finding drained livestock, or seeing a shadowy form bounding in reverse near banana groves. Testimonies are treated seriously within the culture, with people still warning children to avoid walking alone at night. Unlike many cryptids that fade into folklore, the Sigbin continues to command fear as if it were an established predator.

Though mainstream science does not recognize the Sigbin, its description remains unusually consistent across centuries of reports. The combination of anatomical strangeness, predatory behavior, and cultural significance marks it as one of the most distinctive cryptids of Southeast Asia. Whether natural or supernatural the Sigbin stands as a striking example of how living traditions and field testimonies can maintain a creature's reputation long after its first account was made.

A 60 pound Sigbin lashes out at unsuspecting villagers, revealing its horrific vampiric nature. Copyright © Lochlainn Seabrook.

SKUNK APE

A gigantic, 7 foot tall Skunk Ape in its native habitat: the swamps of America's Southeast. Though conventional science does not acknowledge it, consistent modern sightings keep the creature's legend alive. Copyright © Lochlainn Seabrook.

QUICK FACTS

NAME: Skunk Ape.
FIRST SIGHTING: Early 19th Century.
LOCATION: Florida, USA.
SIZE: Height 6-7 feet, weight estimated at 300-450 pounds.
APPEARANCE: Large, bipedal primate with broad shoulders, long arms, and a bulky frame.
EYES: Red or orange glow reported in night encounters.
SKIN/FUR: Covered in long, dark brown to black hair with occasional reddish tones.
DIET: Omnivorous, feeding on wild hogs, deer, fish, turtles, berries, nuts, roots, and human crops when available. Also reported raiding garbage bins, livestock pens, and citrus groves. Evidence suggests a flexible diet adapted to Florida's wetlands and subtropical environment.
MOVEMENT: Walks upright on two legs but can run swiftly; occasionally drops to all fours when moving through thick brush or swamp.
NOTABLE BEHAVIOR: Strong odor resembling sulfur, rotten eggs, or skunk spray. Known to issue loud screams and whistles. Avoids human contact yet observed near farms and highways. Reported to throw rocks and break branches when threatened.
FIRST REPORTED BY: Seminole tribes and early European settlers.
CREATURE CLASSIFICATION: Unverified hominid, sometimes considered a regional *Homo* relic.
STATUS: Unverified by mainstream science, but sightings continue into the present day.

CREATURE PROFILE

Unlike many cryptids that dwell in remote mountain ranges or deep forests, the Skunk Ape inhabits one of the most distinct environments in North America: the subtropical swamps and wetlands of Florida. Credible accounts describe a large primate-like animal that survives in the dense vegetation of the Everglades, where few humans venture at night. Its name comes from the foul odor that often precedes an encounter, likened to a mix of sulfur, rotten eggs, and the spray of a skunk. This pungent trait sets it apart from other hominid reports worldwide and has become the hallmark by which witnesses recognize it.

Physical descriptions are consistent. The Skunk Ape stands between 6 and 7 feet tall and weighs as much as 450 pounds. Its body is covered in thick, dark hair that sometimes shows a reddish tint in sunlight. The face is said to be more ape-like than human, though some reports note a blend of both. Witnesses frequently mention a glowing effect in the eyes, red or orange in color, particularly visible during night encounters when headlights or flashlights are used. The animal's wide shoulders, long arms, and powerful gait give the impression of immense strength, capable of breaking branches, throwing rocks, or even tipping small boats when agitated.

Dietary reports suggest that the Skunk Ape is highly adaptable. In its natural environment it takes advantage of deer, wild hogs, turtles, and fish. It also gathers berries, roots, and nuts when available, showing an opportunistic approach to food sources. Farmers in Florida have blamed crop raids on the creature, particularly citrus groves, and there are accounts of livestock being taken from pens. The scavenging of garbage cans near rural homes is another recurring observation, which places the Skunk Ape in direct overlap with human territory more often than many cryptids.

Movement is typically bipedal, with a fast and steady stride that allows it to cover swampy ground quickly. In denser terrain, however, the Skunk Ape is seen dropping to all fours, a trait that suggests a primate well adapted to maneuvering through mud, cypress knees, and thick brush. Witnesses often remark on its speed, claiming it can outrun a person even across difficult ground. Its vocalizations are another notable feature. Loud screams, howls, and whistles pierce the night, sometimes compared to a woman's shriek or a distressed animal cry. Such calls echo across the wetlands and have been heard by campers, hunters, and park rangers alike.

The first reports come from the Seminole tribes, who regarded the Skunk Ape as a wild man of the swamps. Early European settlers in Florida also documented encounters, often describing a hairy giant that raided their homesteads. Throughout the 20th Century sightings continued to accumulate, and photographs, plaster casts, and even alleged hair samples have been presented, though none have received scientific acceptance. Still, the frequency of encounters in modern times keeps the legend alive. Hunters, motorists, and hikers report sightings every year, and law enforcement agencies occasionally receive calls from alarmed citizens describing large foul-smelling creatures on the edge of their property.

The Skunk Ape remains outside the accepted zoological record, yet it occupies a prominent place in the folklore and natural history of Florida. Its persistence in reports, combined with its unique odor, primate-like build, and adaptability to a challenging environment, make it one of the most distinctive hominid cryptids in the United States.

For those who believe, the Skunk Ape is not a myth but a flesh-and-blood animal, one that continues to roam the swamps and forests of the Sunshine State, just out of reach of modern science.

A Skunk Ape violently shakes a tree in an attempt to scare intruders from its territory, an unforgettable encounter with one of North America's most elusive and frightening cryptids. Copyright © Lochlainn Seabrook.

SNALLYGASTER

The 15 foot long flying reptilian cryptid known as the Snallygaster, perching ominously on a branch in a Maryland forest. Copyright © Lochlainn Seabrook.

QUICK FACTS

NAME: Snallygaster.
FIRST SIGHTING: Early 1700s.
LOCATION: Frederick County, Maryland, United States.
SIZE: Wingspan estimated between 20 and 30 feet; body length 10 to 15 feet; weight estimated at 500-700 pounds.
APPEARANCE: A dragon-like beast with large leathery wings, a birdlike beak lined with sharp metallic teeth, and tentacle-like appendages extending from its face.
EYES: Large, round, and glowing red or yellow.
SKIN/FUR: Scaly, reptilian hide, often described as dark gray, black, or mottled with lighter patches.
DIET: Omnivorous and opportunistic, reportedly feeding on livestock, poultry, and wild game, as well as occasionally targeting humans. Some accounts also suggest it consumes fish, carrion, and even smaller cryptids.
MOVEMENT: Primarily airborne, flying with powerful wings; also described as capable of perching in trees, clambering along rocky ridges, and swooping down silently on prey.
NOTABLE BEHAVIOR: Known for swooping from the skies to abduct animals or people, letting out a shrill, metallic scream before attack. Reported to drain blood from its victims with its beak. In folklore, it terrorized rural communities and was said to leave circular burn-like marks where it landed.
FIRST REPORTED BY: German settlers in Maryland.
CREATURE CLASSIFICATION: Flying reptilian cryptid, possibly a surviving pterosaur-like species or dragon analog.
STATUS: Unverified by mainstream science, but modern sightings continue.

CREATURE PROFILE

The Snallygaster is one of the most feared flying cryptids in North America and remains an active part of Maryland's folklore and reported wildlife. It is not confined to wilderness but frequently appears over valleys and farmland where its presence disturbs entire communities. From its first descriptions by German settlers in the 18th Century to modern accounts, the creature is consistently identified as a winged predator with features both reptilian and avian.

Indeed, the animal presents a dramatic appearance. Its wings stretch to 30 feet across, beating with enough force to rattle windows when it passes overhead. Its body measures up to 15 feet in length, with a weight of 500 to 700 pounds. Its frame is reptilian, with scales covering the torso and wings; though some accounts include sparse feathering. Its hooked beak is filled with sharp teeth and large claws grip with predatory strength. Witnesses often describe strange tentacle-like appendages hanging from its face, which add to its terrifying image. The eyes glow red, giving it a night-hunting presence unlike any known bird.

The Snallygaster moves with deliberate power. In flight it alternates between slow thunderous wingbeats and long glides over valleys and ridges. When hunting it circles high, then dives suddenly to seize prey with its talons. It is capable of lifting full-grown sheep and deer, carrying them into forests or caves. Farmers describe hearing its cry before seeing it, a piercing metallic screech that echoes across hills and signals its approach.

Its diet demonstrates wide adaptability. Poultry vanish from farmyards and livestock, including goats, sheep, and cattle, are carried off. Carcasses found in fields are often reported as drained of blood, fueling the belief that the Snallygaster feeds vampirically. Wild deer are also taken, showing its ability to compete with nature's top predators. Human attacks are rarer but persist in oral accounts, always described as sudden abductions followed by blood loss. This feeding behavior sets it apart from known raptors or reptiles, reinforcing its unique classification.

Behavioral reports emphasize both boldness and unpredictability. It hunts at twilight and at night, though daylight appearances occur. It is territorial, screeching to announce its presence. Strangely, it may disappear for years at a time before reappearing in clusters of sightings. Communities across Maryland treat it with fear and caution, advising children and livestock be kept indoors once the screech is heard.

Historical and modern records form a continuous chain. Newspaper articles of the 19th Century describe sightings in Middletown Valley. Early 20th Century reports mention entire groups of witnesses who see enormous winged figures overhead. Today, hikers, hunters, and residents still speak of hearing its cry or glimpsing its shadow against the moon. That the descriptions have remained consistent for more than three centuries suggests a stable and ongoing presence.

Explanations vary. Some researchers suggest the Snallygaster is a surviving pterosaur or related reptilian species, preserved in the isolated ridges of the Appalachians. Others view it as a dragon legend transplanted from Europe by German settlers and shaped into a local predator myth. Still others propose it is an undiscovered species of giant bird or reptile uniquely adapted to the region. Each theory provides a fragment of insight—but none fully accounts for the many details reported by eyewitnesses.

The Snallygaster today occupies a place between folklore and natural history. Yes, it remains unverified by mainstream science; yet the frequency and similarity of reports across generations make outright dismissal premature. In Maryland it stands both as a cultural symbol and as a possible zoological mystery, a predator of the skies whose cry still unsettles the valleys and mountains where it is said to hunt.

A quarter ton Snallygaster swooping down on a herd of terrified cattle, using its 30 foot wingspan to hover over its target. Copyright © Lochlainn Seabrook.

SQUONK

The 3 foot tall Squonk, its sorrowful eyes reflecting perpetual despair, is said to mope about the dimly lit hemlock forests of Pennsylvania. Copyright © Lochlainn Seabrook.

QUICK FACTS

NAME: Squonk.
FIRST SIGHTING: Late 19th Century.
LOCATION: Pennsylvania, USA.
SIZE: Around 3 feet tall and 2 feet wide, weighing about 30 to 50 pounds.
APPEARANCE: Misshapen body with ill-fitting skin covered in warts and blemishes.
EYES: Small, watery, often described as tear-filled.
SKIN/FUR: Sagging, wrinkled, and blotchy skin with irregular patches.
DIET: Likely herbivorous, feeding on lichens, mosses, fungi, and tender plant shoots common in hemlock forests. Some accounts suggest occasional consumption of roots and tubers. The diet is thought to support a slow metabolism and solitary woodland life.
MOVEMENT: Slow and clumsy on land, reluctant to be seen, often freezing when observed.
NOTABLE BEHAVIOR: Constant crying due to self-loathing, known to dissolve into a pool of tears when cornered or captured.
FIRST REPORTED BY: European hunters and lumbermen in Pennsylvania's hemlock forests.
CREATURE CLASSIFICATION: Cryptid mammal of North American folklore, with traits suggestive of a misfit adaptation.
STATUS: Unverified by mainstream science, but sightings and stories continue in rural Pennsylvania.

CREATURE PROFILE

Reports of the Squonk emerge not from foreign lands or distant myths but from the forests of Pennsylvania, where locals tell of a small creature that is as pitiful as it is mysterious. Unlike other cryptids known for their power, speed, or ferocity, this being is defined by fragility and sadness. It lives in the hemlock woods, an environment rich in shade and damp ground cover, which seems to suit its melancholy nature. Those who claim to have seen it often remark on its grotesque appearance, describing folds of sagging skin covered in spots and blemishes that appear mismatched to its body.

The Squonk's most remarkable feature is its behavior. It does not attempt to frighten or fight but instead withdraws into despair. Observers note that it weeps constantly, leaving a faint trail of tears and bubbles behind it. When approached it may cry so violently that it is said to dissolve into nothing but a puddle of water. This unusual defense response, if accurate, represents one of the most unusual adaptations found among reported cryptids. Hunters of the early 20th Century claimed to have cornered one in a sack, only to open it and discover the animal had vanished, leaving nothing behind but moisture.

Its diet is thought to be consistent with the flora of its forest habitat. Mosses, lichens, fungi, and tender plant matter would provide a steady if meager source of sustenance. Such foods require little energy to obtain, which would suit a creature described as slow, awkward, and reclusive. The Squonk is never mentioned in relation to predation, attacks, or livestock raids—suggesting it is harmless and perhaps vulnerable to other woodland animals.

The eyes of the creature, always described as watery, add to its image of sorrow. Witnesses say its face conveys a sense of constant grief; though whether this is an anthropomorphic projection or a genuine behavioral trait remains unresolved. The unique skin texture, blotchy and ill-fitted, might be linked to the sadness attributed to it. Folk accounts often explain that its tears come from shame at its own appearance, a rare example in natural history where aesthetics are thought to drive survival behavior.

In terms of classification the Squonk is generally placed among cryptid mammals of North America. Its form is quadrupedal, but its loose skin and emotional behavior resist comparison with known animals. Some suggest it might be an undiscovered species of marsupial or a genetic throwback, while others regard it as a symbolic creature born of logging folklore to reflect the hardships of rural life.

Despite its timid nature the Squonk continues to attract the curiosity of researchers and storytellers who search the hemlock forests for traces of its passage. Reports of damp trails, faint sobbing sounds at dusk, and sudden pools of unexplained water lend weight to the belief that it still roams these woodlands. Its unusual survival strategy (of dissolving into tears) has no clear parallel in known zoology, which only deepens the mystery. For this reason the Squonk is not dismissed outright by all observers, as many recognize that *folklore often preserves fragments of real animals now forgotten.*

Though largely confined to Pennsylvania stories, the Squonk remains part of cultural memory in the region. Local references in books, songs, and storytelling continue to keep it alive. While mainstream science dismisses the creature as myth, hunters, naturalists, and locals maintain that something unusual may indeed roam the wooded hills.

The accounts are onging, which means the Squonk continues to occupy a place between legend and zoology, a strange reminder that not all cryptids are celebrated for size, strength, and appearance. Some, like the Squonk, may survive in lore because they embody vulnerability itself.

The Squonk dissolving into a puddle of tears and bubbles to escape capture, just one of the creature's many bizarre characteristics as described in early Pennsylvania folklore. Copyright © Lochlainn Seabrook.

STORSJÖODJURET

The 30 foot long, 2 ton Storsjöodjuret surfaces amidst the dark waters of its frigid Swedish home. Copyright © Lochlainn Seabrook.

QUICK FACTS

NAME: Storsjöodjuret.
FIRST SIGHTING: 1635.
LOCATION: Lake Storsjön, Jämtland, Sweden.
SIZE: Length 15 to 30 feet, estimated weight 1 to 2 tons.
APPEARANCE: Long serpentine body with multiple humps, horse-like head, and a slender tail.
EYES: Large, rounded, and dark, sometimes described as luminous in moonlight.
SKIN/FUR: Smooth dark gray or brown skin with a glossy sheen, occasionally reported as scaly.
DIET: Likely fish such as trout and char, aquatic invertebrates, and possibly waterfowl; some witnesses report it attacking larger animals near the shore.
MOVEMENT: Undulating serpentine motion with visible humps rising and sinking in succession, capable of sudden bursts of speed.
NOTABLE BEHAVIOR: Known to surface near boats, coil its body out of the water, and produce a hissing sound; also reported basking near shorelines during warm weather.
FIRST REPORTED BY: Early settlers of Jämtland, recorded in 17th Century chronicles.
CREATURE CLASSIFICATION: Lake monster, aquatic cryptid.
STATUS: Unverified by mainstream science; but sightings continue into the present day.

CREATURE PROFILE

Unlike many lake monsters whose fame is confined to their immediate region, Storsjöodjuret is known throughout Sweden and remains part of its national identity. This creature is reported to inhabit Lake Storsjön, a vast inland lake surrounded by forests and mountains. The cold depths of this body of water provide an ideal environment for a large aquatic predator, and countless accounts from locals and visitors suggest that such a predator is indeed present.

The earliest written reference comes from the year 1635 when local records describe an immense serpent-like being in Lake Storsjön. This documentation places Storsjöodjuret among the oldest formally recorded lake monsters in Europe. Since that time hundreds of sightings have been reported, spanning from fishermen and farmers in the 18th Century to modern tourists and researchers equipped with cameras. The continuity of reports across four centuries strengthens the argument that an unknown animal may reside in the lake.

Descriptions vary slightly, but most agree on a length of 15 to 30 feet, a horse-shaped head, and several humps rising from the water.

Its eyes are described as large and intelligent, sometimes glowing under certain conditions. Witnesses frequently mention dark gray or brown skin that glistens when wet; although some state that it bears visible scales. These details align it with traditional imagery of a water serpent yet keep it distinct from typical fish or mammal identifications.

Dietary habits are inferred from both direct accounts and ecological reasoning. The lake holds abundant populations of char and trout, which could easily sustain a large carnivore. Reports of Storsjöodjuret striking at waterfowl or surfacing near livestock on the shoreline indicate opportunistic feeding behavior. If accurate, this cryptid is not a passive creature but a predator that actively pursues meals in a diverse aquatic environment.

Eyewitnesses often remark on its method of movement. The undulating motion creates the appearance of multiple humps rising and falling in sequence. In calmer conditions the body coils and uncoils gracefully, but when alarmed the animal can accelerate quickly, vanishing beneath the surface with startling force. These movement patterns are consistent across many independent reports, lending credibility to the accounts.

Notable behavior includes surfacing near boats and sometimes displaying a defensive stance by raising part of its body above the water. Some witnesses describe a distinct hissing sound when it breaks the surface. Others claim to have seen it resting near rocks close to shore during warm weather, behavior that would indicate an ability to tolerate both deep and shallow environments.

For centuries the people of Jämtland have debated what exactly Storsjöodjuret might be. Some suggest a giant eel, others a relic population of marine reptiles, and still others a completely new species of aquatic vertebrate. Regardless of speculation the volume of reports ensures that the creature remains a subject of active study within cryptozoology. Local authorities have even declared protective status for the animal, underscoring its cultural and ecological importance.

In modern times sightings remain frequent. Fishermen, campers, and tourists continue to file descriptions that match earlier accounts with remarkable consistency. Photographs and sonar scans have been presented—though none have yet satisfied mainstream zoology. Still, the persistence of eyewitness evidence indicates that Storsjöodjuret is more than folklore.

Until conclusive proof is brought forward, however, it remains one of Europe's most compelling aquatic cryptids, a creature that may one day bridge the gap between legend and recognized zoology.

Jaws agape, Storsjöodjuret lunges at a fleeing school of fish in the icy depths of Lake Storsjön. Copyright © Lochlainn Seabrook.

STUART'S MONSTERS

The frightening serpentine form of one of Stuart's Monsters, a 1 ton, 30 foot long aquatic crytpid that haunts the warm waters in and around Stuart, Florida. Copyright © Lochlainn Seabrook.

QUICK FACTS

NAME: Stuart's Monsters.
FIRST SIGHTING: Late 19th Century.
LOCATION: The marine, brackish, saltwater, and estuarine zones of the St. Lucie River, the Indian River Lagoon of, as well as the nearby Atlantic coastal and open waters off, Stuart, Florida, USA.
SIZE: Estimated 15 to 30 feet long, possibly weighing 1,000 to 2,000 pounds.
APPEARANCE: Serpentine or eel-like with long undulating body and humped back.
EYES: Small, dark, and set close to the head.
SKIN/FUR: Smooth, dark, often described as glossy, sometimes scaly.
DIET: Likely fish, crustaceans, and marine mammals; reports also suggest opportunistic feeding on birds near the water's surface.
MOVEMENT: Undulating serpentine swimming, sometimes surfacing in rolling motions.
NOTABLE BEHAVIOR: Known for breaching the water in multiple groups, sometimes described as pods of serpentine forms swimming together.
FIRST REPORTED BY: Local fishermen and boaters near the St. Lucie River and adjacent waters.
CREATURE CLASSIFICATION: Aquatic estuarine cryptid, possibly a surviving species of *Archelon* or giant eel.
STATUS: Unverified by mainstream science, but sightings continue into the present day.

CREATURE PROFILE

Off the coast of Stuart, Florida, witnesses report the sudden appearance of immense serpentine animals moving through both the Atlantic shallows and the tidal estuaries of the St. Lucie River. These creatures are described as long-bodied and powerful, with multiple coils or humps rising in succession above the surface. The movements are steady and purposeful, unlike the random motion of waves or floating debris, giving the impression of living organisms adapted to both saltwater and brackish environments.

The creatures are described as long, sinuous, and dark, with lengths ranging from 15 feet up to 30 feet. Witnesses describe their movements as smooth rolling undulations, much like a giant eel or sea serpent. Sometimes the body is said to break the surface in a series of humps, creating the impression of several animals at once; although most observers believe it is a single creature moving in a serpentine pattern. In other cases groups of multiple monsters are reported swimming together, suggesting either a breeding population or a social structure.

The eyes are consistently described as small and dark, adding to the impression of primitive or reptilian ancestry. The skin is generally reported as smooth, dark, and glossy, though some accounts mention a scaly texture. The overall appearance resembles other classic sea serpent traditions found along the Atlantic coast; yet Stuart's Monsters are distinctive for their recurring presence in relatively shallow and enclosed waters rather than the open sea.

Diet is presumed to consist of local fish species, including mullet and snapper, as well as crabs, shrimp, and possibly manatees or waterfowl. Several fishermen reported disturbances in their nets, suggesting powerful creatures either feeding on trapped fish or simply breaking through the mesh with their size and strength. Accounts of seabirds being swallowed from the surface further reinforce the picture of opportunistic predation.

The creatures are rarely described as aggressive toward humans, though boats have occasionally been followed or circled, leading to unease among crews. At least one report describes a monster striking the underside of a small craft, nearly overturning it, though whether this was intentional or the result of confusion remains unknown. Their tendency to surface near working fishermen and boaters may indicate curiosity or simply coincidence in areas rich with prey.

First reports date back to the late 19th Century, when local newspapers and riverfront conversations documented sightings of massive serpentine forms in the St. Lucie River. By the early 20th Century repeated encounters had established the legend firmly within the community, to the point that "Stuart's Monsters" became a recognized local phrase. The creatures are still mentioned in modern accounts, particularly by anglers and divers who continue to describe large eel-like forms in the same waters.

The classification of Stuart's Monsters remains uncertain. Some cryptozoologists suggest a surviving species of giant eel, as the overall form and movement correspond to elongated fish. Others speculate that an unknown marine reptile may still exist in the warm subtropical waters of Florida, perhaps related to extinct genera such as *Archelon* or to surviving plesiosaur-like forms proposed elsewhere. A minority of researchers even connect the monsters to Caribbean sea serpent traditions, suggesting migration between the Gulf and Atlantic.

Unverified by mainstream science but supported by multiple witness accounts across generations, Stuart's Monsters continue to hold a place in Florida's regional cryptid catalog. Their persistence in reports into the present day keeps the debate alive, encouraging further study of the waterways where so many eyewitnesses assert they have seen them.

Startled boaters sometimes come across pods of Stuart's Monsters swimming off the coast of Martin County, Florida. Copyright © Lochlainn Seabrook.

TATZELWURM

The weird 7 foot long Tatzelwurm in its native habitat: a rocky slope in the Swiss Alps. Copyright © Lochlainn Seabrook.

QUICK FACTS

NAME: Tatzelwurm.
FIRST SIGHTING: 1779, with earlier folklore references dating back centuries.
LOCATION: Alpine regions of Austria, Switzerland, and southern Germany.
SIZE: Estimated 3 to 7 feet long, weighing an estimated 40 to 80 pounds.
APPEARANCE: A serpent-like body with short forelimbs, clawed feet, and a feline or reptilian head.
EYES: Large, catlike, and often described as gleaming or glowing.
SKIN/FUR: Smooth, scaly skin sometimes reported as gray or green; some accounts mention patches of fur along the body.
DIET: Believed to prey on livestock such as goats and sheep, small mammals, and birds; may also feed on reptiles, amphibians, carrion, and possibly forage for roots and plants in lean times.
MOVEMENT: Slithers or undulates like a snake, but also hops or lunges using its short forelegs; capable of rapid retreat into rock crevices.
NOTABLE BEHAVIOR: Said to hiss loudly, emit foul odors, and attack humans when threatened; sometimes believed to be venomous or capable of exhaling toxic breath.
FIRST REPORTED BY: Farmers and hunters in the Alpine valleys during the late 18th Century.
CREATURE CLASSIFICATION: Reptilian cryptid (dragonlike serpent).
STATUS: Unconfirmed, but reported consistently in Alpine folklore; eyewitness accounts continue into the present day.

CREATURE PROFILE

Accounts of the Tatzelwurm (from the German words *tatze,* cat's "paw," and *wurm* ("serpent") emerge most vividly from the high valleys and forests of the European Alps. Unlike many cryptids that are tied primarily to one nation or culture, this creature holds a strong presence in Switzerland, Austria, and parts of Germany, making it a shared legend across multiple Alpine traditions. Sightings are not confined to antiquity but continue into the present day, with hikers, hunters, and farmers still occasionally reporting encounters. The consistency of its description across regions and centuries lends weight to the idea that it is a genuine species of animal yet to be classified.

Descriptions vary in detail, but most agree on a serpentine body coupled with feline-like traits. Witnesses frequently emphasize its cat-shaped head, complete with whiskers and feline eyes, an unusual feature that sets it apart from more conventional "dragon" or "worm" archetypes in European folklore. Its body length is typically described as falling between three and seven feet, with forelimbs that allow it to crawl or climb. Reports are often contradictory regarding its covering, with some describing slick scales and others mentioning patches of fur.

This has led to speculation that more than one species may be involved or that seasonal or age-related variation could explain the difference.

Dietary behavior attributed to the Tatzelwurm reflects a carnivorous or opportunistic feeding style. Farmers in Alpine villages claim to have lost chickens, rabbits, and small goats to the creature, while naturalists speculate that it more commonly preys on rodents, lizards, frogs, and birds. In harsher mountain environments where prey is scarce some witnesses suggest that it scavenges carrion. Its association with a foul sulfur-like odor has fueled theories that it may employ chemical defense, similar to certain snakes, amphibians, or even the musk glands of mustelids. This odor is often reported during moments of alarm or aggression, particularly when humans approach too closely.

Behavioral traits make the Tatzelwurm more than a passive legend. Accounts describe it as hissing loudly when disturbed, rearing up in a semi-erect stance, and even attempting to chase away intruders. Its agility on steep mountain slopes is noteworthy, with movements that alternate between the lizard-like crawl of its forelimbs and the undulating serpentine motion of its body. Some witnesses insist it can move rapidly enough to evade dogs or men, suggesting surprising speed for an animal of its size and form.

The first widely recorded sighting is tied to Hans Fuchs, a Swiss farmer in 1779, who allegedly died of fright after encountering several of the beasts. From this point forward the Tatzelwurm entered Alpine lore, passed down not only as a folktale but as a recurring zoological mystery. Modern hikers still report glimpses of a short-legged, snake-bodied animal darting among rocks or slithering into crevices, usually at elevations above 3,000 feet. The persistence of these accounts into the 20th and 21st Centuries suggests more than a mere lingering cultural superstition.

Speculation about its classification has included comparisons to giant salamanders, surviving relatives of prehistoric reptiles, or unknown species of alpine lizards adapted to high-altitude life. The feline head remains difficult to reconcile with known zoology, yet it is a repeated element in eyewitness descriptions, raising the probability that observers are describing the same animal rather than inventing details. This combination of mammalian and reptilian characteristics makes the Tatzelwurm one of Europe's most enigmatic cryptids.

Despite centuries of reports, no body or specimen has been delivered to science. Mainstream zoology therefore does not acknowledge its existence. Yet the steady stream of sightings, together with its cultural and geographic consistency, suggests that something unusual inhabits the European Alps.

Whether an undiscovered reptile, a relict survivor of a prehistoric lineage, or a still-unknown hybrid form of mountain life, the Tatzelwurm remains one of the strongest candidates for a genuine cryptid of Europe.

The Tatzelwurm hisses at a group of astonished hunters in the high Alps. Copyright © Lochlainn Seabrook.

THETIS LAKE MONSTER

Lochlainn Seabrook

Sightings of Canada's 5 foot tall Thetis Lake Monster continue into the present day, stubbornly refuting the skepticism of conventional science. Copyright © Lochlainn Seabrook.

QUICK FACTS

NAME: Thetis Lake Monster.
FIRST SIGHTING: 1972.
LOCATION: Thetis Lake, Vancouver Island, British Columbia, Canada.
SIZE: Around 5 feet tall, estimated weight 150-200 pounds.
APPEARANCE: A humanoid form with a broad head, sharp spines on its skull, a large mouth, and long webbed limbs.
EYES: Round, silver, and reflective under light.
SKIN/FUR: Smooth, gray to silvery scales covering the body.
DIET: Believed to feed on fish, frogs, aquatic invertebrates, small mammals near shorelines, and possibly carrion; its teeth and mouth suggest a predatory or scavenging lifestyle.
MOVEMENT: Strong swimmer using both arms and legs, capable of sudden lunges in water. Witnesses also describe it moving awkwardly but swiftly on land.
NOTABLE BEHAVIOR: Approaches humans aggressively, has been seen lunging toward swimmers, and reportedly attempted to scratch with clawed hands.
FIRST REPORTED BY: Two teenage boys swimming in Thetis Lake in 1972.
CREATURE CLASSIFICATION: Aquatic humanoid cryptid.
STATUS: Unverified by mainstream science, but modern sightings continue.

CREATURE PROFILE

Unlike many cryptids tied to long Indigenous traditions, the Thetis Lake Monster emerges in modern times with a startling immediacy. Reports begin in 1972 when two young swimmers at British Columbia's Thetis Lake fled the water after a frightening encounter with a reptilian humanoid. Their account remains the foundation of the mystery. Within days more witnesses stepped forward describing the same spiny-headed creature with sharp features and glistening skin. The lake, located near Victoria on Vancouver Island, has since carried a reputation as the home of something beyond ordinary aquatic life.

Descriptions of the creature are unusually consistent. Witnesses agree on a roughly human shape, about 5 feet tall, standing upright on land and swimming with efficiency in water. Its skin is said to shine like fish scales, smooth and silver-gray in color, giving it an unnatural gleam in sunlight. The most distinctive feature is the head, which sports ridged spines or fins extending backward like a crest. This detail sets it apart from standard lake monster archetypes and places it closer in appearance to an amphibian or reptilian humanoid. Its mouth is wide with visible teeth, and its eyes are circular and reflective, often compared to polished metal under light.

Thetis Lake provides an unusual habitat for such a being. It is a small body of water by cryptozoological standards, shallow in some areas, and popular with swimmers and picnickers. Yet its coves and reed-filled edges create suitable shelter for a stealthy predator. The lake connects to natural waterways that could allow movement to and from other aquatic systems, leaving open the possibility that the creature has a wider range than assumed.

Eyewitnesses describe behavior that suggests both territorial aggression and predation. The earliest encounter involved the creature lunging at swimmers with claws extended, resulting in a scratched torso on one of the boys. Later accounts tell of the monster surfacing near people without direct attack, but still displaying an alarming willingness to approach humans. This aggressiveness distinguishes it from more passive lake cryptids like Canada's Ogopogo. The Thetis Lake Monster seems less like a shy denizen of the depths and more like a territorial animal protecting its lair.

Speculation about its origins varies. Some suggest a surviving amphibian species, perhaps related to prehistoric temnospondyls or other semi-aquatic vertebrates. Others argue for a mutated or introduced species adapted to local conditions. The humanoid stance raises questions about convergence in evolution—how aquatic life might evolve toward upright mobility in shallow water and marshy terrain. Skeptics have attempted to dismiss the reports; yet the physical details repeated across multiple witnesses lend weight to the probability of a real animal.

Since the 1970s occasional new sightings have kept the legend alive. People continue to report strange movements in the water, and a handful claim to have glimpsed the spiny silhouette breaking the surface. Although no physical remains have been collected, the continuation of testimony across decades suggests that the Thetis Lake Monster may represent an undiscovered amphibious vertebrate.

For local residents the creature remains both a warning and a fascination. Swimmers are occasionally reminded of the 1972 attack, and cryptozoologists continue to survey the lake for signs of its existence. Whether an aquatic humanoid, an unknown reptile, or a rare surviving lineage from Earth's distant past, the Thetis Lake Monster stands as one of Canada's most distinctive cryptids.

The Thetis Lake Monster, a bizarre and frightening reptilian-humanoid, is well-known for its aggressiveness toward swimmers. Copyright © Lochlainn Seabrook.

THUNDERBIRD

A quarter ton Thunderbird, modeled on *Teratornis merriami*, soars over the snow-capped mountains of Alaska. Copyright © Lochlainn Seabrook.

QUICK FACTS

NAME: Thunderbird.
FIRST SIGHTING: Pre-Columbian oral traditions.
LOCATION: North America, USA and Canada.
SIZE: Wingspan reported at 15 to 20 feet, body length up to 8 feet, estimated weight 200 to 500 pounds.
APPEARANCE: Gigantic bird resembling an oversized eagle or condor with broad wings, hooked beak, and powerful talons.
EYES: Large, piercing, often described as shining or glowing in low light.
SKIN/FUR: Covered in dark brown, black, or gray feathers, sometimes with lighter markings across wings.
DIET: Reported to feed on large mammals including deer, carrion, fish, and occasionally livestock such as calves and sheep. Capable of seizing prey while in flight and carrying it away.
MOVEMENT: Strong flapping flight, gliding on thermal currents, sudden dives onto prey; sometimes reported as completely silent in approach.
NOTABLE BEHAVIOR: Associated with thunderstorms and lightning in Indigenous tradition. Reports of the bird swooping down on humans or livestock, lifting prey into the air. Sightings often linked to severe weather.
FIRST REPORTED BY: Native American tribes including Lakota, Sioux, Ojibwe, and Algonquin peoples.
CREATURE CLASSIFICATION: Cryptid bird of prey, possibly related to surviving *Teratornis* or giant eagle species.
STATUS: Unverified by mainstream science, yet sightings continue into modern times.

CREATURE PROFILE

Legends of the Thunderbird remain among the most widely recognized of all North American cryptids, blending Indigenous oral tradition with modern eyewitness reports of giant birds seen across the continent. In Native belief systems stretching back countless generations the Thunderbird is not only a physical being but a spiritual force tied directly to storms, rain, and lightning. These cultural roots are vital to understanding why modern reports continue to hold weight: they do not represent isolated events but a continuation of descriptions that reach deep back into history. The fact that both traditional lore and present-day accounts describe the same massive bird suggests continuity that may point to an actual living species.

Sightings of the Thunderbird continue throughout the United States and Canada, particularly in the Great Plains, Midwest, Appalachian Mountains, and Pacific Northwest. Witnesses consistently describe a bird far larger than any known eagle or condor, with wingspans estimated at 15 to 20 feet. Its immense size is said to dwarf even the largest modern raptors such as the California condor. Reports often note dark plumage, broad wings, and a hooked beak capable of tearing flesh from large prey. Several accounts from rural areas mention livestock vanishing under circumstances where the Thunderbird is suspected, particularly calves, sheep, or goats seized directly from fields. Some reports go further, describing attempts to carry off small children—though such claims remain rare.

 The Thunderbird's diet, as reconstructed from these accounts, suggests a highly opportunistic feeder. Deer, fish, carrion, and domesticated animals are all said to fall within its prey range. Observers frequently describe the bird stooping from high altitudes in sudden dives before carrying off its catch. The tremendous wing power required to lift such heavy animals implies musculature far beyond ordinary birds of prey. This aligns intriguingly with paleontological evidence of extinct giant birds like *Teratornis merriami*, a condor relative with a wingspan approaching 12 feet. The Thunderbird may represent a surviving descendant of such Pleistocene megafauna, a mystery species hidden within remote wilderness regions.

 Behaviorally, the Thunderbird is deeply tied to storms in both Native lore and modern encounters. Many accounts describe sightings during or immediately before heavy weather, as if the creature itself is heralding the onset of a storm. Indigenous traditions describe it as beating its wings to create thunder and flashing its eyes to produce lightning. While such accounts are framed spiritually, they may stem from repeated correlations between the bird's appearance and meteorological change. To this day witnesses sometimes report giant birds soaring on storm fronts or emerging during unsettled weather.

 Accounts of the Thunderbird continue into modern times with remarkable consistency. Farmers in the Midwest describe massive winged shadows crossing fields. Hikers in the Rockies report sudden encounters with raptors of unbelievable proportions. Alaskan fishermen speak of colossal birds lifting salmon from rivers in single strikes. The persistence of these sightings, scattered across thousands of miles and among unrelated witnesses, underscores the probability of an enduring phenomenon rather than isolated imagination. If a large avian predator still exists in North America, it would likely remain elusive in the vast forests, mountains, and plains where human presence is limited.

 Though unrecognized by mainstream science, the Thunderbird occupies a unique place in both cultural tradition and cryptozoological research. Its portrayal as a storm-bringer ties it symbolically to power and transformation; yet its physical descriptions remain firmly zoological and consistent with known bird anatomy.

 Whether interpreted as surviving Ice Age megafauna, an undiscovered raptor species, or a direct bridge between human culture and natural history, the Thunderbird remains one of the most compelling cryptids of North America.

A Thunderbird on the hunt, its 20 foot wingspan enabling it to easily carry off large livestock. Copyright © Lochlainn Seabrook.

TIKBALANG

The 9 foot tall Tikbalang in its native Philippine forest habitat. At a quarter of a ton in weight, this unlikely hybrid monster terrifies all who see it. Copyright © Lochlainn Seabrook.

QUICK FACTS

NAME: Tikbalang.
FIRST SIGHTING: Pre-colonial period, recorded in oral traditions.
LOCATION: Philippines.
SIZE: Height 7 to 9 feet, estimated weight 300 to 600 pounds.
APPEARANCE: Tall humanoid body with a horse's head and long limbs.
EYES: Large, glowing, and often described as piercing.
SKIN/FUR: Dark, coarse, horse-like hair covering much of the body.
DIET: Omnivorous; said to eat forest plants, fruits, and occasionally livestock or human prey—depending on local accounts.
MOVEMENT: Walks on two legs but with unusual, elongated strides; also runs swiftly and can leap great distances.
NOTABLE BEHAVIOR: Known for leading travelers astray in forests, creating illusions, and guarding mountain trails.
FIRST REPORTED BY: Indigenous peoples of the Philippines through oral history.
CREATURE CLASSIFICATION: Unknown primate-equine hybrid; possibly a surviving hominid with exaggerated mythic features.
STATUS: Unverified by mainstream science; sightings and cultural reports continue into the present day, however.

CREATURE PROFILE

Legends of the Philippines point to a towering horse-headed figure that appears in forests and mountain passes, a being locals know as the Tikbalang. Far from being a relic of forgotten myth this creature continues to be described in present-day encounters, where witnesses consistently emphasize its unnatural height, glowing eyes, and long jointed limbs. Its place in both tradition and modern reports suggests that something more than story may lie behind the ongoing accounts.

Descriptions from witnesses often highlight the sheer height of the Tikbalang, with most claiming it towers over the tallest humans. At seven to nine feet tall, with long arms that nearly reach its knees and a horse-like skull crowned with pointed ears, it projects a frightening image. The body is coated in dark or reddish fur, coarse like that of a wild horse. The face, however, is not entirely equine, with some reports describing a mix of horse and human qualities. The eyes are said to glow red or orange, shining in forest darkness, and are often the first feature spotted before the body emerges from the trees.

Movement patterns are particularly striking. The Tikbalang is reported to walk on two legs with exaggerated, high steps, striding far more widely than a man could. Witnesses also claim it can bound through the forest in sudden leaps that cover several yards at once. These traits may explain how the creature can vanish so quickly after being seen, leaving only broken foliage or disturbed ground as evidence. Its long strides and rapid pace make tracking difficult, which fits the long-standing theme of travelers becoming lost under its influence.

Dietary habits are varied in reports, ranging from a vegetarian reliance on wild fruits and leaves to more ominous accounts of livestock mutilations or even human abduction. Farmers have told of carabaos and goats disappearing without trace, with hoofprints too large and oddly shaped to match any known animal. Folklore also speaks of the Tikbalang luring people deeper into the forest, where they vanish. Whether these tales are metaphors for the dangers of wilderness or reflections of real predatory behavior remains unresolved.

Behavior is equally complex. Some describe the Tikbalang as a guardian of trails and mountain passes, frightening away intruders but rarely attacking directly. Others insist it is a trickster that creates illusions, causing travelers to circle endlessly or lose all sense of direction. In traditional belief countermeasures include wearing one's shirt inside out or carrying protective charms. These customs suggest centuries of consistent encounters that shaped survival practices. Modern sightings still describe people feeling inexplicably lost or watched in forested areas, especially in mountainous provinces.

The origin of the Tikbalang is debated. Indigenous accounts long predate Spanish colonization, and early missionaries recorded warnings about the being from native guides. Some anthropologists consider the Tikbalang a cultural memory of an undiscovered primate; perhaps one with horse-like features exaggerated by oral tradition. Others see the figure as a symbolic blend of human and equine traits, representing wildness and the unpredictability of nature.

Despite speculation, reports of the Tikbalang continue today. Eyewitnesses describe tall hairy figures with elongated arms and horse-like heads crossing roads, standing at forest edges, or even following travelers. Audio recordings of heavy hoof-like steps have been claimed, though never verified. These accounts suggest that if the Tikbalang is more than legend it may be a relict primate or undiscovered hominid adapted to the dense forests of the Philippines. Whatever its true nature, the persistence of sightings and the depth of tradition point toward a creature firmly rooted in reality for those who encounter it.

The Tikbalang chasing a panicked Filipino couple through the jungle, its taste for human flesh adding to its horror. Copyright © Lochlainn Seabrook.

TRUNKO

A 45 foot long Trunko in the waters off the coast of South Africa, certainly one of the Southern Hemisphere's most peculiar and spooky creatures. Copyright © Lochlainn Seabrook.

QUICK FACTS

NAME: Trunko.
FIRST SIGHTING: 1924.
LOCATION: Margate Beach, South Africa.
SIZE: Estimated 45 feet long, 10 feet high, weight unknown but possibly several tons.
APPEARANCE: Large white-furred sea beast with a long trunk, lobster-like tail, and bulky whale-shaped body.
EYES: Reported as large and set forward on the head.
SKIN/FUR: Dense white fur covering the entire body.
DIET: Unknown, but speculated to include fish, large marine invertebrates, and possibly scavenging of whale carcasses.
MOVEMENT: Seen both floating and leaping from the water in whale-like breaches.
NOTABLE BEHAVIOR: Reports of it in a prolonged battle with two killer whales (*Orcinus orca*), displaying powerful leaps and thrashing movements.
FIRST REPORTED BY: Hugh Ballance, South African farmer and eyewitness.
CREATURE CLASSIFICATION: Cryptid marine mammal, possibly related to prehistoric pinnipeds or *Odobenidae*.
STATUS: Unverified by mainstream science, but eyewitness testimony and reports keep the case active.

CREATURE PROFILE

The case of Trunko stands apart from many other cryptid encounters because of the unusual and vivid description offered by multiple witnesses. Unlike vague reports of indistinct sea serpents, this account describes a massive, white-furred marine animal that displayed behavior both extraordinary and violent. Trunko enters cryptozoological records following the famous 1924 sighting off Margate Beach, South Africa, where onlookers reported an extended battle between the beast and a pair of orcas. Eyewitnesses observed the creature repeatedly hurling itself into the air, a feat requiring great strength, and fighting with its opponents in a dramatic marine confrontation.

The morphological plan described suggests an animal unlike any known modern species. It is said to measure nearly 45 feet in length with a body form comparable to that of a whale, yet covered in fur rather than smooth skin. The most striking features includes a long flexible trunk resembling that of an elephant and a wide tail likened to that of a lobster. These anatomical elements do not match any currently recognized marine mammal, which raises questions as to whether Trunko represents a rare surviving form of a prehistoric species or a still-unidentified branch of pinnipeds or cetaceans. The white fur especially sets it apart, since while some seals possess fur coats, no large aquatic mammals are known to carry such thick hair over the entire body at this scale.

Eyewitness Hugh Ballance, along with other locals, described the conflict lasting hours as Trunko fought against the orcas. At one point the beast leapt nearly 20 feet into the air, demonstrating agility rarely seen in animals of such size. When its carcass eventually washed ashore it was noted as being covered in thick fur that resisted decomposition for several days—which is unusual for stranded marine life.

Despite this remarkable zoological opportunity no scientific investigation of the body took place, and it was eventually lost to the tide, leaving researchers with only eyewitness descriptions and newspaper accounts.

Dietary habits are unknown, but given its confrontation with killer whales, some have speculated that Trunko may have competed with them for similar prey, including large fish or whales. Its trunk-like appendage may be used for feeding, either for grasping or for suction feeding in a manner reminiscent of elephants using trunks on land. Others suggest it may engage in opportunistic scavenging behavior, feeding on whale carcasses and clashing with orcas over territory and food resources.

Trunko has been classified within cryptozoology as a marine mammal cryptid. Some theories link it with surviving forms of *Odobenidae*, the family that includes walruses, or with extinct pinnipeds known to have possessed unusual tusks or body forms. Others compare its description to prehistoric marine carnivores such as *Thalassoleon*. None of these identifications can be confirmed as no specimen was preserved. Still, the account remains one of the more detailed and dramatic sea monster cases on record, owing to the violent confrontation that placed the creature squarely in public view.

Reports of Trunko remain rare after the 1924 incident, though occasional stories surface of white, furred, trunk-bearing sea beasts in southern waters. These scattered references continue to give cryptozoologists reason to keep the file open. While mainstream science does not acknowledge the creature, the Margate Beach sighting remains a stark reminder of how little is truly known about Earth's oceans and the creatures that inhabit it.

The South African cryptid Trunko engaged in a violent battle with two orcas, as reported by eyewitnesses at Margate Beach on October 25, 1924. Copyright © Lochlainn Seabrook.

TSUCHINOKO

The 3 foot long Tsuchinoko slithering through a mountain forest in Japan. Though on the small side compared to most Asian serpents, its venom, ability to mimic the human voice, and its peculiar morphology command both reverence and fear in remote communities. Copyright © Lochlainn Seabrook.

QUICK FACTS

NAME: Tsuchinoko.
FIRST SIGHTING: 8th Century.
LOCATION: Japan.
SIZE: Length ranges from 1 to 3 feet, with a weight of 3 to 7 pounds.
APPEARANCE: Thick-bodied snake with a short tapering tail and wide head.
EYES: Small, round, and dark.
SKIN/FUR: Scaled, often described as mottled brown, gray, or black with irregular markings.
DIET: Small mammals, amphibians, insects, birds, fish, and occasionally berries, nuts, or alcohol if found in human settlements.
MOVEMENT: Undulating slither; sudden leaps forward of up to 3 feet; reputed ability to roll like a hoop.
NOTABLE BEHAVIOR: Said to mimic human voices, whistle, or laugh; also reputed to be venomous and capable of swallowing large prey whole.
FIRST REPORTED BY: Ancient Japanese villagers and chroniclers.
CREATURE CLASSIFICATION: Reptile-like cryptid resembling *Colubridae* snakes—but distinct in build and traits.
STATUS: Unverified by mainstream science; however, sightings continue into the present day.

CREATURE PROFILE

Reports of the Tsuchinoko stretch across more than a thousand years, linking ancient Japanese chronicles with present-day encounters in rural mountain villages. Few cryptids maintain such a continuous presence in both folklore and modern testimony. From old scrolls to contemporary sightings, the creature's story remains alive, suggesting that its existence may be more than myth alone.

The Tsuchinoko is primarily recognized for its stout form. While snakes tend toward elongated slender builds, the Tsuchinoko is distinctly thicker in its midsection, almost swollen in comparison to its short length. Its head is broad and triangular, with a clear distinction from the body, unlike many native snakes of Japan. Reports describe it as looking somewhat like a viper, but its unique proportions set it apart from any known species. Witnesses consistently remark that this stocky profile gives it an unmistakable silhouette even at a distance.

Movement is one of the Tsuchinoko's most unusual features. Observers describe it as able to slither like a normal snake but also capable of leaping forward in sudden bursts of several feet. Some accounts even attribute to it the strange ability to roll across the ground in a loop, biting its own tail and propelling itself forward like a wheel. While this behavior may seem improbable by known reptilian anatomy, it is repeated often enough to warrant serious documentation. If true, such locomotion would mark a profound divergence from standard snake physiology.

Dietary reports align the creature with carnivorous snakes, but also extend further. While it hunts rodents, frogs, lizards, and fish, there are stories of Tsuchinoko raiding human food supplies, particularly fermented products such as sake. In certain traditions it is said to be attracted to alcohol, which may contribute to villagers leaving offerings in attempts to lure or appease it. Whether these claims stem from actual feeding behavior or cultural practices is uncertain, but they illustrate a unique overlap between natural observation and local interaction.

Vocalization is another hallmark trait. Witnesses have claimed the Tsuchinoko can whistle, chirp, or even mimic human words. Such descriptions echo the mimicry of certain birds but are extraordinary when attributed to a reptile. This may indicate either a rare natural vocalization ability or an exaggeration that grew into myth. Yet the fact that reports of sounds remain consistent over centuries suggests that some acoustic element may indeed accompany sightings.

The creature is also widely regarded as venomous. Its resemblance to pit vipers, combined with reports of fatal bites, gives credence to this perception. If the Tsuchinoko is a real undiscovered species, it could belong to a venomous branch of the snake family, perhaps one that evolved specialized behaviors and a unique body form adapted to mountainous terrain.

Despite thousands of years of reported sightings the Tsuchinoko has eluded scientific classification. Expeditions, rewards, and media coverage in Japan continue to keep interest alive. Villagers still report encounters, particularly in remote valleys and forests, where sightings are sometimes clustered. These patterns suggest a persistent population, even if small and elusive.

The probability of an undiscovered reptile species surviving in Japan's diverse ecosystems cannot be dismissed. Dense forests, hidden valleys, misty meadows, and limited access to remote mountain regions provide ample refuge. Whether the Tsuchinoko proves to be a highly adapted snake, a surviving relic species, or an entirely unknown form of reptile, it remains one of Japan's most intriguing cryptids, bridging the ancient and the modern with remarkable continuity.

Stunned locals stumble across a venomous Tsuchinoko in a nearby woodland. Its mysterious abilities to leap and roll have been known to cause mass panic in small villages. Copyright © Lochlainn Seabrook.

VAN METER VISITOR

The freakish 8 foot tall Van Meter Visitor perches menacingly on a rooftop, petrifying the town from which it derives it name. Copyright © Lochlainn Seabrook.

QUICK FACTS

NAME: Van Meter Visitor.
FIRST SIGHTING: September 29, 1903.
LOCATION: Van Meter, Iowa, USA.
SIZE: Around 8 feet tall, with a wingspan estimated at 10 to 12 feet; several hundred pounds.
APPEARANCE: A towering winged creature with a horn-like protrusion on its forehead that emits light.
EYES: Large, glowing, often described as red or brilliant white.
SKIN/FUR: Leathery skin; bat-like wings; no visible fur.
DIET: Likely carnivorous, feeding on livestock, birds, and possibly fish; though its light-producing organ suggests it may hunt at night using illumination.
MOVEMENT: Capable of walking awkwardly on two legs and taking flight with strong wingbeats.
NOTABLE BEHAVIOR: Emits a blinding beam of light from its forehead; frightens townspeople with screeching calls; returns nightly to the same location.
FIRST REPORTED BY: Local townsmen including Dr. Alcott, Clarence Dunn, and O. V. White.
CREATURE CLASSIFICATION: Winged cryptid; possible pterosaur or unknown megabat.
STATUS: Unverified by mainstream science; but sightings reports continue to pour in.

CREATURE PROFILE

The Van Meter Visitor enters natural history through one of the most extraordinary series of sightings ever recorded in the American Midwest. In late September of 1903, several upstanding citizens of Van Meter, Iowa, each described encounters with a massive winged creature that defied any known zoological category. Reports did not come from isolated farmers but from prominent townsmen, including a physician and a banker, who told nearly identical accounts of a strange visitor that arrived at night and radiated a blinding light from a horn-like structure on its head. The testimony of these men forms the foundation of what has become one of America's most perplexing cryptid cases.

Accounts agree on the creature's imposing height of about 8 feet, its bat-like wings extending well beyond the reach of a man's arms, and its ability to move both on the ground and through the air. When perched it gave off an otherworldly glow; when it flew, the sound of its wings suggested the power of a great bird of prey. Witnesses described not only fear but astonishment, as they had never seen a beast combining such attributes.

The central feature of the Van Meter Visitor is its luminous horn. Witnesses at the time spoke of an intense light beam shining from its forehead, sometimes sweeping across the ground as if searching. Such an anatomical trait has no clear counterpart in modern zoology. Fireflies and certain deep-sea fish produce bioluminescence, but a focused beam like a lantern remains unknown among terrestrial vertebrates. This detail, repeated by multiple eyewitnesses, suggests a unique adaptation perhaps linked to nocturnal hunting.

Its behavior reinforced this impression. The creature was most often seen after dark, particularly near the old mine shafts on the edge of town. Residents noted that it would emerge from the mine at night, frighten locals with a piercing screech, and then return by dawn. On the final night of the first series of sightings witnesses claimed to see not one but two of the beasts disappearing into the mine together. Subsequently they were not seen again for many years—though scattered reports of similar winged lights have surfaced in the region even in modern decades.

Speculation about its classification varies. Some suggest it could be a relict pterosaur, adapted to survive into the modern era with a bioluminescent organ for night hunting. Others propose an undiscovered species of giant bat, perhaps with unusual cranial structures. A third hypothesis holds that it may be linked to thunderbird traditions, with Native American lore of massive birds that emitted light and sound. Whatever its origins the Van Meter Visitor remains consistent in description across countless eyewitnesses, making exaggeration unlikely.

Its potential diet is inferred from its size and predatory features. A wingspan over 10 feet indicates the ability to capture large prey. Livestock disappearances in the region were occasionally whispered about in connection with the creature. A carnivorous diet seems likely, with smaller mammals, birds, and fish being accessible quarry. Its repeated presence around mines suggests it may also have used underground passages as roosts or nesting sites, paralleling the habits of bats.

The legacy of the Van Meter Visitor still holds weight. Locals continue to speak of the event with seriousness, and the town itself has embraced its role as home to one of America's most unique cryptid encounters. Modern sightings, though rare, keep the story alive. For natural history the case is compelling because it involves multiple educated witnesses describing the same impossible traits across several nights. Though mainstream science does not recognize the creature, the persistence of the account leaves open the probability that something unusual was—and perhaps still is—taking place in Van Meter, Iowa.

Fear spread wildly when the Van Meter Visitor took over the town of Van Meter, Iowa, in the fall of 1903. Sporadic sightings continue to this day. Copyright © Lochlainn Seabrook.

WATER HOUND

Lochlainn Seabrook

The massive 8 foot long, quarter ton Water Hound is known to haunt the edges of Celtic lakes. Its eerie stare, unnatural hybrid appearance, and reputation for dragging people underwater, make it one of the most feared creatures across Ireland and Scotland. Copyright © Lochlainn Seabrook.

QUICK FACTS

NAME: Water Hound (Dobhar-chú).
FIRST SIGHTING: 17th Century.
LOCATION: Ireland and Scotland.
SIZE: Between 6 and 8 feet long, weighing 300 to 500 pounds.
APPEARANCE: Doglike aquatic beast with a long body, powerful limbs, and an otterlike tail.
EYES: Large, dark, and luminous in low light.
SKIN/FUR: Coarse fur, often described as black or dark brown; slick when wet.
DIET: Feeds on fish, waterfowl, livestock drinking at rivers, and occasionally carrion.
MOVEMENT: Swims with strong strokes; capable of quick bursts both in water and on land.
NOTABLE BEHAVIOR: Said to lunge at animals and drag them underwater, sometimes emitting piercing cries.
FIRST REPORTED BY: Rural farmers and fishermen along rivers and lochs.
CREATURE CLASSIFICATION: Amphibious mammal-like cryptid.
STATUS: Unverified by mainstream science, though modern sightings continue.

CREATURE PROFILE

Across the lochs and rivers of Ireland and Scotland local people still whisper about the Water Hound—known in Ireland as the Dobhar-chú. This creature is regarded as one of the most feared water-dwelling beasts in Celtic lands. Its reputation is not built on distant legends alone but on modern reports that sustain its mystery. Farmers, anglers, and travelers along remote waterways continue to describe encounters with an animal that behaves unlike any known species in the region.

The Water Hound is said to be roughly the size of a large dog or small bear, though adapted for an aquatic life. Its body is long and muscular with a thick otterlike tail that propels it through rivers and lochs. Witnesses often describe its fur as heavy and dark, slick with water yet coarse when dry. The beast leaves a strong musky odor near places it frequents, which some believe helps identify its presence even when it is not seen.

The eyes of the Water Hound are among its most striking features. They are described as large and shining, reflecting moonlight when the creature surfaces at night. Accounts often mention that the eyes seem to glow, giving the beast a spectral appearance when it emerges from dark water. The cry it produces is equally memorable—a sound compared to the scream of a woman or the howl of a dog—echoing across valleys and sending livestock into panic.

Dietary habits are central to reports of the Water Hound. It is said to prey on fish and waterfowl. Yet, farmers in past centuries blamed it for livestock losses, particularly sheep and calves taken while drinking from rivers. Some accounts even tell of the creature dragging animals beneath the water, leaving only churned foam on the surface. More chilling are the stories of people being attacked, seized by the creature, and pulled under before vanishing in deep pools. Local drownings of unexplained origin were often attributed to the Water Hound, reinforcing its fearsome reputation. Carrion is also reported as part of its diet, with stories of the beast feeding on drowned carcasses along riverbanks.

Its movement is another defining characteristic. The Hound is fast and agile in water, swimming with smooth strokes that allow it to cross wide stretches in moments. On land it is slower, yet still capable of sudden lunges, moving with a doglike gait when emerging from the shallows. This dual ability to navigate both terrains reinforces the idea that the creature is amphibious rather than strictly aquatic.

Local tradition treats the Water Hound with caution. Stories passed down through families describe it as dangerous to both animals and humans. Children were warned not to play near rivers at dusk, and fishermen carried charms or recited prayers before venturing into deep waters thought to be part of its territory. In some cases, the Water Hound has been linked to folklore involving guardian spirits of waterways—though these interpretations vary from one community to another.

Some researchers propose that the Water Hound may represent a remnant population of an unknown pinniped or otterlike species adapted to freshwater. Others suggest it could be a unique branch of mustelid, larger and more aggressive than the European otter. The persistence of similar descriptions across multiple centuries and locations makes it difficult to dismiss the accounts as mere folklore. If such an animal exists it would represent a rare example of a large predatory mammal hidden in the waterways of the British Isles.

First recorded sightings date back to the 17th Century, often in rural villages where farming life depended on rivers. While scientific authorities do not recognize the creature, ongoing reports from the 20th and 21st Centuries suggest it remains active in isolated regions. Its long life in both oral tradition and eyewitness testimony supports the high probability that an unidentified aquatic mammal still dwells in the waters of the British Isles.

The Water Hound, or Dobhar-chú, pulling a sheep into the murky depths of Glenade Lough in County Leitrim, Ireland. A woman, Gráinne Ní Conalai, is said to have been drowned by the beast in this very lake in 1722. Copyright © Lochlainn Seabrook.

WENDIGO

A 15 foot tall, half ton Wendigo stalks a northern Michigan forest, one of the most terrifying anthropophagous beasts in world history. Copyright © Lochlainn Seabrook.

QUICK FACTS

NAME: Wendigo.
FIRST SIGHTING: 17th Century.
LOCATION: Northern USA (Minnesota, Wisconsin, Michigan's Upper Peninsula), and remote areas in Ontario, Quebec, Manitoba, Alberta, and Saskatchewan, Canada.
SIZE: Height estimated at 8 to 15 feet. Weight estimated between 400 and 1,200 pounds.
APPEARANCE: Tall emaciated figure with elongated limbs, sharp claws, and skeletal features. Sometimes reported with antlers or a skull-like head.
EYES: Glowing, often described as yellow, red, or white.
SKIN/FUR: Ashen gray or pale decayed skin, occasionally covered in thin patchy fur.
DIET: Known as a cannibalistic predator; said to prefer human flesh, but will also eat animals. Some accounts claim it devours entire villages, never satisfied, driven by an insatiable hunger.
MOVEMENT: Moves with unnatural speed for its size. Long strides; able to run across snow or through forests silently; climbs trees with ease.
NOTABLE BEHAVIOR: Drawn to human settlements. Said to mimic voices to lure prey. Associated with winter, famine, and isolation.
FIRST REPORTED BY: Algonquian-speaking tribes of North America.
CREATURE CLASSIFICATION: Carnivorous humanoid cryptid.
STATUS: Undocumented by mainstream science, though sightings continue.

CREATURE PROFILE

The Wendigo is tied more closely to cold and famine than nearly any other cryptid on record. Found in stories and sightings across the northern USA and Canada, this being is described as both a physical predator and a force that thrives when human survival is most threatened. Its association with frozen forests and long winters gives it an unmistakable ecological niche, one that aligns with the places where people are most vulnerable.

Eyewitness descriptions remain remarkably consistent despite the time and physical distance between reports. The Wendigo is described as a towering gaunt being, skin stretched tight over its bones; or in some cases a horrific combination of human and deer-like traits. Its elongated arms, sharp claws, and unnaturally thin frame give it a skeletal outline that witnesses cannot erase from their memories. Some claim to see antlers sprouting from its skull-like head, while others insist the figure is completely human-like—but with twisted proportions. This variability has led researchers to suspect the Wendigo may not be a single creature but a species with regional variations.

    The diet of the Wendigo is a central part of its lore and its reputation. More than any other cryptid it is defined by its appetite. Nearly every report agrees that it feeds on human flesh. The creature is said to hunt lone travelers, families, and even entire camps. Accounts emphasize its inability to feel full, no matter how much it eats. Stories describe villages abandoned overnight, with signs of slaughter and mutilation attributed to the Wendigo. Even when prey is scarce it is said to continue prowling, its hunger insatiable. Some researchers consider this one of the strongest indications that the creature is a biological predator, adapted for survival during long northern winters where food is scarce.

    Movement patterns further distinguish the beast. Witnesses report a massive being capable of moving faster than a human can run, even over deep snow. Yet despite its bulk it travels in silence, able to appear without warning and vanish into the wilderness just as quickly. Its ability to climb trees and strike from above has been mentioned in several encounters, making it as much a danger from overhead as from the ground. These traits suggest an apex predator highly adapted to boreal forests.

    Reports of mimicry give the Wendigo an additional layer of menace. Hunters, loggers, and travelers describe hearing familiar voices in the woods, sometimes of loved ones calling for help, only to encounter the creature waiting. This tactic is remarkably similar to predatory strategies in the animal kingdom, where calls are imitated to lure prey. Its association with supernatural cold is also notable. Temperatures reportedly drop when the Wendigo appears, and the creature itself radiates a chill, reinforcing its tie to winter.

    The first formal accounts come from Algonquian-speaking peoples, who have long regarded the Wendigo as both a physical and spiritual killer. Early European settlers soon recorded their own sightings, often linking the creature to isolated deaths during harsh winters. While modern science has not confirmed the species, reports continue into recent years, particularly in the northern wilderness where human activity meets deep unbroken forest.

    Today the Wendigo is still considered an active threat in remote Canadian and northern American regions. Hunters and campers report strange tracks, chilling howls, and massive shadowy figures in the trees. Local traditions maintain strict warnings about traveling alone in the winter woods.

    While mainstream science dismisses the accounts, the ongoing testimonies—spread across multiple generations and regions—suggest the Wendigo may represent one of the most dangerous unverified predators on the continent.

While campers slumber peacefully, a Wendigo creeps through their campsite in search of an easy human meal. Copyright © Lochlainn Seabrook.

WEREWOLF

An 8 foot tall werewolf stalks a forest clearing in Defiance, Ohio, site of one of the most famous multiple eyewitness "Dogman" accounts in history. Copyright © Lochlainn Seabrook.

QUICK FACTS

NAME: Werewolf (*Homo lupus*).
FIRST SIGHTING: Ancient antiquity, with references dating back to Mesopotamian, Greek, and Norse texts.
LOCATION: Worldwide, but most frequently reported in Europe, North America, and South America.
SIZE: Typically reported as 6-8 feet tall when upright, weighing 200-300 pounds.
APPEARANCE: A hybrid of human and wolf traits; elongated snout, sharp teeth, clawed hands, muscular build, digitigrade legs, and covered in fur. Often reported shifting between human and lupine form.
EYES: Glowing red, yellow, or green, depending on the account.
SKIN/FUR: Thick fur ranging from gray and black to brown or reddish hues; some accounts mention patchy hair in transitional states.
DIET: Carnivorous, primarily livestock, wild animals, and occasionally humans. Some reports suggest opportunistic omnivory when meat is scarce. Witnesses describe feeding on fresh kills and, in folklore, a craving for blood or raw flesh.
MOVEMENT: Quadrupedal or bipedal; capable of rapid sprinting, leaping long distances, and moving silently through forests. Said to possess uncanny stamina and agility beyond human or wolf capabilities.
NOTABLE BEHAVIOR: Territorial aggression, nocturnal activity, transformation at the full moon, heightened senses of smell and hearing, and a tendency to stalk prey before striking.
FIRST REPORTED BY: Classical writers such as Herodotus and Petronius, with widespread medieval accounts recorded by European chroniclers.
CREATURE CLASSIFICATION: Therianthrope (human-animal shapeshifter).
STATUS: Unverified by conventional science, but sightings and encounters continue unabated.

CREATURE PROFILE

Werewolves are among the oldest and most perennial cryptids known to humankind. Reports of men transforming into wolves, or wolf-like beings walking upright, appear in the earliest human records. In Mesopotamia, for example, inscriptions describe wolf-men serving as guardians and warriors. In Greek literature lycanthropy (from *lykos*, "wolf") is mentioned by writers such as Herodotus, who recorded the tale of the Neuri people of Scythia transforming into wolves once a year. Norse sagas describe warriors wearing wolf pelts and gaining wolf-like powers, blurring the line between ritual, reality, and transformation.

Throughout medieval Europe werewolf encounters surged in number, often tied to remote forests and villages. Farmers reported mutilated livestock, mysterious tracks larger than those of ordinary wolves, and shadowy creatures glimpsed under moonlight. Court records from France, Germany, and Eastern Europe document hundreds of werewolf trials between the 15th and 18th Centuries, where witnesses swore under oath that men in their villages had transformed into ravenous beasts. These testimonies, preserved in detail, provide an immense body of ethnographic evidence supporting the persistence of belief in a tangible recurring phenomenon.

Eyewitness descriptions consistently emphasize physical power beyond that of natural wolves. Reports mention individuals standing taller than any man, with broad shoulders, digitigrade legs, and hands ending in clawed fingers. Some describe half-transformed beings with a mix of human skin and fur. Their eyes are often described as luminous, sometimes reflecting light in the same way as nocturnal predators. Witnesses also describe unnerving vocalizations: not quite a human scream, not quite a wolf's howl, but a hybrid sound unlike anything in the known animal kingdom.

Modern encounters continue, particularly in North America where they are often referred to as "dogmen." Witnesses describe large wolf-headed bipeds with human-like chests and arms. In Michigan, Wisconsin, and the Appalachian regions, multiple independent reports include road crossings, livestock killings, and stalking incidents. Law enforcement officers, truck drivers, and hunters have filed reports describing these creatures, lending more credibility to the accounts. In South America similar beings are called *lobisón* or *lobisomem*, where belief in hereditary werewolves remains strong.

From a biological perspective, the werewolf is often classified among therianthropes: beings with both human and animal qualities. Cryptozoologists theorize that the werewolf may represent an undiscovered hominin or canid hybrid, adapted for nocturnal predation and territorial defense. Others suggest a connection with altered states of consciousness, inherited traits, or rare genetic conditions that may explain partial physical transformation reports. Regardless of the explanation, the consistency of global testimonies across time and culture strongly suggests that the werewolf phenomenon has a basis in reality.

The creature's behavior is characterized by stealth, aggression when threatened, and nocturnal hunting. They are commonly associated with the full moon—though whether this is symbolic or biologically linked remains unknown. Their predatory habits align with large carnivores, though reports of selective attacks on humans suggest an intelligence beyond that of natural wolves. Territorial displays, stalking behavior, and sudden retreats into deep forest cover have also been widely documented.

Werewolves remain one of the most well-documented cryptids in history. Their prevalence in written accounts, folklore, and modern testimony places them in the forefront of cryptozoological study as probable real creatures that have yet to be identified and classified by mainstream science.

The 300 pound cryptid, known as the Mineral Point Werewolf, prowls the roads of Mineral Point, Wisconsin, terrifying both residents and motorists. Copyright © Lochlainn Seabrook.

WHITE RIVER MONSTER

The half ton White River Monster, also known as "Whitey," emerges at dusk in the waters near Newport, Arkansas. Copyright © Lochlainn Seabrook.

QUICK FACTS

NAME: White River Monster.
FIRST SIGHTING: 1915.
LOCATION: White River, near Newport, Arkansas, USA.
SIZE: Estimated 12-40 feet in length, possibly weighing 1,000-1,500 pounds.
APPEARANCE: Large grayish, elephant-like body with smooth ridged back, long tail, and sometimes described with horns or a spiny crest.
EYES: Small and dark, set low on the head.
SKIN/FUR: Thick leathery gray skin resembling that of an elephant or giant fish.
DIET: Thought to feed on fish, turtles, waterfowl, and possibly small mammals or carrion in the river system. Local accounts claim it may upset boats to access food.
MOVEMENT: Slow rolling motion at the surface, but capable of sudden surges or dives when startled.
NOTABLE BEHAVIOR: Surfaces regularly in summer months, sometimes bellowing or thrashing; known to frighten livestock and cause riverbank damage.
FIRST REPORTED BY: Farmers and fishermen of Newport, Arkansas.
CREATURE CLASSIFICATION: Aquatic cryptid.
STATUS: Unverified by mainstream science; but sightings continue into the present day.

CREATURE PROFILE

The waters of the White River in eastern Arkansas have long been associated with a mysterious presence that locals call the White River Monster. The earliest widely known reports of "Whitey" come from 1915 when fishermen on the river encountered an enormous creature that disrupted their nets and frightened livestock on the banks. Over the decades that followed repeated sightings turned the river into one of the South's most discussed cryptid hotspots. Even today residents of Newport and surrounding communities describe encounters with an immense aquatic animal that defies classification.

Descriptions of the White River Monster vary, but there is surprising consistency in certain features. Witnesses describe a body ranging anywhere from 12 to 40 feet in length, making it one of the largest freshwater cryptids reported in the United States. The animal is said to possess a broad gray body, thick leathery skin, and a long tail capable of powerful propulsion. Several accounts mention a spiny or ridged back, while others note horn-like projections near the head. Such descriptions suggest a creature adapted for protection in the turbid waters of a large river system.

The eyes of the White River Monster are always depicted as small and dark, overshadowed by the rest of its massive bulk. Observers frequently compare its texture to the hide of an elephant, with folds and ridges that glisten when it breaks the surface. Its size alone suggests it would need a diet rich in protein. Most accounts claim it consumes fish and turtles, but others maintain that it also takes ducks and muskrats, as well as carrion left in the current. Local lore warns that the creature occasionally overturns small boats, possibly as a hunting method or simply as a defensive act when disturbed.

Movement patterns seem deliberate and slow. Eyewitnesses describe the creature rolling just beneath the surface, creating a broad wake. At times it has been observed lying still, only to surge forward with startling speed when approached. Loud bellows or groaning sounds are also part of its reputation, leading some to compare the noise to that of a distressed cow or bull. Farmers along the river in the early 20th Century even reported livestock becoming panicked when the animal surfaced nearby, suggesting the sound carried far across the floodplain.

The cultural importance of the White River Monster cannot be overlooked. During the 1930s newspapers spread reports of the beast widely, leading to national attention and tourism in Newport. The town eventually recognized its role in local identity, and in 1973 Arkansas went so far as to declare a section of the river a protected refuge for the White River Monster. This official recognition sets it apart from most cryptids and demonstrates the seriousness with which locals regard their legendary creature.

Modern sightings continue, particularly during hot summers when the river level drops and visibility improves. Some fishermen still report broken nets or unusual wakes in calm water. Others recall seeing the gray form breach briefly before sinking again into the deep channel.

Although mainstream science has not verified the animal's existence, the frequency of these sightings, combined with the consistency of its descriptions across more than a century, strongly supports the probability that a large unidentified animal inhabits the White River.

Whether the White River Monster is a surviving relic of an ancient lineage, a misidentified known animal, or an entirely new species, it remains an important case in North American cryptozoology. The persistence of reports and the cultural traditions that surround it point to more than mere folklore.

In the quiet stretches of the Arkansas waterway the creature continues to reveal itself to those who keep watch, ensuring its place as one of the most famous river cryptids in the United States.

The 40 foot long White River Monster threatens a small fishing boat in eastern Arkansas. Copyright © Lochlainn Seabrook.

WILDMAN

The 9 foot tall Wildman: supreme guardian of the natural world. Copyright © Lochlainn Seabrook.

QUICK FACTS

NAME: Wildman.
FIRST SIGHTING: Antiquity, with references in European chronicles dating back to at least the 9th Century.
LOCATION: Reported worldwide, especially in Europe, Asia, and North America.
SIZE: Estimated 6 to 9 feet in height, weighing 400 to 800 pounds.
APPEARANCE: Broad-shouldered, muscular, humanoid figure covered in thick hair, often described as primitive yet humanlike.
EYES: Deep-set, dark, sometimes glowing or reflective at night.
SKIN/FUR: Fur ranging from black to brown, occasionally reddish; rough, coarse texture. Skin beneath described as gray, dark, or ruddy.
DIET: Omnivorous; reported to consume roots, berries, nuts, leaves, wild game, fish, livestock, carrion, and occasionally cultivated crops. Accounts suggest opportunistic feeding, with evidence of both hunting and scavenging.
MOVEMENT: Walks upright with a heavy, lumbering gait; can move swiftly when threatened; capable of climbing and swimming.
NOTABLE BEHAVIOR: Shy and reclusive but occasionally aggressive when confronted; known for terrifying vocalizations, stone throwing, and livestock raids; folklore describes them as abducting women or children.
FIRST REPORTED BY: Early medieval chroniclers and travelers across Europe and Asia; later by European settlers in North America.
CREATURE CLASSIFICATION: Anthropoid hominin; possibly a surviving archaic human or unknown primate.
STATUS: Unverified by conventional science; yet considered extant by many field researchers.

CREATURE PROFILE

The Wildman is one of the most ancient and widespread cryptid traditions, with records extending across continents and centuries. From the medieval "Woodwose" of Europe to the yeti-like figures of Central Asia and the "hairy men" of North America, the archetype remains consistent: a large, manlike being, covered in hair, living in remote forests and mountains, and occupying a liminal position between human and beast. Unlike mythological beings, however, the Wildman tradition is remarkably uniform across cultures, strongly suggesting it is based on real encounters.

Medieval European chronicles describe the Wildman as a hairy, speechless man of the woods, sometimes depicted in church carvings and illuminated manuscripts. Reports speak of them dwelling in forests, shunning civilization, but occasionally being captured and displayed in villages. Some accounts describe them as possessing great strength and endurance, capable of overpowering armed men. In Central Asia related traditions of hairy giants—such as the Almas—suggest a close link to archaic hominins like *Homo erectus* or the Denisovans. These beings are said to be intelligent, tool-using, and family-oriented, but living outside the structures of human society.

In North America stories of "wild men of the woods" predate European settlement, found within Native American oral traditions from coast to coast. Tribes describe them as forest dwellers, with some groups revering them as guardians of nature, while others fear them as dangerous abductors. Early colonial newspapers carried reports of settlers encountering giant hairy men roaming the frontier, reinforcing the continuity of this legend into modern times.

Descriptions of the Wildman are strikingly consistent: towering height, immense strength, deep-set eyes, heavy brow ridges, and a body entirely cloaked in hair. The creatures are usually solitary, though some accounts describe small patriarchal family groups. Their footprints resemble human prints but are larger and broader, sometimes with signs of midtarsal breaks—anatomical features that align with known fossil hominins. Their vocalizations range from howls and growls to whistles and humanlike cries, often reported as unnerving or unearthly. Stone-throwing, branch-breaking, rock-clacking, and tree-knocking are among the many documented intimidation behaviors.

Dietary habits, based on reports, suggest opportunism. Witnesses have described them raiding gardens, orchards, and livestock pens, as well as hunting deer, elk, and wild boar. Foraging for nuts, berries, mushrooms, and tubers also appears common. Such a wide dietary range would have enabled survival in multiple climates, from Europe's temperate forests to Asia's mountains and America's wilderness.

Modern cryptozoologists propose that the Wildman may represent an undiscovered species of large primate or a relict population of archaic humans. Parallels to *Gigantopithecus* have been suggested, though this particular creature's known fossils suggest a primarily Asian origin. Others point to Neanderthals or Denisovans surviving in isolated regions into historical times. While no physical specimen has been recovered by science, the sheer volume of reports across centuries and cultures strongly indicates a biological basis.

What about comparisons between the Wild Man and Bigfoot? Interestingly, the Wildman tradition is much older in literature and folklore than the more modern Bigfoot tradition. Indeed, the European Woodwose or Wildman dates back at least a thousand years, appearing in chronicles, carvings, and even heraldry, while, by contrast, the word "Bigfoot" only emerged in mid-20th Century North America—even though indigenous oral traditions predate it by centuries.

That said, the descriptions of the two beasts are strikingly similar: large, hairy, humanlike, reclusive, sometimes dangerous. Perhaps the Wildman is the Old World version of the New World Sasquatch/Bigfoot; in other words, they may represent the same phenomenon expressed through different cultures—possibly a surviving archaic hominin or large primate distributed across continents.

Whatever one's personal views on the matter, the Wildman as a singular cryptid in its own right remains one of the most compelling unknown creatures due to at least one simple fact: it bridges folklore, anthropology, and natural history. Its continuation across geography and time, combined with physical evidence such as footprints and hair samples of unknown classification, supports the probability that these beings are more than legend.

At nearly half a ton in weight, the Wildman can easily defend its territory when necessary. Copyright © Lochlainn Seabrook.

YEREN

The 10 foot tall Yeren in its natural habitat: a Shennongjia forest in Hubei Province, China. Copyright © Lochlainn Seabrook.

QUICK FACTS

NAME: Yeren.
FIRST SIGHTING: 3rd Century B.C.; mentioned in ancient Chinese chronicles.
LOCATION: Remote mountain ranges of central and southern China, especially Hubei, Hunan, and Sichuan Provinces.
SIZE: Reported height ranges from 6 to 10 feet; weight possibly 400 to 700 pounds.
APPEARANCE: Tall, powerfully built, bipedal hominid resembling both ape and human, with broad shoulders, long arms, and a sloping forehead.
EYES: Small and deep-set, usually reported as dark in color, reflecting light at night.
SKIN/FUR: Covered in thick reddish-brown or dark auburn hair, sometimes described as gray in older individuals. Skin of the face and hands visible, usually dark and leathery.
DIET: Accounts describe a wide-ranging omnivorous diet, including wild fruits, berries, bamboo, roots, nuts, fish, small animals, livestock, and occasionally crops such as corn or sweet potatoes. Reports also note opportunistic scavenging of carcasses.
MOVEMENT: Typically bipedal with long loping strides, but capable of running swiftly across steep mountain slopes. Witnesses have also described quadrupedal movement in rough terrain.
NOTABLE BEHAVIOR: Known for vocalizations ranging from howls to grunts, a pungent odor often reported near sightings, stone-throwing when threatened, and apparent curiosity toward humans; occasionally raids rural farms.
FIRST REPORTED BY: Ancient Chinese historians, notably in the *Shan Hai Jing*.
CREATURE CLASSIFICATION: Unknown hominid, possibly a surviving *Gigantopithecus blacki* or related primate.
STATUS: Unverified by mainstream science, but strongly supported by centuries of consistent reports, ongoing eyewitness testimony, and alleged physical traces.

CREATURE PROFILE

The Yeren, sometimes called the "Chinese Wildman," is one of Asia's best known cryptids. Accounts span over two thousand years, with references in early Chinese texts describing a "manlike beast" inhabiting remote mountain forests. Its most frequent modern sightings occur in Hubei Province, particularly around the Shennongjia Forest Region, an area of rugged terrain, deep valleys, and dense subtropical forest that remains largely inaccessible. This isolated environment provides a plausible refuge for a large mammalian species to exist unnoticed by mainstream science.

Descriptions portray the Yeren as a large upright hominid, standing well above average human height and covered in reddish or auburn hair. Unlike most apes it is consistently reported walking upright for long distances. Witnesses describe long muscular arms, a pronounced brow ridge, and a face blending both ape and human characteristics. Tracks attributed to the Yeren are humanlike but much larger, with footprints measuring up to 16 inches in length. In some encounters witnesses report clawlike nails, suggesting a divergence from strictly human morphology.

Behavioral reports indicate intelligence and adaptability. Farmers in rural areas claim that Yeren occasionally raid crops or chicken coops, showing opportunistic feeding. Vocalizations are diverse: witnesses describe shrieks, grunts, and resonant howls that carry across mountain valleys. Many also note a distinct musky odor preceding sightings—a characteristic often associated with large primates. Stone-throwing, tree-shaking, and deliberate displays of intimidation have been described, paralleling behaviors in real world primates such as gorillas and chimpanzees.

One of the most compelling aspects of the Yeren mystery is the possibility of its connection to *Gigantopithecus blacki*, a massive prehistoric ape that lived in China until, allegedly, roughly 300,000 years ago. Fossil evidence suggests that Giganto stood over 10 feet tall and weighed more than 1,000 pounds. The Yeren's reported size, hair color, and geographic distribution overlap closely with what would be expected if descendants of this species had survived into the modern era in remote mountain refuges.

Chinese scientists have taken Yeren reports seriously. In the late 1970s and early 1980s official expeditions to Shennongjia gathered footprints, hair samples, and hundreds of eyewitness accounts. While no specimen has been captured, ongoing sightings from farmers, hunters, and even soldiers has fueled continued investigation. Some of the hair samples collected remain unidentified, showing traits inconsistent with known local fauna.

For many rural Chinese communities the Yeren is accepted as a genuine inhabitant of the wilderness, a living relic that demonstrates how little is truly known about Asia's remaining wild landscapes. If proven real the Yeren would not only represent a remarkable survival of a prehistoric lineage, but would also force a reevaluation of human evolutionary history, especially concerning the persistence of unknown hominids.

The Yeren is reported to raid rural farms in search of food. Usually the only traces of the incursion are footprints and a foul smell. Copyright © Lochlainn Seabrook.

YETI

A 10 foot tall Yeti in its natural Himalayan environment. Accounts of the beast date from ancient times all the way into the present, making it one of the most persistent and widely reported mystery animals in recorded history. Copyright © Lochlainn Seabrook.

QUICK FACTS

NAME: Yeti.
FIRST SIGHTING: Reported in ancient Himalayan folklore, with written accounts appearing in the 19th Century.
LOCATION: Himalayan mountain range, including Nepal, Tibet, Bhutan, and northern India.
SIZE: Estimated height between 6 and 10 feet; weight between 400 and 800 pounds.
APPEARANCE: Large bipedal primate-like creature with broad shoulders, powerful limbs, and a conical head shape.
EYES: Small deep-set, often described as dark and reflective.
SKIN/FUR: Thick, shaggy coat of brown, black, reddish, or whitish hair adapted for alpine cold. Skin is grayish or dark.
DIET: Reported to eat roots, tubers, fruits, and leaves; also linked to hunting smaller animals, livestock raids, and scavenging carrion. Some reports suggest opportunistic predation on larger mammals such as yaks or deer.
MOVEMENT: A true facultative quadruped, it is primarily bipedal, but is also capable of quadrupedal locomotion; reported as an agile climber and a swift runner, even at high altitudes.
NOTABLE BEHAVIOR: Leaves large humanoid footprints in snow; reported vocalizations range from howls to whistles; associated with stone-throwing and avoidance of human contact; sometimes enters villages or herder camps.
FIRST REPORTED BY: Indigenous Himalayan peoples, including Sherpa, Lepcha, and Tibetan communities.
CREATURE CLASSIFICATION: Undescribed primate, possibly a relict species of *Gigantopithecus* or other hominin.
STATUS: Scientifically unverified, but supported by centuries of indigenous tradition, physical traces, and eyewitness accounts.

CREATURE PROFILE

The Yeti, also sometimes known as the "Abominable Snowman," is one of the most widely reported cryptids in human history. Indigenous Himalayan communities have described the creature for centuries as a large, hairy, bipedal being inhabiting snowy peaks, forested valleys, and alpine meadows. Unlike many folkloric creatures the Yeti is consistently reported across diverse cultures of the Himalayas, where it is regarded with reverence, caution, and, just as often, fear.

Descriptions portray the Yeti as a powerfully built, upright primate-like animal, often standing between 6 and 10 feet tall, though smaller individuals are occasionally reported. Its body is covered in long shaggy fur adapted to the severe cold of the Himalayan highlands. While coloration varies the most common reports describe brown or dark reddish coats—though lighter specimens are sometimes mentioned. Observers frequently note its broad shoulders, strong arms, and a head shape tapering to a conical crown, features that distinguish it from known apes.

The Yeti is widely associated with large humanoid tracks found in snow at high altitudes. These prints often measure 12 to 15 inches in length and reveal a stride consistent with bipedal locomotion. Despite harsh environmental conditions tracks have been documented by explorers, mountaineers, and scientists throughout the 19th and 20th Centuries, sparking debates about their origin. Notably, expeditions led by British, Russian, and American mountaineers have all reported encountering unusual tracks in otherwise remote and inaccessible areas.

Behaviorally, the Yeti is elusive and wary of humans, generally avoiding contact. However, accounts continue to come in which tell of it raiding herder camps for food, carrying off livestock, and on rare occasions, intimidating or threatening humans who venture too near. Some witnesses report loud howls, whistles, or guttural calls echoing across valleys, all attributed to the creature. Others describe it throwing rocks, a behavior paralleling that of apes defending their territory.

Dietary reports suggest the Yeti is omnivorous, consuming roots, tubers, berries, and alpine vegetation while also supplementing its diet with small mammals, fish, and scavenged carrion. In harsher winters it may resort to preying upon livestock such as goats and yaks. This varied diet is consistent with survival in the difficult conditions of the Himalayas.

From a scientific perspective the Yeti has been proposed as a surviving population of *Gigantopithecus blacki*, an immense prehistoric ape known from Asian fossil remains. Others theorize it could represent an unknown hominin species, possibly a relict population of *Homo erectus* or Neanderthal adapted to the high-altitude environment. The creature's adaptations—thick fur, large body size, and powerful musculature—would all serve to withstand the cold, rugged terrain of the Himalayas.

The persistence of consistent reports across cultures and centuries, coupled with physical evidence such as footprints, makes the Yeti one of the most compelling cryptids on record. While physical remains have yet to be confirmed, the convergence of indigenous knowledge, eyewitness testimony, and unexplained traces strongly suggests that the Yeti is more than a mythic legend.

With a reputation for extreme territoriality, it is not surprising that a number of accounts include attacks on local mountain villages. Copyright © Lochlainn Seabrook.

YOWIE

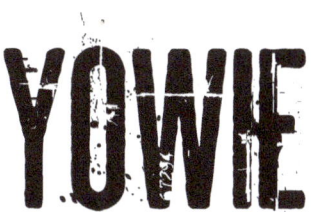

The Yowie is Australia's Bigfoot: sometimes aggressive, always elusive.
Copyright © Lochlainn Seabrook.

QUICK FACTS

NAME: Yowie.
FIRST SIGHTING: Early 19th Century, with Aboriginal oral traditions dating back thousands of years.
LOCATION: Remote forests, mountains, and bushlands of eastern Australia, especially New South Wales and Queensland.
SIZE: Height ranges from 6 to 12 feet, with an estimated weight between 400 and 1,000 pounds.
APPEARANCE: Large, bipedal primate-like being with a broad chest, long arms, and massive shoulders. Possesses a sloping forehead and a protruding brow ridge.
EYES: Deep-set, dark eyes that glow red or amber in low light, often described as piercing and unsettling.
SKIN/FUR: Covered in long shaggy hair ranging from dark brown to black, though reddish coats have also been reported. Skin beneath the fur is typically dark and leathery.
DIET: Omnivorous; reports suggest consumption of roots, fruits, nuts, and vegetation, supplemented by small animals, reptiles, fish, and occasionally livestock. Some accounts claim it scavenges carrion and raids human camps for food.
MOVEMENT: Walks upright with a lumbering gait, though capable of rapid bursts of speed and silent movement. Leaves large humanlike footprints with broad, splayed toes.
NOTABLE BEHAVIOR: Emits loud howls, growls, and shrieks; throws rocks; breaks trees or branches as intimidation. Often avoids humans but may shadow travelers. Aboriginal lore associates it with abductions.
FIRST REPORTED BY: Aboriginal Australians, later documented by European settlers in the 1800s.
CREATURE CLASSIFICATION: Hominid cryptid.
STATUS: Unverified by conventional science, but supported by widespread folkloric and modern eyewitness testimony.

CREATURE PROFILE

The Yowie is Australia's most famous cryptid, often described as the continent's counterpart to the North American Bigfoot or Sasquatch. Aboriginal oral traditions, in which it is referred to as the Yahoo, include references to hairy giants long before European settlement, indicating that this belief is deeply rooted in the continent's cultural memory. Known by a variety of regional names among Aboriginal groups, the Yowie is often portrayed as both a guardian of the wilderness and a dangerous entity capable of harming those who entered its domain without respect.

Physical descriptions vary, but most reports emphasize great size, muscular build, and ape-like features combined with a distinctly human posture. The creature's head is described as dome-shaped or conical, with a heavy brow ridge and flat nose. Its hands and feet are large and humanlike, but often more splayed and adapted for rough terrain. Witnesses frequently remark on its pungent odor, similar to wet animal fur mixed with decay, which is said to precede encounters.

Footprint evidence has been reported across eastern Australia, ranging from 14 to 20 inches in length. Casts show wide impressions with broad toes, supporting claims that the Yowie is bipedal. Sounds attributed to the creature include guttural roars, howls, and bone-chilling screams, often heard in remote bushlands at night. Some witnesses describe a heavy stomping noise or tree-knocking behaviors similar to those reported in North America with Bigfoot.

Dietary habits are inferred from Aboriginal accounts and modern sightings. The Yowie is said to dig up roots, raid orchards, and take bush tucker such as yams and berries. Other reports link it to predation on kangaroos, wallabies, or feral animals. Farmers have occasionally blamed it for livestock disappearances. In survival terms such an omnivorous diet would support its presence in Australia's varied ecosystems, from subtropical forests to arid mountain ranges.

Behaviorally, the Yowie is both elusive and confrontational. Many encounters describe it as avoiding direct contact, quickly retreating into thick vegetation when noticed. Yet others recount frightening displays: rock-throwing, wood breaking, and shadowing people at night. Aboriginal traditions include stories of abductions, particularly of women and children, underscoring its fearsome reputation.

Cryptozoologists have proposed that the Yowie may represent a surviving hominid lineage, possibly related to *Gigantopithecus blacki*, which once roamed Asia, or to other unknown australopithecine-like primates. Its distribution in rugged sparsely populated regions would have aided survival into modern times. Skeptics cite misidentifications of large kangaroos, escaped primates, or hoaxes. But the persistence of reports from both Indigenous and settler populations suggests a deeper phenomenon.

Modern investigations continue, with researchers collecting footprint casts, audio recordings, and eyewitness testimony. Despite the lack of physical remains the sheer number of consistent reports across centuries keeps the Yowie firmly embedded in both Australian folklore and cryptozoological study. Its continual presence in Indigenous stories gives it further weight as a creature deserving serious scientific inquiry.

A half ton, rock-throwing Yowie attempting to drive human interlopers from its forest domain. Copyright © Lochlainn Seabrook.

ZUIYO-MARU CREATURE

The Zuiyo-maru Creature as it might have looked in life. Its true identity remains a cryptozoological mystery. Copyright © Lochlainn Seabrook.

QUICK FACTS

NAME: Zuiyo-maru Creature.
FIRST SIGHTING: April 25, 1977.
LOCATION: Off the coast of New Zealand, South Pacific Ocean.
SIZE: Estimated length 32 feet; weight approximately 4,000 pounds.
APPEARANCE: Long neck, small head, large body, four large flippers, long tail.
EYES: Not clearly observed due to decomposition.
SKIN/FUR: Described as rough, pale whitish with reddish-brown patches; no fur observed.
DIET: Likely carnivorous, preying on fish, squid, and other marine animals; scavenging behavior possible.
MOVEMENT: Aquatic, propelled by four large flippers and tail; no surface locomotion observed.
NOTABLE BEHAVIOR: Carcass retrieved from trawl net at a depth of 1,000 feet; creature remained intact long enough to allow sketches and measurements.
FIRST REPORTED BY: Crew of the Japanese fishing vessel *Zuiyo-maru*.
CREATURE CLASSIFICATION: Possible surviving plesiosaur (*Plesiosauria*) or large unknown marine reptile.
STATUS: Unconfirmed by conventional science; yet its carcass remains as overt evidence that large unknown animals may yet exist in the deep ocean.

CREATURE PROFILE

The Zuiyo-maru Creature is one of the most compelling cases in modern cryptozoology because it involves trained observers, a physical specimen, and scientific documentation.

On April 25, 1977, while operating off the coast of New Zealand, the Japanese trawler *Zuiyo-maru* brought up a large carcass from a depth of roughly 1,000 feet. The remains were so unusual that the crew took numerous photographs, made sketches, and recorded detailed measurements before discarding the decomposing body back into the sea to avoid contamination of their catch.

The carcass measured approximately 32 feet in length and weighed close to two tons. It displayed a long tapering neck of about 5 feet, a small head, and a massive torso. Four large flippers were noted, each over 3 feet long, suggestive of strong aquatic propulsion. A long tail extended nearly 7 feet. The body had little external tissue remaining in some areas, with skin described as rough and fibrous, whitish-gray with reddish patches. No fur or scales were reported.

The skeletal proportions strongly resembled those of a plesiosaur, a group of long-necked marine reptiles believed to have gone extinct around 65 million years ago. Japanese scientists who examined the photographs and tissue samples initially proposed that the find was consistent with a surviving *plesiosaurid*. Zoologist Dr. Yoshinori Kimura and others argued that the body proportions, particularly the long neck and small head, excluded the possibility of a shark.

The diet of such a creature, if living, would likely mirror that of ancient plesiosaurs: fish, cephalopods, and other medium-sized marine animals. Given the deep-sea recovery of the carcass, scavenging behavior is also probable.

Skeptics later suggested the carcass was that of a decomposed basking shark (*Cetorhinus maximus*), whose body shape can mimic that of a plesiosaur when soft tissues decompose. In this state the head, gills, and lower jaw of a shark slough away, leaving a long "neck-like" structure and a torso with wing-like appendages. However, tissue analyses conducted by Japanese scientists reportedly showed collagen protein structures distinct from typical sharks, and several experts noted discrepancies between basking shark carcasses and the *Zuiyo-maru* specimen.

Throughout history sailors and coastal communities have reported sightings of long-necked, flippered sea creatures that bear striking similarities to the *Zuiyo-maru* carcass. Accounts from the North Atlantic, South Pacific, and even freshwater lakes often describe serpentine bodies, elongated necks, and movements consistent with a plesiosaur-like form. The *Zuiyo-maru* discovery therefore provides a rare physical link between modern eyewitness testimony and the possibility of surviving relict populations of ancient marine reptiles.

The *Zuiyo-maru* discovery is significant because it cannot be dismissed as mere folklore. The event was documented by professional fishermen and examined by Japanese scientists with training in marine biology. While the original carcass was discarded, the surviving photographs, sketches, and data continue to be studied.

If the Zuiyo-maru Creature was indeed a plesiosaur, it would mean that a lineage of these ancient marine reptiles survived undetected in the vast and unexplored depths of the world's oceans. Even if it was a basking shark, the case underscores how little we know about deep-sea decomposition and the mysteries that still surface from the ocean's depths.

Either way, the Zuiyo-maru Creature remains one of the most credible cryptid cases of the modern era. Whether the mystery of its identity will ever be solved remains open-ended.

The carcass of the Zuiyo-maru Creature as it looked when it was first hauled up by Japanese fishermen in 1977. While the true identity of the beast remains unknown, photographs of the body, along with detailed tissue analyses by Japanese scientists, ensure that the mysteries surrounding it will not fade away any time soon. Copyright © Lochlainn Seabrook.

APPENDIX

CRYPTIDS BY CONTINENT
112 CYRPTIDS ALPHABETIZED - COVERING ALL 7 CONTINENTS

AFRICA
Agogwe
Emela-ntouka
Hairy Dwarf
Inkanyamba
Kalanoro
Kongamato
Mokele-Mbembe
Nandi Bear
Ngoubou
Popobawa
Trunko

ANTARCTICA
Giant Antarctic Ice Worm
Ningen

ASIA
Ahool
Almas
Barmanou
Buru
Mongolian Death Worm
Orang Pendek
Tsuchinoko
Wildman
Yeren
Yeti

AUSTRALIA / OCEANIA
Adaro
Bunyip
Phantom Kangaroo

Sigbin
Tikbalang
Yowie
Zuiyo-maru Creature

EUROPE
Am Fear Liath Mòr
Beast of Bodmin Moor
Beast of Exmoor
Beast of Gevaudan
Beithir
Black Dog
Brosno Dragon
Cait Sidhe
Devon Devil
Each-Uisce
Ellén Trechend
Fairy
Green Man
Kelpie
Kraken
Lagarfljót Worm
Lindorm
Loch Lochy Monster
Loch Morar Monster
Loch Ness Monster
Merfolk
Owlman
Selkie
Storsjöodjuret
Stuart's Monster
Tatzelwurm
Water Hound
Werewolf

NORTH AMERICA
Ahuitzotl
Akhlut
Altamaha-ha
Batsquatch
Bear Lake Monster
Beast of Bray Road
Beast of Busco
Big Bird
Bigfoot
Black Panther

Cadborosaurus
Champ
Chupacabra
Dogman
Dover Demon
Enfield Horror
Flathead Lake Monster
Flatwoods Monster
Fouke Monster
Goatman
Hopkinsville Goblins
Jersey Devil
Kushtaka
Lake Tahoe Monster
Lake Worth Monster
Lizard Man of Scape Ore Swamp
Loveland Frogman
Lusca
Mantis Man
Minerva Monster
Momo
Mothman
Ogopogo
Onza
Ozark Howler
Pascagoula River Aliens
Pterosaur
Pukwudgie
Reptoid
Rougarou
Shunka Warakin
Skunk Ape
Snallygaster
Squonk
Thunderbird
Van Meter Visitor
Wendigo
White River Monster

SOUTH AMERICA
Mapinguari
Mono Grande
Nahuelito

My favorite mystery animal: The Loch Ness Monster. Copyright © Lochlainn Seabrook.

BIBLIOGRAPHY

And Suggested Reading

Aldridge, Bernard. *Monsters of the Deep: Marine Mysteries from the Depths of the Ocean*. London, UK: Neptune Press, 1982.
Allen, Peter. *The Bunyip and Other Mythical Monsters and Legends*. Sydney, NSW: Kangaroo Press, 1997.
Ancelet, Barry Jean. *Cajun and Creole Folktales: The French Oral Tradition of South Louisiana*. Jackson, MS: University Press of Mississippi, 1994.
Andrews, Cecelia Svinth. *Shanyat'ii: Wisdom of the Tlingit People*. Juneau, AK: Sealaska Heritage Foundation, 1994.
Andrews, Roy Chapman. *On the Trail of Ancient Man*. New York: G. P. Putnam's Sons, 1926.
Arment, Chad. *Cryptozoology: Science and Speculation*. Landisville, PA: Coachwhip Publications, 2004.
Armitage, George. *Mysterious Creatures of the Canadian Lakes*. Toronto: Maple Leaf Press, 1976.
Arrowsmith, Nancy. *Field Guide to the Little People*. New York: Hill and Wang, 1977.
Balfour, Henry. *Legends of Madagascar*. London, UK: Oxford University Press, 1898.
Ballance, Hugh. *Eyewitness Account of the Margate Sea Monster Battle*. Margate, South Africa: Personal Testimony, 1924.
Barber, Paul. *Vampires, Burial, and Death: Folklore and Reality*. New Haven, CT: Yale University Press, 1988.
Barger, Ralph. *Strange Creatures of the Woods: Tales from the Allegheny Plateau*. Harrisburg, PA: Keystone Press, 1904.
Baring-Gould, Sabine. *The Book of Were-Wolves: Being an Account of a Terrible Superstition*. London, UK: Smith, Elder and Company, 1865.
Barker, Gray. *They Knew Too Much About Flying Saucers*. Clarksburg, WV: Saucerian Books, 1956.
Barrett, Frank. *Philippine Folk Tales*. Chicago, IL: A.C. McClurg, 1916.
Bartholomew, Paul. *Champ: Beyond the Legend*. White River Junction, VT: Whitford Press, 2002.
Bartholomew, Robert E. *Bigfoot: Encounters in Ohio, Illinois, and the Great Lakes Region*. New York: Prometheus Books, 1998.
Bartholomew, Robert E., and Joe Nickell. *American Hauntings: The True Stories Behind Hollywood's Scariest Movies—From The Exorcist to The Conjuring*. Guilford, CT: Lyons Press, 2015.

Bauer, Henry H. *The Enigma of Loch Ness: Making Sense of a Mystery*. Urbana, IL: University of Illinois Press, 1986.
Bauer, William. *The Hodag and Other Tales of the Logging Camps*. Madison, WI: University of Wisconsin Press, 1947.
Beyer, H. Otley. *Philippine Folklore and Folklife*. Manila, Philippines: University of the Philippines Press, 1916.
Bindernagel, John. *North America's Great Ape: The Sasquatch*. Courtenay, British Columbia: Beachcomber Books, 1998.
——. *The Discovery of the Sasquatch*. Courtenay, British Columbia: Beachcomber Books, 2010.
Binns, Archie. *Northwest Gateway: The Story of the Port of Seattle*. New York: Columbia University Press, 1941.
Birtles, Terry. *Big Cats Loose in Britain*. London, UK: Robert Hale, 2001.
Black, Ronald. *The Gaelic Otherworld*. Edinburgh, Scotland: Birlinn, 2008.
Blackburn, Lyle. *Monsters of Texas*. San Antonio, TX: Anomalist Books, 2010.
——. *The Beast of Boggy Creek: The True Story of the Fouke Monster*. San Antonio, TX: Anomalist Books, 2012.
Blackman, W. Haden. *The Field Guide to North American Monsters*. New York: Three Rivers Press, 1998.
Blanc, Claude. *Faune de Madagascar*. Paris, France: ORSTOM, 1984.
Blom, Jan. *Myths and Monsters of Madagascar*. Amsterdam, The Netherlands: Noord-Holland Press, 1934.
Blum, Howard. *Out There: The Government's Secret Quest for Extraterrestrials*. New York: Simon and Schuster, 1990.
Boas, Franz. *The Central Eskimo*. Washington, D.C.: Bureau of American Ethnology, 1888.
Bord, Janet and Colin Bord. *The Bigfoot Casebook*. London, UK: Granada Publishing, 1982.
——. *The Great Lake Monsters of the World*. London, UK: Granada, 1982.
——. *Bigfoot Casebook Updated: Sightings and Encounters from 1818 to 2004*. San Antonio, TX: Pine Winds Press, 2006.
Bottrell, William. *Traditions and Hearthside Stories of West Cornwall*. Second Series. Penzance, UK: Beare and Son, 1873.
Bousfield, Edward D., and Paul H. LeBlond. *Cadborosaurus: Survivor From the Deep*. Victoria, BC: Horsdal and Schubart, 1995.
Boyer, Pascal. *Religion Explained: The Evolutionary Origins of Religious Thought*. New York: Basic Books, 2001.
Briggs, Katharine. *The Fairies in Tradition and Literature*. London, UK: Routledge, 1967.
——. *A Dictionary of Fairies: Hobgoblins, Brownies, Bogies, and Other Supernatural Creatures*. London, UK: Penguin, 1976.
Bruford, Alan. *The Grey Neighbours: The Sea-Kings and Other Supernatural Beings of the Highlands and Islands*. Edinburgh, Scotland: Polygon,

1991.

Burnham, Philip. *The Forest People of Madagascar: History and Belief.* New York: Harper and Row, 1965.

Campbell, Elizabeth Montgomery. *The Loch Ness Monster: The Evidence.* London, UK: Birlinn, 1986.

Campbell, Gordon T. *The Loch Morar Monster: The Search for Morag.* Edinburgh, Scotland: Birlinn, 1972.

Campbell, John Gregorson. *Superstitions of the Highlands and Islands of Scotland.* Glasgow, Scotland: James MacLehose and Sons, 1900.

Carey, John. *A Single Ray of the Sun: Religious Speculation in Early Ireland.* Andover, MA: Celtic Studies Publications, 1999.

Carmichael, Alexander. *Carmina Gadelica.* Edinburgh, Scotland: T. and A. Constable, 1900.

Carr, Geoffrey. *Phantom Hounds of the British Isles.* London, UK: Robert Hale, 1979.

Carroll, Cynthia McRoy. *Arkansas Ozarks Legends and Lore.* Cheltenham, Gloucestershire, UK: The History Press, 2020.

Christiansen, Per. *The Scandinavian Lindorm Legends: Serpents and Dragons of the North.* Copenhagen: Nordic Folklore Press, 1998.

Clark, Jerome. Clark, Jerome. *The UFO Encyclopedia: The Phenomenon from the Beginning.* Detroit, MI: Omnigraphics, 1998.

——. *Unexplained!: Strange Sightings, Incredible Occurrences, and Puzzling Physical Phenomena.* Detroit, MI: Visible Ink, 1999.

Clarkson, Peter. *Cold Ocean Biology.* Cambridge, UK: Cambridge University Press, 1982.

Cohen, Daniel. *Monsters, Giants, and Little Men from Mars.* New York: Dodd, Mead, 1975.

Cole, Fay-Cooper. *Philippine Folk Tales.* Chicago, IL: A.C. McClurg and Company, 1916.

Coleman, Loren. *Mysterious America: The Revised Edition.* New York: Paraview Press, 2001.

——. *Mysterious America: The Ultimate Guide to the Nation's Weirdest Wonders, Strangest Spots, and Creepiest Creatures.* New York: Paraview Pocket Books, 2001.

Coleman, Loren and Clark, Jerome. *Cryptozoology A to Z: The Encyclopedia of Loch Monsters, Sasquatch, Chupacabras, and Other Authentic Mysteries of Nature.* New York: Fireside, 1999.

Collie, J. Norman. *Adventures in the World's Wonderlands.* London, UK: T. Fisher Unwin, 1929.

Colvin, Andrew. *The Mothman's Photographer II: Meetings with Remarkable Strangers.* Charleston, WV: New Saucerian, 2007.

Costa, Flávio. *Bichos e Seres Míticos da Amazônia.* Manaus, Brazil: Valer Editora, 2002.

Costa, Joseph D'Lacey. *Haunted Massachusetts.* Guilford, CT: Globe Pequot Press, 2009.

Costello, Peter. *In Search of Lake Monsters.* New York: Aldus Books,

1974.

Crenshaw, Jim. *Fouke Monster of Boggy Creek*. Memphis, TN: self-published, 1974.

Cupp, Robert. *Legends of Pennsylvania's Wilderness*. Philadelphia, PA: Franklin Press, 1921.

Cutler, Ivor. *Scottish Monsters and Sea Serpents*. Edinburgh, Scotland: Polygon, 1993.

Da Silva, Fabio. *Mysterious Creatures of the Amazon*. São Paulo, Brazil: Horizonte Press, 1998.

David, Paul. *Life in Extreme Environments*. Oxford, UK: Oxford University Press, 2001.

Davidson, H. R. Ellis. *Gods and Myths of Northern Europe*. London, UK: Penguin, 1964.

Davis, Christopher. "Close Encounters at Kelly." *Fate Magazine*, Vol. 45, Issue 10, 1992. Lakeville, MN: Llewellyn Worldwide.

Davis, Patrick. *Utah's Folklore and Legends*. Salt Lake City, UT: University of Utah Press, 1985.

De Laguna, Frederica. *Under Mount Saint Elias: The History and Culture of the Yakutat Tlingit*. Washington, D.C.: Smithsonian Institution Press, 1972.

Dendle, Peter. *The Zombie Book: The Encyclopedia of the Living Dead*. Detroit, MI: Visible Ink Press, 2014.

Devereux, Paul. *Mysterious America*. San Francisco: Harper and Row, 1982.

Dinsdale, Tim. *Loch Ness Monster*. London, UK: Routledge and Kegan Paul, 1961.

———. *The Story of the Loch Ness Monster*. New York: Lippincott, 1975.

Doel, Fran, and Geoff Doel. *The Green Man in Britain*. Stroud, UK: The History Press, 2013.

Donnelly, Ignatius. *The Great Devon Mystery*. London, UK: Chapman and Hall, 1855.

Downes, Jonathan. *The Owlman and Others*. Bideford, Devon: CFZ Press, 1997.

———. *The Smaller Mystery Carnivores of the West Country*. Bideford, UK: CFZ Press, 2010.

Downes, Tony. *The Owlman and Others*. London, UK: Fortean Times, 1996.

Drewal, Henry John (ed.). *Mami Wata: Arts for Water Spirits in Africa and Its Diasporas*. Los Angeles, CA: Fowler Museum at UCLA, 2008.

Drury, Robert. *Madagascar: A Captive's Account of Fifteen Years*. London, UK: James Knapton, 1729.

Durán, Diego. *The History of the Indies of New Spain*. Norman, OK: University of Oklahoma Press, 1994.

Eberhart, George M. *Mysterious Creatures: A Guide to Cryptozoology (A–M volume)*. Santa Barbara, CA: ABC-CLIO, 2002.

Ellis, Catherine. *Haunted Bayou and Other Cajun Tales*. Gretna, LA:

Pelican Publishing, 2000.
Ellis, Richard. *Monsters of the Sea*. New York: Alfred A. Knopf, 1994.
———. *The Search for the Giant Squid: The Biology and Mythology of the World's Most Elusive Sea Creature*. New York: Lyons Press, 1998.
Emmons, George T. *The Tlingit Indians*. Seattle, WA: University of Washington Press, 1991.
Eugenio, Damiana L. (ed.). *Philippine Folk Literature: The Myths*. Quezon City, Philippines: University of the Philippines Press, 1993.
Evans-Wentz, Walter Yeeling. *The Fairy-Faith in Celtic Countries*. London, UK: Henry Frowde, 1911.
Firkins, Mary Beth. *The Legend of Boggy Creek: The Fouke Monster of Arkansas*. Little Rock, AR: Arkansas Folklore Press, 1981.
Forth, Gregory. *Between Ape and Human: An Anthropologist on the Trail of a Hidden Hominoid*. New York: Pegasus Books, 2022.
Fort, Charles. *The Book of the Damned*. New York: Boni and Liveright, 1919.
Foster, Michael Dylan. *Pandemonium and Parade: Japanese Monsters and the Culture of Yōkai*. Berkeley, CA: University of California Press, 2009.
Freeman, Martha Ward. *Voodoo Queen: The Spirited Lives of Marie Laveau*. Jackson, MS: University Press of Mississippi, 2004.
Gagnon, Joseph W. *The Search for Champ*. Plattsburgh, NY: North Country Books, 1985.
Gerhard, Ken, and Nick Redfern. *Monsters of Texas*. Gretna, LA: Pelican Publishing, 2008.
Gibbons, William and Hennessy, Jonathan. *Searching for Ropens and Finding God*. Longwood, FL: Creation House, 2006.
Golden, Christopher D. and Jean Comaroff. "The Human Health and Conservation Relevance of Food Taboos in Northeastern Madagascar." *Ecology and Society*, June 2015. Waterloo, Ontario, Canada: Resilience Alliance, 2015.
Goodman, Steven M., and Jonathan P. Benstead (eds.). *The Natural History of Madagascar*. Chicago: University of Chicago Press, 2003.
Gosse, Philip Henry. *The Romance of Natural History*. London, UK: James Nisbet, 1861.
Gould, Rupert T. *Oddities: A Book of Unexplained Facts*. London, UK: Geoffrey Bles, 1928.
Green, John. *Sasquatch: The Apes Among Us*. Blaine, WA: Hancock House, 1978.
———. *The Best of Sasquatch Bigfoot*. Blaine, WA: Hancock House, 2004.
Guiley, Rosemary Ellen. *The Encyclopedia of Vampires, Werewolves, and Other Monsters*. New York: Facts On File, 2005.
———. *The Encyclopedia of Demons and Demonology*. New York: Facts On File, 2009.
Guillermo, Paul. *Living Pterosaurs: The Ropen of Papua New Guinea*. Portsmouth, UK: CFZ Press, 2010.

Haley, Chad Lewis, and Kevin Nelson. *The Van Meter Visitor: A True and Mysterious Encounter with the Unknown*. Onalaska, WI: Unexplained Research Publishing, 2013.

Haley, J. Foster. *Mythical Beasts of the Lumber Camps*. Pittsburgh, PA: Forest and Field Publishing, 1937.

Halpert, Herbert, and Gower, John. *Folklore of the Logging Camps*. St. John's, Newfoundland: Memorial University of Newfoundland, 1961.

Hall, Mark A. *Thunderbirds: America's Living Legends of Giant Birds*. New York: Paraview Press, 2004.

Harding, Mike. *A Little Book of the Green Man*. London, UK: Aurum Press, 1998.

Hartland, Edwin Sidney. *The Legend of Perseus: A Study of Tradition in Story, Custom, and Belief*. Vol. 2. London, UK: David Nutt, 1895.

Healy, Tony, and Paul Cropper. *Out of the Shadows: Mystery Animals of Australia*. Sydney, NSW: Strange Nation, 2006.

———. *The Yowie: In Search of Australia's Bigfoot*. San Antonio, TX: Anomalist Books, 2006.

Heuvelmans, Bernard. *On the Track of Unknown Animals*. New York: Hill and Wang, 1959.

———. *In the Wake of the Sea-Serpents*. London, UK: Rupert Hart-Davis, 1968.

Holiday, F. W. *The Great Orm of Loch Ness*. New York: W. W. Norton, 1968.

Holmes, George, Thomas Aneurin Smith, and Caroline Ward. *Fantastic Beasts and Why to Conserve Them: Animals, Magic and Biodiversity Conservation*. Cambridge, UK: Cambridge University Press, 2018.

Hoshino, Takashi, and Satoshi Tanaka. *Life in the Ice: Microbial Communities of Polar Regions*. Tokyo: Springer Japan, 2013.

Hutton, Ronald. *How Pagan Was Medieval Britain?* Oxford, UK: Oxford University Press, 2023.

Hynek, J. Allen. *The UFO Experience: A Scientific Inquiry*. New York: Ballantine Books, 1972.

Iwasaka, Michiko, and Toelken, Barre. *Ghosts and the Japanese: Cultural Experience in Japanese Death Legends*. Logan, UT: Utah State University Press, 1994.

Jocano, F. Landa. *Outline of Philippine Mythology*. Quezon City, Philippines: Centro Escolar University Publications, 1969.

Jones, Nigel. *Haunted Britain: Supernatural Realms of the United Kingdom*. London, UK: New English Library, 1992.

Kan, Sergei. *Memory Eternal: Tlingit Culture and Russian Orthodox Christianity through Two Centuries*. Seattle, WA: University of Washington Press, 1999.

Kearney, Patrick. *Northwoods Legends and Lore: The Hodag, Paul Bunyan, and Other Fearsome Critters*. Duluth, MN: North Star Press, 1985.

Keel, John A. *Strange Creatures from Time and Space*. Greenwich, CT:

Fawcett Publications, 1970.
——. *The Mothman Prophecies*. New York: Saturday Review Press, 1975.
——. *The Complete Guide to Mysterious Beings*. New York: Thunder's Mouth Press, 1994.
Keightley, Thomas. *The Fairy Mythology: Illustrative of the Romance and Superstition of Various Countries*. London, UK: Whittaker, Treacher and Co., 1828.
Kent, Raymond K. *Early Kingdoms in Madagascar, 1500–1700*. New York: Holt, Rinehart and Winston, 1970.
Koch, John T. (ed.). *Celtic Culture: A Historical Encyclopedia*. Santa Barbara, CA: ABC-CLIO, 2006.
Komatsu, Kazuhiko. *An Introduction to Yōkai Culture: Monsters, Ghosts, and Outsiders in Japanese History*. Kyoto, Japan: International Research Center for Japanese Studies, 2017.
Koster, John. *Operation Sea Monster: The Zuiyo-maru Discovery and the Plesiosaur Question*. Tokyo, Japan: Maruzen Scientific, 1980.
Krantz, Grover S. *Big Footprints: A Scientific Inquiry into the Reality of Sasquatch*. Boulder, CO: Johnson Books, 1992.
Larson, Laurence M. (ed.). *The King's Mirror (Speculum Regale—Konungs Skuggsjá)*. New York: The American-Scandinavian Foundation, 1917.
Laugrand, Frédéric, and Jarich Oosten. *Inuit Shamanism and Christianity: Transitions and Transformations in the Twentieth Century*. Montreal, QC: McGill-Queen's University Press, 2010.
LeBlond, Paul H. *Cadborosaurus: Survivor From the Deep*. Victoria, B.C.: Horsdal and Schubart, 1995.
LeBlond, Paul H., and Edward D. Bousfield. *Anatomy of Cadborosaurus: A North Pacific Sea Serpent*. Victoria, BC: Amphipacifica, 1992.
León-Portilla, Miguel (ed.). *Aztec Thought and Culture: A Study of the Ancient Nahuatl Mind*. Norman, OK: University of Oklahoma Press, 1963.
Lindemans, Michael. *Mermaids and Mermen: A Global History of Mythical Water Beings*. London, UK: Thames and Hudson, 2000.
Lund, Gerald. *Cryptid Chronicles of the American South*. Little Rock, AR: Natural Heritage Books, 2005.
Lyons, Andrew P. and Harriet D. Lyons. *Irregular Connections: A History of Anthropology and Sexuality*. Lincoln, NE: University of Nebraska Press, 2004.
Lyons, Daniel. *Sea Serpents and Lake Monsters of the British Isles*. London, UK: Robert Hale, 1975.
Machado, Rui. *Folklore and Cryptids of Brazil*. Rio de Janeiro, Brazil: Editora Nacional, 1974.
Mackal, Roy P. *Searching for Hidden Animals: An Inquiry into Zoological Mysteries*. Garden City, NY: Doubleday, 1980.
——. *A Living Dinosaur? In Search of Mokele-Mbembe*. New York: E.J. Brill, 1987.

Mackenzie, Donald A. *Wonder Tales from Scottish Myth and Legend*. New York: Frederick A. Stokes, 1917.
MacKillop, James. *Dictionary of Celtic Mythology*. Oxford: Oxford University Press, 1998.
Magnus, Olaus. *Historia de Gentibus Septentrionalibus*. Rome: Apud Ioannem Mariam de Viottis, 1555.
Magraner, Jordi. *Hominids in the Hindu Kush*. Peshawar, Pakistan: Société d'Anthropologie de Paris, 1992.
Mann, Charles C. *1491: New Revelations of the Americas Before Columbus*. New York: Vintage Books, 2006.
Mansi, Sandra, and Katy Elizabeth. *Champ Search: On the Trail of Lake Champlain's Mystery Monster*. Burlington, VT: Champlain Press, 2019.
Manterola, Jorge. *The Onza: Mystery Cat of Mexico*. Mexico City: Fondo de Cultura, 1991.
Mather, Cotton. *Magnalia Christi Americana*. London, UK: Thomas Parkhurst, 1702.
McCloy, James F., and Ray Miller Jr. *The Jersey Devil*. New Brunswick, NJ: Rutgers University Press, 1976.
McGowan, Bob. *Phantom Cats of the British Countryside*. London, UK: Robert Hale, 1988.
———. *The Beast of Bodmin Moor: Fact or Legend?* Truro, UK: Cornwall Folklore Society, 1999.
McKechnie, Gary. *Lake Champlain: Sailing Through History*. Middlebury, VT: Middlebury College Press, 1996.
McKillop, James. *Dictionary of Celtic Mythology*. Oxford: Oxford University Press, 1998.
McNally, Raymond T. and Radu Florescu. *In Search of Dracula: The History of Dracula and Vampires*. Boston, MA: Houghton Mifflin, 1994.
McNeill, F. Marian. *The Silver Bough, Volume 1: Scottish Folklore and Folk-Belief*. Glasgow, Scotland: William MacLellan, 1957.
Meldrum, Jeff. *Sasquatch: Legend Meets Science*. New York: Forge, 2006.
Menger, Paul. *Ropen: The Search for the Bird That Time Forgot*. Burbank, CA: Whitcomb, 2007.
Merrick, Thomas. *Maritime Legends of Europe and Beyond*. Boston, MA: Houghton Mifflin, 1985.
Merritt, Stephanie. *Wildman: The Elusive Orang Pendek of Sumatra*. London, UK: CFZ Press, 2012.
Meurger, Michel and Claude Gagnon. *Lake Monster Traditions: A Cross-Cultural Analysis*. London, UK: Fortean Tomes, 1989.
Meyer, Matthew. *The Night Parade of One Hundred Demons: A Field Guide to Japanese Yōkai*. Somerville, MA: Self-published, 2012.
———. *The Hour of Meeting Evil Spirits: An Encyclopedia of Mononoke and Yōkai*. Somerville, MA: Self-published, 2015.
Miller, Josephine. *Spirits of the Mountains: An Ethnographic Survey of*

Philippine Forest Beings. Manila, Philippines: Ateneo de Manila University Press, 1989.

Mölkänen, Jenni. *Living with Spirits and Environmental Conservation Efforts in Rural Northeastern Madagascar*. Helsinki, Finland: University of Helsinki Press, 2025.

Monaghan, Patricia. *The Encyclopedia of Celtic Mythology and Folklore*. New York: Facts On File, 2004.

Monro, Hector Hugh. *Folk Tales from the Scottish Highlands*. London, UK: Thomas Nelson and Sons, 1930

Murray, Daniel. *A Chronicle of the Devil's Footprints in Devon*. London, UK: J. & A. Churchill, 1855.

Myster, Roland. *Thunderbirds: America's Living Legends of Giant Birds*. Minneapolis, MN: Llewellyn, 1994.

Mysterious Universe. *The Dover Demon: Massachusetts' Bizarre and Creepy Mystery Creature*. Sydney, Australia: 2020.

Napier, John. Bigfoot: *The Yeti and Sasquatch in Myth and Reality*. New York: E. P. Dutton, 1973.

Newberry, Mark. *Beasts of the Backwoods: Cryptid Creatures of North America*. Springfield, MO: Frontier Publishing, 2011.

Newton, Michael. *Encyclopedia of Cryptozoology: A Global Guide to Hidden Animals and Their Pursuers*. Jefferson, NC: McFarland, 2005.

Nickell, Joe. *Mysterious Creatures: Creating a Paranormal World*. Lexington, KY: University Press of Kentucky, 2001.

Norman, Jeremy. *Oceanic Myths and Legends*. London, UK: Hamlyn, 1979.

Obata, Ichiro, and Yoshinori Kimura. *Reports on the Carcass of an Unidentified Animal Trawled off New Zealand by the Zuiyo-maru*. Tokyo, Japan: Department of Natural Science, 1978.

Obeyesekere, Gananath. *The Work of Culture: Symbolic Transformation in Psychoanalysis and Anthropology*. Chicago: University of Chicago Press, 1990.

——. *Imagining Karma: Ethical Transformation in Amerindian and South Asian Traditions*. Berkeley, CA: University of California Press, 2002.

O'Donnell, Elliott. *Irish Wonders: The Ghosts, Giants, Pookas, Demons, Leprechauns, Banshees, Fairies, Witches, Widows, Old Maids, and Other Marvels of the Emerald Isle*. New York: E.P. Dutton, 1903.

——. *Dangerous Ghosts*. London, UK: Rider and Company, 1954.

Ó hÓgáin, Dáithí. *Myth, Legend and Romance: An Encyclopaedia of the Irish Folk Tradition*. New York: Prentice Hall, 1991.

——. *The Lore of Ireland: An Encyclopedia of Myth, Legend and Romance*. Woodbridge, UK: Boydell Press, 2006.

Olsen, D. Robert. *Utah's Strange Monsters*. Logan, UT: Utah State University Press, 1982.

Oren, David C. *A Voz do Sertão: Mitos e Lendas da Amazônia*. Belém, Brazil: Museu Paraense Emílio Goeldi, 1993.

Otten, Charlotte F. (ed.). *A Lycanthropy Reader: Werewolves in Western*

Culture. Syracuse, NY: Syracuse University Press, 1986.

Owen, Richard. "On the Tracks Found in the Snow in Devonshire, February 1855." London, UK: *Royal Society Papers*, 1855.

Parkin, David J. *Palms, Wine, and Witnesses: Public Spirit and Private Gain in an African Farming Community*. Prospect Heights, IL: Waveland Press, 1991.

Patterson, Patrick H. *The Lost Giants of South America*. São Paulo, Brazil: Editora Horizonte, 2007.

Peterson, Russell F. *Silently, By Night*. New York: McGraw-Hill, 1964.

Piccardi, Luigi, and W. Bruce Masse (eds.). *Myth and Geology*. London, UK: Geological Society, 2007.

Plasencia, Juan de. *Customs of the Tagalogs*. Manila, Philippines: 1589.

Pontoppidan, Erik. *The Natural History of Norway*. Copenhagen: A. F. Stein, 1753.

Priscu, John C. *Antarctic Microbiology*. Washington, D.C.: American Society for Microbiology Press, 1998.

Prugh, Jeff. *Bigfoot in Missouri: Momo the Monster*. Columbia, MO: Missouri Folklore Society Press, 2012.

Pyle, W. Haden. "The Enfield Horror." *Fate Magazine*, vol. 26, no. 7, July 1973.

Radford, Benjamin. *Lake Monster Mysteries: Investigating the World's Most Elusive Creatures*. Lexington, KY: University Press of Kentucky, 2006.

———. *Tracking the Chupacabra: The Vampire Beast in Fact, Fiction, and Folklore*. Albuquerque, NM: University of New Mexico Press, 2011.

Raglan, Lady. "The 'Green Man' in Church Architecture." *Folklore*. London, UK: The Folklore Society, 1939.

Ramos, Maximo D. *Creatures of Philippine Lower Mythology*. Quezon City, Philippines: University of the Philippines Press, 1990.

Randle, Kevin D. *History of UFO Crashes*. New York: Avon Books, 1995.

———. *Alien Encounters*. New York: Berkley Books, 1997.

Randles, Jenny. *Supernatural Pennines*. London, UK: Robert Hale, 1990.

———. *Alien Contact: Window on Another World*. London, UK: Hale, 1991.

Rasmussen, Knud. *Intellectual Culture of the Iglulik Eskimos*. Copenhagen, Denmark: Gyldendal, 1929.

Redfern, Nick. *Three Men Seeking Monsters: Six Weeks in Pursuit of Werewolves, Lake Monsters, Giant Cats, Ghosts, and UFOs*. New York: Paraview Pocket Books, 2004.

———. *The Monster Book: Creatures, Beasts and Fiends of Nature*. New York: Visible Ink Press, 2016.

———. *Monsters of the Deep*. London, UK: Visible Ink Press, 2021.

Regal, Brian. *The Secret History of the Jersey Devil: How Quakers, Hucksters, and Benjamin Franklin Created a Monster*. Baltimore, MD: Johns Hopkins University Press, 2018.

Rink, Henry. *Tales and Traditions of the Eskimo, with a Sketch of Their*

Habits, Religion, Language and Other Peculiarities. Edinburgh, Scotland: William Blackwood and Sons, 1875.

Roberts, C. R. "Mount Rainier-area Youth has Close Encounter in the Foothills." Tacoma, WA: *The News Tribune*, April 24, 1994.

——. [Follow-up article on Batsquatch] Tacoma, WA: *The News Tribune*, May 1, 1994.

Roosevelt, Theodore. *Hunting the Grisly and Other Sketches*. New York: G. P. Putnam's Sons, 1893.

Ross, Anne. *Pagan Celtic Britain: Studies in Iconography and Tradition*. London, UK: Routledge and Kegan Paul, 1967.

Sahagún, Bernardino de. *Florentine Codex: General History of the Things of New Spain*. Santa Fe, NM: School of American Research and University of Utah, 1950–1982.

Sanderson, Ivan T. *Follow the Whale*. New York: Little, Brown and Company, 1956.

——. *Abominable Snowmen: Legend Come to Life*. Philadelphia: Chilton, 1961.

——. *Investigating the Unexplained: A Compendium of Disquieting Mysteries of the Natural World*. Englewood Cliffs, NJ: Prentice-Hall, 1972.

Scott, William Henry. *Barangay: Sixteenth-Century Philippine Culture and Society*. Quezon City, Philippines: Ateneo de Manila University Press, 1994.

Seabrook, Lochlainn. *Britannia Rules: Goddess-Worship in Ancient Anglo-Celtic Society - An Academic Look at the United Kingdom's Matricentric Spiritual Past*. 1999. Franklin, TN: Sea Raven Press, 2010 ed.

——. *Carnton Plantation Ghost Stories: True Tales of the Unexplained from Tennessee's Most Haunted Civil War House!* 2005. Franklin, TN, 2016 ed.

——. *Christmas Before Christianity: How the Birthday of the "Sun" Became the Birthday of the "Son."* Franklin, TN: Sea Raven Press, 2010.

——. *Everything You Were Taught About the Civil War is Wrong, Ask a Southerner!* 2010. Franklin, TN: Sea Raven Press, 2024 ed.

——. *Jesus and the Law of Attraction: The Bible-Based Guide to Creating Perfect Health, Wealth, and Happiness Following Christ's Simple Formula*. Franklin, TN: Sea Raven Press, 2013.

——. *The Bible and the Law of Attraction: 99 Teachings of Jesus, the Apostles, and the Prophets*. Franklin, TN: Sea Raven Press, 2013.

——. *Christ Is All and In All: Rediscovering Your Divine Nature and the Kingdom Within*. Franklin, TN: Sea Raven Press, 2014.

——. *Jesus and the Gospel of Q: Christ's Pre-Christian Teachings as Recorded in the New Testament*. Franklin, TN: Sea Raven Press, 2014.

——. *The Articles of Confederation Explained: A Clause-by-Clause Study of America's First Constitution*. Spring Hill, TN: Sea Raven Press, 2014.

——. *Everything You Were Taught About American Slavery War is Wrong, Ask a Southerner!* Spring Hill, TN: Sea Raven Press, 2015.

——. *Confederacy 101: Amazing Facts You Never Knew About America's Oldest*

Political Tradition. Spring Hill, TN: Sea Raven Press, 2015.

———. *Seabrook's Bible Dictionary of Traditional and Mystical Christian Doctrines*. Spring Hill, TN: Sea Raven Press, 2016.

———. *Everything You Were Taught About African-Americans and the Civil War is Wrong, Ask a Southerner!* Spring Hill, TN: Sea Raven Press, 2016.

———. *Abraham Lincoln Was a Liberal, Jefferson Davis Was a Conservative: The Missing Key to Understanding the American Civil War*. Spring Hill, TN: Sea Raven Press, 2017.

———. *The Ultimate Civil War Quiz Book: How Much Do You Really Know About America's Most Misunderstood Conflict?* Spring Hill, TN: Sea Raven Press, 2017.

———. *America's Three Constitutions: Complete Texts of the Articles of Confederation, Constitution of the United States of America, and Constitution of the Confederate States of America*. Spring Hill, TN: Sea Raven Press, 2021.

———. *Vintage Southern Cookbook: 2,000 Delicious Dishes From Dixie*. Spring Hill, TN: Sea Raven Press, 2021.

———. *Secrets of Celebrity Surnames: An Onomastic Dictionary of Famous People*. Cody, WY: Sea Raven Press, 2023.

———. *Seabrook's Complete Battle Book: The War Between the States, 1861-1865*. Cody, WY: Sea Raven Press, 2023.

———. *Rocky Mountain Equines: A Photographic Collection of Horses, Donkeys, and Mules of the American West*. Cody, WY: Sea Raven Press, 2024.

———. *Rocky Mountain Bison: A Photographic Collection of Bison of the American West*. Cody, WY: Sea Raven Press, 2024.

———. *Mysterious Invaders: Twelve Famous 20th-Century Scientists Confront the UFO Phenomenon*. Cody, WY: Sea Raven Press, 2024.

———. *Your Soul Lives Forever: Documented Victorian Case Studies Proving Consciousness Survives Death*. Cody, WY: Sea Raven Press, 2024.

———. *Authentic Victorian Ghost Stories: Genuine Early Reports of Apparitions, Wraiths, Poltergeists, and Haunted Houses*. Cody, WY: Sea Raven Press, 2024.

———. *The Greatest Jesus Mystery of All Time: Where Was Christ Between the Ages of 12 and 30?* Cody, WY: Sea Raven Press, 2024.

———. *Manmade: Male Inventors Who Created the Modern* World. Cody, WY: Sea Raven Press, 2025.

———. *Jesus and the Gospel of Thomas: A Christian Mystic's View of Christianity's Most Important Ancient Text*. Cody, WY: Sea Raven Press, 2025.

———. *The Hunter-Gatherer Principle: Evolutionary Biology and the Case for Sex-Based Female Sports*. Cody, WY: Sea Raven Press, 2025.

———. *When Monsters Ruled: The 25 Scariest Animals of the Prehistoric World*. Cody, WY: Sea Raven Press, 2025.

———. *If They Were Alive Today: How Famous Historic Americans Might Look if They Lived in the 21st Century*. Cody, WY: Sea Raven Press, 2025.

Searle, Frank. *Nessie: Seven Years in Search of the Monster*. London, UK:

Coronet Books, 1976.
Seneca, C. J. *The Kalanoro: A Legend from Madagascar.* New York: Overlook Entertainment, 2024.
Shackley, Myra. *Still Living? Yeti, Sasquatch and the Neanderthal Enigma.* London, UK: Thames and Hudson, 1983.
Sharp, Lesley A. *The Possessed and the Dispossessed: Spirits, Identity, and Power in a Madagascar Migrant Town.* Berkeley: University of California Press, 1993.
———. *Wayward Pastoral Ghosts and Regional Xenophobia in a Northern Madagascar Town.* Cambridge, UK: Cambridge University Press, 2001.
Sheaffer, Louis. *The Snallygaster: America's Dragon.* Frederick, MD: Middletown Historical Society, 1978.
Shuker, Karl. *Mystery Cats of the World: From Blue Tigers to Exmoor Beasts.* London, UK: Robert Hale, 1989.
———. *In Search of Prehistoric Survivors: Do Giant "Extinct" Creatures Still Exist?* London, UK: Blandford, 1995.
———. *The Beasts That Hide From Man: Seeking the World's Last Undiscovered Animals.* New York: Paraview, 2003.
———. *Here's Nessie! A Monstrous Compendium from Loch Ness.* Bideford, UK: CFZ Press, 2016.
———. *This Cryptid World: A Global Survey of Undiscovered Beasts.* London, UK: Herb Lester Associates, 2020.
Siegert, Martin J. *Antarctica: Earth's Own Ice World.* London, UK: Natural History Museum Publishing, 2002.
Silver, Timothy. *A New Face on the Countryside: Indians, Colonists, and Slaves in South Atlantic Forests, 1500–1800.* Cambridge, UK: Cambridge University Press, 1990.
Simpson, Jacqueline, and Steve Roud. *A Dictionary of English Folklore.* Oxford, UK: Oxford University Press, 2000.
Sjoestedt, Marie-Louise. *Gods and Heroes of the Celts.* 1949. Mineola, NY: Dover Publications, 2000 ed.
Skinner, Charles M. *Myths and Legends of Our Own Land.* Philadelphia, PA: J. B. Lippincott, 1896.
Smith, Charles. *Legends of the Amazon.* New York: Harper and Brothers, 1879.
Smith, David J. *Florida's Skunk Ape: The Everglades Bigfoot.* Tampa, FL: Pineapple Press, 2008.
Smith, Jim. *Legends of Louisiana: From the Rougarou to Marie Laveau.* Lafayette, LA: Acadian House, 2011.
Smith, Malcolm. *Australian Bigfoot: The Yowie.* Sydney, AU: Self-published, 1996.
Smith, Mark A. *Creature of Legend: The Ohio Grassman and Other Bigfoot Sightings.* Columbus, OH: Ohio Cryptid Press, 2009.
Smith, Paul. *Terror of the Gévaudan: The Mysterious Man-Eating Beast.* London, UK: Futura Publications, 1976.

Smith, William L. *Boggy Creek Casebook*. Texarkana, TX: Southern Cryptid Research, 1990.
Smith, William Ramsay. *Aboriginal Legends: Animal Tales*. London, UK: J. B. Lippincott Company, 1930.
Smyers, Karen A. *The Fox and the Jewel: Shared and Private Meanings in Contemporary Japanese Inari Worship*. Honolulu, HI: University of Hawai'i Press, 1999.
Sodikoff, Genese Marie. *Forest and Labor in Madagascar: From Colonial Concession to Global Biosphere*. Bloomington, IN: Indiana University Press, 2012.
Speck, Frank G. *Penobscot Man: The Life History of a Forest Tribe in Maine*. Philadelphia: University of Pennsylvania Press, 1940.
Spence, Lewis. *The Magic Arts in Celtic Britain*. London, UK: Routledge, 1945.
———. *The Minor Traditions of British Mythology*. London, UK: Rider and Co., 1948.
Spritzer, Don. *Flathead Lake: From Glacier to Stump Town*. Missoula, MT: Pictorial Histories Publishing, 1996.
Sproule, Anna. *Mystery at Lake Champlain*. Toronto: Kids Can Press, 1991.
Steadman, Lyle. *The Cultural Ecology of the Solomon Islands*. Belmont, CA: Wadsworth Publishing, 1971.
Steenstrup, Japetus. *On Unidentified Marine Mammals and Globsters*. Copenhagen, Denmark: Royal Danish Academy, 1933.
Stonor, Charles. *The Apa Tanis and Their Neighbours: A Primitive Civilization of the Eastern Himalayas*. London, UK: Routledge and Kegan Paul, 1960.
Story, Ronald D. (ed.). *The Encyclopedia of UFOs*. Garden City, NY: Doubleday, 1980.
Strand, Erik. *Monsters of the North: Cryptids and Dragons in Scandinavian Lore*. Stockholm: Boreal Books, 2009.
Strickler, Lon. *Phantoms and Monsters: Cryptid Encounters*. Hanover, PA: Dark Forest Press, 2013.
Sullivan, Timothy D. *Texas Cryptid Chronicles*. Austin, TX: Lone Star Press, 2017.
Summers, Montague. *The Werewolf*. London, UK: Kegan Paul, Trench, Trubner and Company, 1933.
Swanton, John R. *Tlingit Myths and Texts*. Washington, D.C.: Bureau of American Ethnology, Smithsonian Institution, 1909.
Swick, James. *Voices in the Hills: Folklore of the Ozark Mountains*. Norman, OK: Red Oak Press, 1987.
Sykes, Bryan. *The Nature of the Beast: The First Scientific Evidence on the Survival of Apemen into Modern Times*. London, UK: Coronet, 2015.
Tewes, Michael E., and Everett C. Hibbitts. *Wild Cats of North America: Ecology and Conservation*. College Station, TX: Texas A&M University Press, 2004.

Thalbitzer, William. *The Ammassalik Eskimo: Contributions to the Ethnology of the East Greenland Natives*. Copenhagen, Denmark: Meddelelser om Grønland, 1914.

Torquemada, Juan de. *Monarquía Indiana*. Mexico City: Pedro Balli, 1615.

Trey, Edward. *The Brain-Eaters of Nandi: An Inquiry into East African Cryptids*. Nairobi, Kenya: East Africa Press, 1972.

Trumbull, James Hammond. *Natick Dictionary*. Washington, D.C.: Government Printing Office, 1903.

Turner, Patricia Rickels. *Louisiana Folk Tales: Oral Narratives from the Cajun and Creole Traditions*. Baton Rouge, LA: Louisiana State University Press, 1985.

Turnquist, Kristi. "Batsquatch of Mount St. Helens Explores NW Legend." Portland, OR: *The Oregonian*, August 18, 2021.

Tyler, Royall. *Japanese Tales*. New York: Pantheon Books, 1987.

Underwood, Peter. *The Supernatural*. London, UK: F. Muller, 1973.

Vallee, Jacques. *Confrontations: A Scientist's Search for Alien Contact*. New York: Ballantine Books, 1990.

Ventura, Varla. *Banshees, Werewolves, Vampires, and Other Creatures of the Night*. San Francisco: Weiser Books, 2013.

Wallace, David. *The Thunderbird Mythos: Native Traditions and Modern Sightings*. Oklahoma City, OK: Red Earth Press, 2007.

Walsh, Bill Gibbons. *Monsters of Maryland: Mysterious Creatures in the Old Line State*. Mechanicsburg, PA: Stackpole Books, 2010.

Wamsley, Jeff. *Mothman: Behind the Red Eyes*. Point Pleasant, WV: Mothman Museum and Research Center, 2005.

Watson, Peter. *Supernatural Scotland*. London, UK: Batsford, 1981.

West, Harry G. and Todd Sanders (eds.). *Transparency and Conspiracy: Ethnographies of Suspicion in the New World Order*. Durham, NC: Duke University Press, 2003.

Westwood, Jennifer, and Jacqueline Simpson. *The Lore of the Land: A Guide to England's Legends*. London, UK: Penguin, 2005.

Whitcomb, David. *Dragons in America: Folklore and Fact*. Baltimore, MD: Heritage Press, 1999.

Whitcomb, Jonathan. *Searching for Ropens: Living Pterosaurs in Papua New Guinea*. Longwood, FL: CFZ Design and Publishing, 2007.

White, Richard. "Inventing the Hodag: Folklore and Fraud in Wisconsin Logging Culture." *Journal of American Folklore*, 92, No. 364 (1979): pp. 325–340.

White, Tim. *The Bunyip: Australia's Folklore Monster*. Melbourne, Victoria, Australia: Oxford University Press, 1985.

Whyte, Constance. *More Than a Legend: The Story of the Loch Ness Monster*. London, UK: Hamish Hamilton, 1957.

Williams, Gareth. *A Monstrous Commotion: The Mysteries of Loch Ness*. London, UK: Profile Books, 2015.

Williams, Rex Gilroy. *Out of the Dreamtime: The Search for Australasia's Unknown Animals*. Katoomba, AU: URU Publications, 1998.

Wohlwend, Hans. *Sagen aus Graubünden*. Chur, Switzerland: Calven

Verlag, 1959.
Wood, Jennifer. *The World's Most Mysterious Creatures*. London, UK: Octopus, 1978.
Woodley, Michael A. *In the Wake of Bernard Heuvelmans: The History of Cryptozoology*. New York: CFZ Press, 2008.
Wooley, Seth Breedlove. *The Minerva Monster: Bigfoot in Ohio*. Wadsworth, OH: Small Town Monsters Publishing, 2015.
Woolfall, Peter. *Alien Big Cats in Britain*. Exeter, UK: Wildtrack Publishing, 2004.
Yeats, W. B. *Fairy and Folk Tales of the Irish Peasantry*. London, UK: Walter Scott, 1888.
Yoda, Hiroko, and Matt Alt. *Yokai Attack! The Japanese Monster Survival Guide*. Tokyo, Japan: Kodansha International, 2008.
Young, Mark. *Appalachian Monsters: A Cryptozoological Survey*. Charleston, SC: Southern Folklore Publications, 2005.
Young, Stanley P., and Edward A. Goldman. *The Puma: Mysterious American Cat*. Washington, D.C.: American Wildlife Institute, 1946.
Zhou, Guoxing. *The Mystery of the Chinese Wildman*. Beijing: China Travel and Tourism Press, 1982.

Mokele-Mbembe: a living dinosaur in Africa? Copyright © Lochlainn Seabrook.

MEET THE AUTHOR

"Bestselling author, award-winning historian, and esteemed nature writer Lochlainn Seabrook straddles multiple genres with ease, seamlessly weaving together history, science, politics, philosophy, and spirituality with the authority of a scholar and the flair of a storyteller." — SEA RAVEN PRESS

AMERICAN POLYMATH LOCHLAINN SEABROOK is a bestselling author, award-winning historian, and acclaimed multidisciplinary artist. A descendant of the families of Alexander Hamilton Stephens, John Singleton Mosby, Edmund Winchester Rucker, and William Giles Harding, the neo-Victorian scholar is a 7th generation Kentuckian, and one of the most prolific and widely read traditional writers in the world today. Known by literary critics as the "new Shelby Foote," the "American Robert Graves," the "Southern Joseph Campbell," and the "Rocky Mountain Richard Jefferies," and by his fans as the "the best author ever," he is a recipient of the United Daughters of the Confederacy's prestigious Jefferson Davis Historical Gold Medal, and is considered the foremost Southern interpreter of American Civil War history—or what he refers to as the War for the Constitution (1861-1865).

A lifelong litterateur, the Sons of Confederate Veterans member has authored and edited books ranging in topics from ancient and modern history, politics, science, comparative religion, diet and nutrition, spirituality, astronomy, entertainment, military, biography, mysticism, anthropology, cryptozoology, photography, and Bible studies, to natural history, technology, paleography, music, humor, gastronomy, etymology, paleontology, onomastics, mysteries, alternative health and fitness, wildlife, alternate history, comparative mythology, genealogy, Christian history, and the paranormal; books that his readers describe as "game changers," "transformative," and "life altering."

One of America's most popular living historians, nature writers, and Transcendentalists, he is a 17th generation Southerner of Appalachian heritage who descends from dozens of patriotic Revolutionary War soldiers and Confederate soldiers from Kentucky, Tennessee, North Carolina, and Virginia. Also a history, wildlife, and nature preservationist, the well-respected scrivener began life as a child prodigy, later maturing into an archetypal Renaissance Man.

Besides being cofounder and co-CEO of Sea Raven Press, an accomplished writer, author, historian, biographer, lexicographer, encyclopedist, neologist, publisher, editor, poet, creative, onomastician, etymologist, and Bible authority, the influential prosateur is also a Kentucky Colonel, eagle scout, entrepreneur, businessman, composer, screenwriter, nature, wildlife, and landscape photographer, videographer, and filmmaker, artist, artisan, painter, watercolorist, sculptor, ceramic artist, visual artist, sketch artist, pen and ink artist, graphic artist, graphic designer, book designer, book formatter, editorial designer, book cover designer, publishing designer, Web designer, poster artist, digital artist, cartoonist, content creator, inventor, aquarist, genealogist, ufologist, jewelry designer, jewelry maker, former history museum docent, teacher's assistant, and a former Red Cross certified lifeguard, ranch hand, zookeeper, and wrangler. A contemporary songwriter (of some 3,000 songs in a dozen genres), he is also a pianist, organist, drummer, bass player, rhythm guitarist, rhythm mandolinist, percussionist, electronic musician, synthesist, clavichordist, harpsichordist, classical composer, jingle composer, film composer (currently his musical work has been featured in 11 movies), lyricist, band leader, multi-instrument musician, lead vocalist, backup vocalist, session player, music producer, and recording studio mixing engineer, who has worked and performed with some of Nashville's top musicians and singers.

Currently Seabrook is the multi-genre author and editor of over 100 adult and children's books (totaling some 30,000 pages and 15,000,000 words) in over 100 categories, books that have earned him accolades from around the globe. His works, which have sold on every continent except Antarctica, have introduced hundreds of thousands to vital facts that have been left out of our mainstream books. He has been endorsed internationally by leading experts, museum curators, award-winning historians, chart-topping authors, celebrities, filmmakers, noted scientists, well regarded educators, TV show hosts and producers, renowned military artists, venerable heritage organizations, and distinguished academicians of all races, creeds, and colors.

He currently holds two interesting world records: He is the author of the most books on American military officer Nathan Bedford Forrest (12 in total), and he was the first to publicize and describe the 19th-Century platform reversal of America's two main political parties, namely that Civil War era Democrats (primarily in the South—the Confederacy) were Conservatives, while Civil War era Republicans (primarily in the North—the Union) were Liberals.

Of northern, western, and central European ancestry, he is the 6th great-grandson of the Earl of Oxford and a descendant of European royalty through his Kentucky father and West Virginia mother. A proud descendant of Appalachian coal miners, trainmen, mountain folk, and wilderness pioneers, his modern day cousins include: Johnny Cash, Elvis Presley, Lisa Marie Presley, Billy Ray and Miley Cyrus, Patty Loveless, Tim McGraw, Lee Ann Womack, Dolly Parton, Pat Boone, Naomi, Wynonna, and Ashley Judd, Ricky Skaggs, the Sunshine Sisters, Martha Carson, Chet Atkins, Patrick J. Buchanan, Cindy Crawford, Bertram Thomas Combs (Kentucky's 50th governor), Edith Bolling (second wife of President Woodrow Wilson), Andy Griffith, Riley Keough, George C. Scott, Robert Duvall, Reese Witherspoon, Lee Marvin, Rebecca Gayheart, and Tom Cruise.

A constitutionalist, avid outdoorsman, wilderness conservationist, and gun rights advocate, Seabrook is the author of the international blockbuster, *Everything You Were Taught About the Civil War is Wrong, Ask a Southerner!* He lives with his wife and family in the magnificent Rocky Mountains, heart of the American West, where you will find him writing, hiking, and filming.

For more information on Mr. Seabrook visit
LochlainnSeabrook.com

Praise for Author-Historian-Artist
Lochlainn Seabrook

Comments from our readers around the world

★ "Lochlainn Seabrook is a genius writer!" — STEVEN WARD

★ "Best author ever." — EMILY (last name withheld)

★ "We get asked a lot what books we use and read. We don't do many modern historians, but we make an exception for some, and Lochlainn Seabrook is one of them. His works are completely well researched from original documents, and heavily footnoted and documented." — SOUTHERN HISTORICAL SOCIETY

★ "Looking forward to more Lochlainn Seabrook books, my favourite historian!" — ALBERTO IGLESIAS

★ "Lochlainn Seabrook is one of the finest authors on true history in this century. His books should be on every student's desk." — RONDA SAMMONS RENO

★ "All of Col. Seabrook's books are great. I have bought most of them and want to end up buying them all." — DAVID VAUGHN

★ "Lochlainn pulls together such arcane facts with relative ease, compiling these into ordinary prose that strike to the heart with substance, no fluff-speak. I am awestruck! Really. He is an inspiration to me. . . . He is truly a revolutionist. He dares to speak what others whisper; he writes with a boldness and an authoritative knowledge that is second to none." — JAY KRUIZENGA

★ "Mr. Lochlainn Seabrook is . . . the most well researched and heavily documented author I've ever read. His books are must haves. Everything he writes should be required reading! I assure you, you won't be disappointed. One simply cannot go wrong with his books. Mr. Seabrook is awesome! . . . I have never read any other author as well researched and footnoted as him. I've been in love with Mr. Seabrook for almost 5 years now. His quick wit and logic is enough reason to purchase his books. But the mere fact that he's so extensively researched is icing on the cake. Mr. Seabrook is my favorite, hands down." — LANI BURNETTE RINKEL

★ "My favorite book is the Bible. Lochlainn Seabrook wrote my second favorite book." — RICHARD FINGER

★ "I have a new favorite author and his name is Lochlainn Seabrook." — J. EWING

★ "Lochlainn Seabrook is an incredible writer and I love all of his books on the South. . . . His writing is brilliant. . . . I look forward to reading more of his masterpieces. Thank you." — JOEY (last name withheld)

★ "It's hard to choose just one of Lochlainn's books!" — ROSANNE STEELE

★ "Mr. Seabrook, thank you ever so much for blessing us with your most enlightening works." — LAURENCE DRURY

★ "I recommend anything written by Lochlainn Seabrook." — HOTRODMOB

★ "Awesome books . . . by a great writer of truth, Lochlainn. Thank you so much. Keep up the great work you do." — WILDBUNCH19INF

★ "I love Lochlainn Seabrook's style and approach. It's not the 'norm.' What a miracle his books are. . . . He is a literal life changing author! Amazing books!" — KEITH PARISH

★ "I adore Mr. Seabrook's style and I love his books. I love an author that does proper research, and still finds a way to engage the reader. Mr. Seabrook does an admirable job of both." — DONALD CAUL

★ "Lochlainn Seabrook's books are much more well researched and authoritative than those eminently celebrated as being the authorities on the subjects he writes on. You can always trust to find the truth in his writings. . . . He does not rewrite history, but instead shows it as it is." — GARY STIER

★ "I love all of Colonel Seabrook's books. They are informative and enlightening, and his warm Southern hospitality writing style makes you feel right at home." — KEITH CRAVEN

★ "Lochlainn Seabrook's work is an absolute treasure of scholarship and historic scope." — MARK WAYNE CUNNINGHAM

★ "Mr. Seabrook's command of . . . history is breathtaking. . . . He deserves great renown—check out his books!" — MARGARET SIMMONS

★ "I love Seabrook's writings. LOVE!!! . . . So grateful to know the truth! Keep writing Lochlainn!!!" — REBECCA DALRYMPLE

★ "Lochlainn Seabrook . . . [has] probably [written] the best book on mental science in existence by a living author. Along with Thomas Troward, Emmet Fox, and Jack Addington, Mr. Seabrook is one of the top four mental science authors of all time, since biblical times." - IAN BARTON STEWART

★ "Glad I discovered Mr. Seabrook! . . . He writes eye opening books! Unbelievable the facts he unearths - and he backs it all up with truth, notes, footnotes, and bibliography! . . . He always amazes me! His books always see the whole picture. His timelines and bibliographies are incredible. He always provides carefully reasoned arguments! He's the best. To me I think he's better than the late great Shelby Foote! America needs more like Lochlainn Seabrook. I can't wait to own all of his books on the war someday. Everyone who wants the Truth, who seeks the Truth and wants the full story, should read his books." — JOHN BULL BADER

★ "I love all of Colonel Seabrook's books!" — DEBBIE SIDLE

★ "Lochlainn Seabrook is well educated and versed in what he writes and I'm impressed with the delivery." — THOMAS L. WHITE

★ "Lochlainn Seabrook is the author of great works of scholarship." — JOHN B. (last name withheld)

★ "Thank you Lochlainn Seabrook for your wonderful books! You are the real deal! You are an amazing author and I love your books!!" — SOPHIA MEOW CELLIST

★ "I really enjoy Mr. Seabrook's books! His knowledge is beyond belief!" — SANDRA FISH

★ "Love Lochlainn Seabrook. Awesome!!" — ROBIN HENDERSON ARISTIDES

★ "Kudos to Lochlainn Seabrook who is a very good and informative professional truthful historian. We need more like him!" — AMY VACHON

Nurture Your Mind, Body, and Spirit!
READ THE BOOKS OF
SEA RAVEN PRESS

Visit our Webstore for a wide selection of wholesome, family-friendly, evidence-based, educational books for all ages. You'll be glad you did!

Artisan-Crafted Books & Merch From the Rocky Mountains

SeaRavenPress.com

Visit our sister sites:
LochlainnSeabrook.com
YouTube.com/user/SeaRavenPress
YouTube.com/@SeabrookFilms
Rumble.com/user/SeaRavenPress
Pond5.com/artist/LochlainnSeabrook

A Selkie haunting Ballyness Bay, Falcarragh, County Donegal, Ireland. Copyright © Lochlainn Seabrook.

If you enjoyed this natural history book you will be interested in some of Colonel Seabrook's popular related titles:

- When Monsters Ruled: The 25 Scariest Animals of the Prehistoric World
- North America's Amazing Mammals: An Encyclopedia for the Whole Family
- The Concise Book of Owls: A Guide to Nature's Most Mysterious Birds
- The Concise Book of Tigers: A Guide to Nature's Most Remarkable Cats
- Rocky Mountain Equines: A Photographic Collection of Horses, Donkeys, and Mules of the American West
- Rocky Mountain Bison: A Photographic Collection of Bison of the American West

Available from Sea Raven Press and wherever fine books are sold

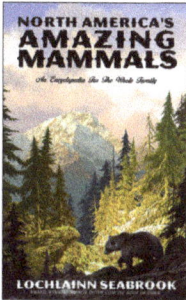

PLEASE VISIT OUR WEBSTORE FOR COLONEL SEABROOK'S BOOKS, FINE ART NATURE & WILDLIFE PHOTO PRINTS, WALL POSTERS, AND BUMPER STICKERS

SeaRavenPress.com

www.ingramcontent.com/pod-product-compliance
Lightning Source LLC
Chambersburg PA
CBHW041436300426
44114CB00025B/2898